J. B. Watson

The Founder of Behaviourism

J. B. Watson

The Founder of Behaviourism

A Biography

David Cohen

Routledge & Kegan Paul
London, Boston and Henley

First published in 1979
by Routledge & Kegan Paul Ltd
39 Store Street, London WC1E 7DD,
Broadway House, Newtown Road,
Henley-on-Thames, Oxon RG9 1EN and
9 Park Street, Boston, Mass. 02108, USA
Set in 10 on 12pt Palatino
and printed in Great Britain by
Caledonian Graphics

British Library Cataloguing in Publication Data

Cohen, David, b. 1946

J. B. Watson.
1. Watson, John Broadus   2. Psychologists –
United States – Biography
150'.19'4320924   BF109.W/   79-40210

ISBN 0 7100 0054 5

Contents

Acknowledgments

I should like to thank the following people who gave me extremely useful information and help: Jim Watson and Polly Hartley, the only surviving Watson children; Ruth Lieb, Watson's long-time friend; Curt Richter, the pyschologist who was a student of Watson's.

Cedric Larson, who has spent many years studying Watson, also provided me with some help and drove me up to Watson's home in Westport, Conn. Julia Morgan of the archives at Johns Hopkins University ferreted out a wealth of material. I am also grateful to the MS Divisions of the Library of Congress, the University of Chicago, the Yale Medical Library and of the Information section of J. Walter Thompson for much help, and to Cornell University. Philip Pauly of the Smithsonian Institution kindly let me see an unpublished paper of his on the history of psychology at Johns Hopkins. Dr G. Clayton, the librarian of Furman University, gave me access to much material on Watson's early life and on South Carolina generally at the time.

Professor Brian Foss has kindly read and criticised much of the book and made a number of helpful suggestions. The errors remain mine, of course. I have also had much encouragement from my literary agent, Sheila Watson, and my editor, David Godwin. Finally, Aileen Latourette read most of the book and offered many useful criticisms. I must thank her and our sons, Nicholas and Reuben, for putting up with an awful lot of Watson in the recent past.

Introduction

In 1928 when he was at the height of his fame, John B. Watson wrote an article called 'Feed Me on Facts'. It is enough to intimidate any biographer. Watson said:

> I do want to say one word about the modern craze for biographies! How can we keep people from writing them? How can a thoughtful person get anything but amusement out of them especially out of the psychological or psycho-analytic biographies? Many bio-graphers take their characters back to infancy and childhood, in order to secure a certain continuity in the life trends of the person biographed. View any of these biographies now, in the light of what the behaviourist has taught us about conditioning and slanting in infancy and their inaccuracies become apparent at once. In the first place, no one can write a worth while biography unless one knows something about the infancy of the person written about. Bio-graphies based on incidental facts or public achievements may make interesting reading. They may even make good literature. But they are not biographies. To write a biography one needs to be a Boswell and even a Boswell can write only one biography. To grind 'bio-graphies' out two or three to the year on the basis of the flimsy records we have, even of living people – not to speak of those long dead – is a pedantic and humorous, if not commercial undertaking.

But there seems to me to be a need for a biography of Watson. Watson probably influenced psychology as much as, or even more than, Freud did. Watson's 'public achievement' certainly should make 'interesting reading', especially as much of it has hardly been explored. In itself, that would be reason enough for a book about him.

Watson led an interesting and unusual life. In his story, there is much that is tragic. He was one of the youngest men ever to make it into Who's Who and yet he seems to have died a bitter man. It is hard 'to secure a certain continuity in the life trends' because Watson's life

1

changed radically a number of times. Sometimes he made the change himself; at other times, he reacted to some disaster by doing his best to alter his life. As a result, Watson almost had a number of careers. There was the poor young man from down South who became professor of psychology at Johns Hopkins before he was thirty. There was the brilliant professor who was sacked. Forced out of academic life, Watson went to work in advertising. He became one of the key figures in making American advertising what it is today. He tried to continue doing some research – without much success. But then, at a certain point, he clammed up. He stopped thinking about advertising. He stopped doing any psychology. He lived the life of a rich commuter who had precious few ideas. He refused to write and, for about twenty years until his death, he remained silent, intellectually dead, a remarkable silence for a man whose achievements Bertrand Russell compared to Aristotle's. All these shifts make him fascinating and, of course, difficult to write about.

Watson did not mean to help any biographer. He had many of his papers burned just before he died. He did not leave too much information about his infancy though, fortunately, enough remains to build up some picture of his early life to enable us to understand at least some things about his character.

Watson's contribution to psychology and to American culture also needs to be put into perspective. B. F. Skinner has become so famous as the behaviourist that it is vaguely assumed that Watson just influenced him. To found behaviourism was merely to pave the way for the great operant conditioner. Watson did more than merely 'found' behaviourism. He did much pioneer work in a variety of subjects like learning, sex research and child development. He invented behaviour therapy in 1919 though no one else actually did much behaviour therapy till the 1940s. Skinner and Eysenck, incidentally, both hint that they really invented it. But the 'founder' of behaviourism was radical in his ideas as well as his life. He believed, as many critics of psychology now do, that the subject should get out of the laboratory. It was too artificial. Psychologists should observe people in real-life situations. Psychology should be practical as well as scientific so that people could use it. Watson stressed the necessity for observation repeatedly and did much work that would now be called ethological. Traditionally, behaviourists dismissed ethology as unscientific.

Watson also moulded two important areas of American life. He made Madison Avenue aware of the usefulness of psychology and he very much contributed to making American advertising the powerful force it is today. Watson also became an authority on child care in the

1920s. His book *The Psychological Care of the Infant and Child* was a best seller and influenced government health policy. It became something of a parents' bible like Dr Spock is today. Spock's own book is often a direct reaction against Watson. Watson also helped make America, as he put it, 'psychology mad' by writing a stream of good popular articles on psychology which took the discipline out of the university and exposed it to the public.

The 'public achievements' would make in themselves 'interesting reading'. But Watson himself is an intriguing man. The radical changes in his life and his career need to be described and explained. More than most psychologists he tried to live his own psychology. He used behaviourism on himself and his children. His ideas did not stay abstract, out of his life. I hope the book will also explore the relationship between Watson's ideas about human beings and how he, as such a human being, lived. In view of the radical changes in his own life, this seems an especially interesting area to me.

In his attack on biographies, which was part of a general attack on most novels, plays, biographies, autobiographies around in 1928, Watson declared: 'There are no mysterious individuals in real life; why can't we keep them out of books?' Watson did much that makes him appear mysterious. By the end of the book, I hope he will be something less of a mystery.

1

The Making of a Behaviourist
1878–1900

When you go to Greenville, South Carolina, it is difficult to imagine what the town must have been like in 1878. Today, the roads into Greenville are lined with motels, bill boards and eating places that offer that fast, junky food which seems to be America's latest oral obsession. At any moment I expect to see South Carolina Fried Chicken. To one side of the road there are three old railway carriages which have been splendidly restored and turned into a French restaurant, the robust technology of one age becoming the chic decor of another. But, the taxi driver explained to me, the railway restaurant was not doing well. It took too long to get food there. Greenville is not the fairly sleepy Southern town it once was.

In 1797 a town was planned on the site of Greenville. But it was called Pleasantburg. In 1831 the name was changed to Greenville. The town was surrounded by country then. Even now, half a mile off the main road, the countryside is very lovely. There are still lots of farms and fields. When I went to the town the branches of the trees sparkled in the December sun and a perfect rainbow, a total arc, capped the sky with its colours. John B. Watson was always something of a country boy.

When Watson was born in 1878, Greenville was a small town. It was, he said, 'a village of 20,000 souls'. Souls was an apt word, for it was a very religious place. In 1825 the Baptist Theological College set up in Greenville. The Baptist influence was strong in the town when Watson was growing up. In many churches, long and emotional religious meetings were frequent. A very fundamental God was also, as we shall see, a strong influence in the Watson home, for his mother was very much a believer.

There had been a Watson family in the area since before 1797. We know a tedious amount about the ancestors of J. B. Watson because one of his brothers was obsessed by genealogy and was as indefatigable in his search for his own roots as ever Alex Haley was. Watson's brother managed to trace the family back to Alfred the Great. This is, I am told, a common trait in the South where what counts is not what you are or what you do but who you can claim descent from. After this royal start in life, the family did not do too well, for the next most illustrious ancestor it could cull from history was Sir William Petre who was a Lord Mayor of London round 1656 and a rich wool merchant. These exalted ancestors were all on the Roe side, the side of John's mother.

On the paternal side, a John Watson had come from County Down to America in 1752. John lived in South Carolina but this ancestor got little attention. The man wasn't a king or a Lord Mayor and he didn't even have the ancestral decency to be rich. His son, another John, was a mere sergeant in the America Revolutionary Army. This second John lived on until 1823 and had thirteen children. One of these children was James Madison Watson who was the grandfather of the behaviourist.

James Madison Watson was a farmer. When he died, he left his farm in Travellers Rest (which is some six miles from Greenville) to his son, Pickens Watson. It was a small farm that backed on to the Reedy River after which the local Baptist church was named. It might be small but this farm was to play an important formative role in John B. Watson's life. His first years were those of a country boy Pickens Watson worked the farm.

In 1868, Pickens, who was then in his middle twenties, married Emma K. Roe. Emma was beautiful, strong, quite intelligent and, it seems, insufferably religious. She may have married a little beneath herself – one of her relatives, for example, had the important job of running the Reedy River Church Sunday school – but Pickens was a lively and attractive man. At first the marriage went well. Before John was born the couple had three other children: Edward, who was to become as religious as his mother; Thomas Stradley, who died when he was only twenty, and Watson's only sister, Mary Alice.

The Watson family was poor. They claimed, like many other poor whites, to have lost their riches in the Civil War. Emma had to work on the farm. She did have a black nurse to help look after the children, but a Southern white family then would have had to have been utterly destitute to have no help at all. Emma's main interests were her farm, her children and her religion. She went constantly to the local Baptist church at Reedy River and she was also one of the principal lay organisers for the Baptists in the whole of South Carolina. When John B. Watson was born, he was born into a house where God and the Devil were both firmly, and fundamentally, entrenched.

John Broadus Watson was born on 9 January 1878. His mother was then thirty years old. He was a bright and healthy child.

It must have been an austere house if Emma had her way, as she usually did. Fundamentalist Baptists do not drink or smoke. Dancing is not permitted. The Reedy River Church compensated for all this strictness by having long and very emotional 'meetings' which might last two or three days. Religion was fervent and exciting. Often these meetings led to ecstatic conversions. Frequently 'brothers' or 'sisters', as the Baptists called themselves, got up and denounced themselves as wretched sinners. They often specified a whole miscellany of sins. Watson's mother clearly loved it as well as believing in it. With Emma's church, there came a strong accent on morality and, with morality, there came a strong emphasis on cleanliness. Her children had to be, literally, impeccable.

No records survive of John's toilet training, but it must have been a difficult experience for it seems to have marked him quite deeply. When Watson wrote about children he was fierce and rigid in arguing that children had to be trained from when they were six months old: it is hard to believe such passion did not stem from his own experiences. His own children were set on the pot from when they were about four months old. It would fit well with the whole atmosphere of Emma's house for her to insist on cleanliness. It was crucial to be clean. Dirt was the mark of the Devil.

Watson never took the exceptional step of writing about his own toilet training but he did often write about the way he had been trained to fear the dark. The nurse Emma employed told him that the Devil lurked in the dark and that if ever Watson went a-walking during the night, the Evil One might well snatch him out of the gloom and off to Hell. Emma seems to have done nothing to stop the nurse instilling such terrors in her young son. Most likely, she approved. To be terrified of the Devil was only right and prudent. As a fundamentalist Baptist, she believed that Satan was always prowling. All this left Watson with a life-long fear of the dark. He freely admitted that he studied whether children were born with an instinctual fear of the dark because he had never managed to rid himself of the phobia. He tried a number of times to use his behaviourist principles to cure himself but he never really managed to do it. As an adult Watson was often depressed, and when he got depressed he sometimes had to sleep with his light on. I suspect that this nice, clear consequence of religion in the home was not the only one.

The Reedy River Church believed not only in 'strict discipline' but also in mutual spying. Brothers and sisters were meant to report on each other's sins. In 1887 a sister was dismissed for drinking and, a few years later, a brother was denounced for having gambled on a horse.

Watson could not but be affected by this atmosphere. The authority of God and the power of the community left Watson with a peculiar ambivalence about people who had authority over him. He wanted to defy them: but it was not something that came easily or nonchalantly to him.

Emma was a very energetic and social person. Her home was a centre for frequent meetings about Baptist affairs. The minister from the local Reedy River Church often dropped in. Emma even managed to persuade her husband Pickens (who was to find religion less and less to his taste) to become a deacon of the Reedy River Church. As soon as he could walk John Watson went to church. When he was six he trudged two miles to the local school where the education he received was very much based on the Bible. As a child Watson had no choice but to be religious.

It seems, however, that all Emma's attempts to mould her son into a religious person failed. From the time that he was six or seven, Watson seems to have done his best to escape from the relentless religion of his mother. He took to roaming the countryside. He always liked the country. As often as he could, he missed Sunday school – which was taught by a Roe – and just wandered across fields and farms. He kept pets. He learned to ride. He got his father to teach him a whole variety of manual skills. Pickens, who was finding Emma's religious fervour more and more constricting, probably encouraged his son to think critically of all those rigid Baptist ideas. Father and son got on well. They enjoyed doing practical things together and when he had children, Watson loved to spend time with them doing things like riding and building. He believed it was the best way of being a close family. By the time that he was nine, Watson could handle tools and he could sole shoes. He knew how to milk cows. He had acquired many practical skills. In a number of crises in his life he always said he could fall back on doing rather than brooding. At ten, I think, the young Watson had learned to withdraw from his mother's insistent faith when he could. He was also a little shy. He liked animals and was good at dealing with them, preferring them to people, he said sometimes. It is surely no accident that when Watson had all the money he needed to live in the house of his dreams, he chose a farm. He liked the outdoor life and he learned much from being brought up on a farm. It gave him confidence with animals and his father confirmed the very practical bent in him. Watson wrote: 'At 12 I was a pretty fair carpenter. This manual skill has never lost its charm.' I think it offered Watson not only charm but a means of escape from family tensions. As we shall see, it was an escape that he needed.

In 1890, when Watson was twelve years old, the family moved closer in to Greenville. His father began to do some work at a sawmill on the other side of Greenville and Watson went often enough to help him. The family still lived on a small farm west of the Augusta Bold Road. Watson moved from the small school in Travellers Rest to the local public school in the town. Watson did very poorly at his new school but he never began to explain why. And yet the reason was simple enough.

We have seen that Watson's mother, Emma, was energetic and religious. Her husband Pickens, however, was not really a very suitable spouse. He was far from being a hard worker. Where Emma was responsible and pious, Pickens had a wild streak in him – a streak that was often to be found in his son. Emma tried hard to make her husband the pillar of small town society that he should have been but the truth is that the older he grew, the more Pickens became a kind of hill-billy character. Pickens might be a deacon of the Reedy River Church but his main interests in life were swearing, drinking whisky and chasing women. All this must have been very mortifying for Emma.

Pickens cared less and less about appearances and the marriage between him and Emma became more and more a marriage of true incompatibles. Apart from all the drinking and swearing, which were bad enough for a decent Baptist to put up with, there were the women. Unlike that modern Baptist, President Carter, Pickens did not keep his lust to his heart, he acted on it. He was good-looking in a rough kind of way and women did not dislike him. To make matters worse, it seems that Pickens got in the habit of going off with Indian women. According to Polly Hartley, John B. Watson's daughter, Pickens probably had two Indian 'wives' in the vicinity of Greenville. When Emma and her church and her morality got too much, Pickens seems to have gone off for some sensual consolation among the so-called savages. All these exertions did not exhaust him, for he lived to be eighty-six.

Emma had for some time put up with Pickens's wanderings. But round 1891 something drastic happened. Pickens left home. There is no way of knowing whether Emma finally got so exasperated with her ne'er-do-well husband that she kicked him out or whether Pickens got so exasperated with his wife that he left. But leave he did.

When his father left home Watson was thirteen years old. He never wrote what the effect of losing his father in this way was, but the effect was profound. Watson was close to his father and felt that the man betrayed him. Years later, in the 1920s, when Pickens was in New York he got in touch with his now famous son. But John refused to see the old man even though Pickens was by then well over eighty. He rejected his father as his father had rejected him, though he did send him a little money so that Pickens could buy some clothes. Watson felt the loss of his father, and of his teacher in carpentry, very keenly.

It is clear, also, that in many ways John was like Pickens. He was already a good-looking boy at thirteen. And like his father, he had a rough and impulsive side to his character. As John grew older it would become clear that many of Pickens's 'bad' habits had rubbed off on to his son. Like his father, John Watson swore a great deal. Like his father, he drank a good deal and he always drank bourbon whisky, his father's favourite drink. And like his father, John Watson liked women rather too much for a decent Baptist. Pickens was always chasing women. John had the good fortune to be so attractive that women were always chasing him, according to many sources. In all these dissolute ways, John was very much his father's son.

When his father left home John's anger and his impulsiveness at once began to manifest themselves. At school Watson began to be rather vicious and violent. He was obviously intelligent but he was lazy, 'somewhat insubordinate', he remembered, and he never made a decent grade. He mocked teachers. And as soon as the teachers were out of the room, he and a friend of his called Joe Leech would box until one or the other of them drew blood. Fighting was much better than studying. Watson wrote that he had 'few pleasant memories of these years'. He did not like school at all. And school would seem to have no reason to like him.

Joe Leech and Watson did not stop at doing violence to themselves. They also engaged in that charming Southern pastime of 'nigger fighting'. On their way home from school every day they would pick out a black man and set courageously upon him. Twice Watson was arrested. Once it was for 'nigger fighting'. The second time Watson did not even have the excuse of taking out youthful high spirits on some unfortunate black, for he started to fire a gun in the middle of Greenville. So much violence seems to have been Watson's response to a situation he could not cope with when Pickens left home. This might be expected of the son of the disreputable Pickens but it was hardly what Emma expected of her son.

The files of the Greenville papers in which these events might have been recorded were destroyed in a fire and Watson does not seem to have kept any press clippings of that period! Watson was confused, angry and he wanted to be defiant. It is not surprising that he should be spurred on to be so violent. I think, however, that he began to feel a need to control it. He cast about for ways to cope. It would have been easier for him if he could have immersed himself in religion and blamed his father for being such a sinful bastard. But even then Watson could not take refuge in religion. He never listened to the sermons. And there was probably something in him that admired how very defiant Pickens had been not just in leaving but in leaving to co-habit with Indians. Watson would always find defiance very attractive. His father would have approved.

The departure of his father also made Watson treasure his manual skills even more. Manual work became a consolation and a refuge. It allowed him to be by himself and it allowed him to become totally absorbed in whatever it was that he was doing. Later Watson would define true happiness as forgetting oneself. When one was really happy, one did not think, and, certainly, one did not brood. And the thirteen-year-old boy had, after all, plenty to brood about.

The departure of Pickens also affected John's relationship with his mother. Watson never wrote about this relationship but he always seems to have accepted Freud's view that childhood experiences were crucial to the way adults developed. His only quarrel with Freud was that he made all these things into unconscious mysteries. Watson often spoke of his fear of the dark as a legacy from childhood. I think he seized on that specific because he did not want to think too much about his feelings for his mother. When Pickens upped and left, Emma may well have started to dote on her son John. He must have reminded her of the attractive qualities in Pickens. He was at an age when mothers and sons can tend to become very close. His older brother Edward seems to have been a religious prig from an early age. Clever, good-looking and with not a little of his father's rumbustiousness rubbed off on him, John must have been the apple of his mother's eye. Watson was ambivalent about this. He basked in it and fretted over it. He was always to warn that too close an attachment to a mother or father might make it very difficult to make 'marital adjustments' later on.

Watson also was tremendously afraid of homosexuality. He knew how close he had been to his mother. Emma had a considerable hold over him and that hold did not pass till she died.

One can speculate interminably over the psychohistory of a psychologist. But, because of what was just about to happen, it is important to get a sense of what Watson was like at fifteen. He seems to me to have developed into a curious, chaotic youngster. His mother had taught him to be energetic and hard-working. But beside this respectable discipline, there was all the intense emotion of her religious fervour. She had failed to make her son religious but Watson would always tend to defer to figures in authority as his mother had taught him one should defer to God and to the church. He saw how intense emotions were. His disreputable father gave him very different

11

characteristics. Pickens was impulsive, rough, rebellious and also had a great zest for life and its simple pleasures.

Then, at the age of fifteen, Watson achieved something quite unexpected. In the introduction, I said that his life took a number of radial turns. This was the first of them. He pulled off his first of many academic coups. He got himself admitted to Furman University. Despite the royal line of descent from Alfred there was no family tradition of going to college. Watson was a lazy troublemaker at school. He hardly seemed destined for an academic career. There was no money to pay for college. Emma might reasonably have expected him to start work and help pay some of the bills. Why did he decide to go and how did he manage to get himself admitted? Watson left no account of why he went, but it is not hard to see why he might decide to go to college. All the chaos of his father leaving, his problem at school and his inability to be religious made Watson sense that he wanted something very different out of life. He had seen how his father had kicked against all the local morality. He was doing the same, getting into trouble with the law. Unless he took himself in hand he would end up running a farm or a shop and trapped down South. He would be condemned to a narrow and boring life if he stayed in Greenville which was dripping with religion. He wanted to get away and the only way that he could do that was to get an education. He realised, too, that he had to do something to escape from the atmosphere of his family with its tensions and its perpetual stress on God. Without being able to say so, he seems to have known that he had to plunge into something or he would end up doing all manner of violence to himself and to others. Two arrests by the age of fifteen did not promise well. Watson was to study quite feverishly at Furman and to look to the university as a way of making himself ready for 'real life'. A college education offered all kinds of escape and it would make a different world his oyster.

Watson's motives are comprehensible. But how did a poor white boy with a record of laziness and violence at school get the very respectable Baptist Furman University to accept him? And at fifteen? Watson very much wanted to get an education. He must have somehow persuaded the President of Furman that despite his poor school record he was intelligent and very much in earnest. Watson already had some sense of how to present himself in order to make a good impression. In later life, Watson was usually to have a knack of getting things done when he really wanted them. President Montague of Furman was impressed and persuaded. Some of Emma's Baptist connections may have helped but Watson gave her no credit either for helping him decide to go to Furman or helping him actually to get in. Usually Watson acknowledged his debts. Going to Furman and getting accepted there

12

was very much his own idea and his own achievement.

In 1894 Furman University was in Greenville. The campus was pretty and set up on a hill. It was studded with trees and had a country air. In the mid-1950s the university sold the site which had now become a piece of valuable real estate, and where the Baptists once taught students there is now a gigantic supermarket called Piggly Wiggly! None of the old Furman buildings remain. Furman's main academic aim in 1894 was to churn out Baptist ministers, but the college offered many other courses. Watson did as little Bible study as he could get away with. The classes at Furman were open to women, which was to prove important. Like many people, it was at college that Watson would discover sex.

But before he could dally with sex, Watson had to pay for his education. He still lived at home, often quarrelling with brother Edward who disapproved of him. To pay fees, Watson did all kinds of odd jobs. Then after two years Watson began to help out in the chemical laboratory. That paid his way from then on.

At Furman Watson took a wide variety of courses. In his first year he did algebra and modern history as well as Latin, Greek and some elementary science. In doing the history of England, he came across David Hume for the first time. But it was Hume's *History of England* rather than his philosophy which Watson read.

The classics were Virgil and Cicero as well as studying the myths of Greece and Rome. In his first year Watson did rather well in the final examinations, though he liked to pretend he was not so good a student.

In his second year Watson returned to the study of the classics. He worked on Goodwin's *Revised Xenophon's Anabasis*. But, perhaps more important, it was in 1895 that Watson first met Gordon Moore and that he first started to do philosophy. Moore was a clergyman and he was probably the first person to have a real intellectual influence on Watson. He was something of an eccentric and something of a heretic – at least by Baptist standards. In 1900 he was removed from Furman University and went to work at the University of Chicago. Moore recognised that Watson was a young man of great promise and their relationship meant a great deal to Watson. For the course in logic, Moore used Fowler's *Logic*, Mill, Hamilton, Bain and Davis's *Theory of Thought*, a tome which does not appear to have lasted the test of time.

In 1895 Moore also gave a course in 'the elements of psychological knowledge' which Watson took. What Moore taught was very conventional. Psychology was largely the study of consciousness. There was much emphasis on intuition and thinking. Young Watson probably had to take part in introspective exercises. Introspection in 1897 was

13

not an embryonic encounter group. You did not search out your soul, your feelings or the reasons why you could not cope. What you did was to sit in front of a screen and to watch certain stimuli like three dots or the number five or a blue slide. You then had to report what went on in your consciousness when you saw these stimuli. For example, a number five might be accompanied by a sensation of effort in the mind together with tingling sensations in the belly. The aim of all this introspection was to define what made up consciousness. Not for the last time in their existence, psychologists were apeing physics. Physicists had dissected the constituent elements of matter. Psychologists hoped to be able to arrive at a formula for the constituents of mind. They hoped, for instance, that a formula could be devised for the experience of seeing blue which would be as tight as the formula for carbon dioxide. It may sound absurd now but this aim dominated psychology from 1880 to 1914.

The important point to grasp is that Watson did not immediately react against this kind of introspection. It took him about eight years to reject it in private. The rugged and practical young man did not at once hate introspection because it meant that he had to think about his feelings and anxieties. He was not being asked to do that kind of introspection. And, second, he was far from confident enough intellectually to be much of a critic. It may have seemed bizarre but, for the moment, he accepted it.

Moore also taught a great deal of Wundt. Wundt was a German psychologist who had founded the first psychological lab at Leipzig in 1879. Wundt firmly believed introspection could dissect out the elements of consciousness. Watson probably also first read William James during this period. James argued that the main task of psychology was to understand the stream of consciousness. But Gordon Moore seems to have spent much more time teaching Wundt than he did teaching James. It was only as a graduate student at Chicago that Watson would come to grips with James really properly.

Moore's course in junior psychology also included topics like the imagination and 'sentiments', which Moore divided from the emotions, though his catalogue of courses leaves little clue as to how he performed this nice division. Watson also took classes in the psychology of memory which must have covered Ebbinghaus's pioneering experiments in memorising nonsense syllables. Watson must have seen from these that it was possible to study human behaviour without having to rely on introspection. Moore also offered courses on 'Desire and the Will' which led to a 'defence of personal freedom'. Moore believed man was free. It is interesting to know that Watson faced this problem at the start of his studies for, I shall try to show, Watson believed rather more than his theories allowed that people were free to plot their destinies, to change their lives, and he even suggested that people might use psychology to help them do so.

Watson liked Moore very much. He wrote that the only topics he really enjoyed in Furman were philosophy and psychology. He said that Moore preached the only sermon he had ever listened to and that it was more a poem about evolution in blank verse than anything godly. Since Baptists believed in the Bible as the literal Word of God, it is not surprising Moore eventually got into trouble. 'Under him [Moore] I devoured Bowne's *Metaphysics*, Davis' *Psychology*, Weber's *History of Philosophy* and some considerable collateral reading including Wundt,' Watson wrote. Watson certainly enjoyed his psychology course enough to put his name down for the senior course that year. He would have more to devour. But in his examinations it was his worst subject. He got a mere 78 per cent. Most of his scores were round 90 per cent.

If Watson was doing well at his work, he was not too happy in the life of the college. He felt unsocial and he had few friends. His association with Joe Leech, with whom he had bullied 'niggers', seems to have come to an end. His only close friend was a boy called George Buist who would eventually become Professor of Chemistry at Furman. They spent a lot of time together in the chemistry lab in which Watson worked. A number of factors contributed to make Watson quite withdrawn. He was still having to cope with the after-effects of his father leaving home. He was conscious of being a poor white student whose family had no tradition of being educated. Many of the students at Furman may well have been more than a little snobbish towards him. He got saddled with a nickname that he detested, 'Swats'. The meaning of the word was never clear to him and it is probably not an American form of the British 'Swot'. But Watson hated being called that 'especially when I was introduced to pretty girls'. Apart from those troubles, Watson seems to have had problems with his older brother, Edward, who apparently regarded him as a ne'er do well and far too much like the abominable Pickens, who showed no signs of repenting but who continued to disgrace the family by cavorting with Indians close to town.

It was round about 1895 or 1896 that sex first appears in Watson's life. For all that he might be unsocial, he still managed to be attractive to women. In his autobiographical note, Watson wrote that he fell in love with one of the three co-eds at Furman. He did not say if he made much progress with this affair. Watson's daughter told me that she had good reason to believe that before her father graduated from Furman he had already had an affair with an older woman. Certainly Watson was good-looking, determined and charming. He may even have been successful enough with girls to make other men notice the fact with some envy.

Bennett Geer, who was an assistant on the campus, recalled meeting Watson on a train many years after Watson left Furman. Watson was the 'same old Broadus' he had been in college who thought highly of himself and, Geer added vituperatively, 'a little too highly'. Geer also said that Watson's eldest brother, Edward, had decided that John was the black sheep of the family. Edward can have formed this unflattering opinion only, I suspect, because of women or of religion. Watson was probably already making it quite plain that he had little faith. And the worthy Edward had probably heard something of Watson's romances at college. In a small town like Greenville, everyone thought it his or her Christian duty to spy out any scandal there might be. Satan was always a-prowling. Emma must have feared for her son's soul. There is no doubt that by the time he was seventeen, Watson was very interested in pretty girls. It was a sign of how fundamentally sexual he was that he should fall for one of the three girls on the Furman campus. There is some circumstantial evidence to suggest that Watson consummated one of these affairs while he was still at Furman. He was always a passionate man; he was always successful with women; he was attractive. There was enough of Pickens in him not to make him feel as ashamed of his desires as his religious mother would have wished. Watson was shy and would have felt any rebuffs quite deeply. But sex was not that frightening to him. Yet if he had been found out, the university would probably have dismissed him. It was a temple of study, not of lust.

Apart from his romantic and sexual escapades, Watson continued to do well at college. In his third year he did economics, geology, some Bible studies, French and German as well as physics. He got high marks in all these. He also took Moore's senior psychology course which was 'a more minute and extended examination of the powers and processes of the human mind'. Moore still taught 'ideal feeling', whatever that may be, and expounded 'the divisions of sensibility', a topic more suited to Jane Austen, one might think. But this year Moore also offered a new emphasis on psychophysics and physiology. Watson learned about visual illusions and the perception of tones; he learned, too, the basic layout of the nervous system. Moore used an up-to-date text but he still mixed in metaphysics. And, again, there was much discussion of personal freedom.

Watson by 1897 knew that he was academically very bright. But it is unlikely he knew what it was that he wanted to pursue. He had ambition but it was a kind of compulsive, chaotic ambition. He obviously worked very hard, almost compulsively. But the subjects at which he worked did not matter much. He slaved at Greek as he did at physics. Even if he hated the subject he insisted on doing well. He noted with some pride that he was the only one of his fellows who passed the final year examination in Greek. 'I only did it because I went to my room at two o'clock the afternoon before the exam, took with me one quart of Coca Cola syrup and sat in my chair until time for the exam the next day,' Watson wrote. He had to succeed.

But though he had to succeed, there was no clue what he was to succeed in. And in looking at Watson's career in 1897 and 1898 it is hard to understand just why he chose to pursue philosophy and psychology. He was doing even better in all the hard science courses. He was good enough at chemistry to be employed as a technical assistant in the laboratory. In his examinations in physics and astronomy he usually scored around 94 per cent, scores that were much better than those he obtained from Moore. He had always had a practical bent. A career in the sciences was quite possible. And yet Watson never seems to have been drawn to that.

It seems that what decided Watson was Moore. He liked and he respected Moore. And it was a period in his life when he needed a man he could respect. If any teacher in the sciences had begun to inspire him, he would have turned to that. Psychologists seem often to have been influenced to take the subject up as a career not because of its content but because of the way a particular teacher attracted them to it. In what should have been his final year, Watson studied ethics under Moore as well as mathematics, physics and chemistry. The course on ethics included Kent whom Watson was to grow to loathe. It also seems that Watson took a course in civics under Moore.

Watson should have graduated in the summer of 1898. But he worked himself up into a state of frenetic anxiety before the final examinations. He always tended to suffer from sleepless nights when he really got worried. And now his anxiety also came out in an odd way. In class Moore said just before the examinations that he would always flunk a man who handed in papers backwards. Eccentric Moore could no doubt find some metaphysical justification for such an act. Moore meant more to Watson than any other teacher at Furman and the warning stayed very much in Watson's conscious, and his subconscious mind.

Come the examinations, what did Watson do? In all the papers that were not marked by Moore, he did excellently as ever. But the paper on civics which Moore was to mark, Watson handed in backwards. He wrote what was probably a perfectly acceptable paper but then handed the sixteen pages in backwards. True to his eccentric decree, Moore failed the young man. Watson had to stay an extra year. Watson's reaction was defiant. 'I made an adolescent resolve then to the effect that I would make him seek me out for research one day,' Watson wrote in 1936. And, as we shall see, his adolescent resolve did nearly come true.

Watson said that he handed in the papers backwards 'by some strange streak of luck'. For a man who believed in Freudian slips, this was an unconvincing admission. Watson was fearful of how well he would do and doing well for Moore was very important to him. By handing in the paper backwards, he made it impossible in psychological terms really to fail because he could not pass the exam because of a technicality. He was opting out of the examination. It was also an act of defiance and a challenge. If Moore really believed in Watson he could still have passed him. There may have also been another reason for Watson's failure at this time. It meant that he did not quite yet have to choose what he would do with himself and, I suspect, he knew when he made that choice he would have to leave Greenville and his mother. Their bond was, indeed, very close.

So Watson stayed another year at Furman. He never particularly enjoyed college life there. He wrote that 'little of my college life interested me'. He wanted the college to give him guidance and to prepare him for life in a broader way than his family experiences could. But Furman could not do that. 'Those years made me bitter, made me feel that college only weakens the vocational slants and leads to softness and laziness and a prolongation of infancy with a killing of all vocational bents,' Watson added. He wanted to be independent; he wanted to be free of the influence of his mother and, also, his now gone father. He hoped that Furman would somehow teach him that kind of independence and wrench him from that 'infancy'. But he was asking for something which he needed as a person but which the university could not provide. It is a sign of how conflicted he was about wanting to be independent and yet not being able that he failed his examination and, second, that even when he had graduated with a Master's degree he did nothing much for a whole year. For a boy who had been resourceful enough to get to college, such inactivity seems surprising.

Moreover, Furman offered boys and girls very little by way of preparation for daily living. Watson was to argue that colleges ought to allow pre-marital sex and that there should be places where students could, almost, experiment in living. Yet the universities of the 1890s were morally strict places. If Watson had indeed consummated his romantic affairs, it must have been very clandestine or he would have risked being dismissed. Watson would have enjoyed the free campuses of the 1960s. Until universities could become places where the young could learn to live, Watson wrote 'we must look tolerantly upon college as a place for boys and girls to be penned up in until they reach majority – then let the world sift them'. He felt that being at Furman had been a kind of marking time. He had wanted to go to a place to grow up in emotionally and socially. He felt that he had not been allowed to do that. He needed an environment in which he could flower and Furman had not been that. The world had yet, he felt, to sift him.

Watson was twenty one when he became an MA. He now had to choose what to do. He knew that he did not really want to stay in the South. There were few good universities there and, as an ambitious young man, Watson knew enough about academic realities to realise that he had to get a PhD at a college of some standing. Furman was not that. But there was also the problem of Emma. She was ill. Watson would have found it hard to leave her anyway. The fact she was so ill must have made it almost impossible for him to go. So, after he had graduated so well, Watson took what was for a man of his academic standing a really lowly job. He became a teacher in a one-room school house. Later, he puffed out this position to 'The Principal of the Batesburg Institute'. It is true that he was the Principal but he was also the only teacher, a chief without any Indians.

The Batesburg Institute seems to have completely disappeared from the official records of Greenville education. According to Ben Field, who went there when he was ten, it was a small private school for about twenty children. They were all white, of course. Watson taught all twenty in one class. The parents of the children could only afford to pay him $25 a month which was a pittance even in those days. To add to that, Watson got free board and lodging. Every week he would stay and eat with a different family. It must have been a little humiliating going from house to house. But the job meant he could be close to his mother. He even joined a church again to please her as she lay dying. He did not have to worry about quarrelling with his brother Edward since he was no longer at home. And by living in Greenville, but not at home, Watson was in effect weaning himself away from his mother's powerful influence.

As a teacher, Watson was a success. He was attractive, funny and interesting. He did not believe in the kind of formal teaching he had received most of his life. 'He liked to take us kids in the yard and play games with us,' Field says, 'and he made a practice of telling stories.' The stories must have been good, for the children listened, Field remembers. And while Watson could be charming, he had a sharp temper. He did not put up with anyone behaving in the way that he and Joe Leech had done at school. If things went well, he was delightful; if things went wrong, he could flare up fast. Field recalls that once Watson got furious with him because he talked too much in class.

At the school, Watson apparently kept a number of rats. He had what Field calls 'his house of rats'. And these rats were not just there to be admired. Watson had, it seems, done some training with these animals. They had been conditioned – though, of course, he did not know the word conditioned – to run in circles when he played some particular sound noise. Field said that these rats were able to do a number of other tricks including running in particular directions. In one way, it would be foolish to read too much in this. All it shows is that the young Watson was interested in animals and able to train them. On the other hand, it also suggests that way back in 1900 Watson knew how to do what B. F. Skinner later scientifically perfected – to 'shape' the behaviour of animals.

On 3 July 1900 Emma Roe Watson died. Her death freed Watson in some way of which he was not aware. Until she died he seems to have been unable to make any serious effort to go to graduate school. Yet by 20 July Watson had persuaded the President of Furman, A. P. Montague, to write a glowing letter of recommendation to the University of Chicago, and also one to Princeton. The letter to Chicago survives. The President praised Watson's brains and his character. He wrote: 'Mr. Watson is one of our strongest men, an alumni who reflects credit upon his alma mater. He is a gentleman of marked ability, very studious, a successful teacher and a man of high character.' Obviously word of Watson's affairs had not reached the President. Montague added that Watson would have it in his power to attract other students (who had money) to Chicago and that 'he will do you much honour'.

But Watson had first to decide whether it was to Chicago or Princeton that he really wanted to go. Princeton, that most olde worlde of American universities, probably attracted the snob in Watson. Mark Baldwin, the professor of philosophy there, was a very lively man. Watson wrote to Baldwin who replied that Princeton still insisted on a reading knowledge of Greek and Latin. 'That settled it,' wrote Watson. He was not going to sweat through verbs, tenses and Xenophon ever again, Coca Cola or no Coca Cola. Watson makes it seem that it was Princeton's insistence on the classics that turned him against it. I think that this is far from the truth.

Moore had gone to Chicago. Moore had been something of a mentor to Watson. He represented a kind of security for the young man and Watson flamboyantly wanted to prove to Moore how very brilliant he was. Moore made Chicago sound attractive for he wrote to his ex-student and extolled John Dewey who was then the professor of philosophy there. 'I was more interested in philosophy than in psychology at that time,' Watson wrote. To study under Dewey promised much and, to cap it all, Watson actually had a relative at the University of Chicago. John Manly was an English scholar who, like Watson, had gone to Furman and from Furman had joined the faculty at Chicago. Manly was Watson's brother's brother-in-law. Watson chose Chicago and wrote to President Harper that he was 'very anxious to go to Chicago and I believe you will find me an earnest student'. Watson was aware of how limited Furman was. He told Harper that he had resigned his teaching job 'in order to do advanced work in a real university'. Furman, by implication, was a dolled-up college. Watson's ambition comes through clearly. 'I know now I can never amount to anything in the education world unless I have better preparation.' He pleaded either for a scholarship or for free tuition. But he was already acute enough to suggest that he could probably get another student, who had money, to go up with him to Chicago in a year or so. Watson also wrote to John Dewey, the professor of philosophy at Chicago, and set out his eagerness and his qualifications. Chicago must have been impressed. The letter of recommendation from the President of Furman was glowing and, in those distant days, people believed letters of recommendation. Moore probably spoke up for Watson. Although Watson had only applied to Chicago in July, by September all the arrangements had been finalised. Watson had the knack of getting things done, even then.

In all his work, Watson stressed that the habits which were formed in one's youth were crucial. He objected to biographies because most biographers failed to grasp the point. In 1928 by then the witty Dr Watson moaned: 'How can we keep people from writing them [biographies]? . . . no one can write a worth while biography unless one knows something about the infancy of the person written about.' When he left Greenville in 1900 Watson had already been, to use a word he got very fond of, 'slanted' in many directions.

The young Watson was practical, good with his hands and skilful with animals. He loved designing gadgets and had confidence in his abilities with things. He was less sure of himself with people. He had tried desperately hard to overcome all the chaos of his adolescence and, to some extent, he had succeeded. But he was left very vulnerable by what had happened at Greenville because he wanted some man to be the father to him that Pickens had never been.

From the age of fifteen Watson had driven himself very hard. He knew he was ambitious and that he wanted to make his mark in the world. His mother had given him a model of constant energy. One had to be doing things, always. And after Pickens left, she relied a great deal on her son. He was close, possibly too close, to Emma. One of the ways in which he reacted to this was to withdraw from intimate personal contacts. He found it hard to give of himself and he was always worried that his own children would be too close to him, too attached, too dependent. Emma probably did her son a great favour by dying when she did, for her death appears to have freed him in some kind of way so that, after July 1900, he could really go his own way.

Emma had not managed to instil the religious habit in her son. But she did leave him with a strange need for authority. There would often be in Watson a need to defer to certain people who had authority over him. His letters show him to have been remarkably obsequious at times.

There was also Pickens's influence, however. Pickens was rough, rebellious and defiant. His son learned much from him, including a taste for defiance. In 1900 Watson would probably have denied that he owed his father anything but I will argue that much of the psychologist's best work came when he had to balance his tendencies to defer and to defy. When he became too defiant, he rampaged beyond the realism of sense: when he was too deferential, he had to keep his originality in check. It offended too many people. It would take Watson a long time to become confident enough not to be too deferential. And to state behaviourism, of course, he would need to defy most established psychological ideas.

But Pickens not only gave his son a sense of defiance, he also betrayed him. Watson would be fearful of too much intimate contact. He was close to his father who left him and he was close to his mother who tended to overwhelm him with too much love. It became difficult for the young Watson really to give himself totally to anyone though he did rather hanker after father-figures, it seems.

After he left South Carolina, Watson probably never set foot in church again. He only uttered the name of the Lord when swearing. It has been argued that, though Watson rejected religion, he turned behaviourism into a creed. In the 1930s one acid reviewer lampooned him as the Billy Sunday of behaviourism. In a doctoral thesis 'John B. Watson and American Social Thought', Lucille Birnbaum admits that she is religious herself and then claims Watson produced a revivalist psychology. His science had to be fundamentalist though his faith could not be. This seems too pat to me. Watson did not become rigid in his psychological ideas until 1930 after he had suffered a variety of personal and professional vicissitudes. Between 1900 and 1925, certainly, he often shifted his positions. He put forward a particular method of doing psychology; he did not ossify that method into a fixed system. He never required fervour. As editor of the *Psychological Review*, he published many papers that were either frankly hostile to behaviourism or, at least, very different. Billy Sunday and the other fundamentalists did not so accommodate the Devil or, even, Catholics.

Greenville left Watson also with a certain sense of inferiority. He was often very aware of that in Chicago. The South was more famous for its manners than for its minds and it was intellectually that Watson wanted to excel. And though the 'nigger fighter' had become the academic youth, Watson always had a not very pleasant streak of racial intolerance in him. Otherwise, though, he was a sharp and likeable young man.

The morality of Greenville, with the fear of the Lord on everyone's lips, also left Watson with a keen eye for social hypocrisy. When Pickens left home, the boy must have had to put up with much charitable Christian concern that was humiliating. The Fields, for instance, seem always to have been coming round to see how Emma and her poor abandoned family were doing. There was only their Christian duty. It contributed to making Watson shy. And, in a society where mutual spying was a way of life, it must have seemed an advantage to develop into a loner.

When Watson left Greenville at the start of September 1900, he left it for good. He had no lingering fondness for the place. When he went back South he went on business always at the expense of some university. In 1919 he returned to Furman to collect an honorary LID but he never became romantic about his roots. When he left for Chicago in 1900 he may not have been quite sure how it was that he wanted to make a mark on the world, but he knew he wanted to make that mark. He also knew that his life would be very different from that of his family in the staunch Baptist town. Watson was glad to get out of Greenville. The place had done much to form him and, when it found out the details of his eventual career, the town was duly and devoutly shocked.

2

Chicago

Watson took the train up to Chicago at the end of August. He had saved $50 out of his meagre pay at the Batesburg. He was twenty-two. He was not sure what he wanted to study: he was not sure how he would eat. He felt himself to be unprepared and undisciplined for what he chose to call a 'real university'. Eight years later, Watson would leave Chicago with a national reputation as an animal psychologist, having been appointed professor at Johns Hopkins at the remarkably young age of twenty-nine. By then, Watson would also have arrived at many of the ideas that were to shock and change psychology. But, for the moment, he believed himself to be much more interested in metaphysics than in rats.

The faculty at Chicago was a lively one. Watson soon met the famous Dewey and the controversial French physiologist, Jacques Loeb. Also at Chicago were the philosopher George H. Mead, the physicist Albert Michelson, and a young sociologist, William Thomas. But the man who was to have the greatest influence on Watson at Chicago was James Angell. Angell did not even become assistant professor of psychology until 1901 but he was a man who was almost calculated to impress the young Watson. Angell was thirty-one. He was very able, elegant and stylish. He came from an old New England family and did not have to rummage history for his ancestors, as some of his folk had come over on the *Mayflower*. Angell's father had been President of the University of Michigan. Angell seemed to have all the social and intellectual graces. Watson liked him, and Chicago, at once. 'I entered then and felt at once I had come to the right place.'

It might be the right place but the lectures in the autumn of 1900 and the spring of 1901 soon showed philosophy was the wrong subject. As always, Watson worked terribly hard. He studied the history of philosophy, Kant and the Greek philosophers but he got nothing out of any of them. One of the philosophy faculty, Tufts, taught a private course on Wilhelm Wundt, the German philosopher and psychologist who had set up the world's first psychological laboratory at Leipzig in 1879. Despite that laboratory, Wundt was committed to introspection as the way of doing psychology. Watson got very little out of any of these courses. At first he blamed himself for his failure to 'flower in philosophy'. He drove himself to work harder at it.

The only philosophy Watson found at all congenial was that which was taught by his old mentor, Gordon Moore. Moore taught Locke, Hartley, Berkeley and Hume. Hume soon fascinated Watson who said that the Scottish philosopher 'freed him intellectually' because he had shown that 'nothing is fixed, final or sacrosanct'. We cannot logically prove that the sun will rise in the east tomorrow but we believe it will do so because the sun has always risen in the east. Our beliefs are very much a matter of habit. And Hume also suggested that our beliefs are tremendously influenced by our feelings. We are much more emotional than logical creatures though once we have committed ourselves to a particular belief we like to dress that faith up with all kinds of arguments. After all the religious certainties of Greenville, Watson felt exhilarated by Hume. Hume gave him, too, some authority for being sceptical. The only other sceptic Watson had known was Pickens, who scoffed at conventions but who was hardly an intellectual.

Hume emphasised that nothing was sacrosanct – and certainly not the philosophy and psychology of 1900. But if Hume was a boon, Dewey was a disaster. Watson wrote that he got 'strange to say least of all out of John Dewey. I never knew what he was talking about and unfortunately I still don't.' In 1936 when Watson so dismissed Dewey, he could afford ironies. In 1900 he was disappointed and worried.

In many ways it is odd that Watson should have been so negative about Dewey. Dewey became famous for his pragmatism and Watson would become a most pragmatic psychologist. Dewey had, in 1896, written a rather interesting article on the reflex in psychology. Dewey suggested that the 'entire organic situation' affects the way that we perceive the stimulus and helps 'to determine what the stimulus shall be and do'. What seems to be the same stimulus from the outside is not necessarily perceived as the same stimulus. If you are sick, *steak tartare* (the stimulus) does not provoke the usual response of greed, delight and brandishing of knife and fork but is perceived as horrible raw meat and is pushed away with a slight shudder. This idea interested Angell, who must have made Watson read Dewey's article. But for Watson, the great John Dewey was incomprehensible.

'God knows,' wrote the irreligious Watson, 'I took enough philosophy to know something about it. But it wouldn't take hold. I passed my exams but the spark was not there.' The subject felt wrong

25

to Watson. It was too abstract and, though he liked some of the philosophers like Tufts, Mead and Moore, he really did not find them compelling. 'I attach no blame to them for my failure to flower in philosophy,' he wrote, but they had not commended his total respect.

Psychologists often seem to have drifted into the discipline either by accident or because some teacher inspired them and steered them into it. In the midst of all this metaphysical disillusion, there was Angell. Watson always admitted the debt he owed to Angell. 'Mr. Angell's erudition, quickness of thought and facility with words early captured my somewhat backwards leaning towards psychology,' he wrote.

Angell was the ideal man for Watson to give himself to. He had intellectual presence and he was willing to take Watson under his wing. One result of Pickens's departure, I believe, was that Watson felt a need for a man he could look up to. Angell hardly reminded Watson of his father but he did become something of a father-figure to Watson. And, as a result, Watson gave him tremendous affection and loyalty. Watson would have, in the end, to struggle to free himself from Angell. But in 1901 Angell fulfilled the need Watson felt for a real teacher who would teach him psychology (or something else) rather in the way that his father had taught him carpentry. (It is curious that Jacques Loeb, who was a far greater scientist than Angell never evoked any of this intensity in Watson.)

From the intellectual standpoint, Angell was conservative. He had studied at Harvard under William James. James made a very deep impression on Angell. His knowledge, his observations and 'above all, the fascinating literary style, swept me off my feet'. Angell would stay swept off for the rest of his career. He taught the psychology James had taught him – the main task of the psychologist was to analyse the stream of consciousness. Habits, the Self and how we knot it together, the Will and the Soul were the other main topics in the study of man, and woman, kind.

Because of Angell's influence, Watson would always have a soft spot for James. Even when Watson was a full-blooded behaviourist and denounced consciousness as metaphysical nonsense, he wrote with some admiration for James. But Angell was to have a more critical say in Watson's career Loeb suggested when he do his doctoral thesis under him on the physiology of the dog's brain. But Angell felt that Loeb was not a 'safe' man for a 'green PhD candidate'. If Angell thought he was unsafe, then Loeb must be unsafe. In 1915 Watson wrote to Loeb to say he was sorry he had been so swayed by Angell's mania for caution but, for now, Angell was too important personally and intellectually for Watson to refuse his advice.

Both Angell and Henry Donaldson, who taught neurology, believed that Watson should use his talents on animals. Watson was not yet sure enough to actually pick a subject for his thesis all on his own. He let Angell guide him towards the study of 'animal education'. The idea must have appealed to Watson after his good times with the animals and rats back in Greenville. And it was fortunate that Watson at this point avoided studying people. If he had done so, he would have soon had to face the stark fact that he disagreed totally with Angell's position. Watson was far too insecure for that kind of confrontation. So, instead of burrowing into some aspects of consciousness, Watson would turn his attention to the general area of 'animal education'. He already had the acumen to set himself an important problem; how did rats learn and what were the limits to which they could be trained. The psychology of learning, which was to become one of the most important areas of psychology, had hardly began in 1900; Watson was to be one of its pioneers.

To understand the way Watson worked at this time, it is important to realise how he lived. He had to slave to make money. His $50 was soon exhausted. He had a room in a students' boarding house and, to pay for that and his food, he worked there as a waiter which made him the princely sum of $2.50 a week. Watson had to rush back from his rats to help serve dinner. He disliked being so poor – though he had known nothing different, it was much worse than being poor in Greenville. Angell paid Watson $1.00 week to 'dust his desk' and be an assistant janitor in the laboratory. Later, Donaldson gave Watson $2.00 to keep his white rats for him. Watson enjoyed his job as 'private nurse to a cage full of white rats'. All these financial strains meant Watson could afford to do very little but work. At most he had $6.00 a week to survive on. He said later that he would also have studied medicine if he had the money. He was ambitious and he would have worked hard at his thesis anyway. But his poverty made him concentrate on work the more. He felt driven to succeed. He spent many evenings and most Sundays in the laboratory. If Emma was looking down from Heaven, she would have feared for her son's soul as he spent Sunday playing with rats instead of praying in church. In the autumn of 1901 Watson became a compulsive worker.

In 1900 very little was known about the true abilities of animals. Only circuses had been concerned about what animals could or could not do. But suddenly in the 1890s the question of animal intelligence became a major issue. Most psychology now looks at human behaviour and tries to see what there is in it that is like animal behaviour. After Watson, many behaviourists would study learning in rats and argue that people also learned just like that. Ethologists now kept on telling us how many of the things we do are merely sophisticated versions of what monkeys, apes or lions do. But in 1890 scientists wanted to see not if they could reduce human beings to the level of animals but, rather whether they could raise animals to a more human status. The trend was to suggest that animals could, indeed, 'Reason'. Much attention was paid to remarkable cases like Clever Hans, the horse who could do square roots and speak in Russian. The horses of Eberfeldt also had remarkable mathematical abilities, especially for horses. Dr Doolittle would have felt at home, though, in their all too human vanity, it never occurred to any investigators to ask whether these intellectual animals could talk their own language. No one tested whether the horses of Eberfeldt had a horse language. Watson was to devote an ironic chapter in *Behaviour* to some of these extraordinary animals. In 1901 they were taken seriously. The French psychologist, Claparède, went twice to examine these beasts. Finally even Clever Hans would turn out to be a fraud, but 'Animal Intelligence' was the burning serious topic of the moment and also the title of Romanes's book (published in 1882) which was much discussed then.

Scientists wanted to know just what animals could manage intellectually. And they could do this only through observing animals. But observing an animal was only necessary because it was the only way of getting at the introspections the animal would have if only the brute could speak. Had animals had the gift of tongues, scientists would have been much less interested in animal behaviour. In 1890 scientists relied on the argument by analogy. If an animal behaved in a way that a person behaved you could argue, by analogy, that the animal must therefore think and feel as a person would in such circumstances. Lloyd Morgan had issued his canon of parsimony which stated that you must account for the animal's behaviour in as lowly terms as possible but the mood of the time seems to have favoured finding that animals were rational.

It is worth giving an example from the main study of the white rat before Watson to make clear how scientists tried to introspect for animals. Small (1901) put a rat in front of various problem boxes – animal puzzle boxes which had to be solved. He watched what happened. Small is describing a rat who has found a door of a box closed:

> The pausing of the rat when the door unexpectedly failed to open
> might seem to imply reflection but this is not so in any strict usage of
> the term reflect. Surprise and disappointment will quite suffice to
> restrict activity for the time and those affections would preclude
> the possibility of reflection unless reflection is merely used in a
> descriptive sense to designate the transition from this passive to an

active state under the resurging impulse of hunger. That the rat *feels* 'why' and 'what' is certain, that she thinks 'why' or 'what' is both doubtful and unnecessary.

Small published his study on the white rat in 1901. Much of it was couched in these terms, making very nice distinctions. Did the rat feel 'whether' or 'what'? Could the rat have feelings? Its behaviour was studied essentially as a clue to these matters.

It was against this kind of background that Watson set out to do a number of things. He wanted to see how young the rat could solve certain problems: he wanted also to see what were the limits of the problems that rats could solve. If Watson had trained young rats to do all kinds of tricks back in Batesburg, he may have suspected their abilities were extensive. Watson also wanted to see how the development of the rat's brain correlated with its abilities. He was especially interested in medullation, the process by which nerves acquire a sheath of protective material, and how that related to the abilities of the animal.

Today a psychologist might start by taking a particular litter of rats from birth and putting them through their paces. But Watson had no idea of the capacity of rats as there was, apart from Small, no literature on the subject. He had no technology, though Thorndike had published *Animal Intelligence* in 1899 and had established a standard set of puzzle boxes for cats. Watson was very much feeling his way.

Between autumn 1901 and the end of March 1902, Watson was to work feverishly on this problem. As at Furman, he plunged himself into the topic. He worked Sundays and left himself little time for relaxation, especially as he still had to do the various jobs that earned him his living. He noted in his thesis each day on which he carried out each portion of each experiment so there is a sense of the way he wrestled with each new problem and moved from one difficulty on to the next. Watson wrote: 'I enjoyed the years in neurology and physiology and my research on the rats. I worked day and night and established work habits that have persisted the rest of my life.' Some of these work habits were compulsive. Watson always tended to overwork. He was very fertile and liked to immerse himself in doing research; and also, because he was somewhat insecure, he felt it very necessary to work so hard in order to excel.

Watson usually worked by himself and he tested each of his animals himself. When he rewarded them with food, the food was not a pellet that came impersonally down a chute but it was bread that Watson had soaked in milk and handed to the rats. Watson became fond of the animals. He very honestly noted mistakes that he made, as when he confused two animals. Experimenting on animals was a novel art and science; Watson's thesis offers flashes which show how haphazard it must have been at times. The expensive technology that now dominates modern animal laboratories is very different. Precisely because Watson was so close to his rats, he often observed their behaviour acutely. Many of his observations read just like an ethologist's, though ethology did not exist then.

Watson began his experiments on 19 November 1901. He was to work in his feverish way at them throughout the winter, spring and early summer. With those beloved manual skills of his, he built a cubical wire box. In its middle he put food. He concealed the entrances to the box by placing sawdust in front of them. The rats had to find their way to the food. It was the first, and the simplest, of the problems that Watson would set them. Later on he put food in the middle of labyrinths that grew ever more complex. Then Watson would devise a piece of apparatus where the rats had to pull a string that sprang a latch that opened the door to the food. Finally Watson would get the rats to walk a plank. When they reached a certain point on the plank, their weight counterbalanced the latch to spring the door behind them, and thus made it possible for the rats to get at the food.

It soon became clear that rats could make their way to food in a wire box. In a complex box with two entrances, the fastest animals learned to make their way in 75 seconds. On 2 December Watson put his rats through labyrinths which had four entrances. The rats had to push their way through a blind to each entrance. Three of the entrances did not lead to the food but rather out of the other end of the labyrinth. At first the rats did not go through the blinds at all.

Watson noted acutely that one rat 'ran frantically around, smelling at the food and clambering up the sides of the fence. This was the first time he had to obtain food without first removing sawdust from the entrance'. The rat tried to bite its way through the labyrinth and then Watson had to go and serve at dinner in the boarding house. When Watson got back to the laboratory, he found this rat 'sitting on the fence looking the picture of discouragement'. Watson had to show the rats how to push through the blinds. But once he had done that, they learned the task quickly enough. By the next day, running through on 'true pathway' that led to the food had become 'almost a reflex'. The fastest rat did it in 17 seconds. The rats could learn a complex labyrinth.

Watson found that young rats who were about 30 days old did learn quicker than mature rats of 63 days of age. But as he moved on to more difficult problems, the older rats seemed to do better. By 1 January the rats had graduated to the problem in which a string had to be pulled to spring the latch that got to the food. Watson celebrated the new year by noting that one rat's record showed how learning develops. A typical rat first pulled the string that opened the latch in 12 minutes. Then his record ran: 12 minutes; 12 minutes; 3 minutes; 8 minutes; 2 minutes; 3 minutes. So far an improvement rather than an 'aha' leap. But then the times were 0.33 minutes; 0.33 minutes; 0.16 minutes; 0.08 minutes; 0.108 minutes. Watson had made a fundamental discovery in the psychology of learning. Learning is not an even process at all. It is a question of slow haphazard improvements followed by a sudden solution.

Previously the rat had always seen the result of its actions. It dug through sawdust and, lo, there was the food; it pulled the string, behold, the bread soaked in milk. The plank was different. The rat had to walk out far enough to counterbalance the friction of the string and latch. But the food was behind the rat. It could not be seen at once. Watson did not think the animals could solve it. At first, they were confused. But on the second day, after twelve accidental successes, one rat began to master the problem. It took another eighteen trials before the rat could solve it consistently. Other rats were slower but they solved it too.

Watson could have gone on to see if rats could manage even more complicated problems. Instead, he wanted to see if the rats could solve those same problems younger. In those months he had come to like the young rats. 'It is a pleasure to watch them,' he wrote, 'they fly from place to place trying everything.' He identified with their energy.

Watson now took a new litter of rats. He put the rats in a box with their mother. The rats could find their way back to their mother across the box with an obstacle in it at the age of 12 days. 'This was a definite and businesslike procedure.' At 15 days of age the infant rats knew exactly what they were doing and 'scrambled over one another in their eagerness to get back'. At 18 days he put them in one of the labyrinths but they did not grasp the problem at all. Instead they curled up and went to sleep. They were too young.

Watson then weaned these rats at 20 days. He put them to work on the problems. They solved them all, the boxes, laybrinths and string and planks at a much younger age than the first rats. Another litter was weaned at 16 days. These rats raced through the battery of problems even younger. Watson said a little importantly: 'We may safely conclude that the rat reaches psychical maturity between 23 and 27 days of age.'

As you read *Animal Education*, you get a feeling of the way Watson was absorbed by the work. The rats fascinated him. They amused him. He felt that he could understand them. But in order to make sense of their behaviour he did not have to construct elaborate analogies about what humans who behaved in the same kind of way might be intro-specting. Even now, early in his career, Watson was careful not to ascribe to the rats anthropomorphic feelings.

The psychological part of his thesis done, Watson turned to neurology. He knew what the rats could do at various ages. He now sacrificed rats who were aged from 1 day to 30 days and examined the state of their brains at each age. He wanted to link their psychological abilities with the physiological development of their cortex. It was a sensible, and new, attempt to marry psychology and physiology.

Small had noted that the rat at birth is able to smell, able to make co-ordinated movements, and is sensitive to taste. Watson now showed it had all these capacities without any medullated fibres. He then tried to correlate the abilities he had unearthed in the rat from ten days on. 'From fourteen days to twenty-four days,' Watson wrote, 'we had a development on the psychical side not paralleled by a like increase in the development of medullation.' The presence of medullated fibres in the cortex was not a *sine qua non* of the 'rat's forming and retaining definite associations'.

After 24 days, there was an enormous increase in the number of medullated fibres. First, Watson asked: 'Should we grant that there is no increase in the psychical life of the rat after twenty-four days?' He argued that while older rats in the wild undoubtedly would be more skilful at finding food and would have a 'larger stock of associations', the 'young rat will be master of the situation even more quickly than the adult'. Confronted by a novel problem 'pure' mental ability did not increase after twenty-four days. Watson always believed that abilities flowered young. Second, Watson was tempted to ask what the signi-ficance of these medullated fibres was. He phrased the question in German, a sign of the hold German psychology had over the Americans at the time. 'Wass überhaupt', he asked, was the significance of those medullated fibres. He knew the rat could form associations without them but that did not tell him what they were for. But Watson did not really pursue this problem.

During the time in which Watson ran the experiments he became more and more under strain. He was working obsessively hard at something that fascinated him. He knew he was doing good work and that gave him enough confidence to begin to wonder about the whole way in which psychology was done. He read Hume again to see the Scot argue again that nothing was sacrosanct, final or fixed.

In his laboratory with his rats, Watson had been very isolated. Visitors were rare, though both Angell and the philosopher George Mead dropped in from time to time. Watson became confident of his experimental ability. No one in the whole USA had, by the end of 1902, as much experience as he did of working with rats.

But all Watson's confidence evaporated when it came to writing up the thesis. The extent to which it worried him shows how much he felt himself to have been poorly trained at his 'unreal' first university. Angell helped him. Watson generously admitted in 1936 that Angell 'worked with me on every sentence I wrote on my thesis, Animal Behaviour. He taught me rhetoric as well as psychology.' Ironically, Watson was to learn to write with great clarity and wit: Angell never achieved the same easy style.

It was while he was writing up the notes, that the first vague glimpses of behaviourism occurred to Watson. He had been too busy with the details of running the rats to mull over the implications of the research. But now he could start to wonder if it could be possible to study human beings in the same kind of way. If you could understand rats without the convolutions of introspection, could you not understand people the same way? But he knew that such an idea would be heresy. In 1936 Watson wrote: 'At Chicago I first began a tentative formulation of my later point of view.' Watson broached the subject to Angell in 1904. I think he was thinking his way towards it late in 1902. It would be a mistake to think he had arrived at any very systematic formulation. But he just *felt* – and *felt* seems a key word – that there was no reason not to look at people the objective way he had done with rats. Human beings were not so special, not so soulful nor absolutely different from other species. And Watson not only liked animals but he knew the limitations of introspection.

'I hated to serve as a subject. I didn't like the stuffy artificial instructions given to subjects.' A criticism very familiar in modern psychology. 'I always was uncomfortable and acted unnaturally.' The introspective Watson added that, 'With animals I was at home. I felt that, in studying them, I was keeping close to biology with my feet on the ground. More and more the thought presented itself: Can't I find out by watching their behaviour everything that the other students are finding out by using Os?' Students who used Os – observers – gave human subjects instructions to observe their own consciousness.

Watson knew well enough that such an idea would appal Angell. Yet Watson *felt* the value of what he was groping towards. At the same time, it frightened him. If he had mentioned the idea to Angell, the reaction would be hostile, for his mentor believed man was a thinking and spiritual being in an utterly different category from rats or any other animal. Watson looked up to Angell. It was a terrible dilemma. And there were also practical questions. Watson was ambitious. He wanted to deserve and to get an excellent doctorate and he needed

Angell's support both for that and to get a position. He could not bear to quarrel with Angell on a personal level and he could not afford to quarrel with him on a professional level. Unformulated as his ideas were, Watson knew that what he wanted to say, what he felt, was a complete anathema to the people on whom he depended. He was unable to defy and could not really in his heart of hearts defer to them. He resolved this conflict in a classic way. He had his first breakdown.

Again, the young Watson was unable to quite complete his work – as he had been unable to complete his degree at Furman – without a trauma. At Furman he had handed his papers in backwards in order to fail. Now, after so much gruelling and creative mulling, Watson had an attack of anxiety. His own short account of what happened is the only one.

'In the fall of the year before I graduated [1903] I had a breakdown – sleepless nights for weeks – a typical Angst. Getting up at 3 am to walk eight or ten miles.' Watson was to suffer from such insomnia and depression surprisingly often. It is hardly surprising that Watson wrote he had 'received little encouragement' and that he was bitter at how his tentative ideas were frostily received. It is important, however, to realise that his behaviouristic ideas were very tentative, amounting to not much more than a 'What if we tried to study humans in this way. . .?' Until 1909, he still taught introspective psychology as well as animal behaviour. In 1902 he was just starting to toy with some of the ideas that would crystallise into behaviourism. But even toying was bad enough as far as Angell and the rest of the faculty at Chicago went.

As well as his intellectual problems, he had financial and sexual ones. Let us put sex before money. He was clearly a man with considerable sexual needs; in the supposedly chaste atmosphere of the times these needs were hard to satisfy. Watson would later recommend 'wholesale necking' among students. To add to his intellectual problems, Watson fell desperately in love as he had done with one of the co-eds at Furman. It seems to have been nerve-racking. His beloved, apparently, indulged in some widespread wholesale necking of her own which though it was what Watson later recommended was not something that he could at that time put up with. He was always very jealous. Poor, frustrated and in a dreadful dilemma about what to do with his ideas, it is not strange that Watson should succumb to a breakdown.

Watson was right about Angell. When he did muster the courage to broach the subject, in 1904, Angell would tell him he was ignorant. Man was not a soft, soulless machine. He should stick to animals. That reduced Watson to silence for about four years. And when finally he did come out publicly with his by then systematic ideas about what the future of psychology should be, Angell's reaction was curt. His protégé was crazy. Watson's breakdown in 1902 was an understandable response. He dealt with the crisis sensibly.

He went off for his first vacation in three years with his friends the Van Pelts in Norwood, Michigan. 'A month there during which I went to bed only with a light turned on.' The phobia from the past reappeared in the crisis. The strain had brought up Watson's old fear of the dark and, perhaps, it is not too fanciful to suggest that he sensed his ideas on how to study human beings were a final blow, a crowning act of defiance to his dead mother and her Baptist beliefs.

But Watson coped very sensibly with his *Angst*, as he called it. He left Chicago for the countryside. The Van Pelts seem to have been very friendly and relaxed. Watson would always recommend to people that the way to cope with depression was to get out into a new environment even if that meant leaving all one's family behind. He argued – and, as we shall see, his arguments seem to have that peculiar sharpness that comes out of these being experiences that he had had himself – that it was very foolish to decide to commit suicide while one was depressed. He always stuck to this advice for himself.

The new environment worked. Watson noted that he made: 'A sudden recovery and back to work. This, in a way, was one of my best experiences in my university course. It taught me to watch my step.' Watson was always one to try and put his experiences to good account. He also got intellectual benefits from his *Angst*. He added that it 'in a way prepared me to accept a large part of Freud when I first began to get really acquainted with him around 1910'. He returned to Chicago, eager for 1903.

Watson completed *Animal Education* and submitted it to the university as his thesis. In many ways the degree was something of a triumph for Watson. He was the youngest PhD that Chicago had ever had. Donaldson felt very strongly that the thesis could be published. In those days, academic publishing cost the author money since there was not much of a university market for what were, in effect, monographs. Watson could not afford the cost so Donaldson insisted on lending him the $350 it took to publish the thesis. He did not manage to repay the debt for 20 years.

But while it was pleasant to have his thesis published, Watson also received a tremendous blow to his intellectual confidence. He was awarded his doctorate 'Magna Cum Laude' – with great praise. Instead of merely congratulating him on that fact, they pointed out at once that his thesis and examinations 'was much inferior to that of Miss Helen Thompson who had graduated two years before with a Summa Cum

Laude'. The *highest* praise was, clearly, more praiseworthy than simply *great* praise. It seems a particularly malicious act on the part of Dewey and Angell to have spoilt Watson's doctorate in this way. Perhaps they both wanted to put this iconoclastic young student in his place. It would be typical of Angell to want to make sure that Watson knew his place. It certainly wounded Watson. 'I wondered then if anybody could ever equal her record. That jealousy existed for years,' Watson wrote. And if, on the one hand, it was a powerful spur, the whole experience left with Watson, he reckoned, 'my first deep-seated inferiority'. That he should be so concerned about the opinions of the incomprehensible Dewey seems to show how great Watson's need for intellectual recognition was. (Incidentally, Helen Thompson does not seem to have made any major contribution to psychology.) Watson felt rejected and dejected.

There were some consolations. The technical learned journals in the field received Watson's work very well. So did the relatively intellectual *Nation*. But the more popular press was outraged by the cruelty of sacrificing rats in order to study the brain. *Life* seized on the story, spurred on by angry anti-vivisectionists. It pilloried Watson. He was criticised in print and caricatured in cartoons as a killer of baby rats. And all to what end? To see how the animals could learn their way round a maze. Watson was deeply affected by the controversy. He went to some lengths in his 1907 monograph on orientation in the rat to state that the animals he used then were well cared for and happy.

Despite the controversy and despite the fact that he had not equalled the record of Helen Thompson, Watson had a number of offers of jobs. Donaldson offered him an assistantship in neurology. 'I am proud of that to this day,' Watson noted in 1936. But he felt that he wanted to develop his studies of animal behaviour and to pursue his novel notions of how to do human psychology. He was about, in fact, to accept an instructorship in psychology at the University of Cincinnati when Angell fell ill. In order to make money, Angell was spending the summer of 1903 teaching at the University of California. It was the final straw and he collapsed due to overwork.

Angell recommended that Watson be hired as an assistant in order to cope with this emergency. Angell wrote to President Harper that Watson had had a 'long and flattering notice in the *Nation*' and was beginning to acquire an 'enviable' reputation in animal psychology. Angell noted shrewdly that there was a great 'boom' in animal psychology and that therefore it made much sense to appoint Watson.

It is typical that Watson's first letter after he got his job was to complain about the salary. The university offered $600: Watson claimed Angell had told him he would get more. In the end Watson accepted the job and he was to remain chronically short of money. The lack of cash was a frequent theme in all his letters.

But Watson did not let money depress him. He plunged into teaching. He set up new courses in animal psychology. He built new equipment with those charmed hands of his. He did teach some human psychology but it was conventional stuff. Angell would not have allowed anything else. Watson was very diffident after 1904 about his ideas on how to study people objectively. He had felt the hostile reception deeply. It had forced him in on himself and made him doubt his ideas. Until 1909 Watson would use Titchener's manuals when he taught human psychology and Titchener was, even more than William James, a believer in introspection.

The sagas of late 1902 and early 1903, the breakdown, the slightly tarnished degree, and being jilted all brought Watson to a point where he felt a great need for love and security. There was a student in his laboratory called Mary Ickes. Her handsome professor impressed her. She fell in love with him. Watson appreciated being loved so completely. He did not have the means to marry but he decided to propose to Mary. He knew that this time he would not be rebuffed. As it turned out it was not quite that easy. Her brother, Harold Ickes (who was to be Roosevelt's Secretary of State) disliked Watson and disapproved of him. The man seemed an adventurer. Ickes may have heard rumours of Watson's previous liaisons; he may even have heard, from John Manly, about the disreputable Pickens with his lusts for ladies of all colours. Ickes sent his sister away to Altoona to forget Watson. But Mary was not minded to forget him. She was completely determined to marry the attractive young psychologist. Her brother might try to dissuade her but to no avail.

Watson followed Mary to Altoona. Shy and unsure of himself, he had been deeply hurt by his most recent romantic experiences. It was delightful to find a woman who loved him more than he loved her. Mary was never to make him jealous. In Altoona they decided to get married. Watson even made some sort of peace with the disapproving Harold Ickes, for the wedding reception took place in Ickes's house.

When Watson married he was twenty-five. His prospects were very uncertain. He would often say later that he had married too young, by which he meant, among other things, too poor. $600 was not much money on which to keep a wife and, within eleven months, a child. But Watson needed to marry. He was tired of being by himself. Everything reported about Watson and everything that he wrote on sex suggests that it was very important to him. Emma Roe had not managed to quash the sensuality in her son despite all her religion and morality: in that, Pickens had triumphed. Watson was a lustful chip off the parental block. Watson wanted to share his bed night after night. He also wanted some emotional security at last. And also, marriage to a girl who came from a good family would, in some way, assert his place in society. Angell attracted Watson partly because of his social standing. Mary, like all the women Watson seems to have wanted, was a pretty high-class girl. He wanted such conquests in order to confirm his own place in society. Watson acted, as he often did, impulsively. Despite all the financial and family difficulties, he quickly decided to marry Mary. And he got his way.

It was to be a good marriage for many years. Watson may have been a little on the rebound but he cared for his wife. Mary was intelligent. She often worked with her husband. She helped him edit his writings and was, apparently, an excellent proof-reader. She did some reviews for the *Psychological Bulletin* and she comes over as a sensible, though hardly inspired, author.

In 1904, Watson began to correspond with a young student of animal behaviour called Robert Yerkes. They were interested in each other's research. But both men also confided in each other. Most of the information about Watson's marriage comes from asides in letters between Watson and Yerkes who was a young physiologist at Yale. They wrote very often to each other after August 1904. Most of their letters were about professional matters but Watson felt, for some reason, great personal sympathy with Yerkes. He could confide in him and he felt that he needed someone to confide in. He admired Angell but he was always aware that Angell was somehow too distant and superior to be a real friend.

Watson speaks in his early letters of his new son, John, who was born in 1904. 'A baby is more fun to the square inch than all the rats and frogs in creation. Honest,' Watson told Yerkes who had not yet taken the plunge into marriage. When Yerkes married, Watson offered very whole-hearted congratulations. When Mary Ickes was seriously ill, it was to Yerkes that Watson spoke of his anxieties and of how he nursed his wife. When Yerkes was married and either of them could afford it, they planned to meet. But both of them were poor. When Yerkes and Watson finally did meet, they liked each other personally as much as they had done in their letters. Yerkes was to be Watson's most important professional friend for many years. And Mary Watson's reaction to her husband meeting Yerkes shows just why it was that she had been so determined to marry John. She was infatuated with intelligence. She worshipped brains. She wrote to Yerkes that she had been enthralled to listen to him and John 'talk shop'. Some women might hate such serious scientific talk but not her. What a thrill it was to sit not just at the feet of the professor but also to lie in his bed! It was

Mary Watson who did most of the loving between the two of them. Watson never quite really gave himself to her. Perhaps, with all the traumas of South Carolina not far behind, it was too hard for him really to trust a person in that kind of intimate way. (Watson does not seem to have revisited Greenville with Mary, incidentally.) Nevertheless, it seemed a happy enough marriage. When they could afford it, round 1908, the Watsons went off to Canada across the Great Lakes. Watson still loved the countryside. He liked being head of his family and enjoyed doing things with his small children as Pickens had enjoyed doing things with him. At first Watson was faithful.

That year, Watson also met one of the leading introspective psychologists, Edward Bradford Titchener, who was a very proper Englishman. He was to prove a major influence.

Watson also acquired teaching responsibilities. With Angell gone until May 1904, much of the running of the department fell on to Watson's young shoulders. He had much teaching to do. Setting up the animal laboratory for his courses involved a great deal of effort. Watson was always haggling with suppliers of lenses and other scientific equipment. He was always building new bits of apparatus. He enjoyed his own energy.

Watson did find the time to write a short note on 'Some Unemphasised Aspects of Comparative Psychology'. He argued that there was no point in studying animals' behaviour in order to infer what the state of their consciousness was. The behaviour of animals was intrinsically worth studying. Everything about animals could be learned by studying their behaviour and their biological make up. This points very much to Watson's mature views. He would eventually make the same claim about the study of human behaviour. But it was not too outrageous to suggest that animals could be understood by observation. Watson attacked the argument by analogy which claimed to reveal what the beasts would say and thought if they could voice their opinions. Such complications were unnecessary. He did not try again to discuss his ideas that tended towards behaviourism. This time he just concentrated on animals.

In order to prepare for a new study on rats, Watson arranged to spend the summer of 1904 in Baltimore studying a new operative technique under Dr William Howell of Johns Hopkins Medical School. This plunged Watson into more financial trouble, for the university did not pay his modest salary for the period of May to September. He was broke but he enjoyed his time at Johns Hopkins. He met Mark Baldwin again. Baldwin had been at Princeton when Watson was seeking a 'real university'. He liked Watson and he was to remember the impression Watson made on him.

In 1904 there were plans to form a separate department of psychology at Chicago. Dewey had left Chicago. In order to counter the 'depressing influence' of Dewey's departure Angell wanted to promote 'vigor and vitality' by setting up a department of psychology separate from that of philosophy. This would mean that Angell would finally have to be made professor. While Angell politicked, Watson had to take on more of the teaching. He was also asked to help edit a new journal, the *Journal of Comparative Neurology and Psychology*. Ambitious as he was, he could not turn that down even though he knew it would mean more hard work.

Work also meant continuing battles with the university over money for equipment. Watson was expected to teach animal psychology without spending a cent on animals or anything else. In February 1905 there was the saga of the projection lantern. Watson wrote to President Harper explaining he needed it to teach the nervous system and the sense organs. He dared to remind Harper that he had been told by Professor Judson (who later became President of Chicago) that $100 would be set aside in 1905 for the lantern. Never, riposted Harper. Perhaps a generous friend of the university might be persuaded to donate such a lantern but to provide money was out of the question. Watson must have made some caustic reply. By 15 February Harper wrote to Angell saying Watson's letter to him (lost alas) was either 'an indication of insanity or intentional impertinence'. Impertinence was, of course, worse. Angell tried to smooth things over and must have succeeded. But by 26 May Watson was in trouble again. He again pressed Harper for funds for equipment and did so more than it was polite or politic to do. Watson had to apologise for impertinence. His letter verges on the obsequious. He regrets he used 'a certain freedom of expression which I see now might easily have been thought to be impertinent'. He pleads, 'I did not intend the letter to be such.' He prostrates himself: 'You have always been kindness itself to me and you have never given me the slightest right to be impertinent.' University presidents never gave anyone the slightest right to be impertinent: grovelling gratitude for their posts was what was expected of junior academics. Watson duly was apologetic and lowly in many letters to Harper and later to the President of Johns Hopkins. He was far too unsure of his position in the academic world and society as a whole to flaunt these conventions. He prided himself on being a 'Southern gentleman'. But these apologies also suggest that he was susceptible to those who had formal authority over him. His mother kowtowed to the authority of God. For a long time, her irreligious son kowtowed to the authority of university presidents.

After these apologies it must have been galling later in 1905 when

Watson ran out of money. Having a baby was dear. When the summer came, his money had gone. He had no one to turn to but Angell. Again, Angell was kind. He wrote to Harper and asked that the university fund give Watson a loan. Watson lived modestly but had heavy expenses. Harper obliged. He sent Watson $200 repayable in a year at 4 per cent.

In May 1905 Watson wrote to Yerkes outlining the plans he had to extend the work on rat learning. Watson wanted to find out what happened when a rat who had learned to run a maze from start to food box was set down in the middle of that maze. Would the rodent cope? There was also the more fundamental question of how the rats learned. Which of their senses was crucial? The answer Watson came up with was to influence much of his psychology.

Watson collaborated with Harvey Carr, a doctoral student whose meticulous attention to detail Watson admired. They constructed the most elaborate maze any rat had yet had to face. To get to the food, a rat had to make eight correct turns and it was 40 feet from the entrance to the food. No one had studied how rats might cope with something of this complexity apart from Small who, as was typical, had made an elementary methodological error. Small had allowed his rats to spend a night in the maze before he began to test them.

Watson and Carr tested their rats every day. Again, Watson's report is full of interesting observations that recall or, more accurately, precede ethology. One note runs:

> The food, at first, apparently exerts little or no influence in drawing the animal to the food box. The stimulus of the new surroundings is more potent and the animal's 'attention' roves freely from one part of the maze to the other. This type of behaviour stands out in bold relief with that of the fully trained animal. In the latter case, the food is the emotionally exciting object. It compels his attention from beginning to start and retains its power to the end.

It was not till 1956 that other psychologists began to discuss curiosity as a drive.

The rats learned the maze quickly again. The first run took an average of 29 minutes; the third run took an average of 12.31 minutes. By the 16th trial the average was down to 0.63 minutes and by the 35th the animals scampered through in 0.42 minutes. Again, younger rats were learning more quickly. Watson had shown yet again the nature of the progress of learning in the rat. At first, learning is slow: then there is a period in which progress is very quick – from 12 minutes on trial 3 to 0.6 on trial 16. But then any improvement has to be much more marginal because the rats get to the point where they know how to run

41

the maze perfectly well but they would have to be Speedy Gonzales to get their times down any further. It becomes a question of their muscles not their minds.

Having shown that the rats learned this complex maze, Watson wanted to know how they did it. He assumed that it had been by one – and one only – of their senses. Such an assumption would seem naïve now, perhaps. But the previous studies in the field were few. Small had tried to see if blind rats could run a maze but he had not even managed to blind his rats competently, it seems. There was a study by a man called Rowse. Rowse put hoods over the heads of birds and, during three trials, these hooded birds adamantly refused to learn a maze. Ergo, birds learn by seeing. 'May we not suppose', sniped Watson, 'that the poor record on these first three trials were due, in part, at least, to the presence of fear and excitement.' Fright made the birds freeze; they refused to budge. How would you feel if you had a hood put over your head and were placed in an utterly unfamiliar place? Watson saw to it that his rats were neither frightened nor shocked when he asked them to run his maze.

Watson's first look at vision failed. He and Carr had not made sure the rats were hungry and so when they were placed in the maze in the dark they fell promptly asleep. A new group of rats was tested in the dark. 'It would apparently take a microscope to find the influence of vision,' commented Watson drily. The rats learned the maze in the dark perfectly well.

But Watson wanted better evidence. In March 1906 he began to operate on a group of six-month-old rats who had previously learned the maze. He made one group blind by removing their eyeballs; he made another group deaf by removing their middle ear; he did not quite remove the noses of the last group but he took out their olfactory bulb to make sure they could not smell. There could be no doubt that each group was deprived of its respective sense. Watson admitted these were cruel operations but he took great care to see the rats recovered properly. The blinded rats were frolicking and playing 24 hours after the operation.

It did not seem to matter which of their senses they lost. The rats always managed to learn the maze over again. On their first run after being blinded, the rats made it to the foot in a mere 2.39 minutes. The deaf and the anosmic (non-smelling) rats did nearly as well. Watson and Carr then went on to test a group of blinded, deaf and anosmic rats who had never learned the maze. Again, there was no evidence that any of these rats found the maze hard to learn. They did not butt into the alleys and they seemed able to make the correct turns without too much trouble. They behaved much like the normal rats did.

42

In the summer of 1906 Mark Baldwin visited Watson and suggested that the key might be the whiskers. These enabled the rats to get round the maze so well. At once Watson snipped the whiskers off two rats. It had no effect. He gave other rats local anaesthetics to make sure it was not something to do with their touch sensations. Even the sense of taste was tested though Watson always wondered how a rat might use its sense of taste to learn the way round a maze. But as the rats were so undiscriminating that they happily drank water with .01 per cent solution of quinine, a vilely bitter brew that no human would touch except if parched in the middle of the Sahara, Watson could not see how they could make use of taste. Blind, deaf, anosmic, whiskerless, anaesthetised, the rats still learned the maze. Did they have to be dead to fail?

The one sense that Watson had not managed to extirpate was the muscle or kinaesethetic sensations. Elegantly, Watson set out to show that when their kinaesthetic sensations were confused, the rats had much more trouble with the maze.

New mazes were built. They were either longer or shorter than the ones on which the rats had learned. When the alleys were shorter, the rats kept on running into walls at their end. They hugged to the walls: one rat frantically kept butting the walls. The animals were confused. Watson argued that they had been looking for the turning points which their muscles remembered from the first maze.

When the alleys in the maze were lengthened, the rats tried to turn at precisely the points where they used to turn. They were disturbed when they found that impossible. The rats again ran into the walls. To check that it was not the strangeness of the new mazes that were perplexing the rats, Watson and Carr put some rats down in the middle of a maze they had learned. It took the animal only two and a half turns to get its bearings in that situation. Watson felt that he had showed clearly that the rat learned the maze through its 'intraorganic sensations'. He thought it his best work, he told Yerkes, though he thought that some work Yerkes had done was even better. Even as late as 1936, Watson wrote: 'The research he [Carr] and I did together on the lengthened and shortened mazes still brings a bit of a kick when I think of it.'

It all left him, he wrote to Yerkes, heartily sick of rats. 'I never want to see another rat go round the maze.' But he had gained a sense of his own abilities. He did not have to seek Angell's help in writing it up this time. Watson noted: 'I felt a certain independence on the maze work.' He was becoming a little more confident.

The value of Watson's work on how rats learn mazes was tremendous. It was the first model of well controlled research in the field of animal learning. Watson really helped to establish the idea that learning takes place gradually at first and then reaches a point where it cannot get any better. Since Watson, psychologists have been probably more interested in learning than in any other activity. You could be forgiven for thinking that for the psychologist to be is to learn. Recently, of course, we have learned that we can learn while we are asleep, drowsy, attending to something else or suspended in a yogic trance. We cannot blame Watson for everything that subsequently took place in the psychology of learning but his thesis and the papers in 1907 and 1908 sparked off much interest. For many years other psychologists copied what Watson had done. They studied how rats learned in mazes. They copied him rather badly for they made their mazes simpler and concentrated on the finest points of manipulating the rat. By 1910 or so Watson was thinking beyond the rat. Watson did not believe that once you understood how the rat learned you understood learning which, alas, most of his successors either believed or behaved as if they believed. Watson would return to the rats in 1916 when he produced what seems to me a vital experiment which no one really understood for twenty-five years.

Public recognition also came his way. In 1906 Watson was asked to edit certain issues of the *Psychological Bulletin*, one of the leading journals of the time. Watson also became editor of the *Psychological Index*. This publication was not a list of forbidden psychological texts but just gave annually every paper that involved scientific psychology. It was useful, though putting it together must have been difficult and dull. Watson worked on it partly because it added a little extra to his salary. Watson's growing reputation also attracted more and more students to Chicago. In August, he wrote to Yerkes: 'I hope to God you are getting more rest this summer than I am.'

And throughout 1905 and 1906 the correspondence between Watson and Yerkes developed. They saw each other as young ambitious men who were destined for important careers. By April 1906 Watson was suggesting that he, Yerkes and Jennings should write a book to consolidate their 'fleeting' ideas on how to study animals. They often moaned to each other about the need for better facilities to study the higher animals.

By accident Watson was to find himself soon in an ideal situation for looking at animals' behaviour in the wild. With the work on rats behind him, Watson persuaded Chicago to give him the funds to buy four monkeys. Going as ever for ambitious projects, Watson wanted to see whether monkeys could imitate, but he could not start at once on the study.

Round 1900 universities did not pay their academic staff for July and

August. Education ground to a halt early in June. After the end of the month professors were meant to fend for themselves. The best thing was to be independently rich. If not, you either had to be frugal or to find extra work. Broke as he always was, Watson was looking for summer work. He did not want to teach if he could help it. In 1906, he met Dr Alfred Mayer who ran the Marine Biological Station of the wealthy Carnegie Institution. Mayer offered Watson work for the summer. Watson was delighted. The extra $255 meant that he and Mary could hire a maid for a few months. They could go out a bit together leaving their children with her. It was very welcome.

The Carnegie had a base in Key West, Florida. Near Key West were the Tortugas, some deserted and desolate islands where noddy and sooty terns came to nest in the summer. Watson was excited by the idea of observing these terns for two reasons. First, he wanted to establish their life history, to do what ethologists would call an 'ethogram', a full account of the way that they lived. Second, there were stories that these terns were expert at homing. In 1907, that was called 'distant orientation'. No one had proved that birds really did home. If the terns really could get back to the Tortugas, they would have to navigate over hundreds or thousands of miles of sea in which there were no landmarks. Could the terns do it? And if they could, how did they? Watson meant to find out.

There was much to concern Watson on the islands apart from the birds. He had been saddled with a taciturn Swedish cook who hardly ever spoke a word. Watson complained to Yerkes of the man's Scandinavian silences. Less silent were the four monkeys. The purpose of Watson's trip to the islands was, of course, to study the noddy and sooty terns. But he decided that he would take down to the islands the four monkeys from his lab, he let these monkeys loose on the islands. Watson wrote to Yerkes: 'I dislike the idea of taking them back and trying to get reliable results in a lab.' That might do for chickens, rats or cats. 'But when you get to the monkeys there is a spontaneity which I have never seen in the north.' Watson enjoyed the monkeys' spontaneity. I believe his observations of the monkeys on this trip confirmed his feeling that one should observe people too in their natural habitats. Unfortunately, after Watson, most behaviourists preferred to get reliable results in the lab rather than to witness too much spontaneity. In the lab, life is more easily controlled.

Despite the cook, Watson enjoyed life on the desolate Tortugas. At times, the solitude was oppressive. He told Yerkes: 'For God's sake write me a letter to keep me in touch with civilisation. If you see a picture of a good beefsteak and a bottle of beer on ice would you send that along too.'

From March 1906 Watson and Yerkes had discussed collaborating on a study of colour vision in animals. Watson became very involved in designing the kind of apparatus he would need for this study. His letters to Yerkes are full of excited scrawls all over the margins. Watson longed to meet his friend to discuss the project. 'If I can beg, steal or borrow,' he would go East to see him. When he failed to do any of these, Watson said he would 'cover my head with sack cloth and ashes'. He was far away enough from his Baptist past to begin to poke gentle fun at it; fundamentalists were always draping themselves in sack cloth and bathing in ashes. Reading their letters, it is clear that Yerkes meant a good deal to Watson, but it was a very equal relationship. Watson was not tempted to defer to his friend. He accepted his criticisms with good spirit usually. Once Watson responded to an attack on his style in a particular paper by writing 'I promise faithfully never to write such English again.'

As Watson came to trust Yerkes more, he began to hint that he was still working away at his ideas on 'behaviour'. Watson was reading all the literature from the *Origin of the Species* onwards in preparation. He wanted to be well prepared before he broached the subject of human behaviour again. Watson was still very diffident about revealing his ideas in public. In October 1907 he told Yerkes: 'To my mind, it is not up to us behaviour men to say anything about consciousness.' But Watson knew he was stalling. The complete 'behaviour man' would have ripe things to say about consciousness. But he was still not ready for the confrontation that he knew his views would bring. And Chicago with the soulful and conservative Angell as professor was too hostile to it all. But Watson kept on reading all the literature and allowing his iconoclastic ideas to mull. He was still very young.

In many ways Watson was quite content. He enjoyed the work in the lab. Tinkering with lenses, cells and filters for the experiments on colour vision gave him the chance to satisfy the would-be engineer in him. The work in the Tortugas gave him the chance to fulfil what there still was of the country boy who loved the wild. Angell was a kind of mentor still. As ever, Watson worked a little too hard. He complained of being overworked and of not sleeping too well. But he was beginning to be restless. He was not confident enough to take matters in his own hands, but when an offer to leave Chicago came Watson was interested.

Johns Hopkins University specialised in graduate work. Its professor of psychology was Stratton who had made one notable contribution to psychology. Stratton decided to test the relationship between sight and touch by wearing distorting lenses so that the world 'looked' upside down to him. He then studied the problem of how one tried to manage in an upside-down world. It was a brave and striking piece of experimentation which proved, among other things, what a long slow process it is to re-educate our senses. But by 1907 Stratton was bored with Johns Hopkins and decided that he would take up a job at the University of California. Watson was invited to go to Hopkins as assistant professor of psychology.

A letter from the biologist H. Jennings who taught at the medical school at Hopkins to Baldwin shows that Baldwin had every academic reason for inviting his friend. 'Watson would certainly be a great acquisition for us,' wrote Jennings. 'There is hardly anyone else doing the grade of work he is doing in comparative psychology . . . I would rejoice to see him here.' The President of Johns Hopkins agreed. Watson was offered the post of assistant professor at the salary of $2,500. But Watson hesitated. He gave Angell's name as a reference.

Angell, who had finally badgered and blackmailed Chicago into making him professor of psychology, was also fulsome in his praise. 'I would not lose him if I could possibly help it for I should be swamped without him but I am more solicitous for his welfare than for my personal comfort.' Angell said Watson would need to be tempted by at least $2,000 and he noted shrewdly Watson would be influenced by 'considerations of rank'. He was still just an instructor at Chicago despite his achievements.

Baldwin delivered both rank and salary. He could offer Watson $2,500 to become Assistant Professor of Psychology. Up against it, Chicago, however, finally decided to appoint Watson to the rank of Assistant Professor Elect. It was not quite clear what he would have to do actually to get elected. Watson hesitated. He did not want to leave Chicago. He said that he even did not want to leave Angell who, obviously, had some strange power to hold Watson. He did not want to leave the research he had going including the work on colour vision. The lab he had wired up and added to all the time was also a powerful reason for staying in Chicago. 'I hated to leave Chicago,' he wrote. And yet he did leave it.

Watson's attitude to Chicago is curiously contradictory. He hesitated to leave it and he wrote in 1936 that he had totally enjoyed his time there. Yet in 1908 he wrote to Yerkes that 'I hope to have all kinds of talks with you. I have lived so much alone as I told you once before that I sometimes wonder whether I am on the right track at all or not.' He had a sense of isolation at Chicago. Since 1905, he had made sure that Angell had had very little to do with his research details and had ceased in any way to be intellectually inspiring. Yet Watson still found it hard to snap the bonds.

But by the beginning of 1908 Baldwin came up with an offer which it would have been pathological to refuse. Watson was offered the chair of psychology at Johns Hopkins. He was not quite thirty. It was irresistible.

I wonder if Watson ever read the recommendation Angell wrote and, if he had done so, whether it helped to dispel that deep-seated inferiority of only – only! – getting a Magna Cum Laude. Angell wrote that Watson 'is an A1 man in running a laboratory, technically proficient in every direction from electricity to etiquette'. Angell said he would rather have the ambitious and indefatigable Dr Watson 'twice over any man of his generation. He is better balanced, better trained and more effective as a university man than any other fellow of his generation.' If such a recommendation landed on one's desk today given the cut and thrust of university politics one might wonder why Angell wanted to get rid of him!

The other reference came from Donaldson, the neurologist, who described Watson as full of enthusiasm and 'with that gift of Heaven of getting things done'. Donaldson added, wryly, that he had no reservations and 'I appreciate that this is a rather unusual condition of affairs'.

With such testimonials, it is not surprising that President Ramsden decided that 'it is clear to my mind that he is the man for us'. Ramsden also asked for an opinion from Howell who was Dean of the Johns Hopkins Medical School. Howell could only speak of Watson's work. His comment is interesting for it shows that Watson was really only thought of as an animal psychologist. Howell noted that 'the underlying idea of applying the experimental Method to the study of the complex consciousness of acts of animals appeals to me very strongly and I think Watson is showing originality and strength in carrying it out.' Howell had never heard of the attempts Watson had made to broach the subject of human psychology in 1904.

It is a sign of how reluctant Watson was to leave Chicago that he did not at once accept the offer. First of all he tried to use it to bargain for a better salary at Chicago. He could hardly ask for Angell's chair, but some more dollars would be welcome. The new President of Chicago, Judson, who had reneged on the projection lantern was just as rigid as Harper. By 1 March 1908, Watson wrote to Baldwin that as he and his friends had failed to get a rise out of Judson: 'I had practically decided to telegraph my acceptance to you today: this plan was disturbed by a letter from Thorndike inviting me to pay a visit to Columbia for the purpose of meeting Dean Russell.'

Watson had offers from two excellent universities. It was even more flattering that Thorndike, the doyen of animal behaviour, should want to hire Watson. It is a mark of the man's hold over him that Watson turned to Angell for advice on how to handle such a surprisingly favourable situation. 'Prof. Angell tells me to write you frankly,' said Watson, 'and I ask for a few more days indulgence.' By then, he would know whether Thorndike was 'serious and prepared' for he had told him that, otherwise, 'he'd better not spend his good money on me'.

On 3 March Watson sent his telegraph. The cable arrived in the middle of a meeting of the Academic Board of Johns Hopkins. He accepted the chair. 'I felt', Watson wrote, 'I was foolish not to go.' His salary would be $3,000.

At this time Watson also began to work with a young zoology student, Karl Lashley. Lashley was born in West Virginia in 1890 and, like Watson, he had started university by the time he was sixteen. His first love was Latin, but then a teacher introduced him to zoology. There were similarities between him and Watson. The young Lashley loved wildlife and was fascinated by gadgets. He appeared to have a very intimate relationship with his mother's sewing machine which he kept on dismantling and reassembling again. In 1910 Lashley was doing his master's degree at the University of Pittsburgh and discussed the observation of baby monkeys. Watson, who had been so taken with the four adult monkeys on his trip to the Tortugas, wanted to study the behaviour of the monkey from birth on. In 1911 Lashley came to Hopkins to study for his PhD in zoology and psychology. Watson took to this young man, and for the next few years they worked and talked together a great deal. In 1910 they found two pregnant monkeys, observed the birth of their babies, and logged their every developmental step from then on. They were on their way to becoming the Piagets of the apes.

Between March and August Watson was busy with preparations. He continued to observe the two infant monkeys. The animals then travelled to Baltimore with Watson. He got to his new home early so that he would have time to do some of the decorating himself. And he prepared himself for what he knew was his big opportunity. Watson wrote to President Ramsden with a humility that came from his own nervousness: 'I realise that this important position is not given to me because of my attainments but rather as an expression of confidence in my ability to do valuable work. . . . I wish to assure you that I shall do my utmost to deserve, as soon as possible the honour Johns Hopkins has conferred on me.' He had come a long way from Greenville to a real chair at a real university. But he was still not quite sure he deserved so much.

Watson's feelings about his time at Chicago were more contradictory, I think, than he knew. He had learned much from Angell, Donaldson and Loeb. His research was methodologically more thorough than anyone else's. He had had a host of fruitful ideas for animal work. Chicago had given him a great deal of opportunity. The only thing that had proved impossible was to take an M.D. Watson never wanted to practise medicine but he felt a medical degree would be useful for research, especially with humans. But Watson had also been under too much supervision. Angell, especially, mattered too much to Watson for Watson to be really able to develop his revolutionary ideas on the study of human behaviour. To become a full-blooded behaviour man who studied human beings objectively would have threatened his relationship with Angell. So Watson largely suppressed that side of his thinking. He could not defy Angell enough to concentrate on it. So he did his very useful, often very beautiful, research on animals. It is no accident that two months after he went to Baltimore Watson went to Harvard. There, free of the dominion of Angell, he expounded his views that a scientific psychology should study the way human beings behaved as objectively as animals were studied. Yerkes was worried by that. And Watson's ideas were criticised by other scientists at Harvard. But, as we shall see, Watson now felt much freer to go his own way.

For another five years, Watson would develop his ideas on human behaviour more or less in private. He would still remain quite cautious. But as he took the train down to Baltimore, he was certain he was on the right lines. As he travelled, he may well have reflected – for he was given to evaluating himself – that he had done well for a young man who had come to Chicago in 1900 with $50 in his pocket, not much self-confidence and not very clear ideas in his head.

At Johns Hopkins, Watson was to flower and become the man who, according to Bertrand Russell, had done more for psychology than anyone since Aristotle.

3

The Young Professor 1908–13

Baltimore was a conservative city. It was not a very pretty place and Watson grew to loathe it. He detested the damp climate and, after Chicago, it often seemed rather provincial. The campus of the university, some miles away from the industrial heart of Baltimore, was very different. Small, modern and elegant, Johns Hopkins had quickly established itself as a major American university. It had only been founded in 1876 but it had an original purpose; to enable students to do postgraduate work. In the 1880s very few American universities granted the PhD. Many psychologists had gone to Germany to obtain a doctorate simply because they could not get one in the USA. By 1908 many other universities were starting to award doctorates but Johns Hopkins had already made itself felt as a very respectable university. Watson had got a good chair.

But the university was under the financial control of the town. Johns Hopkins had nearly always deferred to the conservative spirit of Baltimore. Stanley Hall, its first professor of psychology, had deliberately made himself sound pious in order to be an acceptable professor. In 1887 the university stopped receiving any dividends from the Ohio and Baltimore Rail Road (in which Johns Hopkins had a 30 per cent stake) because the railway was going bankrupt. That failure meant the university had to solicit even more money from Baltimore. The academic staff often resented the autocratic way in which the rich businessmen who sat on the board of the university took decisions. No university president dared risk offending the spirit of Baltimore, as Watson would soon find out.

John Broadus Watson arrived in Baltimore in August 1908 and began to prepare himself for what he saw as the greatest challenge of his young career. He was determined to excel. To avoid the distractions of too much society the Watsons took a house in the suburbs. Not to be too well placed also suited Watson's pocket. He and Mary needed to economise. Eight years in Chicago had left Watson in debt to the tune of $2,300, nearly two-thirds of his grand new annual salary. The young professor desperately wanted to repay those debts so that he would be free from money anxieties. Owing money nagged at him, especially perhaps because it reminded him of his youth. As part of the economy programme, Watson decorated their new house himself. He did a good job, of course, with those skilful hands of his. By the start of September everything was in order. The house was painted; Mary and the children were settled in; even the monkeys had arrived by train. Watson was ready to start work as one of the youngest professors America had ever seen.

The department of psychology at Johns Hopkins was part of the department of philosophy, psychology and education. The professor of philosophy, Mark Baldwin, was head of the department. He also part-owned and edited the *Psychological Review*, one of the leading journals in the field. Baldwin was a brilliant man in many ways. He was both a philosopher and a psychologist; he skirmished over sensations with Titchener. But Baldwin had absolutely no knowledge of animal behaviour and very little skill in experimental technique. He hoped that Watson would be able to build up a psychological laboratory again. The university had starved Stratton of the means to run one properly. When Watson arrived, there was little equipment and no technical assistance. Watson had to work feverishly to build the most basic things needed to teach animal behaviour. It took a great deal out of him. He apologised to Yerkes for the state of his correspondence: 'my general physical condition accounts for the vagaries in the letters'. He was not getting enough sleep.

The other problem Watson had to face was that he would have to teach far more human psychology than he had ever done at Chicago. In 1908 and 1909 he relied heavily on Titchener's manuals, for he was not yet confident enough on the human side to rebel against introspective psychology. Watson admired the sheer hard work that had gone into compiling the manuals and he liked Titchener despite their theoretical differences which Watson was only beginning to articulate. Watson even often wrote to Titchener about the problems he faced as he organised his new department and laboratory.

But in his first two months at Baltimore there was one marvellous event. Watson and Yerkes finally met. On 4 November Watson, having first inquired how much the cheapest rail fare was, took the train to Boston to see his friend. The two men took to each other in person as much as they had done on paper. They talked for two or three days on a whole variety of topics. Yerkes admired Watson's work with rats but he was far more cautious about using the same kinds of observational methods with humans. Psychology was more than mere behaviour. Watson spoke to a seminar at Harvard. There was a chilly response to his tentative ideas on the study of human behaviour. After that meeting Yerkes was so distressed that he even wrote to Titchener to ask him to guide Watson into being a proper psychologist rather than a 'behaviour man'. Yerkes's attitude was one of a number of influences that made Watson feel cautious and persuaded him to keep his silence for a few more years yet. On 11 November, back in grimy Baltimore, Watson wrote to his friend: 'I start work today with a lot more inspiration than I should have had if I had not had my talks with you.' Yerkes's friendship meant very much to Watson.

When Watson returned to Baltimore, he expected to have Baldwin's help in organising the laboratory. Baldwin was very energetic and influential within the university. On 30 November Watson wrote to Ira Ramsden, the President of Johns Hopkins, with detailed requests for new equipment. Baldwin added his own enthusiastic support, saying that 'the work would do us great credit'.

In early December Watson was robbed of Baldwin's enthusiastic support. The lively philosopher committed a heinous academic crime; he was caught in a negro brothel in a position that could not be described as philosophical. Rumour even had it that Baldwin was with a minor. Conservative Baltimore was utterly shocked. Professors were meant to be pillars of virtue. The university was not quite as conservative as the town but it did not dare to offend. Ramsden told Baldwin he would have to leave at once. Baldwin tried to gain time. He suggested he go for a long holiday and return when the scandal had died down. But Ramsden insisted on resignation. Baldwin had to comply.

Distressed, Baldwin at once walked into Watson's office. Dramatically he said that Watson was now editor of the *Psychological Review*. Watson was literally struck dumb for a minute. Baldwin explained what had happened. The news flabbergasted Watson. By the next day, Baldwin was moving his things out of Johns Hopkins. Europe and Mexico henceforth would have the benefit of his brains. Watson watched him go with mixed feelings. He liked Baldwin and he could have relied on him for support and even some guidance. As professor of philosophy, Baldwin had been head of the combined department of philosophy, psychology and education. But though it was distressing that Baldwin was forced to resign, it also meant that for the first time in his academic life Watson was really on his own. No one, apart from Ramsden, was in any sense his superior. He was free. 'The whole tenor of my life was changed. I tasted freedom in work without supervision.' As professor of psychology, Watson would not, of course have been supervised but he would always have been conscious of Baldwin as somehow there above him. Watson revelled in his new independence.

At Hopkins, too, there was the biologist H. B. Jennings, who believed, like Loeb, in neuromechanism. Only when we understood the physiological, physical and chemical processes that underlay each 'bit' of behaviour could we arrive at the real truths about behaviour. Psychology was inadequate physiology. Watson felt that this was an unrealistic view. Centuries might pass before neurophysiologists could specify just how the nervous system operated when a person saw an apple or felt depressed. In the meantime, Watson was not prepared to see psychology go into hibernation. Though he did not state it in quite these formal terms, Watson seems to have understood that there was a psychological level of explanation of behaviour as well as a physiological level. The psychological level was important in itself, not *faute de mieux*. Neuromechanism was, in one sense, Utopian for it did not seem very likely that the neuroscientists would soon give a proper account of the mechanisms and, in another sense, it was incomplete. Watson would elaborate these points very thoughtfully in 1914. Meanwhile, he liked Jennings and took some courses he gave on evolution and lower organisms such as snails, and amoebas. To argue, as has been done, that Watson filched Jennings's ideas is misguided. Apart from the fact that Watson toyed with behaviourism as early as 1904, long before he met Jennings, such an argument glosses over the differences between behaviourism and neuromechanism. To accept that man is a machine, as Watson did, was neither to deny the complexity of human behaviour (which Jennings and Loeb tended to do), nor to deny the need for psychological explanations. Pure neuromechanism would rob psychologists of any true role; behaviourism succeeded partly at least because it offered psychologists a specific, scientific function.

Two older men at Hopkins were also to befriend Watson. He liked Arthur Lovejoy, the professor of education, and he also came to like Ira Ramsden, the president of the university. Ramsden had some psychological background, for he had attended the classes of the pious Stanley Hall in 1881. Ramsden did his best to provide Watson with the facilities he needed. There were no silly rows such as that over the lantern at Chicago. Watson constructed much equipment with his own hands; Ramsden approved of such economies. Watson felt he was treated 'very finely' by him. Ramsden would never have the intense influence over Watson that Angell had had but the young professor transferred some of that intense loyalty for an older man to his president.

The other older man in Watson's intellectual life was, oddly enough, Titchener. He held the great apostle of introspection in something like awe. Watson was for some years a member of the 'experimental society', an informal group of psychologists who looked to Titchener as their leader. It is very important to understand their friendship. It reveals a great deal not just about Watson's character but also about the state of American psychology at the time. In December 1908 Watson wrote two telling letters to Titchener. He first told Titchener that he had just spent some time with Yerkes at Harvard and Holt at Yale. They 'frequently took your name in vain. Yerkes and I come to the firm conclusion that it is time for you to come back into the field.' Titchener had temporarily stopped being very active in psychology in 1907 because of a series of bitter disputes that centred round the American Psychological Association. Titchener felt he ought to be its President. Watson looked with dismay at those men who should be 'patriarchs' in the field. They had either stopped work altogether or stopped publishing or had gone into administration. At this time Watson made no mention of the great differences between Titchener and himself. Psychology needed Titchener. The young professor went even further; he needed Titchener. 'I shall always remember the contact I had with you at St. Louis, brief though it was. It did me a world of good. I feel the need of seeing you, of having you in the laboratory, of getting your criticism, kindly and certainly.'

Titchener replied in a very friendly manner for Watson wrote back on 19 December: 'Your letters to a certain extent pay up for the fact that you will not be here to cuss at my laboratory.' Then came a section in which Watson moaned about his own debts and commiserated with Titchener who had money problems of his own. Watson said money troubles made him be 'on pins and needles'. He then expressed his admiration for Titchener in such a very fulsome way that it says much about Watson's need for a mentor.

> I think I wrote you once about my regard for you. Angell and Donaldson have been like parents to me and I am sure that they will live in my memory as long as I live. My first debt is to them. It is an intellectual, social and moral debt. After these two men I have always placed your work and what I know of you personally. I am not so sure that I do not owe you as much as I owe them, I think if I had to say where the stimulus for hard persistent research came from I should have to point to you. I did not know a great deal of experimental psychology until your Instructor's Manual fell into my hands. I went to work on that and then I began to see the amount of work you must have done in order to have written that.

Watson always admired hard work. He told Titchener that the famous Munsterberg, the sociologist Jastrow and Raymond Cattell 'might never have lived as far as influencing my work'. He felt able, also, to tell Titchener of his doubts:

> In the summer if I can come I want to talk over the field with you. Some people tell me I am making a mistake in not doing work on the human side. Perhaps I am. But I am sure no one can do good human work and good animal work at the same time. I get discouraged because I can't. I sometimes think that a reputation won on animal work must be very ephemeral. True there is a good deal of interest in it at the present time but for how long? I feel that it is kind of up to me to stick to it and make it a respectful business. I imagine Yerkes has his dark moments too. I hope he sticks to it. I should value a frank statement from you. I shan't promise to agree with you if you think animal work unsafe but I should value the opinion just the same.
>
> Here's hoping we will see you at the next meeting. The papers don't amount to a tinker's damn. As for the presidency, I say go hang. I do get a lot out of the fellows I meet and smoke with.

The letter reveals very well the extent to which human work made Watson nervous after the bad reception his tentative ideas had received from Yerkes and others. He admired Titchener: that admiration made Watson move even so slowly in formulating his views.

There was one man in Johns Hopkins who was more favourably inclined to Watson's ideas, but he was only a junior member of staff, Knight Dunlap. Dunlap had been a pupil of Stratton's – Watson's predecessor in psychology – and, when Stratton left for California, he left Dunlap behind. Dunlap had published some work on hearing and pitch. He was aggressive and appeared self-confident. But Stratton's departure bothered Dunlap. The new professor however, seemed inspiring when it came to animal work. For his part, Watson was not that impressed with Dunlap. He wrote to Titchener in 1909 that he had had to tell Dunlap that he was not satisfied with his work, 'that unless he could take a problem and stick with it I would not recommend his appointment for more than the coming year. It is very hard to turn a man down but I am anxious for Hopkins to come into its own.' The ambitious professor was dismayed by having an assistant who was less good than he ought to be.

Early in 1909 Watson had settled in well enough to turn his mind to research again. Yerkes came to see him. They discussed working together on colour vision. Watson was very excited by the project. Throughout 1909 they wrote screeds to one another, sometimes three letters a week each. Most of this mass of correspondence deals with minute technicalities about lenses, colour filters, prisms, selenium cells and other experimental details. The project inspired Watson to enormous energy. All previous studies of colour vision had used either coloured papers or colour filters. Both these methods were unsatisfactory. It was impossible to control the precise wavelength of the light that the animal perceived. With the help of some physicist friends, Watson devised a new apparatus which allowed precise control of the light that fell on the animal's retina. His letters to Yerkes now were about the designing of this magnificent new machine. Watson always loved to draw out a map of it in all its complex glory.

Ramsden assisted this project greatly, for he provided $900 for the equipment and also, as Watson gleefully told Titchener, 'a competent mechanician', Charley Childs. In the light of such bounty, Dunlap's mediocrity was irritating. 'With a good man in the field of human psychology', Watson told Titchener, 'I am sure we can make our institution a real power.' Watson did not tell Ramsden, however, of his feelings about Dunlap. He would genuinely give him a chance to improve.

The experiments on colour vision aimed to test how well animals could see colours. 'I do not much expect to find colour vision outside of the monkey till we come to birds,' Watson wrote to Yerkes. These expectations were proved wrong. The omnicompetent rat turned out to be as good at distinguishing colours as the monkey. Different colours appeared to present different problems to the animals. Red seemed to be the one that was often the hardest for them. Watson did not obtain results that were exact enough for him to say confidently that animals stopped seeing colour at such and such a wavelength. But even the monkeys did not see red too well. It was much easier for all species to discriminate blue and yellow hues. The early work in 1909 showed how useful the new apparatus would be but it did little to solve the whole range of problems in colour vision that Watson saw as interesting. What is telling methodologically, of course, is that at this stage it was animal colour vision that really concerned Watson. Human beings were not yet his kind of subject.

The summer of 1909 was to prove busy and fraught. When the academic year ended at Hopkins in May, Watson was supposed to go to teach at Columbia for the summer. He badly needed the $600 he would be paid for two months' work. But he had also arranged to go back down to the Tortugas to continue studying the noddy and sooty terns at the expense of the Carnegie Institute. There was a slight clash of dates. Unless Columbia excused Watson a few days early, he would miss the boat for Florida. By the time the next boat cast him on the lonely islands, all the birds might have flown off anyway. The risk of that was too great for the Carnegie to stand the cost of Watson's trip. Columbia refused to excuse him. 'I am disappointed but I do not blame Columbia,' Watson wrote. So Mary came up to spend a few days in Manhattan with her husband. The two had a very gay time, away from their small children for once. They spent rather more money than they could afford. The $600 was meant to pay off some of those stubborn debts. Watson had to write Yerkes an apologetic note in which he confessed he could not just now repay $10 Yerkes had loaned him.

A mere $10 might soon be too small a sum to bother Yerkes. With less than tact, Yerkes informed Watson that he might be about to secure a chair at Yale with a salary of $10,000. 'I wouldn't be in your class if you got that, 'observed Watson wryly. Yerkes responded with the thought that Harvard might be interested in offering Watson a chair of experimental education with a much better salary than $3,000. Watson was sanely sceptical. He reckoned there was one chance in a hundred that Harvard would make him such an offer. And even then he would be torn. 'It is needless to tell you I am unhappy professionally with the crowd I have to run with,' he told Yerkes. Only Jennings was an intellectual ally. But, for all that, Ramsden treated him finely, it was possible to work, and while he was 'determined to get a living wage', Watson saw no reason either to leave or 'even to give rein to my unhappy feelings'. Watson moaned that if only he had the cash to join a golf club, he would feel much less frustrated.

Despite being sceptical about Harvard, Watson saw it as a way of bringing pressure on Ramsden. He went so far as to write Ramsden a long letter in the middle of August when the President of Johns Hopkins was away on holiday. Watson exaggerated wonderfully saying that he had just been 'approached' by a member of the Harvard psychology department 'with regard to the conditions under which I should be willing to take the chair of experimental education'. He was happy at Hopkins but he had three nagging anxieties. Before Baldwin left he had appointed as professor of education a certain George Buchner. Watson was acid at his expense. Buchner, he lamented, 'is not a University man in my opinion.' He might be well versed in the history of education but he was no more qualified in 'experimental education' than Watson was in ballet. 'I am sorry thus to write to you about my colleagues, but I feel that it is better to tell you about it than to let it rankle in my soul.' Having been so aggressively rude, Watson added; 'I know I have put myself in a position to be rebuked by you and I shall humbly accept it if you administer it.'

The capacities of Buchner mattered because education and psychology were within the same department. Watson felt that the affairs of the joint department were at a crisis. He hoped Ramsden might now give his 'general opinion' about moving 'towards giving me a separate organisation'. He wanted to be head of his own department of psychology and nothing but psychology. 'There is really no kind of connection between my work and the work in philosophy. I would rather, far rather stand in intimate relation with biology than with philosophy.' Watson apologised for making this request after only a year at Johns Hopkins but he felt very strongly about it. It was, of course, partly symbolic. It was vital to cut the bonds with metaphysics for psychology to establish its scientific credentials.

When it came to money, Watson's letter was again a mixture of menace and meekness. He was not sure enough to ask for more than a 'general opinion' again. This time, Ramsden had to opine 'as to whether I can hope to have my salary increased in the years to come. What I should desire would be some kind of yearly increase until say $4,000 was reached. I am in debt and the strain of living and trying to get off indebtedness is very discouraging. Please understand I am not "dickering".' In reality, Watson had little to 'dicker' with but he made it sound as if a lavish offer from Harvard was likely. Finally, returning to meekness, Watson wrote that: 'I do however desire to unburden myself to you and to be largely guided by your advice. If my letter has been too frank and undiplomatic, I crave your forgiveness.'

Ramsden did forgive, by and large. On the qualities of Buchner, he was tactfully silent. Ramsden said that he was also in favour of a separate department of psychology. He asked Watson to submit detailed proposals and warned that they would take two to three years to implement. Finances could be improved more quickly. He held out some hope that an annual raise could be arranged for Watson.

Towards the end of 1909 Watson began to feel that he would like to expound his more acceptable ideas to a wider public. He suggested to *Harpers* that he write them an article on the 'new science of animal behaviour'; *Harpers* accepted the suggestion and offered what seemed to be the amazing sum of $75. Round this time, too, the young professor began to discuss the possibility of writing a book on animal psychology for Henry Holt and Co. In preparation he was reading very widely, combing the biological literature of the nineteenth century. Watson worked through Darwin's writing and through everything else he could find in the field of animal behaviour. This intensive reading did nothing but confuse him at first. On 29 October 1909, he wrote to Yerkes: 'Damn Darwin'. The neo-Darwinians, it seemed, 'are in a worse hole than psychologists . . . I am terribly at sea as to finding a proper place and scope for psychology. What are our simple pre-suppositions and what is our scope and what are we good for?' If Watson had been a pure neuromechanist there would have been no problem for him. While he was trying to sort out his ideas, he had written a chapter entitled 'behaviourism as a biological problem'. The use of the word *behaviourism* clearly emphasises the direction of Watson's thinking. All this concentration made him wonder if he was a psychologist at all, for he thought one could handle the theory of natural selection, even applied to man, without mentioning consciousness at all or deviating from a biological point of view. 'Am I a physiologist? Or am I just a mongrel? I don't know how to get on.'

It was a plea from the heart. Watson saw one simple solution. Forget all theories! One could continue doing interesting experiments and publishing the results. He was getting more and more frustrated. But without a theory into which experiments could fit and could grow out of, psychology would not be very satisfying. 'Unless I am big enough to do the other [i.e. be theoretical] what is the use of results? I will go back to truck farming.' That would be what he was fit for.

By 22 November Watson told Yerkes that he had rewritten the chapter and was ready to throw the whole thing 'out of the window'. The struggle with past theories confused him and confusion cramped any fluency he had. But something else cramped Watson too. He told Yerkes: 'I simply cannot write swiftly and easily nor can I say the things which I feel ought to be said.' The second part of that sentence is critical. It suggests very clearly that Watson felt that he ought to say that psychology should make its decisive break and become an objective natural science. Consciousness, introspections and all the other relics of metaphysics could be left to philosophers to sort out. People as well as animals ought to be studied objectively, with detachment, as if they were objects. But to make such a radical case would infuriate Titchener and Angell, those precious father-like figures. Yerkes would fume too. Such powerful influences combined to make Watson hesitate. The defiant streak in him longed to shock them and, as important, to say what he wanted to say and felt ought to be said. But he could not quite muster the confidence yet. All these struggles with theory took their toll. On 4 January 1910 Watson was so exhausted by them that he spent a whole day in bed, 'an exquisite pleasure, a pleasure which I had not tasted for some 7 to 8 years before.' That was when he had stayed with the Van Pelts to recover from his first breakdown.

There were a number of ways in which Watson could have developed his ideas. Remarkable as it now sounds, Watson had actually had to argue the case for the study of animal behaviour as an important field in itself. Beasts deserved research not just for the light their antics cast upon human behaviour. Moreover, their behaviour did not have to be gilded with attempts to infer the consciousness that animals might admit to if only they could talk. Animal behaviour could be explained without any reference to animal consciousness. But though Watson had to argue this, there was much scientific sympathy for it. The controversial crux would come, Watson well knew, when he tried to extend this line of reasoning to human behaviour. Even here though he had options. He could claim that there was a need for the objective study of human behaviour as well as for introspective studies. Yerkes, certainly, would have accepted that. In effect, that was the soft position. But Watson's instinct was to go further and to maintain that, as far as psychology went, to be is to behave. Consciousness could be cut out. It was irrelevant to the understanding and prediction of human behaviour. It was this last radical position which would really shock the established psychologists like Angell and Titchener. It denied the human species its unique status as being somehow a qualitative cut above the rest of evolution. But this radical position was that which appealed most to Watson. He wrestled from 1908 on with this dilemma.

There were also other pressures on Watson. He had had to learn the business of editing an academic journal when Baldwin handed him the editorship of the *Psychological Review*. There were all kinds of strains. Those whose papers he rejected were often offended; printers were inefficient. Yet, anyone reading the *Psychological Review* from 1909 on is bound to see that Watson did not turn papers down because they clashed with his own views. He was a tolerant editor. But it all took enormous attention. In December 1909 he moaned to Yerkes: 'God damn that Review! It is just eating my time and sapping my energy.' Yerkes counselled rest though he was hardly the one to give advice on healthy living. A few weeks previously Yerkes had gone down with ptomaine poisoning because he had been buying cheap food in order to save the money to buy a car. So poor were academics! But Watson was too restless, too close to formulating his iconoclastic views to take things calmly and not to overwork.

By the beginning of 1910, Watson was getting very near to the position he argued in his famous paper in 1913 which is usually taken to mark the beginning of behaviourism. In 1910, Watson published his article in *Harpers* on the 'new science of animal behaviour'. The article shows clearly that Watson was well on the way towards behaviourism but that he was still holding back some crucial criticisms of introspective psychology. Watson argued that animals should be studied only by observation and experiment. The argument by analogy from the animal's behaviour to its would-be-expressed consciousness was absurd. Observation and experiment would lay bare why animals behaved as they did. Watson hinted that human psychology could

61

well benefit from having some research of this sort done but the unassertive way that Watson put that made it seem such research would just be a useful complement to introspective psychology; it would not compete for the whole terrain of psychology. Watson did not launch into a total attack on the study of consciousness. On those essential elements of being human, language, feeling and thinking, the will, the article was silent. It was a piece, after all, on animal behaviour and, as far as *Harpers* were concerned, people were not animals. Yerkes objected to some passages in the article. Watson replied that the article had been useful in informing people of new developments. 'I am in a community which practically has not heard of psychology,' he reminded his friend.

On 6 February 1910 Watson told Yerkes that, in fact, 'I would remodel psychology as we now have it.' He would like to expound behavourism and to put consciousness in its place as an irrelevance but, 'I fear to do it because my place here is not ready for it. My thesis developed as I long to develop it would certainly separate me from the psychologist. Titchener would cast me off and I fear Angell would do likewise.' The main obstacles were Watson's own inner loyalties. Yerkes urged caution.

It was no good turning to the cautious Yerkes for inspiration. Round the end of 1909 Knight Dunlap began to play an important role in helping Watson. In June of that year, Watson had been most unimpressed with his assistant. Yet Watson wrote of late 1909 that 'about this time I began to perfect my point of view about behaviourism. To Dunlap I owe much.' In his autobiography Dunlap claimed that Watson really owed him everything. Dunlap said that he had discarded the old doctrine of 'images' while Watson still accepted it. In 1936 Dunlap claimed:

> Watson had not at that time [1909] developed his behaviourism and his thinking was to a large extent along conventional lines. He was violently interested [surely an odd adverb] in animal behaviour and was looking for some simplifications of attitude which would align that work with human psychology. Hence, he was interested in the iconoclastic activity I was developing and was influenced by my views but carried them to extremes.

Dunlap's attack here becomes confusing. On the one hand he accuses Watson of just taking Dunlap's ideas to illogical extremes. Dunlap said he had himself: 'denounced introspection as held by the orthodox psychologists. Watson carried this further to the exclusion from his psychology of everything to which the word "introspection" could be applied.' Dunlap 'rejected images as psychic objects' but, in his senseless enthusiasm, Watson ruled out not just images but also the imagination. Where the sensitive Dunlap questioned the possibility of observing consciousness, Watson just chucked consciousness out of psychology.

Yet while Watson was vandalising the contents of the mind, Dunlap also accused him of 'hopeless Titchenerian bias'. When Dunlap confronted Watson with this deviation and simply 'urged him to study behaviour as behaviour, he admitted the apparent Titchenerian bias but opined he could get away from that in his later writings. He did eventually but only after American psychology had generally moved ahead.' Dunlap also said that all Watson was interested in was finding 'physiological substitutes' for perception, thought and feeling.

When he wrote his autobiography, Dunlap was so busy heaping critiques upon his old professor that he failed to notice how the critiques contradicted each other. Titchener whom Watson was biased towards did not have the least interest in physiology. Yet Watson was, on the one hand, just seeking 'physiological substitutes' for mental state and, on the other, being a Titchenerian. Apart from such contradictions, some of Dunlap's claims were just false. Long before the two men met, Watson had been toying with behaviouristic ideas. Watson never denied the existence of the imagination though he would argue that imagination had nothing to do with images. Long before he met Dunlap, Watson studied behaviour as behaviour. And even the criticisms that Dunlap made of introspection differ greatly from Watson's. In 1912, Dunlap wrote 'The Case Against Introspection' and Watson published it in the *Psychological Review*. The gist of Dunlap's argument is philosophical. Introspection is conceptually confused. To be aware of an awareness is an odd sort of awareness. It is not like being aware that there is a red blot on my notebook. To ask a subject to scrutinise their consciousness and report on it must alter the nature of their consciousness at that moment. When I see red, I usually see red. When I also happen to be introspecting, I see red and I am thinking of what am I conscious as I see red. This is not ordinary seeing red. Dunlap did not conclude that introspection was an invalid technique, but he wanted its uses and its complexities clarified. With modifications, it would have its good points. Even if Dunlap had all these ideas he put forward in 1912 back in 1909, it is clear that they are very different from Watson's excommunication of introspection.

In 1936, however, Watson confessed that he owed much to Dunlap and that Dunlap had 'in his own biography . . . stated my indebtedness to him better than I express it myself'. This last statement was surely meant to be ironic. To harp so much on what another scientist owes you is to puff yourself up. But Watson then added that 'what he says is true'. Watson may well have had reasons by 1936 for not quibbling about how much Dunlap helped him. He did not want then to get involved in more bitter quarrelling. He was tired. And he may have been inclined to remember what seem to me to have been the two main reasons for being grateful to Dunlap. First, Dunlap was the first psychologist to be enthusiastic about Watson's ideas. Everyone else gave him a chilly response when he suggested that human beings might be studied objectively; Dunlap did not. And Dunlap was an experimental human psychologist. Second, Dunlap did help Watson to clarify his ideas about mental images. Since one of the prime functions of consciousness was to be conscious of these images which were then, somehow, translated into thoughts or feelings, Watson had to resolve the issue. He had always been uncomfortable when trying to read off the images in his own mind. Dunlap, who questioned that 'images were psychic objects', enabled Watson to go further and claim, not that images did not exist, but that they were not relevant to psychology. The talks with Dunlap did help Watson to see that and, at least as important, Dunlap's support gave Watson some self-confidence in his tentative, but revolutionary, feelings.

But while Dunlap did influence Watson in this way, his claim to be the true father of behaviourism rings a little hollow. In 1936, when it was made, many psychologists were only too willing to pillory Watson. It was acceptable to say not only that behaviourism was wrong but that Watson had cribbed it from someone else. Dunlap did play a part in the evolution and development of Watson's ideas and of his determination to utter them. But it was no more than his part.

Watson was also excited by anthropology at this time. Sumner published *Folkways*, a massive tome that described the different customs of tribes all over the uncivilised world. The rich romantic observation fascinated Watson. Sumner delighted in showing that what was taboo and immoral for one people was classed as first-rate moral behaviour somewhere else on earth. Morality was a question of geography. The Baptists with their rigid morality, insisting that certain acts were of necessity sins, displeasing to God, and would land one in ever-flaming Hell, were shown to be provincial bigots as far as Watson was concerned. He now had evidence to back up his convictions. Gods differed widely; marriage customs differed widely; sexual behaviour differed widely. In one spot, polygamy was the norm: in others, polyandry. In some societies adultery was no sin. Many tribes encouraged their young to frolic sexually before they got married on the grounds that a proper spouse had to be expert in the arts of love. It was heady stuff for Watson and would influence both his personal and professional life. The anthropologists were, of course, soon to be attracted by the universals that existed in all cultures. They nearly all seemed to have marriage, family, customs that surrounded property and death, and some kind of religious activity. For Watson, the fascination of *Folkways* was different. An adequate psychology would have to explain why 'human nature' took, in these various cultures, an endless diversity.

Watson was also titillated to learn that every well-to-do man in Bassar, Togo, had has three wives because 'children are suckled for three years' and that 'the Arabs in Jerusalem take three or four wives as soon as they have sufficient means'. In Russia it often happened that fathers arranged for their sons to marry a young girl and promptly snatched the maiden away to be their own concubine. All these folkways were not the ways of Baltimore or of Greenville. Yet they were human. And, to Watson, they also sounded like fun.

For the time being, he was happy with Mary Ickes. Watson liked being a father. He enjoyed his children. By 1910 John was six years old and Polly was four years old. They were fun to play with and to watch grow up. Mary helped him often enough in his work. She was sick once more and he tended her with loving care. Watson was not looking for excuses to be unfaithful but he often dipped into *Folkways* again. Both from a professional and a personal point of view it was a stimulating book and it was not a little ironic that Sumner, its author, had been an evangelical minister who had found the cloth too constricting.

Having written his article for *Harpers*, Watson now continued with his work on his book for Holts. He also had much to plan for the summer of 1910. He intended that year to get to the Tortugas to continue the work on the birds and he also found that he had to give much attention to plans for a Congress of Psychology.

The object of a Congress of Psychology was that it should be an international gathering of all the leading figures, national and international, in the field of psychology. The attempt to organise it was to annoy Watson considerably until the middle of 1911. But Watson was, paradoxically, to gain much from what turned out to be a fiasco in which psychologist after psychologist behaved more like an opera prima donna than a serious man of science. At first Titchener, who was not a member of the American Psychological Association, refused to join in plans for the Congress. This suited a number of other psychologists, especially James McKeen Cattell, very well. Cattell urged that Titchener, though he was a very eminent psychologist, could not be a vice-president of the Congress because he was not a member of the American Psychological Association. Titchener had founded in 1904 his 'experimental society' to which Watson, Holt,

Yerkes and a few others had belonged. Titchener disapproved of the American Psychological Association. Cattell, who was an ambitious man, seems secretly to have hoped that he would be asked to preside over the Congress. If that was not to be, then he hoped at least to be the king-maker. The obvious choice for president was William James. But James was sick and in Paris. James at first accepted and then declined and then accepted again on the most bizarre of conditions. He would only be nominally president; on the first day of the Congress he was to be allowed to resign and to name the person who would take over the chair. James's decision would be final. Watson had been elected secretary of the committee that would organise the Congress and he, somewhat reluctantly, agreed to James's plan. Cattell then somehow managed to arrange that Ladd, a physiological psychologist whose textbooks Watson had used at Furman, should get nominated as the person who would inherit the presidency from James. Watson was furious. A number of universities including Harvard, Yale and Hopkins would pull out because Ladd had no great reputation.

Watson felt he was hopeless as a politician. Eventually in December 1910 some sort of compromise was reached. All the past presidents of the American Psychological Association and Titchener as well would serve as vice-presidents of the Congress. Watson wrote to Titchener that he was 'sincerely weary of having my soul tired to death'. There remained the question of whether the errant Baldwin who had been a president of the American Psychological Association should be included in the roll of vice-presidents; eventually, morality won out. Baldwin was excluded. Titchener finally agreed to join the association. Watson was glad and wrote, not without jealousy, that he hoped he, Yerkes and Holt had 'contributed a little toward bringing about this result'. By January 1911 Titchener was being difficult again. He was refusing to serve on the executive committee of the Congress. 'Titchener, I beg of you in the name of all the gods, to reconsider this decision. . . . The time is ripe for a good one [Congress] and the foreigners will come if we subsidise them.' Watson was sure that could be managed if the Congress committee was strong enough. Titchener seemed essential to that. Watson confessed he did not know what he would do if Titchener would not join the Committee. He added 'but if you will come in I shall take heart and take off my coat at the same time.' Watson's pleas, in the end, persuaded the stiff Titchener to join. The date of the Congress was to be some time in the summer of 1913.

I have tried to describe as briefly as possible all these political moves because they are only of the scantiest interest now. But they did affect Watson. At the start of 1910 he was still very much impressed by the patriarchs of his profession as men. There was something close to reverence in his feelings for Titchener, Angell, even James as people. He had come close to being distraught again in late 1909 because he realised that what he wanted to say would so upset the leading old men in his profession. By the beginning of 1911 they had lost much of their awe. He had seen them posturing, politicking, pirouetting on their dignities *ad nauseam*. These days, we accept that academic politics are at least as bitchy as any others. But Watson had a faith in learning, in the academic ways of life. 'University men' did not act in such a petty manner. But he had seen them act just so for a whole year. Witnessing this helped to free him to oppose them.

Watson also had positive reasons to be more confident. His students were turning out good work, in the field of animal learning especially Ulrich had shown that the number of times a day rats were made to work on a problem affected the rate at which they learned it. The most practice, five times a day, did not make for the best learning. Ulrich also showed that it was better to have the rats tackle more than one problem at a time. Dunlap was producing good work at last. Watson felt he was head of a laboratory that had some standing. Ramsden approved of much of Watson's work and, in the summer of 1910 told his young professor that his salary would be raised to $3,500. Watson wrote to Yerkes: 'I don't deserve it and I am ashamed to take it but I do need it. Now I can clear away my debts and go to Europe some summer. It's embarrassing never to have been.'

Meanwhile, however, Watson set sail for Florida rather than for Europe. He had arranged his contract with Columbia more skilfully this year so that he could get down to the Tortugas to continue work on the terns. Watson sailed in April and stayed in the islands until the end of June. From there, he still had to write about the affairs of the ill-fated Congress. That politicking would last all summer and beyond. But at least down in the islands Watson had peace, quiet and an exciting project to continue with.

In 1907 Watson had made some preliminary observations on the behaviour of noddy and sooty terns. These were a prelude to his study of homing in these birds. Watson extended his observations from before the birth of the birds. He found that the noddy terns constantly covered the eggs. Each member of a breeding pair sat on the eggs by turns; they kept the eggs moist by wetting their feathers in the sea and then brushing them against the shells; they turned the eggs round and round with their beaks. The birth of the young affected the terns remarkably. While minding the eggs and when their offspring were very young, the parents would fight any intruder into their space. As the chicks grew, the parents became much less quick to respond aggressively.

Watson went on to map the development of the young terns. At the moment of birth they were very unco-ordinated and they could hardly take the food from their parents. By twenty days, they could consume food as fast as their parents could regurgitate it; at eight to ten weeks, the terns left the nest. Their feeding habits were fairly regular; the birds searched for food at intervals that ranged between two and five hours. Watson described their feeding and drinking movements.

The fighting of the tern was also very characteristic. It had a very sharp bill and Watson had had blood drawn from his hands often enough. The terns fought by locking bills and battering each other with their wings. They were brave and vicious enough to attack large Man O'War birds when the latter tried to roost on the nests of noddies. Watson also described how noddies fought each other. Usually this was when a large strange bird tried to usurp a nest, to steal straws or 'in general to encroach upon the neighbourhood of the nest', an interesting anticipation of the idea of territory which was to engage so much ethological attention. Watson saw that the territory depended on the birds' biological condition; a brooding bird 'saw' or had a much larger territory round the nest at least in the sense of attacking intruders more readily. 'As soon as the egg is laid the instincts of the bird again change. Before the egg is laid the birds are timid and will fly up at the slightest disturbance. After the egg is laid the birds become exceedingly bold,' Watson wrote.

He noted a number of other curious aspects of the behaviour of the birds. They sunned themselves for long periods and spent much time standing motionless on housetops or pieces of driftwood. He observed how they built their nests. Very young birds, often lay completely still, 'death shamming', or, sometimes, shamming lameness. Some aspects of the birds' behaviour baffled Watson totally. One of 'the most interesting ones is its inveterate system of nodding to every bird that comes near to it and its mate.' This nodding often preceded a fight, a change of nesting site or sex. The birds sometimes completely stopped doing anything for long periods of time. This total lack of any behaviour bemused Watson: he could not explain it at all.

If the birds homed across water, could they swim? Watson ducked noddies and sooties under water. Most of the birds could cope with this treatment. They kept their sense of orientation and rose 'in a beautifully co-ordinated way' when Watson let go of them two feet under water. After a night in a cage that was partially submerged, the birds' ability to fly off was quite unaffected.

On 16 May 1910 Watson marked 12 noddies and 12 sooties. They were meant to go to Mobile and be released there to see if they would fly the 720 miles back to the islands. But bad weather prevented the necessary boat connections being made and so the birds were released at Key West some 66 miles away; 12 of the 24 birds were back in Watson's hands within 44 hours at the most. At the end of May Watson tried again. This time, he did manage to ship the birds to Mobile and another set to New York. But many of the birds died in transit because they were packed too close together and because they did not have enough minnows to eat. Watson felt very badly about this. There could not be any proper test of the birds' ability to home until the conditions under which the birds were asked to perform were rather more adequate. The next time round, he would need a properly qualified assistant to travel with the birds.

The solitude on the Tortugas made Watson wry. He wrote to Ramsden that 'a letter from civilisation' informed him Ramsden had given a fellowship to a man Watson approved of. 'My two months', wrote Watson, 'is costing the Carnegie [Institution] $1,500 and more than one of us will be disappointed if I don't get any returns.' Watson sent the letter off before he knew the fate of his birds. For his part, Ramsden replied nicely. He wished he might have the chance to see Watson working with the birds. That must be exciting. And this prompted Watson to tell Ramsden that 'you have certainly given me encouragement by the way you have treated both me and the lab.' In the next few months Watson would obtain from President Ramsden two sums of $100 each for graduates in financial straits, an increase in Dunlap's salary, a further allocation of $100 so that he could hire Ulrich to tend the rats in the laboratory, a job that Watson remembered as being crucial to the functioning of a good department, and, to cap it all, the part-time services of a stenographer because Watson had more than forty letters a week to write with the business side of the *Psychological Review* and the new *Journal of Animal Behaviour* to cope with. Ramsden was generous. And Watson, for his part, was always aware of the financial hardships of those under him. He had been very poor himself for a long time: now he was just poor.

By 1910, then, Watson had added to the reputation of Johns Hopkins in psychology. He had more and more students and, therefore, more and more work. The standing of the psychology department within the university increased. Though Watson complained of having to work too hard, he was very pleased with the success he was having as a professor. Slowly it made him surer of himself.

Another influence also began to make itself felt at this time. Watson began to meet regularly with Dr Adolf Meyer. Meyer was a psychiatrist who had just been appointed to head the Phipps Psychiatric Clinic at the Johns Hopkins medical school. Watson never warmed to Meyer personally but the two men liked each other's ideas. The arrival of

Meyer also pushed Watson towards studying problems of human psychology. Watson spent much time preparing a new course for medical students which would involve them taking a minor in psychology. Psychology should begin to affect medicine. In 1911 Watson published a short paper on this course in the *Journal of the American Medical Association*. Human memory, attention and emotions should all be studied in an objective way urged Watson. He was getting ever closer to his revolutionary postiion.

Animal colour vision still fascinated Watson. Early in 1911 Mary was training chicks to make colour discriminations. Watson admired her ability to handle the animals and the new apparatus he was using 'since what she knows about the apparatus could be quickly and easily said'. He actually included her as co-author on the paper that eventually emerged. Watson was also planning the monkey research with Karl Lashley.

But Watson could not get away from human psychology for too long. The papers submitted to the *Psychological Review* and *Psychological Bulletin* suggest that the whole question of consciousness and introspection was beginning to agitate many American psychologists though none of them urged anything as radical as the break Watson did. A paper by John Boodis wondered just what the uses of introspection were; Dunlap published his 'Case against Introspection' in 1912; Max Meyer, a neurologist, published a book called *The Fundamental Laws of Human Behaviour* in which he argued, like Jennings, that every psychological action or reaction was rooted in some physiological response and that, therefore, psychology was essentially useless. The fundamental laws of human behaviour were not laws of behaviour or psychology at all but laws of physiology. This was not Watson's view and Meyer did not speak of the question of consciousness as such, but the book certainly suggested that psychology needed a more scientific approach to compete as a science. Watson could see plainly that the orthodoxies of Titchener and Angell were no longer the only kinds of position that were being discussed.

These questions exercised Watson particularly in March 1911 when he had to review a book of Titchener's. Much of Titchener's book dealt with the question of *imageless thought*. Debate had raged for twenty years on whether it was possible to think with or without having concurrent visual images. Some introspectionists argued that much thinking was imageless; others maintained that without imagery thinking was impossible. Watson wrote to Yerkes 'I don't give a damn about imageless thought', but his review was not in the end so brutal. Still, if Watson needed any reminding, reading Titchener would have showed him the irreconcilable differences between different kinds of introspectionists. For most sensations had the attributes of *quality, duration, intensity and extension*: Titchener believed there was also the attribute of *clearness*. It was all less and less convincing to Watson. His own views became more bold.

In April 1911 Yerkes came to Baltimore and they discussed yet more work on colour vision. For the rest of the year Watson's letters to Yerkes have little to say about either consciousness or introspection. I think Watson knew that their views differed too much to want to argue them. They discussed whether monkeys learned by imitation. Grandly Watson informed Yerkes that Yerkes's best work, on the dancing mouse, was better than Watson's best work, on the rats. In the letters Watson also noted that he quarrelled with Miss Washburn, a pupil of Titchener's, over an article she wrote and there were troubles with printers both for the *Review* and the *Journal of Animal Behaviour*, the first issue of which appeared in February 1911. Watson also had to bicker with the Carnegie Institution because they refused to give him adequate funds to pursue the project on the Tortugas. He perfected the apparatus for the experiments on colour vision. There were five PhD students for him to supervise and many more undergraduates than ever before. Watson felt overworked.

In April 1911 Watson fired off one of his familiar salvoes about salary. He told Ramsden that he had recently been offered $8,000 by Thorndike to become Head of the Peabody School and had been told this might lead to a university presidency. After the threats came the deference. Watson told Ramsden: 'I told him [Thorndike] immediately that I did not care to consider it . . . I told him I'd rather by far work in my lab under a man I knew to be a good president than to ever attempt such a task myself.' But Watson asked for more money for himself and for Dunlap who should also be promoted. Later in the year Watson pressed for funds to appoint a man to teach educational psychology and applied psychology. The importance of these practical fields in human psychology were becoming clear to Watson.

In the summer of 1911 Watson did not go to the Tortugas. He spent some of the time in New York and some of it just thinking about the role of instincts in behaviour. In November Yerkes was in Baltimore again and they were back to the question of work on colour vision. The details of Watson's life in 1911 sound fairly prosaic. Yet it was during this year that he made the decision finally to refine his views and to dare to articulate them in public. It was perhaps because of this that he was sick again between the 1 and 14 January 1912. Two weeks later he wrote to Yerkes that he had agreed to write another article for *Harpers* on the modern trend in psychology 'which will probably make everyone I know mad'. At the same time, Watson was planning his first researches into human learning. The young neurologist, Karl Lashley, had been persuaded to teach a number of people to shoot with bows and arrows. Would these would-be Robin Hoods learn their new skill in the same kind of way that rats learned to thread a maze? Watson wrote to Yerkes: 'I suppose Titchener would be disgusted if he knew about it. 'Watson was well aware of the fact that he would soon cause a furore.

In the midst of this intellectual ferment, Ira Ramsden resigned as President of Johns Hopkins. The timing could not please Watson. Ramsden had just promised that there would finally be a separate department of psychology. To secure his position, Watson mounted a campaign to get Angell made president of the university. An avid Angell visited Baltimore but the campaign failed. Watson did not mind too much. He had become a little less starry-eyed about Angell. Confidentially, Watson told Yerkes that Angell had often been too frightened of damaging his own popularity to really push for his friends. His loyalty was strictly limited.

In October 1912 Watson finished some new work on the spectral sensitivity of the chick which showed that though chicks could see the same kinds of colours as people, it took much more light to stimulate their retina, especially round 520 mu (a shade of green). Two weeks later Watson wrote a critical review of a paper on the nature of the animal mind. He wrote to Yerkes about it: 'I sometimes fear my critical attitude makes me more enemies than friends.' In an ideal scientific world, criticisms should be welcomed. 'I take it as a kindness to have anyone jump upon the weak places in my work,' Watson said. Others took less kindly to that. Partly, of course, Watson was pretending to be surprised by the hostility which criticism aroused' but partly he was so driven to excel that he reacted very well to having his work attacked. It spurred him on and, sometimes, improved his research; others, less rugged, preferred simple, sluggish praise.

In that autumn Watson agreed to give a series of lectures at Columbia in February 1913. These were to mark a crucial turning point in his career. He was nervous and said nothing to Yerkes about these plans. Instead, he told his friend that the two Baltimore monkeys had had a baby whose development would be observed from day to day. Watching the monkeys in the laboratory made Watson aware of the limitations involved. 'I am extremely anxious', he told Yerkes, 'to see field studies develop. I feel that most of our problems are to be raised by field studies and that after we have turned our animals out of the lab we ought to retest our hypotheses in the field.' This was an important point which Watson would develop. But of the lectures he had 'in mind', he said nothing.

It was sensible of Watson not to let Yerkes see the text of any of these lectures in advance for Yerkes would, undoubtedly, have criticised Watson for being too extreme. And now that he had finally worked out what his mind was and decided to speak it, Watson did not want to be pushed into any last-minute revisions.

On 24 February 1913 in New York, Watson gave the first of the lectures that mark, in effect, the beginning of the kind of psychology we know now. They were an immediate success. He attracted large crowds of over two hundred and he wrote to Yerkes that he had been upset by how big they were. Once he had given the first lecture he could write to Yerkes and asked, as ever, to be criticised. 'I am sending you a print of my first lecture. If you don't like it, I hope you will cuss me out,' said Watson who knew well that Yerkes would have reservations. On 26 March, by which time Watson had finished the series of lectures, he wrote to his friend: 'I am sending you a bunch of reprints. I understand Angell thinks I am crazy. I should not be surprised if that was the general consensus of opinion.'

It is not surprising that Watson was so defensive. For all the criticisms of introspection we have mentioned, what Watson had to say marked a decisive break with the past. It marked, for him, the end of a long struggle in which he had restrained himself because there were people who meant so much to him that he did not want to offend them. But Watson had both acquired the confidence to speak out and sensed a growing restlessness with psychology as it was. He could not be forever in thrall to Titchener, Angell and Donaldson.

Watson began his classic lecture 'Psychology as the Behaviourist Views It' in a firm mood. He wrote:

Psychology as the behaviourist views it is a purely objective experimental branch of natural science. Its theoretical goal is the prediction and control of behaviour. Introspection forms no essential part of its methods, nor is the scientific value of its data dependent upon the readiness with which they lend themselves to interpretation in terms of consciousness. The behaviourist, in his efforts to get a unitary scheme of animal response, recognises no dividing line between man and brute. The behaviour of man, with all of its refinement and complexity, forms only a part of the behaviourist's total scheme of investigation.

Watson then attacked the view that psychology is 'a study of the science of the phenomena of consciousness'. If perception or feeling were studied in order to analyse the 'mental states' which led to them, then the study of behaviour *per se* had no value. This was, indeed, what many psychologists claimed. Watson said he had often been asked

73

what the value of animal psychology was and what its bearing on human psychology was. 'I used to have to study over this question. Indeed it always embarrassed me somewhat. I was interested in my own work and felt it was important, and yet I could not trace any connection between it and psychology as my questioner understood psychology.' Watson said it was time to stop making 'false pretences'. Animal psychology had so far contributed little to human psychology. But that was partly because human psychologists had so dismissed the value of animal work. Watson added:

> It seems reasonably clear that some kind of compromise must be effected; either psychology must change its viewpoint so as to take in the facts of behaviour, whether or not they have bearings upon the problems of 'consciousness'; or else behaviour must stand alone as a wholly separate and independent science.

Watson said that if 'human psychologists' did not welcome co-operation it would lead to confrontation. `

Watson then went on to defend the position that it was acceptable to study the behaviour of animals objectively, for example, the manner in which rats learned mazes. There was no reason why 'we should still feel the task is unfinished and the results are worthless, until we can interpret them by analogy in the light of consciousness.' Assume that the variables which affect the rats' learning have all been teased out objectively. 'Although we have solved our problem we feel uneasy and unrestful because of our definition of psychology; we feel forced to say something about the possible mental processes of our animal.' That was quite unnecessary, said Watson. The behaviour revealed all. He then went on to criticise those would-be behaviourists who devoted much energy to working out where on the phylogenetic scale consciousness began to appear.

> More than one student of behaviour has attempted to frame criteria of the psychic – to devise a set of objective, structural and functional criteria which, when applied in the particular instance, will enable us to decide whether such and such responses are positively conscious, merely indicative of 'consciousness' or whether they are purely 'physiological'.

Watson did not even deny the existence of consciousness among animals. He merely questioned the usefulness of the concept:

> One can assume the presence or the absence of consciousness anywhere in the phylogenetic scale without affecting the problems of behaviour by one jot or tittle; and without influencing in any way the mode of experimental attack on them.

Problems of behaviour were not so unimportant, however.

To make consciousness the centre of human psychology, the 'centre of reference for all behaviour', was short-sighted. It meant that psychologists discarded a massive number of facts and experiments as not being psychology because 'unless our observed facts are indicative of consciousness, we have no use for them'. Watson pressed home his attack by pointing to the signal failure of psychology 'during the fifty odd years of its existence as an experimental discipline to make its place in the world as a natural science'. If you failed to replicate my findings, it was not due to some fault in the apparatus you used or in the control of stimuli but 'due to the fact that your introspection is untrained'. It was not so in physics or chemistry. 'If you can't observe 3–9 states of clearness in attention, your introspection is poor. If, on the other hand, a feeling seems reasonably clear to you, your introspection is again faulty. You are seeing too much. Feelings are never clear.' If this sounds like caricature, one should try to read Wundt. Even Titchener was not spared. One psychologist would say that a visual sensation had the attributes of 'quality, extension, duration and intensity'; Titchener would add *clearness*; others would add *order*. Watson said that if one considered colour, it was clear that this whole approach was pointless. Were there an immeasurably large number of colour sensations, one different sensation for each discriminable hue of colour? Or were there just basic sensations of green, blue, red and yellow? Some claimed yellow was a distinct primary sensation but then you could mix blue and green, outside of consciousness, in order to produce yellow. It was no good claiming, as Titchener did, that psychology was young and that answers would be found to these controversies. Watson's point was that the nature of the questions was such that you could never, in principle, find scientific answers to them. He was far from being the philosophical simpleton Angell was to damn him as.

Memory had been experimentally investigated, and to great point, Watson claimed. There was no need to ask about what was happening in consciousness when one remembered. He pointed out again the confusion in the ranks of the introspectionists when it came to feelings. Some said they were attitudes, others that they were different kinds of sensation. Plumbing one's mind had achieved very little in the view of understanding emotions.

In his lecture, Watson then turned to the functional psychologists like Angell. Watson said he had been very surprised when one of them, Pillsbury, started a book by defining 'psychology as the "science of behaviour" '. But after a few pages the science of behaviour was dropped 'and one finds the conventional treatment of sensation, perception, imagery etc.' The functional psychologist, Watson stressed, was forced into a position in which mental states had to have a function and their only possible function was to cause actions. To espouse functionalism was to get trapped in the mind–body problem.

Once he had attacked the nature of contemporary psychology, Watson set out to offer a constructive programme. 'I believe we can write a psychology, define it as Pillsbury did and never go back upon our definition; never use the terms consciousness, mental states, mind, content, introspectively verifiable and the like.' Watson believed that this could be done without sacrificing the complexity of human behaviour. 'It can be done in terms of stimulus and response, in terms of habit formation, habit integrations and the like.'

This kind of attempt was not easy, Watson admitted. He set out some of the ways in which he had tried to carry out a programme of study using such concepts on the terns in the Tortugas. It would be much more difficult to study Australian savages like that. It would be even more difficult to study 'the psychology of the educated European . . . but, . . . I should have followed the same general line of attack.' In principle, the behaviour of all these creatures was susceptible to the same kind of investigation.

Practical considerations also led Watson to argue the value of behaviourism. Educators, doctors, lawyers and businessmen did not all use psychology because it was so impractical. Those few areas which did not depend on introspection, especially psychopathology and the use of tests, were beginning to flourish. Watson was fierce at the expense of those who looked down on practical or 'applied' psychology. There were large fields to conquer, for example, the whole field of the reliability of the memory of witnesses.

> For a 'pure' psychologist to say that he is not interested in the questions raised in these divisions of science because they relate indirectly to the application of psychology shows . . . that he fails to understand the scientific aim in such problems, and secondly, that he is not interested in a psychology that concerns itself with human life.

That last idea was to become a crucial one in the development of Watson's ideas.

As an example of the kind of work he had in mind, Watson quoted the research of Ulrich. Ulrich could compare the effects of having a rat work at a problem once a day, three times a day or five times a day. Ulrich also looked at whether the animal should learn one problem at a time or three problems together. Watson urged the need for similar studies on people. There was no need to invoke consciousness either in the rat or in man to answer such problems.

Towards the end of the paper, Watson acknowledged that man was special in that he could talk. Watson did not rule out the use of data obtained through language but he stressed that this should not be the only form of data obtained. Also, though he did not say so, everything depended on what questions were asked in language. 'The situation is somewhat different when we come to a study of the more complex forms of behaviour, such as imagination, judgment, reasoning and conception. At present the only statements we have of them are in content terms,' wrote Watson. By 'content terms,' he seems to have meant an introspective examination of the contents of consciousness when one thought, imagined or judged. Wundt, for example, made long lists of the images that preceded and, for him, contained the psychological insights he had. The image was the insight. Watson added: 'Our minds have been so warped by the fifty odd years that have been devoted to the study of the states of consciousness that we can envisage these problems only in one way.' Watson admitted that 'behaviour methods' could not immediately resolve all these problems and he spent much of the spring of 1913 grappling with the behaviourist theory of thinking. But his plea was simple. Given time, the behaviourist approach would be able to handle those complex abilities which were taken to be specifically human; 'the introspective method itself has reached a *cul-de-sac* with respect to them.' Watson even suggested that Yerkes, who wanted psychology to study psychics, was wrong in spirit. 'The ignoring of consciousness' was a much better strategy.

Only in the last paragraph of the paper did Watson become defensive. He admitted to having a 'deep bias on these questions. I have devoted nearly twelve years to experimentation on animals. It is natural that such a one should drift into a theoretical position which is in harmony with his experimental work.' He attempted to offer Angell an olive branch. 'There may be no absolute lack of harmony between the position outlined here and that of functional psychology. I am inclined to think, however, that the two positions cannot be easily harmonised.' Watson said he felt there were still many weaknesses in his formulation but, nevertheless, he thought that it was vital to consider the points he had made in order to arrive at a scientific psychology.

In order not to be too shocking, Watson veered between demanding an end to all study of consciousness and suggesting that behaviouristic observation and experiment ought to be added to the study of consciousness but the more he got into his argument, the more irrelevant he made the study of consciousness and mental states appear. A behaviouristic psychology would take its place among the sciences. Its data would be verifiable. Experiments could be properly replicated by different workers. And, most important, Watson claimed there would not be any loss of richness in the data psychology had to handle. We now tend to castigate behaviourism because of its narrowness. It leaves so much of life out. Watson argued that the introspectionists with their obsessive observation of mental states actually were divorced from life. He would return to that point later.

But the most shocking part of Watson's papers was that in which he suggested that the behaviour of man should be studied just like the behaviour of animals. There was no soul; there was no mind that conferred on man his special and unique status. Watson even anticipated that behaviourism might study thinking. All this was to rob human beings of all that seemed to elevate them beyond the other animals. To make matters worse, Watson said that one purpose of behaviourism was the prediction and control of behaviour. This latter phrase has passed into the textbooks as one of the key definitions of psychology. It then marked a complete break with the past for, until then, the object of psychology was to analyse consciousness. And if behaviour could be predicted, what happened to free will, that religious and philosophical necessity?

Titchener responded to Watson's paper with much ingenuity. He deplored some of it but stressed that what Watson really wanted to do was to found a 'technology'. The behaviouristic programme outlined was not scientific: it was, claimed Titchener, a technological plan to control behaviour. It was not in competition with psychology. It was something quite different. Titchener's criticism has, of course, a very modern ring since we now often accuse behaviourism of being a technology whose aim is to manipulate people. Titchener hoped in this way to keep the sanctum of psychology for introspection. Psychology was about the mind: the rest was not so important. Angell, in his first public utterance on the subject, tried hard not to sound too upset. He recognised 'the service rendered by so courageous and lucid a statement of creed although part of the programme seems to me rather Utopian and impracticable and other portions appear to disregard obvious distinctions and difficulties.' But when you took out the Utopian bits, which he never specified, and the obvious difficulties, which he also never specified, Angell had the highest regard for his former pupil. Later on, Angell argued that psychology had to keep some introspection in order to keep its identity. It had to be balanced by objective studies, for, without any study of introspection or consciousness, 'what becomes of the entire system of moral and spiritual values and experiences?' Angell never forgot that James had let him see some of his data on religious experiences. In private, Angell was more scathing about Watson.

A few days after Watson's lecture Angell wrote to Titchener, 'I shall be glad to see him properly spanked even though I cannot join the ceremony.' Titchener wrote a paper in reply to Watson's points in which he still vigorously defended introspective studies and said that Watson was simply too impatient of results. Angell, having read Titchener's paper, complained that 'you have let Watson down more amicably than most persons think he deserved'. Angell would have liked 'to poke a little fun on the historical side of the case. Indeed, I think, if Watson had ever had any historical courses which were developed after he graduated, he could hardly have fallen into some of the facts which have entrapped him.' Angell felt he was too close to Watson to be more biting then he had already been in public. He added to Titchener, 'I am wholly impatient of his position on this issue which seems to me scientifically unsound and philosophically essentially illiterate.' Other psychologists like William MacDougall, Munsterberg, James McKeen Cattell, Woodworth and Thorndike all attacked Watson for being too extreme. Behaviourism and conventional psychology which reserved for psychology the precious realm of the mind could co-exist. Indeed, Angell argued that if psychology denied the existence of consciousness there would be no field that was specifically psychological.

But if there were critics, Watson also won much admiration. There was an impatience with what were felt to be foreign, Germanic methods in psychology. The temper of the times was to be practical. All kinds of reforms were in the air. Watson's manifesto offered the possibility of a psychology that would be practical as well as scientific. George Wells praised Watson for having made 'quite the most conspicuous contribution' to the debate on the nature of psychology. Wells felt that behaviourism was clearly the wave of the future. And many others supported Watson.

In assessing the origins of behaviourism, John C. Burnham has argued that Watson did indeed not create behaviourism all on his own. Burnham accepts that the other scientists who claimed to have founded behaviourism or were nominated by others for that distinction have very poor claims compared to Watson. Many of the contenders were impressive; William James (in parts), William MacDougall (in even fewer parts), Thorndike, Jennings, Dunlap, Loeb, and from history, Comte and La Mettrie. Burnham agrees, though, that, compared to all these, Watson made the crucial contribution. But Burnham stresses the importance of Kuhn's theory (*The Structure of Scientific Revolutions*, 1962) in which he argues that scientific revolutions occur when a field is ready for a change of paradigm. A new discovery forces the whole nature of a scientific problem to alter and, for that to happen, the prevailing mood has to be right. When Watson delivered his famous lectures in 1913, they had such an effect because the prevailing mood among many psychologists was receptive. The objective results in animal behaviour were impressive; there had been some questioning of introspection as by Dunlap and Boodin. There is certainly much in what Burnham says.

But Kuhn's model fits psychology a little uneasily at times. Watson did not make a new discovery that changed the nature of psychological problems. What Watson was doing, in fact, was to frankly offer a new way of doing psychology. Behaviourism was, quite knowingly, a new paradigm. It was a self-conscious revolution against consciousness. Paradoxically that makes it hard to fit under Kuhn's theory which re-interprets the function of what seem to be just discoveries. Watson 'discovered' nothing; he offered a new method.

There is a less paradoxical quibble with the uncritical acceptance of Kuhn's ideas. Somehow, he suggests that the individual makes his revolutionary contribution at the point when everybody is beginning to change their minds anyway. Behaviourism shocked most psychologists and we have seen the many struggles Watson had before he felt able to articulate it publicly. Nor did Watson's vision sweep all other ways of doing psychology away. Psychoanalysis, Gestalt psychology and other 'schools' did not wither away though introspection did. The natural sciences tend to work with one paradigm, with sweet logic, replacing another paradigm after the latter has been 'disproved'. Psychology is different for various paradigms seem to have been in perpetual competition with one another. Kuhn's model does not fit psychology quite exactly.

Finally, this hypothesis downgrades the contribution Watson made and what it cost him personally. It took nine years and at least one breakdown for him to have the courage and the coherence to state his feeling that psychology should be an objective natural science rather than a subjective introspective study. When Watson gave those lectures in 1913, they attracted so much attention partly because people recognised how very radical his ideas were. It took a long time to convince psychologists of the validity of behaviourism and the now repetitive debates between behaviourists and their opponents make it clear that, successful as it has been, behaviourism is only one of a number of models that are battling for the honour of being psychology. Watson knew very well that his views would arouse controversy, make him many enemies, and that many people who mattered to him would never be convinced anyway. Burnham pays little attention to this as well as failing to explore the problems in affixing Kuhn's unmodified ideas on to the psychological battles of 1913.

By March 1913, when he finished his series of lectures at Columbia, Watson was committed to a fully objective psychology, a total behaviourism which applied to human beings as much as to animals. In the next few years he would begin to work out a psychology which was not only objective but also really connected with human life.

4

Towards the Psychology of Real Life 1913–18

Textbooks often make it seem that once Watson had uttered his behaviourist manifesto the rest of psychology withered away meekly. It was neither so easy nor so neat. After 1913 Watson often had to repeat his essential arguments. Very many psychologists refused to accept his ideas for they seemed much too extreme. For his part, Watson wanted to move on. Now that he had outlined his methodology, he wanted to put it into practice and he could only do that by studying human beings. Full of energy and enthusiasm, he meant to show that psychology could be objective even when confronted by the most complex human 'behaviour'. Feeling, thinking, language, all the actions that seem to be essentially the core of what marks us out as human, had to come within the scope of behaviourism. After 1913 Watson started work on observations and experiments on children and adults and also produced a series of important papers that reveal the animal psychologist in a new guise of a student of human behaviour. Now Watson published apace. The year 1913 saw another crucial paper 'The Image and Affection in Behaviour'; 1914 finally saw his book *Behaviour* published; in 1915 Watson published *The Conditioned Reflex and its Place in Psychology* and the year after that he offered a behaviouristic interpretation both of Freud's ideas and of the concept of mental illness. It was a period in which Watson, having broken with the orthodox, brimmed over with new ideas.

Novel as his thoughts might be, Watson had to look to other natural sciences, and their current concepts, in developing his ideas. From biology he took on the concept of the reflex as the basic unit of human behaviour. Both Loeb and Jennings were enamoured of the reflex. They saw it as a very simple and automatic response to stimuli. You tap the knee; it flexes. You puff air towards the eye; the eyelids blink. For Loeb and Jennings the whole of human behaviour was built up simply on this kind of basis. The reflex in 1913 was a rather crude mechanism. But Watson took it as a base.

The success of the lectures in February and March in New York did not go to Watson's head. He was much more often defensive than he was arrogant when it came to discussing how they had been received. When he returned to Baltimore, he was very much aware of the fact that battle was about to ensue. Behaviourism threatened to rob psychologists of much that they believed very precious, the intrinsic difference between people and animals. Darwin had damaged human morale enough by suggesting that we shared the same ancestors as the gorilla. Watson now aggravated the insult: human behaviour was of fundamentally the same nature as that of the gorilla or, even less flattering, we were on a par with the rat. Watson had had so much religion heaped upon him as a child that he took some delight in the theological outrage he was perpetrating but it was more difficult for the young professor to flout the social conventions. He liked to rebel but he also liked to be accepted.

The lectures had another effect on the psychologist's life. He was, for the first time, away from his wife for long periods of time. He was a very handsome man. The lectures were a success and, among those who attended, were a number of intellectual young women. There is no definite evidence to suggest that it was at this point in time that Watson began to be unfaithful to Mary Ickes but it is, according to his daughter, quite probable. The affairs that the psychologist had at this time did not threaten his marriage. They were frolics. Watson, who often referred to *Folkways* as having been a seminal book for him, knew quite well that in many parts of the world a little adultery was moral and that even in America it was far from infrequent. There was too much passion in the young Watson for him to be faithful to Mary Ickes forever.

In Baltimore, Watson prepared for the summer's work in the Tortugas. With Yerkes's help, he persuaded the Carnegie Institution to hire Lashley too. Lashley was to do some original work of his own, help with the birds and escort them to Mobile and New York. Under his eagle eye they might just make the trip in good shape so that they could be set free with some hope of realistically testing whether or not they could home back to Florida.

Lashley made the trip much more exciting. Though he was shy and rather gawky, Watson found him excellent company. They talked incessantly, mostly about the way behaviourism ought to be developed. Like Watson, Lashley was very interested in the concept of the reflex. For once, life on the islands was not so solitary for Watson. For two weeks both men carried out further tests and observations on the birds. Then Lashley took some thirty birds back to the mainland. He had built special cages for them and he made sure, hour after hour, that they were well. He fed them himself and also made certain they had enough water and space. The close attention he gave the birds paid off. When he reached Mobile, which was 720 miles away, the birds were in fine fettle. He released some fifteen birds here. The original plan was to take the other fifteen up to New York but something went wrong and so Lashley decided to take the other fifteen birds 135 miles further on to Galveston. It would still be a good test of their homing abilities. Alone on the island, Watson waited to see if the birds did, indeed, come back home.

Watson did not have too long to fret. On the fourth day after Lashley released the birds, two terns returned. Three more birds arrived on the fifth day; a further two flew in on the sixth day including one bird from Galveston; three more terns arrived on the seventh day; in the next few days, a further three birds flew in. Watson had reason to be excited. They had shown that terns could fly back across nearly 1,000 miles of water to a small island. And, unlike pigeons, these terns had never been trained to home. How did the birds manage such a feat?

It could not be done by vision. Though Lashley had shown that the terns used their eyes to navigate their way round the islands, the birds would have had to soar impossibly high above Mobile to see the distant Tortugas way over the horizon and then head for them. Their visual acuity would have to be phenomenal and Watson's studies of the check made him incline to the view that the vision of birds was slightly less sharp than that of people. Watson and Lashley examined the terns to see if they had a 'special Spursinn', a special organ in the nasal cavity which, it was alleged, was linked with the ability to home. They found no such neurological nugget in the terns' 'nose'. There was no evidence either that homing terns were receptive to 'infra-luminous rays' which guided them back to the island. Watson had to confess he was stumped for an explanation. They had proved that the terns were able to home but they could not begin to explain how they did. Current theories were not very helpful but 'we do not suggest the assumption of some new and mysterious sense'. Watson suggested a number of experiments that might resolve the problem, but after 1913 he lost interest in the powers of birds. Human psychology claimed much attention and, also, he found himself too often at odds with Meyer of the Carnegie Institution to relish the idea of working more for them.

In July, while Watson was still far from civilisation, he published a paper which developed the ideas of behaviourism. 'Image and Affection in Behaviour' tackled two of the strongholds of introspective psychology, mental images and feelings. Watson began by saying that the doctrine of mental images was at the heart of introspective psychology. He then gave an example of a situation that psychology ought to be able to explain. Someone suggests to Watson that he borrow $1,000 to go abroad for a year: 'I think over the situation – the present condition of my research problems, whether I can leave my family etc. I am in a brown study for days trying to make up my mind. Now time between stimulus and response is given over to implicit behaviour (to "thought processes").' This quotation makes clear what a very wide view of 'stimulus' Watson took. The stimulus was the suggestion that he borrow $1,000: the response was days later, when he decided whether or not to do it. In between lay innumerable other 'pieces' of behaviour.

The behaviourist could use external signs to keep a track of the man in the brown study. Did he sweat? Was he agitated? Did he forget his usual routines of life? What did he actually do? But all these observations, however lovingly detailed, could not give 'anything like a complete record of "my mental content" ' or of the 'totality of conscious processes'. To do that, one had to introspect and read off one's private mental image. From external behaviour, it was impossible to be sure whether the man in the brown study was agonising over past sins or deciding whether or not to go abroad. Watson added:

> If we grant this, and such an impulse is very strong, the behaviourist must content himself with this reflection: 'I care not what goes on in his so-called mind; the important thing is that given the stimulation (in this case a series of spoken words) it must produce response, or else modify responses which have already been initiated. This is the all important thing and I will be content with it.' In other words, he contents himself with observing the initial object (stimulation) and the end object (the reaction). Possibly the old saying 'a half loaf is better than no bread at all' expresses the attitude the behaviourist ought to take: and yet I for one dislike to admit anything which may be construed as an admission of even partial defeat.

Behaviourism would have its own theory of thinking as well, Watson determined. What kind of mental images would the would-be borrower have? Introspection into images could not say. Watson pointed out that Angell and Fernald had spent a great deal of energy trying to discover if different thoughts aroused different kinds of images. But the results were a total mess. Watson did not say people never had mental images but he claimed that only a few people in fact used such images in their thinking: 'but I insist that the images of such a one are sporadic and as unnecessary to his well being and *well thinking* as a few hairs more or less on his head.' Psychologists made

85

mental images so central because that appeared to justify the use of **introspection and the perpetual concern with consciousness.** Though the kinds of images that were the object of introspection did not usually *cause* any behaviour, the philosophy behind introspective experiments suggested that a person first has an image in conscious- ness and that awareness of this image makes the person decide to behave in a particular way. All these activities of the mental image took place in the cortex.

The reaction of Watson to all this was, in part, strange. It should by now be clear why he attacked the use of introspection and the central role allotted to consciousness. It is much less clear why he went on to try and diminish the cortex. He identified consciousness with the cortex and attempted to show that psychologists revered the cortex, and made it the lynchpin of the nervous system, because they were desperately seeking a way of smuggling the 'mind', or, *horribile dictu*, the soul, back into psychology. As a result, Watson declared 'there are no centrally initiated processes'. In itself, the brain can conjure up nothing. It is utterly dependent on stimulation from the periphery, either from the sense organs or from the muscles. The cortex is, Watson argued, nothing but 'a mechanism for co-ordinating incoming and outgoing impulses'. Abstract thinking, meditation and musing stem from something we have seen, heard or felt. Nothing originates in the brain for, to Watson, the only things that might originate there of themselves were nefarious mental images.

Of course, the word Watson used, *co-ordination*, in itself still allows the brain many functions. But the argument that downgraded the cortex remains bizarre and, ultimately, unnecessary. Behaviourism could be quite objective without that. But Watson was quite prepared to defend his view. His account of thinking goes some way, at least, to reveal how he meant to employ such a theory. Very young children first learn physical habits, eye–hand co-ordinations, all kinds of movements. At six months, the baby can do many things like reach for a ball, grasp it and begin to manipulate it. Once the body begins to be co-ordinated, the baby begins to develop 'speech habits'. Then language comes apace. Watson said that its development means that 'there arise associations (neural) between words and acts'. When I put my hand out for a toy duck and my mother says *duck* to me, the presence of these two events creates a neural association between the physiological reflexes that make up the movement in my hand and the physiological reflexes that will eventually activate my tongue and larynx to make the sound *duck*. How this masterpiece of neural orchestration was to occur was not specified by Watson, who just wrote that after the baby develops its co-ordinations:

Behaviour then takes on refinement; short cuts are formed
and, finally words come to be, on occasion, substituted for acts.
That is a stimulus which in its early stages would produce an act
(and which will always do so under appropriate circumstances)
now produces merely a spoken word or mere movements of the
larynx.

The problems with such an account of thinking are both physiological
and theoretical. How do the muscles in the body, the springs of those
reflex arcs that make us stretch, come first, to be associated with, then
to trigger, movements of the tongue and larynx? Watson did not seem
to think that this was really a problem. Second, and more fundamental, speech does not develop only after physical co-ordinations
have been established, as Watson would himself come to see. And,
finally, it is hard to see how many utterances ever originally had any
physical response linked to them. I read a three-year-old child a fairy
tale about a bad dragon being fought by a good knight. The child's only
experience of kings and dragons is verbal. But Watson wanted the
body, rather than the brain, to be central. Remembering his rats, he put
our minds in our muscles.

Watson went on to distinguish overt and implicit behaviour. Often a
stimulus produces an overt response. 'I tell John to go to the sideboard
and get an apple taking for granted that he goes.' But, in contrast with
such action which 'involves the larger musculature in a way plainly
apparent to direct observations, we have behaviour involving only the
speech mechanism. This form of behaviour, for lack of a better name, I
will call *implicit behaviour*.' Watson claimed that when there was
deliberation between the stimulus – someone telling him to borrow
$1,000 – and the response – deciding whether or not to do it – that
interval was given over not to any unobservable thought processes but
to implicit behaviour which could, in principle, be observed. It could
be observed because Watson then went on to claim that the implicit
behaviour was of one kind, silent speech. Everyone admitted that
'words spoken or faintly articulated belong really in the realm of
behaviour as much as do the movements of the arms and legs.' But
Watson went further. Any form of thinking had, inside the head, to
take place in words. Only the words were never actually uttered. But,
though the words were not uttered, they were formed in the way that
spoken words usually were. Therefore, a minute analysis of the movements of the larynx, of the tongue and possibly other organs and
muscles would tell one what a person was thinking. 'The larynx is the
seat of most of the phenomena, I believe. If its movements could be
adequately portrayed, we should obtain a record similar in character to

that of the phonograph.' When the psychologist had adequately studied the way his subject spoke, and the movements of his larynx in speech, it should be possible to monitor his larynx while thinking and know his thoughts.

Now this seems a somewhat strange theory, indeed. Watson had confused consciousness with the cortex. In his determination to wipe the study of consciousness out, he seemed to argue that all thinking was verbal and denied the possibility of visual imagery. He also had to assume that silent speech produced the same muscular movements as spoken speech. The whole theory can only be understood in the light of Watson's reaction against introspection. However, speech could still be accepted as psychological evidence. For instance, there was nothing to stop one explaining how one felt when confronted by a particular stimulus. Later behaviourists, however, assumed that Watson disallowed reports on oneself. It was the kinds of self-report one made that mattered, as we shall come to see.

In the second part of this paper, Watson turned to affection. Watson argued that affections or feelings are 'an organic sensory response'. He did not think there were special nerves or nerve endings for pleasure, though he had to accept the probable existence of pain receptors in the skin. 'The first question that concerns us is how it happens that organic processes have come integrated into such well marked, solid groups known as pleasantness and unpleasantness?' He then lapsed into what seems now very antique thinking and said that these feelings 'as they now stand, they are really perceptions (objects) which as at times may be examined as other objects, such as hunger, thirst etc.' He seems to mean that we know quite clearly that we are hungry, we are thirsty, we are in pain. He derided 'Titchener's view that these processes are never clear. It is a plain assumption and a very weak one, arrived at largely in the interest of obtaining a structural differentiation between sensation and affection.' Sensations and perceptions were always clear: feelings never could be, according to Titchener, at least.

The second question was why these 'affective processes' so often accompanied our perceptions in life. You walk down a country lane, see a view, remark it is lovely and experience a feeling of pleasure. Here, Watson leaned on an unexpected source: Freud. This paper contains Watson's first mention of Freud. The psychoanalyst's treatment of sex appealed to Watson. 'Since my first study of the [Freudian] movement I have been rather surprised that no one has connected pleasantness with the activity of the receptors stimulated by tumescence and unpleasantness with those stimulated by a shrinkage of the sex organs.' In other words, pleasure and unpleasure that we take in quite unsexual things has, at bottom, a sexual root. Watson claimed that 'the erogenous areas are in infancy widely distributed through the body surfaces.' Not only the sex organs produced erotic responses. These ideas were not without merit. They explained why different tribes, as *Folkways* showed, took pleasure in such a variety of actions. Stroke your infants while stretching their ears and they will come to regard ear-stretching as a delight. Hug your children while they sit and do their homework on the porch and they will come to love work. Almost nothing apart from stroking of the skin is, in itself, pleasurable. We are conditioned into our pleasures as we are into our fears. But this account could be interpreted in two ways. Either the arousing of the physiological sensations linked with tumescence *is* pleasure, or it is because I recognise that these sensations have been aroused that an act seems to me nice or nasty. Watson spoke of these associations 'actually serving as "personal evaluators of experience" ', an ambiguous phrase that did not decide between the two possibilities.

The problem of what *is* pleasure and the definition of it is, essentially, a philosophical one. More important from the point of view of Watson's thought was that we could be conditioned into loving or hating any thing, person or situation. Nothing was sacred; experience could manipulate us all. What accompanied stroking or erotic arousal became what we took pleasure in. If I admire the *Mona Lisa*, it was because to some extent, the masterpiece evoked the same physiological responses that made me feel physically good and excited. The aesthetics of erection were bound to make Watson few enemies. He stated that his ideas meant 'admitting that the esthetic, artistic and religious sides of life are at bottom sexual' so that for once he anticipated Freud who only made God an outcrop of the Id in 1929. Many psychologists like Angell and Titchener would shy away from such a position. But Watson was, if not past caring, at least past caring too much. This paper marked Watson's entry into human psychology. It was more than methodological and would lead the behaviourist to study both emotions and their origins and to try to prove his notion that thinking was silent speech.

In the summer of 1913 Watson felt he needed a rest. He took his family up to their house in Canada. For the moment he had had enough of psychology. He put some finishing touches to the house and indulged himself in a new hobby. He bought a motor boat and raced it up and down the lake. Much to his dismay, one man had a faster boat. Not to own the fastest boat riled Watson. With Mary and the children, he put the final touches to the gravel path that led up to the house. It was a happy time. Watson enjoyed his children very much though he found it difficult to show them much physical affection. They did things together as a family, as he and his father had done back in Greenville. That was better than a lot of soft hugging and kissing, Watson felt. He wrote to Yerkes that the month he had spent in Canada made him feel much more cheerful. He had been feeling depressed because of the sheer pressure of work he had undertaken.

As the autumn term began at Johns Hopkins in October 1913, Watson had two plans for his department. He asked the new university to allow him to add two men to his staff. Both were to deal with human, not animal, psychology. He wanted an applied psychologist to look at such topics as industrial psychology and he wanted to recruit a man to carry out research in the psychology of drugs. Watson also wrote to put on the record that Ramsden had agreed that psychology should become a separate department and not part of philosophy, psychology and education. Watson also pleaded for more money for Dunlap. The poverty of Dunlap's family caused him concern. In the confusion between presidents, Johns Hopkins was not minded to expand and so Watson did not get his way. In November Watson wrote to Yerkes both to complain and to commiserate. Yerkes was in money trouble again. So was Watson after having spent so much money on his house in Canada. 'The starvation problem', as Yerkes called it, 'is certainly staring me in the face,' said Watson. 'I would certainly have been arrested but for summer schools.' Watson added sensibly that both he and Yerkes felt so distraught about money because 'we have both been trying to do twice as much as we have any right to do'. He wanted to go hunting in Virginia or New Hampshire or Alaska but it was, as ever, a question of the money.

Though the university did not want to expand, Watson's reputation was attracting more students. Watson was pleased but, of course, complained of the extra work. The university administration was not as supportive as Ramsden had been. Despite these problems, Watson involved himself in another project. He badgered the Carnegie Institution for money to set up a station where higher mammals could be observed in something akin to their natural habitat, a place where monkeys could frolic as Watson had seen them do in the wild of the Tortugas. He argued that psychology desperately needed the data that would come from accurate observations at such a station. One week, Mayer of the Carnegie was enthusiastic; the next week, he pleaded that the Carnegie was broke. 'Mayer makes me ill,' Watson moaned to Yerkes, and the behaviourist added that he hoped that while Mayer was visiting the South Seas the Fiji Islanders 'chewed' him up. But as the islanders did not oblige with any cannibalism, Watson was left to cope with Mayer's vacillations. Yerkes thought the plan for such a station sound but the letters between the two men became infrequent now. In February Watson said he missed Yerkes's 'cheering letters'.

In the autumn of 1913 Watson was also seeing through to publication *Behaviour*, the book he had been writing so long. Much of the lectures he had given at Columbia went directly into it and Watson kept adding new data both from his own research and from that of other psychologists. As a result, the book is a curious mixture. Parts expound the basic ideas of behaviourism as related to studying people: other parts cover animal behaviour, and especially learning, in great detail; one whole chapter is devoted to the then topical issue of the 'wonder horses' who seemed able to read and solve simple equations. Watson was very attached to the book, for it had cost him a lot to write, and when Goodnow, the new President of Johns Hopkins, congratulated him on it he was very pleased.

Curious and uneven it might be but *Behaviour* was very important for Watson. It marked the point at which he really turned towards human psychology and a psychology of real life. The book had one overriding theme, the need and value of the behaviouristic approach. But, within that, Watson crammed all manner of facts, speculations and experiments ranging from an analysis of the so-called 'wonder horses' to Freud.

The first chapter was a repetition of the two key papers of 1913. Watson slightly expanded his treatment of sex. He argued that when we see a sexually exciting stimulus it arouses 'reflex arcs' that link receptors and muscles. He spoke of 'erotic tissues' though, in fact, he claimed elsewhere that most of the body could be an erotic tissue. If the stimulus was intense enough, enough reflex arcs would be stimulated powerfully enough for overt seeking behaviour to begin. Presumably that meant the sufficiently aroused man tried to pick up the girl. The essence of Watson's argument was that by a process of substitution, people came to respond to many objects which are not really sexual in the same kind of way as they did to sexual objects. Here Watson dipped into Pavlov. Pavlov had shown how a dog who originally salivated at the sight of food could be made to salivate when a green light flashed. Watson did not here explain exactly how this model applied to human behaviour. He just asserted that a similar process of substitution worked in people. 'Certainly many objects (non affective stimuli, stimuli distantly or not at all connected with sex stimuli) do not, in the beginning, arouse these groups [of reflex arcs] *but through the ordinary mechanism of habit come later to arouse faintly the one or the other.*' The other was, in Watson's scheme, the 'avoiding reaction', which was connected with sensations hostile to sex and so with pain. Watson did not really at this point convincingly explain how all this happened.

But the terms in which Watson spoke of introspective psychology were yet harsher. As behaviourism had absorbed thinking and feeling,

'It would thus seem that there is no field which an introspective psychology legitimately can call its own.' Watson was not prepared to see behaviourism declare thoughts and feelings as being beyond the proper scope of psychology. Without the least introspection, these complex human process could be studied.

Watson then outlined the key problems that psychology should address itself to. These were 'sense organ functions', 'instinctive functions' and 'habit formation'. All behaviour was the product of the interplay of heredity and environment but it was important to tease out what was instinctive and what was learned. Watson hoped to describe in detail the behaviour of various species so that he could construct 'both an ontogeny and a phylogeny of behaviour'. Data from such detailed observations would establish how the behaviour of a species correlated with its physiological structure. If birds did not have the structure of wings, they could not exhibit the behaviour of flying. That is banal. But science knew very little about the connection between an animal's biological make-up and the actions and reactions it was capable of. 'Finally,' said Watson, he wanted 'to achieve the correlation of behaviour and structure with physico-chemical processes.' His use of *correlation* is critical. If the task of psychology was to *reduce* all facts about behaviour to facts about physico-chemical processes, then *correlation* is a curious word. The behaviourist clearly thought that all events in the body had a physical and/or chemical correlate. There was no immaterial soul stuff hovering about. But psychology was not a kind of interim physiology as many of the biologists and physiologists who were so committed to the simple reflex seemed to believe. Watson's concept of the stimulus, for example, was already far too psychological for him to be a simplistic reductionist.

Watson was well aware of the seductive dangers of reductionism. He wrote:

> That the organism is a machine is taken for granted in our work.
> The only point we insist upon is that the machine be made not
> too simple to perform the multitudinous demands which the
> behaviourist must make upon it. There has been a strong tendency
> on the part of many biologists to assume that the mechanisms are
> exceedingly simple.

That had been the cardinal sin of both Loeb and Jennings. 'As long as we have animals in the world it is hard to see how the demand for a study of their methods of living, moving and having their being can ever grow less.' Watson doubted that better physiological or neurological research would make the behaviourist superfluous. One day it might be possible 'to trace the complete set of physico-chemical

92

changes (from the moment of incidence of the stimulus to the end of movement in the muscle). In fact, it is one of the goals of behaviour to assist in making this possible. But again we insist that all of the facts about the response be considered.' Responses were very complex; few were just simple reflexes. Biologists must see that.

Much has been made of Watson's love of the reflex as the basic unit of behaviour. In *Behaviour*, he uses the term reflex in at least two senses. There is a narrow sense in which a reflex is a very small movement such as the flexing of a toe or finger. Such a reflex exists because of an arc, a neural connection, which makes a particular stimulus trigger a particular response. In this case, some stimulus 'causes' the toe to flex and the reflexes might be even more minute. One aim of behaviourism was to analyse both instinctive and learned behaviour into their constituent reflexes. But Watson emphasised that he was interested in 'synthesis as well as analysis' and it is here that the second, wider use of reflex is important. It was important to see how patterns of behaviour fitted together or were joined together by the organism. We do not just react at the level of muscular twitches or flexions of the toe. What it pleases us to call our *actions* were, for Watson, reflexes but complex reflexes that had been joined together. To cry when you left your loved ones was, for the behaviourist, just such a reflex. Behaviourism was, therefore, not just a matter of breaking down reactions into small parcels of physiological reflexes, as has often been suggested. Watson was clearly attracted to the reflex as the basis of behaviour, but he had the sense to warn that his beloved reflex 'is a convenient hypothesis' just as the electron was in the physics of his time.

Instincts were also scrutinised. Observation had shown that when animals were born, they performed far more useless random movements than useful or co-ordinated ones. 'Organised adaptive reflexes and instinctive acts' were few and far between. Quickly the baby animal managed to organise many of these hit and miss movements into 'acts which are usually but not necessarily serviceable to the animal'. Many of these random movements were never organised by the animal into acts that were of any use. Watson was, in fact, questioning that every movement of an animal had to have survival value. The existence of a movement did not mean that it had to have a point. Biologists seemed to him to be making a fetish of the usefulness of each and every movement.

Watson went on to give a long, rather grand list of instincts in various species. Eating, sleeping, playing, vocalising, fighting, migrating, homing were only a few of very many instincts. Watson said it was impossible to be logical at present in the classification of instincts. He suggested that there were two ways in which one might work on instincts. First, field observations were essential. 'Completely worked out, this method would give us the life-history or field activity of animals,' he said. When ethologists began to produce their ethograms it was not such a novel idea. The second method was to take animals into the laboratory and observe 'the order of appearance of instincts, measuring their degree of perfectness'. It would then be possible to see how these instincts improved or waned or were used. Watson would become extremely interested in the question of what instincts human beings were born with. When *Behaviour* was written there was no research on human instincts, so Watson went on to illustrate the kinds of research that had been done on various animal species. He included his own works on terns and monkeys amongst a variety of facts about turtles, fishes, cats, guinea pigs and others.

Since early Chicago Watson had been interested in learning. He now turned his attention for over a hundred pages to the question of how animals and people learned. Habits were learned and could be defined as 'a complex system of reflexes which function in serial order when the organism is confronted by certain stimuli'. Habits were learned at least from the moment the baby came out of its mother's womb. The task of the psychologist was to work out how animals and people formed habits, what habits they were able and unable to form and how these habits could be learned more efficiently. For Watson, learning to solve a problem such as running a maze was learning a habit.

In the section on learning, Watson reviewed much of the available animal research. He presented the learning curve that he had found to exist in rats which showed that, after a number of trials in which the animal improved slowly, there came a point where improvement was rapid till it levelled off. Work on people learning typewriting showed they first improved very quickly but that then improvement tailed off. They reached their typing limits and could get no better. The notion of comparing animal and human learning fascinated Watson and he persuaded Lashley to mount an experiment in this area. Watson also considered the use of incentives or rewards in learning. He doubted that punishment was very effective. Easy tasks might be learned in order to avoid punishment. But the more complex the task, the less likely that seemed.

Watson went on to write again of his work on how rats learned the maze and of his experiments in removing various of their senses. He offered an analysis of the reflexes involved in this experiment. In a simple habit, the stimulus first arouses a whole variety of random movements. These are pared away so that 'on later presentations fewer and fewer random movement. Finally the stimulus arouses the few necessary acts in serial order.' But such a model only applied to simple habits. The more complex the habit, the greater the chain of reflexes it needed so that what Watson called an 'analysis ideal' would be able to state the number, location and order of functioning of each reflex arc from the initial response (the rat being placed in the maze) to the point where the rat reached the food. To be able to establish each arc would also mean being able to pinpoint the 'stimulus which releases each arc'. In a complex habit, many of these stimuli would be muscular or kinaesthetic. A muscle might be the receptor of one reflex and the effector, or activator, of the next reflex in the chain.

It was still left to explain why and how animals learned to chain these reflexes together into useful habits. They were not born with a stock of ready-made behaviours that would last them a life-time. Though Watson had always given his rats food when they solved their problem boxes, he did not want to invoke reward as the cause of learning. 'Producing pleasure', he said, or avoiding pain 'cannot be invoked as the eliminating agent'. An animal did not eliminate its random movements that were useless in performing a habit because of reinforcement. Pleasure and pain fluctuated too much for them to be accorded this role. They also reminded Watson perhaps a little too much of those introspective feelings.

Watson was led to argue, therefore, that the reaction of animals to a particular stimulus is determined by what the last reaction to that stimulus was (technically recency) and also by how often the animal has produced that reaction in response to the stimulus (technically frequency). If the last time Elsie said, 'I love you', I smothered her with kisses; then next time Elsie says, 'I love you', I am likely to smother her with kisses again. Watson gave a less romantic illustration. Say a rat makes ten movements in solving a problem. We label these 1 to 10. The crucial movement is movement number 5. As the rat perfects his habit of solving the problem, when he produces movement 5 the behaviour comes to an end. Put the numbers 1 to 10 in a hat and draw them a number of times. Each is equally likely to be drawn. Each number has the same probability. But if we end each game when the number 5 is drawn, then the probability of number 5 being drawn increases, for the game always stops when it pops out. The other numbers don't have that privilege. So the successful movement 5, like the winning number, gets to appear more often because every time the rat produces it, it means both success and the end of the problem. Watson failed here really to examine the implications of this idea. In many of his own experiments he seemed to ignore it, for he did reward the animals and, in 1916, he even tested the effects of different timing of rewards on problem solving. The notion that learning was based on the frequency of past responses became, for all its inadequacies, surprisingly influential in psychology – even though it has obvious defects. As a theory it suggested learning was very arbitrary and it did not really explain why the movement number 5 should reappear so frequently.

Watson also included the results of Lashley's work on teaching people to shoot with bow and arrows. They did not learn this task too well but in so far as the humans did improve, they improved in a rat-like fashion.

Language and thinking also entered into the book since Watson was determined not to hand these topics to the introspectionists as being beyond behaviourism. He stressed that it was the human capacity to think and to speak that set us apart from other animals. Language was instinctive since children, long before they could speak, uttered a variety of sounds that foreshadowed speech. Watson explained a number of experiments in which an attempt had been made to monitor the movements of the tongue. In one, subjects were told to say and to listen to the phrase, 'Mary had a little lamb'; then they were asked to think of the same phrase. Could the recording instruments pick up similar movements when they spoke, listened and just thought? The evidence was not too convincing but Watson suggested that the apparatus with which the study was done was far too crude. Moreover, the tongue rather than the larynx had been monitored. The behaviourist meant to give his theory a proper sophisticated test. In the next chapters we shall see the fate of these studies. Watson also made the point that it was a mistake to think all thought was verbal. Our bodies and our muscles absorbed and retained thoughts. Again, it was in the muscles, in our motor habits rather than in our brains, that the throne of language lay. Watson had a complex about the cortex, it seems.

Behaviour did not get a uniformly favourable press and *Science*, to Watson's chagrin, did not review it at all. A review in the *Journal of Philosophy* praised the wealth of data presented and said that it would 'doubtless become the accepted text for animal psychology'. But the review condemned the extreme of discarding consciousness. Behaviourism denied, it said, human ability to be aware of our own responses, to be self-conscious and, for all the faults of introspection, it did not do that. To throw out all introspective evidence would be folly though the review piously hoped introspection would become more scientific. How it would achieve this was left unsaid.

In October Watson complained to Yerkes: 'I think you are a pill not to review my book. You must remember that I spent quite a few minutes reviewing yours. You are the one man in the country capable of saying all the mean things about it that ought to be said and for you not to do it disappoints me exceedingly.' Watson remained light about it. He went on to ask 'where in hell did Titchener roast me?' Titchener had finally gone into print with his views on behaviourism. Yerkes did not review the book because he could not have given it a really favourable review. He did not wish to offend his friend. As Yerkes was made tetchy by Watson's criticisms, he presumed the behaviourist would also be riled by a fairly hostile review. Yerkes does not seem to have understood that Watson was at this period so driven, so excited and so absorbed in his ideas that he actually thrived on criticism. He did not get angry because Titchener roasted him. To be so open and so objective was, in some ways, a blissful state: it would not remain with Watson forever.

The year 1914 saw its share of professional honours for Watson. His ideas were winning many converts, especially among the younger psychologists. In July 1914 Watson was elected President of the Southern Society for Philosophy and Psychology. Later in the year the behaviourist received the accolade of being elected President of the American Psychological Association. Angell, who believed Watson to be crazy, cannot have been too pleased. It was only ten years since Watson had been so wounded by being told that, good as his doctorate was, he would never equal the achievements of Helen Thompson. Watson must have allowed himself a moment of self-satisfaction. Though behaviouristic ideas were not suddenly accepted everywhere, the process of changing the way psychology was done was well under way.

It was not all success, though. Watson still had dark moments. He moaned to Yerkes in February that psychologists would never get either a decent salary or their scientific due. Yerkes moaned back in concert.

Throughout 1914, Watson had spent much time with the scholarly Karl Lashley. Lashley had far more influence on the development of Watson's thinking than Dunlap ever did. The two men spent much time talking together and in their daily conversations they refined their ideas on a number of points. By 1914 Watson's relationship with Dunlap was quite cool again. Dunlap was trying to set up his own laboratory and Watson was encouraging him in that. Dunlap was beginning to resent his head of department who showed no signs of moving on and leaving the way clear for Dunlap to inherit the chair. But with the much younger Lashley Watson enjoyed real friendship and real pleasure in working together.

In 1914 they spent much time discussing two problems that were crucial to the development of behaviourism – thinking and the conditional emotional reflex. In his autobiographical note Watson wrote that Lashley had been the first person to coin the terms 'conditioned emotional reflex'. The concept was to play a large role in the development of Watson's ideas. In order to understand it, one has to unravel Watson's relationship with the psychology of Pavlov and Bechterev.

It is impossible to know when Watson first read Pavlov. Pavlov had won the Nobel Prize in 1904 for his work on the physiology of the digestive tract. Watson must have heard of Pavlov during his time at Chicago. In 1909, Yerkes and Sergivs Morgulis published a paper on 'The Method of Pawlow [sic] in Animal Psychology'. It appeared in an issue of the Psychological Bulletin edited by Watson. In 1913, Bechterev published his *Objective Psychology* in German in Leipzig. Watson, who had learned German, ironically, to read Wundt read it eagerly. It ought to be stressed that, for his part, Bechterev acknowledged his own debt in places to Watson. To suggest, as has been done, that Watson simply plagiarised the work of these two great Russian scientists is far too simple.

Reading Pavlov and Bechterev made Watson interested in the possibility of conditioning reflexes. Watson distinguished between conditioned secretion (Pavlov's salivating dogs) and conditioned motor reflexes. Though the idea of conditioning the flow of saliva appeared interesting to Watson, he felt that its usefulness as a technique was limited. So he concentrated on seeing what relationships could be found to exist, and made to exist, between particular stimuli and particular motor actions. With Lashley, he set about exploring this area.

First, Watson and Lashley made subjects listen to a bell. In itself, this produced no reflex. Then they placed a small electrode on the foot of a subject and, through that electrode, the experimenter could give them a small electric shock. They then made the subject hear the bell and suffer a shock simultaneously. With the shock, that subject's toe flexed. Then, they gave the subject the bell again and watched to see whether the toe flexed again. It was on this basic model that Watson and Lashley spent much of 1915.

They tested eleven human subjects. They found that the reflex was not conditioned too reliably. It made 'its appearance at first haltingly'. It came and went until with a few more shocks it was established in most subjects. Some subjects always proved impossible to condition even when the experimenters turned up the shock a little! Watson acknowledged they did not understand why this happened. But having seen that most subjects did condition, Watson went on to test how that conditioned reflex could be played upon. One subject was trained in May and not retested until October. The reflex reappeared after he had been given one reminding shock. (Remember the subjects could not avoid the shock by remembering the reflex as would be the case in most Skinnerian experiments now.) Other subjects did not remember the reflex well and had to be retrained. Fatigue affected the reflex. It seemed that when the reflex was vanishing, it could be revigorated by throwing in with the bell some quite new form of stimulation, and not the electric shock.

Watson and Lashley also tried to see what happened if one tried to condition the pupillary reflex to strong light. After twenty minutes training two subjects developed a small constriction of the pupil when they heard the sound that had been paired with the strong light. But Watson had to abandon this project as subjects complained their eyes hurt too much. They also tried to establish a heart-beat reflex and to see if there was a 'psycho-galvanic reflex'. They reasoned that if a subject received a bell together with an electric shock, there had to be some 'emotional change sufficient to show'. But try as they might, they could not measure any noticeable psycho-galvanic change. The use of the word *reflex* here was odd as may be seen from this sentence: 'the bell would come finally to produce bodily changes sufficient to show on the galvanometer and we would thus have our conditioned reflex.' On such a reading, any response would be a reflex. As well as these niceties of definitions, the enterprise failed because though it made theoretical sense, Watson noted: 'The only fault to be found with such a train of reasoning is that it does not work out when put to practical test.' To produce effects on that galvanometer required violent stimulations like bursting a bulb or burning the subject with a cigarette end. But Watson was sure emotions as well as saliva flows and toe movements could be conditioned.

Despite these difficulties, Watson believed in the value of the reflex method. When subjects received a shock on the foot, they showed the toe reflex and when their fingers were shocked the finger reflex appeared. It could be used to investigate a variety of topics in sensory psychology investigating and perception. Psychologists could test reactions to light, to shape, to pitch, even to smell without polluting themselves with introspection. Watson's enthusiasm here seems to have outrun his methodological good sense. He seems to have thought that once you established a reflex to, say, a green light of intensity, you could then alter the intensity of the light and measure the point up to which the reflex persisted. This did offer an objective measure but there are far easier objective ways of testing human perceptual abilities. Only Watson wanted to get his humans to be as like experimental animals as possible in order to symbolise the break with introspection. Watson's confidence was growing.

In November 1915 Mary Ickes Watson fell gravely ill. She had been in poor physical shape all the year. Suddenly, she collapsed. She had appendicitis and, on top of that, she needed to have an operation on her womb, a 'womb suspension'. Watson was very tender towards her during this illness. He took the children to the laboratory at Johns Hopkins a lot. Mary was in a great deal of pain and, through November, Watson wrote often to Yerkes to describe the way Mary was recovering. By 22 November she was 'making a more rapid recovery than any white rat I ever had to deal with.' By 10 December Watson was quite agog with admiration. 'My wife is actually going out and dancing a little.' She was a strong woman but the operation took its toll. She became more anxious and introverted than she had been before and, critically, her interest in sex began to diminish. For all his tenderness, too, Watson began to see his wife as a woman who was growing middle-aged. The professor still saw himself as a young man and a man who was coming into his prime. It would make for difficulties between them.

Despite Mary's illness, Watson had to go to Chicago in December 1915. He was president of the American Psychological Association and had to chair its annual meeting. He was far too ambitious to miss it. It must have been delightful to Watson to return to Chicago as president of the association. This year he would have not the slightest qualm about saying what he meant. No one held him in thrall now. He began by telling delegates that he made some 'impolite' remarks on the state of psychology in 1913. He would now offer a positive programme rather than just destructive criticism. Watson titled his address 'The Conditioned Reflex – Its Place in Psychology'. He gave an account of the work of Pavlov on secretion reflexes and Bechterev on motor reflexes. He suggested that the ideas and techniques of the Russians could have wide application in psychology. We have already seen that Watson used *reflex* widely so that he applied it both to a muscular twitch and to a well organised action like drawing a revolver, a favourite example of his. In his witty address, Watson had nothing to say about any disparity between these two levels of reflex. He insisted rather on the usefulness of the concept and of the technique. He confessed to a 'bias in its favour' but admitted that 'Time may show I have been over-enthusiastic about it.' He also repeated his message that object work on animals had established a wealth of facts, a sound scientific base, between 1900 and 1916. Let human psychologists learn the lesson. If they became objective, the facts would also fall into their laps. Watson was becoming more adept at such polemics. His address was always confident and often charming. He announced that he intended to study reflexes in more detail and that he would concentrate on their role in emotions. Watson was well received. Many young psychologists were impressed. As usual Watson enjoyed seeing old friends at the Congress. He drank and smoked a good deal into the early hours. Watson had every reason to be happy. Behaviourism was embattled but on the offensive. It had a positive programme for looking at human behaviour. It was no longer just a critical programme that quibbled at the old ways of doing psychology. Watson and his friends were suggesting new, practical ways of tackling some of the key problems in human psychology.

While Watson had been enjoying all this public success, life had not stood still at Johns Hopkins. Watson had kept on asking the new President, Goodnow, to put into effect Ramsden's promise to make psychology a separate department. Goodnow kept on insisting that Watson had never really been given that promise formally. Watson did not endear himself to the new President by spending $500 more than his allocation was in 1914. For that, Watson took all the blame upon himself. He explained that one reason for the high cost of running the department was the high price of rats. Rats were a luxury. Watson suggested to the university and the medical school that they joined forces and begin breeding rats commercially. The proposal made sense. But it took an enormous number of meetings, committees and bureaucratic negotiations. In the middle of the proceedings, Watson did manage to get Hopkins to pay for him to travel to Chicago to study a breeding station that the University of Illinois had just set up. After much research, it was discovered that the medical school spent $2,500 a year on experimental animals. Pressure for the animal farm continued after Watson proved that the university itself spent $3,500 on experimental animals and that the cost would increase tenfold over the next eight years. Watson was alarmed by a dearth of small mammals and, in May 1915, lamented to Goodnow: 'guinea pigs are almost impossible to obtain'.

The behaviourist also had much more radical plans afoot. Sometime in 1915 it began to be clear to him that he really needed to devote his energy to the study of children and, especially, of children's emotional development. Though Watson did not care personally for Meyer, the new head of the Phipps Clinic, the two men saw the need for psychology and psychiatry to work together. It was agreed that Watson should set up a laboratory at the Phipps Clinic and start research on the development of children.

In the early part of 1916 Watson designed and built his new laboratory. Being so close to psychiatric patients had its disadvantages. In February, as Watson walked out of the Phipps, he had an encounter with 'a paranoiac with manic symptoms'. This man kept on talking and talking to Watson who had no idea of how to get rid of him. The

101

encounter bothered Watson mightily. But he did not shrug it off as something to avoid. He decided he would go to a psychiatric convention later in the year to understand a little of the work that was going on in the field of mental illness. At that convention Watson turned out to be the only psychologist. Meyer encouraged this interest in mental illness.

Watson surprised himself by deciding to move to the Phipps and concentrate on the children. It was an impulsive move. When he told Yerkes of it in February 1916 it came as quite a bombshell. Watson reflected that it was an unlikely decision to have made but 'we can never tell about ourselves from moment to moment; I get rather disgusted with trying to make the human character amenable to laws.' A self-respecting behaviourist would have been much more predictable in his actions. It amused Watson that he knew he had never quite managed to make his own character 'amenable to laws'. It was not just that he was too much of a rebel for that. He was, and he liked to see himself as, prey to sudden shifts in his life. Going to Furman and his rapid marriage were instances of that. The decision to work at the Phipps was sudden but the plan to study children was not really quite so sudden for it made excellent scientific sense given the ideal that behaviourism should be a psychology of real life.

As usual Watson plunged into the project with children enthusiastically. He was soon spending twelve hours a day working on it and the rest of the evening puzzling over his results. He was tired. Mary still needed considerable tender nursing. But it did not matter much for Watson felt exhilarated by what he was doing.

The plan Watson had was strikingly simple. He would take forty children and observe them on a daily basis from birth onwards. He would record their movements, their reactions to certain stimuli and chart their maturation. No one had done that before. It would make it possible to see what the normal development of a child was. In addition, Watson intended to test his ideas on the conditioned emotional reflex and on instincts. He would first see what seemed to be the instinctive behaviour of the human baby and then, taking these instincts to be made up of 'congenital reflexes', he would see how he could condition them. Assume that he found that a touch on the toe made the infant coo. Was it possible to condition that child so that other things made him coo too, just as Pavlov had managed to condition his dogs to salivate at green lights and bells? Watson did not really write up this work till 1919, and we shall look at it in some detail in the next chapter.

Changing the focus of his work made Watson cling more than a little to Yerkes as a familiar friend. Yerkes still believed in the value of introspection. At the end of March 1916, Watson wrote to his friend: 'Friendship to me is a far more precious thing than agreement about psychological positions. I have felt this keenly about Titchener and I have felt it even more so with response to you. My feeling for you has nothing to do with the question of whether you think a certain amount of introspection is justifiable.' If one only had friends one agreed with, Watson laughed, he would find himself 'in the land of the friendless'. Yerkes continued to mean a great deal to Watson. He also admitted to Yerkes that money problems, due partly to Mary's illness, meant that he had to take on consulting work outside the university. Watson was much better able than Yerkes to tolerate the fact that they disagreed.

While Watson was beginning his research on children, he was also writing two short but interesting papers which, again, expanded the range of his interest. 'Behaviour and the Concept of Mental Disease' queried the way psychiatrists used the word 'mental'. He confessed his own ignorance of psychiatry but he pointed out that he had over the years read and studied Freud in some detail. Watson argued that what Freud said was true but not in the way that Freud put it. Having swept consciousness out of psychology, the behaviourist was hardly going to dabble in the murks of the unconscious. It was at the biological level that Freud was right. Watson put it like this:

> The central truth that I think Freud has given us is that youthful, outgrown and partially discarded habit and instinctive systems of reaction can and possibly always do influence the functioning of our adult systems of reactions and influence to a certain extent even the possibility of our forming the new habit systems which we must reasonably be expected to form.

For the Oedipus complex, read the Oedipal habit.

The habits that were outgrown and yet clung to need never be ones the subject or patient is conscious of. Watson added: 'and here all I mean by being "conscious" – and all I believe psychopathologists mean by it – is that the patient can not phrase in terms of words the habit twists which have become part of his biological habit equipment.' Neuroses became twisted habits, 'habit disturbances', maladjustments of behaviour. Instead of attributing a mental disease to the patient, Watson said one should try and describe his condition 'in terms of the inadequacy of responses, of wrong responses and of the complete lack of responses to the objects and situations in the daily life of the patient. I should likewise attempt to trace out the original conditions leading to the maladjustment and the causes leading to its continuation.' Watson argued that many of the so-called symptoms of so-called mental diseases were conditioned reflexes in which the conditioning was essentially inappropriate. Lashley had devised apparatus which had shown that it was possible to condition the parotid gland which controlled salivation. If that gland was easy to condition, it was plausible to argue that other glands also were and could be misled, by chance, by some traumatic event, by mis-training, into the most woeful and maladjusted of conditioned reflexes.

Imaginative as he was at this time, Watson asked his readers to pretend they were dog psychiatrists. The canine therapist is confronted by a most bizarre dog. Given red meat, the patient falls into a stupor; brought close to a female dog, the patient starts to cry; spoken to gently, our sick dog puts his tail sorrowfully between his legs shouted at, the 'mad dog' perks up and wags its tail. Finally when the besotted animal falls asleep, it sleeps with its paws sticking up in the air pointing to the moon. Now, the kind Watson would explain to the canine therapist that there is no need to introduce any concept of mental disturbance. 'I tell him that I have *trained the dog* during the past five years to do these things. The trouble with the dog is that its habits are twisted.' With a dog of poor hereditary stock, such bizarre habits would quickly turn it into a truly pitiful object. Once he had worked out the weird origins of disturbance, Watson would begin to retrain the dog, giving him this time more appropriately doggy habits.

Few psychiatrists, not even Adolf Meyer, would agree with Watson, but he claimed that one could understand psychiatric illnesses in people along the same lines. Watson was impressed by particular psychoanalytic tools like word association tests and, even, by the interpretation of dreams. These techniques would allow one to trace the origins and precise nature of the maladjustment or twisted habits. Watson denied that there was any reason for behaviourists not to talk to their patients. Conversion was as much behaviour as playing tennis. But he did stress that one should also take into account the patient's movements and gestures which were as likely to be disturbed as his speech was.

In a very sketchy way, Watson put forward a hypothetical case. The speech defects of a young man point to the ' "incest complex" '. The analysis offered was simple in theory:

> The faulty and unwise behaviour of a mother has led the boy to react to her in many particulars as does her husband. Such a group of integrations on the boy's part seriously disturbs the forming of suitably boyish habits and may bring in its train a vast series of conditioned reflexes which may show themselves in general bodily disturbances.

Tics, paralysis, all kinds of ills that go with and are part of mental illness could result from the mother's faulty behavour.

The importance of this paper was considerable for Watson both personally and also historically. It marked his first step into psychiatric theory. He was to extend his interest in that in the next few years. It was already a confident contribution. And with some justice for here, in 1916, Watson had in effect laid the foundations of what we now call behaviour therapy.

In his letters to Yerkes Watson wrote of the progress of his work on children. By August 1916 the lab at the Phipps was fully equipped and Watson had organised a flock of forty babies who could be observed and tested daily. The work was not as simple as he anticipated. In October he wrote to Yerkes that it was turning out more difficult than he had anticipated. In October, too, Watson made what was to prove a final attempt to explain to Yerkes the need for behaviourism to disavow introspection totally. Watson told his friend that while Yerkes had been trained in biology, Watson had been a psychologist from his first graduate days. Because Yerkes had never had to do any human psychology and had never witnessed the interminable hair-splitting as to sensations and perceptions, introspection could seem more useful to him. But, for Watson, introspection had become more and more of an albatross round the neck of psychology. As a psychologist and nothing but a psychologist, the time came when, as Watson wrote, 'finally my stomach would stand no more and I took the plunge I did in 1912'. Yerkes agreed that Watson had probably analysed accurately the reasons for their differences on introspection. But the differences remained.

For the rest of 1916 Watson worked very hard at the Phipps. His wife, Mary, helped occasionally but she was getting more interested in society than in experiments. In November Watson began to tackle the subject of handedness in babies, eliciting their grasping reflex. He also made some observations on how babies closed their eyes when confronted by strange new objects.

Though war was raging in Europe, America did not enter the war on the side of the allies until 1917. So for most of 1917 Watson's plans seemed academic. He wrote a review of a paper on wish fulfilment which, again, indicated much agreement with Freud's basic ideas. Watson was in no doubt that we had many sexual wishes that we dared not express. The review showed that Watson was familiar with the recent disputes between Freud and Jung and also that he had read Jung's latest book, *The Psychology of the Unconscious*. At Johns Hopkins Watson continued to skirmish with Goodnow. He asked for more money for his secretary, Miss Shoemaker, and talked her into staying on as a technical assistant. After much badgering, her salary was raised to $900 a year. Watson also requested the university to pay Dunlap's expenses to go to the Southern Society for Philosophy and Psychology. He told Goodnow that it would probably 'mean more to us in dollars and cents' than it cost, for Dunlap would probably recruit some students.

At the end of March 1917 the war does begin to obtrude into Watson's life. He wrote to Goodnow suggesting some ideas for the psychological testing of men in the armed forces and asked Goodnow to relay these ideas to Washington. Three days later Goodnow did just that at a meeting of the National Council for Research. It took some time for the Council to decide to make use of the behaviourist.

In the meantime Watson continued with the observations on children. There were a few breaks in this daily routine. In January he had taken his wife to the annual meeting of the American Psychological Association and complained that he had not been allowed to talk seriously with anyone. In February he turned his attention to an important problem, the effect of delayed feeding or reward upon learning. Watson compared six rats who were fed as soon as they solved the problem of pressing a rod to open a box with six rats who did not get any food until 30 seconds after they had solved the problem. Watson found that it was very difficult for him to wait the requisite 30 seconds for the unrewarded rats were very restless, would tear at the box and then leave it. Watson recommended that automatic equipment should replace the hand that fed the rats. But, the actual results showed no significant differences between the rats who were fed immediately upon receiving a reward and those who were rewarded later. Watson wrote 'those who hold that getting hold of the food following usually immediately upon completion of the last successful act stamps in that movement' received no support. Watson then transferred the rats who had been fed with delay to learning a task where they got food the moment they solved the problem and he transferred the rats who had been fed at once to learning a task where they got their food only 30 seconds after they solved their new problem. These manoeuvres had little effect. Watson also noted that after the animals got the problem they seemed to make more, not less, useless random movements. He was much puzzled by this question of why the animals' reflexes did not become more efficient and cut out all these unnecessary movements.

Historically, the paper is of interest since it is one of the first attempts to vary the timing of rewards. Latterday behaviourism has been largely constructed on two kinds of work, that of shaping animals' behaviour so that the psychologist 'trains' a pigeon to play ping-pong and, second, the study of different schedules of reinforcement. Without that phrase, here was Watson doing an early experiment and finding that these two different scheduled ways of timing food led to not very different effects. Watson felt, rather prematurely, that this one experiment settled the issue of whether delayed feeding was different from immediate feeding. By now, he was more interested in people and in real life than in animals and this paper was, almost certainly, the last animal research that Watson did. The behaviour man had truly become a human psychologist.

This paper also, ironically, provoked a row with Yerkes. Yerkes did not like some parts of it (though, unfortunately, Yerkes's letter to Watson is not extant now) and Watson, with pique, withdrew the paper from the *Journal of Animal Behaviour*. He gave it instead to *Psychobiology*, a new journal that he and Dunlap founded. In May 1917 Yerkes and Watson made up their quarrel, but only superficially. They drifted apart and they did not write to each other again for over a year. The time of their intense friendship was over. By now, Watson felt confident enough of himself not to be too affected by that. Watson turned dandy. He often wore a formal morning coat to Johns Hopkins.

When America went to war Watson tried to enlist as a line officer. The patriotic psychologist did not have good enough eyesight, however, and had to resign himself, it seemed, to seeing the war out on the campus. In June 1917, however, the authorities had more ambitious plans for Watson. The Committee on Personnel for the military included among its members Thorndike, who had become a veritable doyen among psychologists. He felt that Watson ought to be recruited for the country needed its best and most practical brains. In time of war, objective psychology would surely come into its own. Introspections about the sensations one had under fire were not the kind of thing to interest the Pentagon. Watson was eager to serve his country. In July Thorndike wrote to Goodnow to ask the university to release Watson and, a few days later, it was agreed that Watson could join the military. Johns Hopkins would pay him half his normal salary and, of course, his chair would be there waiting for him when peace came. In August 1917 Major Watson was commissioned.

Major Watson was, at thirty-eight, one of the most successful psychologists in America. He had finally come into his own. Confident of himself, confident of his ideas, everyone expected him to make a notable contribution. At first things went well. Watson worked day and night organising the boards that would test would-be pilots. In those early days of flight, there was no clear idea of what made a good pilot. Watson was enthusiastic and, left on his own to organise these selection procedures, he was efficient as ever. By 20 September Thorndike could write to Goodnow that the work of Major Watson 'seems to me to be growing in importance every day'.

To weed out those unfit to fly, Watson devised a number of perceptual and motor tests. He wrote to Dunlap and asked that Dunlap come and join him. Dunlap hesitated a while but he found it would have been impossible for him to refuse; so Dunlap enlisted too and was commissioned as a captain. The two psychologists were ordered to concentrate on the problem of how different men reacted to the oxygen deprivation that existed at high flying altitudes. (There were no pressurised cabins in those days, of course.) To test reactions, would-be pilots were slowly asphyxiated while under orders to perform a variety of perceptual and motor tasks. The ability to perform under such conditions, and how long it took for the pilots to lose control and consciousness, made it possible to predict how well they could cope with the hazards of aviation. It was an interesting project.

But the real problem Watson had with the war was that it brought him into contact with the military. The behaviourist soon developed a very poor opinion of soldiers, especially those in command. A Colonel Bingham was put in charge of all aviation scientific effort. Of his Colonel, Watson wrote 'his egoism and self seeking soon made everyone in the personnel section of aviation understand why it is that some officers fail to return from expeditions even when not engaged by enemy troops.' Bingham and Watson quarrelled: Watson was no longer used to being in a subordinate position and he cannot have taken kindly to receiving orders from Bingham. Watson was sent to Texas to work on the military use of homing pigeons. But before the birds could be made part of the war machine, radio became widely available. The homing pigeon's military career came to end. In the Second World War B. F. Skinner had a similar experience. He devised a scheme so that properly conditioned pigeons could guide missiles to their targets. Just as Skinner sold his scheme to the Pentagon – many generals objected apparently because it was cruel to animals! – the atom bomb was perfected. Again, birds lost their chance to shine in conflicts.

Watson was ordered back to Washington and given what seems to be a rather menial task. Thorndike had devised questionnaires which he wanted British pilots to fill in. Watson was perhaps over-qualified for the task of trundling these questionnaires from airbase to airbase but the prospect of going to Europe excited him. He felt he would see real fighting too. He returned to Baltimore for a few days. He had been having an affair in Washington but it was, as usual, a dalliance and nothing that threatened his marriage. Watson had a few good days with Mary. He took a somewhat dramatic leave of his children for he kissed them both. Watson did not believe in showing his children too much physical affection for that might condition them to love you too much. His daughter, Polly, remembers being quite surprised when he kissed her: he had not done that for a long time. But in late 1918 Watson was off to war. The slaughter in Europe was such that he might never return. In such circumstances it was permitted to kiss one's children.

The sea voyage pleased Watson. He was excited to land in France. He was finally seeing Europe. He reported to a General Foullois at Tours. From Tours Watson went to Paris on his way to the Marne front. It was summer and the French countryside was very beautiful. When Watson reached the Marne front he found his orders had been cancelled. The British were too busy fighting to fill in questionnaires. Watson was packed off to Nancy where he actually came under fire. He was not fit enough to go into battle so he hung around, at the edges of action, for about three months. The lack of any real work irritated him so he eventually asked for orders to go home. The British did not seem any more willing than before to fill in Thorndike's questionnaires. It was all rather unsatisfactory.

When Watson finally received orders to return, he decided to go back through Paris and London. He enjoyed the sights of Paris and felt rather proud of the fact that he had witnessed a few air raids. He then crossed the Channel and spent a few days in London. The city impressed him and, to cap the experience, he saw another air raid. In mid-Atlantic Watson also saw some action for he watched a torpedo cross the stern of the *Rochambeau*, the ship he was sailing home on. Watson's account of the war is amusing, for it is obvious that he got a great thrill out of being close, but not too close, to action. He was no coward but he did rather dramatise how near he had been to real conflict. Apparently, a hooter sounded in Nancy some 30 minutes before shelling started.

On his return, Watson was set to do more work on oxygen deprivation. The experiments did not satisfy him much. It was some consolation that as he was in Washington he could continue to have a number of affairs of the heart. But he took little delight in the scientific work he was doing.

Then in the spring of 1918 Watson got into grave trouble over rotation tests. These tests claimed to show how good a person's sense of balance was, a critical quality for a good pilot whose plane might have to turn over, dive, pirouette and go through all manner of acrobatics in order either to kill or avoid being killed. Some doctors promoted the rotation test which used the degree of nystagmus, the oscillation of the eyeballs, to assess the sense of balance. Doubts were growing as to the validity of the tests. A number of men who had been rejected as pilots by the US Air Force had become successful pilots for other air forces. Then professional trapeze artists and whirling dancers whose balance had to be exquisite were shown by the tests to have a dreadful sense of balance. If that was really so, all these acrobats would be dead or maimed. The military authorities suppressed these results. Watson was asked to review the evidence on the rotation tests. He treated this as a scientific, not a diplomatic, task. He concluded the tests were a useless fraud. Worse, he allowed his opinion to become known within the military without having gone through the appropriate channels. He was threatened with court martial. The physiologist, George Wells, who had shown that trapeze artists would fail the balance test, had been sent to the front for his pains. Colonel Crabtree, head of the Aviation Medical Corps, was furious with Watson and meant to devise a proper punishment for his impertinence and injudiciousness: likely death. Watson, who had failed the medical test for a line officer, was sent out of the Aviation Corps with the comment that 'he be not allowed to serve his country in his scientific capacity but be sent to the line'.

Crabtree was especially furious because a scandal was brewing over the rotation tests. Not only did they not stand up scientifically but many men with the right social connections had been accepted as pilots even though they had failed the test. That might have been common knowledge among the military but to naive 'university men' like Watson and Dunlap it was shocking. They were not used to such corruption. When Watson put in writing his fierce attack on the rotation test, he was fuelling a very sensitive situation. He was transferred to the General Staff in order to learn the business of overseas military intelligence. The man whose eyesight was too poor to fight was now going to be put behind enemy lines. It was perhaps not all that melodramatic of Watson to claim that he had been ordered to do this work because his superiors could then guarantee to send him on missions so dangerous that he was likely to die.

One possible way of avoiding this fate was to be sent to Russia. There were plans for a high-level mission to Russia. Watson wrote to Goodnow imploring him to use all his influence to have Watson go on the trip to Moscow. He very much wanted to meet Pavlov and Bechterev and he felt sure that something of the highest scientific value would come out of their meeting. Goodnow sympathised but Watson had made far too many enemies. There was no chance of the behaviourist going to Russia. His fate was to be less comfortable. Watson was bitterly disappointed.

Colonel Crabtree was deprived of the pleasure of seeing Watson killed in action. With scant regard to this issue, the Armistice was signed just as Watson was waiting for orders to go abroad. He was understandably very happy to see the end of the war.

In his autobiographical note, Watson summed up his war pithily:

> The whole army experience is a nightmare to me. Never have I seen
> such incompetence, such extravagance, such a group of over-
> bearing, inferior men. Talk of putting a Negro in Uniform! It is
> nothing to making a Major or Lieutenant Colonel of most of the
> Rotary Club men who went in as officers in the American Army
> (West Point and Naval Academy men excepted). The French and
> British officers were such a superior set of gentlemen that the
> contrast was pitiful; I can liken it only to a fanciful situation of a
> group of Yankee drummers dining at the Court of St. James.

Watson always liked Mark Twain who had written more flattering, of
course, of a Connecticut Yankee at King Arthur's court. It is telling,
though, how even here Watson's belief in academic standard shines
through. The West Point and Naval Academy men are different for in
some way they have a qualification in war. They were almost
'university men'. He was very much a professor.

Watson was probably, it must be said, not the easiest of men to have
under one's command. He was by 1917 very confident of himself and
of his opinions. He was one of the five or six leading psychologists in
the USA. The few people he deferred to were those whom he thought
were his academic equals or betters. His experience of military
commanders from Colonel Bingham on were that they were men of the
feeblest intellect. So it is perhaps not surprising that there should have
been one clash after another. The conflict was, of course, made worse
by the fact that Watson had a dogged commitment to scientific truth
and was genuinely outraged by the rotation tests scandal.

Sexually, however, Watson seems to have had a wonderful time. He
was beginning to tire of his wife. Her own interest in sex diminished
greatly after her operation. Watson was too passionate to be content
with that. He later wrote a great deal on how vital it was for both
partners to be aware of the arts of love. The *macho* man taking his
pleasure at a woman's expense was not the way he saw himself. Away
from home, handsome Major Watson flirted and had affairs. As he
turned forty he was very attractive, witty and clever. Women fell for
him easily enough. If he ever felt the need to justify his actions, he
could always recall *Folkways* with its comforting liberal message. The
sins of one tribe were the glowing moral actions of another in some
other place. A psychologist had to have the best informed morals. And
educated morals made nearly everything a matter of the social
conventions of the time and place.

Between 1913 and 1918 Watson had expanded behaviourism considerably. He had tackled a whole variety of problems in both human and, to a lesser extent, animal psychology. Some of his theories – notably his account of thinking and his attack on the cortex – were very strange unless placed in the perspective of man reacting totally against introspection as he knew it. But Watson's psychology was far from narrow and he was moving toward his aim of a scientific psychology connected with real life. He looked forward to getting back to observing the children again. Watson was delighted about getting back to research. He was much less delighted to be going back to his wife. But his work was in fine fettle and, in the end, that mattered more than anything else.

5

The Complete Behaviourist Programme 1918–20

The only advantage Watson had had from the war was his trip to Europe. Otherwise the military experience did him nothing but harm. It interrupted his work. The commanding officers he met were such marvels of imbecility that, for the first time in his life, Watson became truly arrogant. Much of his life he had had to ward off his own sense of inferiority. He worked so hard partly to prove how good he was. But after 1918 a certain arrogance showed.

The war did not just affect the personality of the behaviourist; it also affected the status of psychology. In the wake of the war, the world looked to science for answers to many problems. A scientific psychology held out the hope of solving all manner of difficulties. Newspapers and magazines were more interested in serious psychology. Freud and Watson both benefited from the fact that their revolutionary theories came at a time of much general interest in the possibilities of psychology. From 1918 Watson was much in demand as a consultant. His ideas on business, on education, on efficiency were called for. He was expert in human behaviour in a world that began to clamour for instant expertise. As we shall see, this trend became much more apparent after 1920.

Johns Hopkins welcomed back its war-weary professor of psychology. Watson wrote to Goodnow on 20 November that he would be coming back 'unless I have been fired in my absence'. Early in December Watson was back in the laboratory. The war had taken its toll. There were few students. The department had, in fact, gone into mothballs with both Dunlap and Watson away. Miss Shoemaker, his secretary, had finally left. But Watson was soon 'getting things done', as was his knack. He got a new stenographer and filed an appropriation for the year that was just starting. The haggling over salary also resumed. The war had led to considerable inflation. Major Watson had been in some financial difficulties and Mary had had to take a job. The work that she did – in an insurance company – earned her a very necessary $1,200 a year but it was the kind of low-level work which Watson thought little of. His wife should have been up to a better position. Despite the fact that he was now established as one of America's leading psychologists, Watson only asked for a modest raise to $4,500. To add weight to his case, in March 1919 the behaviourist sent Goodnow one of those little missives in which he recalled to the university the merits of their professor of psychology. 'I do not wish to blow on my own horn,' trumpeted Watson, 'but I do wish to call your attention to the fact that some of the work we are doing on animals and babies is getting a certain amount of notoriety.' Goodnow was worried by anything notorious; respectable, reputable success was what he expected of professors. Watson, who liked to tease, knew just the effect that a word like *notoriety* would have on the rather humourless Goodnow. But Watson's research was attracting serious interest.

One topic on which Watson's views were notorious at the university was prohibition. Watson was a staunch advocate of the cocktail and bourbon. His return to the university was a happy one. He rejoiced in being among academics again. But he was much less happy to go back to his wife. The war and the affairs he had made him see that he cared much less for her. More arrogant now, he began to feel she was not quite worthy of him. He was in his prime but, he decided with a certain casual cruelty, she was no longer in *her* prime. She reproached Watson for his affairs. But the behaviourist always felt that he had the upper hand with Mary. She loved him too much to threaten him with divorce and he did, after all, always return after his infidelities. He was unfaithful and Mary was waiting. It made for a tense, brittle marriage. The womb operation which had made Mary less and less interested in sex did not help matters either. Rather callously, Watson seems to have dated the end of her prime to not long after she had her womb 'suspended'.

Research was more inspiring. As soon as he got back, Watson made the necessary arrangements to start work on the children again. Though he was also involved in a number of other projects, these studies of children were his first love. He knew their importance. In November, Watson began to write up systematically the observations on children which had been made before he had gone off to war.

Watson saw that the behaviour of a new-born baby was already quite complicated. So young, the organism could already sneeze, hiccup, yawn and cough. Some infants cried very quickly but others did not shed tears till the fifteenth day of their life. Watson also observed smiles and found one case of a four-day-old smiling. A few other babies smiled on the seventh or eighth day, usually when stroked gently or tickled very lightly. Watson was especially interested in testing how good the perception of infants was. Babies, he found, could turn their heads only 30 minutes after birth. A number of babies were then tested to see if they could fixate a light soon after their birth. The babies were put in a darkened room and a light was moved from 15 degrees to the right of the baby to 15 degrees to the left. When the light was moved in this orbit, the baby could co-ordinate its eye movements well enough to fixate it. It took the baby who was fourteen hours old 10 seconds to fixate that light at 10 degrees to the right and 12 seconds to fixate it at 15 degrees. The eye took time to co-ordinate its movements so that it would have been beyond the newly born child's ability to follow a moving light with its eyes. But Watson was impressed by the co-ordination he saw. An infant tested at seventeen hours of age even managed to fixate a light 20 degrees to its left. That took it 30 seconds. Not all the babies managed to co-ordinate effectively in their first 24 hours but most of a group of 20 babies did.

The other behaviours which Watson found to exist at birth are now well accepted. He found that babies had a grasping reflex present more or less at birth. The babies seemed to be able to sustain a weight that was very nearly equal to their own body weight. Watson also tried to test the handedness of babies by seeing which hand could grasp a weight longer in the first days of life. Also, a cunning device was attached to both hands of the child that gave a tracing of the amount of activity of each hand. If the right hand was more active that suggested the child would grow up right-handed and vice versa. Watson wanted to discover whether it was heredity or environment that made children right- or left-handed. For all the cunning of his devices, he admitted he had arrived at inconclusive evidence. But, again, he had spotted an important problem and suggested useful ways of tackling it. He continued to work on it through 1919.

Very young babies also appeared to have 'defence movements'. The method of testing these was 'very crude', for the experimenter first pinched the baby's nose and then watched for the reaction. At four days, one indignant baby's 'hand went up at once and pushed at the experimenter's fingers in three seconds'. Another baby of eight days of age struck at the experimenter's fingers in 3 seconds with the right hand and 4 seconds with the left hand. Pinching the babies' knees also made them kick out. Watson believed that these were impressive muscular co-ordinations for creatures that were so young. They could certainly form the basis for conditioning the most subtle motor habits in the child.

Watson's observations led to some interesting ideas. He argued that since sucking and swallowing seemed to be instinctive, it was important to study any child who had problems in swallowing. That might be a sign of retardation and one of Watson's reasons for studying the normal development of children was to make it possible to diagnose children who were less than normal. Other ideas were frankly weird. Some physiologists argued that, during evolution, human beings had gone through a stage in which we lived in the sea. The embryo had gills. If we were the descendants of fish, then maybe swimming was an instinct. A few-hours-old baby was gently lowered into a tank full of water at body temperature. Panic occurred. The baby slashed in a quite unco-ordinated way with its hands and feet. It was terribly frightened until it was gently lifted out of the water. If swimming was an instinct, it was one long lost.

Watson also tested the sensitivity of infants to loud noises. When there was a loud noise, the baby tended to react by catching its breath, making spasmodic movements of the arms and legs and closing its hands. The behaviourist interpreted these responses as signs of fear. Taking the support away from a child as if he was being dropped also produced the same responses. These were, for Watson, the roots of fear. He argued babies were innately terrified of loud noises and losing physical support. Incidentally, Watson took the greatest precautions in these experiments that not the least scratch should come to an infant. When a child was dropped, Watson dropped him into the arms of an assistant who was kneeling in a bed with a pillow on it for the baby to fall on if the clumsy assistant failed to catch. There were many objections to mapping out the growth of children – if anything should happen to a child, the outrage of the press would be deafening. In his study of fear Watson also often placed children in the dark in the laboratory. As he was still frightened of the dark himself, the issue of whether such fear was instinctive or acquired fascinated him. For if, as he suspected, children were conditioned to fear the dark, it ought to be possible to 'un-condition' the fear. And the behaviourist was more than a little embarrassed by his own anxiety when the lights went off. Watson could find no evidence for an instinctive fear of the dark. It was adults who trained children to be frightened.

Having observed that the new-born baby is capable of moving its head and the rest of its limbs vigorously, Watson observed that when the baby's movements were restrained, he or she screamed. Some of the physical reactions that accompanied this screaming appear very similar to those that Watson classed as fear: 'The body stiffens and fairly well co-ordinated slashing or striking movements of the hands and feet and arms result; the feet and legs are drawn up and down; the breath is held until the child's face is flushed.' Even at birth, a child could be so provoked by clasping its elbow joint tightly or by placing the head in a definite position between cotton pads as had often been done when testing the eye co-ordination of the babies. Often 'the slight constraint put upon the head by the soft pads' made the child so disturbed that the experiment had to be stopped. (While this was done, the lights were still on.) Watson came to believe firmly that the origin of rage lies in the infant's instinctive reactions to having its movements hampered.

The studies of both fear and rage had to be limited and could not be pushed as far as Watson would have liked. Too great a shock might make babies react as the young terns did; they might assume a 'death feint' and become paralysed. Love, the third emotion, put different constraints on Watson. As he had argued in 1914, very young children could be erotically aroused. The empirical facts fitted the Freudian hypothesis. But Watson was careful not to harp too much on these shocking facts. Under 150 days, he observed, children were not much interested in their sex organs; after that, they 'discovered' them and appeared to enjoy touching them. Young boys, Watson saw, had erections. The child discovered its own sexual 'apparatus' before it was six months old. As we have seen, however, Watson believed that erogenous zones extended far beyond the genitalia. The whole skin was a potential source of sensual delight. His observations not only provided some useful evidence of infantile sexuality but he went on to argue that his observations of parents with children showed just how it was that parents conditioned their children to love them. Mother would tickle, hug, stroke, pet and pat her darling baby. Father did much the same thing. Often Watson saw a child who had been crying bitterly change its mood completely when it was stroked or held. Older babies understood this pattern of behaviour perfectly well for they held out their arms in order to be held. This action, a small child holding out his arms, was, Watson noted, 'the forerunner of the embrace of adults'. The comparison was neat and suited Watson's thesis well. We learn our love habits, like our habits, by conditioning in childhood.

The implications of Watson's work were very startling and very relevant to much contemporary debate about the care of children. Watson claimed that his research showed that there was no immediate, instinctive bond between mother and child. A child has no infallible pull towards its natural parents. A child learns who its mother is, and learns to love its mother, because its mother gives it those soft sensations. Mother strokes, embraces, rocks and cuddles her baby. Her baby loves her. But, in fact, anyone who did this would be loved and the provider of sweet sensations did not have to be human. If a robot stroked and petted a child, it would come to love that robot. Love was conditioned. From a neurophysiological point of view, Watson argued that the pathways that were associated with tumescence and detumescence already existed marked out in the infant. They were ready for the child to be conditioned into loving being excited by the soft stimulation of the skin. We were indeed born, as Freud decreed, polymorphous perverts. But where Freud deduced our perversity from the dreams of his patients, Watson observed it in the actual behaviour of young infants. He always acknowledged his debt to the psychoanalyst.

The observations that he carried out between 1916 and 1919 suggested to Watson that the following group of 'emotional reactions' belonged to the 'original and fundamental nature of man; *fear, rage* and *love* (using *love* in approximately the same sense that Freud uses *sex*)'. Watson went on to explain that he hesitated to use the underlined terms because contemporary psychology still saw feelings in introspective terms. He would have preferred to merely label them 'emotional reaction states, X, Y and Z'. But that would divorce these results too much from ordinary experience. Watson did not really manage yet to distinguish convincingly between the physical responses that signified fear and those that signified rage.

The account Watson gave of his work on the children then has a strange gap. There are very few notes on the behaviour or instincts of children between their thirtieth and eightieth day. It seems likely that Watson did not stop watching children between these ages for he did test their ability to blink. He found that the blinking 'reflex' first appeared at fifty-five days and that it needed 'a developing or ripening period' before it took place. Watson never commented on this strange, and damaging, gap in his observations. Any systematic account of the development and maturation of children would need, of course, to fill in its crucial fifty-day divide in which, presumably we now know, babies do more than begin to blink.

Watson performed some much more meticulous observations of how children began to reach for objects. A little girl, L, was observed every day from her eightieth day on. A stick of red peppermint candy was suspended in front of her within easy reaching distance. L sat on her mother's knee. If, after a minute or so, L had not tried to get hold of the candy, Watson would put it in her mouth. Until the ninety-fourth day, L made no attempt to reach out for the candy. Then Watson placed the stick of candy in her left hand to see if she would place it in her mouth. L did not. The psychologist then placed the candy in her right hand and she at once put it in her mouth. A minute later, having somehow retrieved the candy, Watson repeated the process. The little girl repeated the pattern. Her left hand stayed immobile and sticky with candy; her right hand shot the sweet up to her mouth. She still did not reach for it. At 101 days she fixated on Watson rather than the candy but did open her hand and move a little towards it. At 129 days Watson made the candy swing back and forth before L. She followed it with her eyes and, when it was six inches away from her, she struck it with the back of her hand, grasped it with some difficulty using both hands, bumped it against her chin and finally worried it into her mouth. On the next trial, she grasped perfectly; and, at once, she repeated the action exactly. The child now seemed able to reach in a perfectly co-ordinated way. Between the 129th and 150th days, L became quite adept at reaching for the candy. She could do it without the help of her other hand and she could stretch out either while lying on her back or crawling. Her preference, as Watson suspected at 101 days, was for the right hand. By the 171st day, she could grasp the candy with either hand but did it very rarely with the left hand. Two years later Watson noted L was completely right-handed. He had not only analysed the gradual way in which a child developed the co-ordination needed between eye and hand in order to reach out for and grasp some candy but he suggested that this offered an early way of telling whether a baby was right- or left-handed. Watson studied fifteen other infants in this way. The results were 'wholly similar'. It was round the 120th day that the child was first able to co-ordinate perception and movements well enough to get hold of the candy. The period before that was one in which the baby had to mature physi- ologically and also get enough experience and practice to put this action together. Watson wondered if children, like his rats back in 1902, might be trained to achieve this co-ordination earlier.

From candy to candles. During L's time with the candy she was also tested with a candle. From 150 days on a candle was placed close to the child. She reached out for the flame even when it was held as close to her as one-eighth of an inch away from her hand. The candle was then moved in a circle round L. She followed it with her eyes and tried to reach it. She was briefly allowed to touch the flame. Her fingers flexed but, on the next trial, she reached out again for it though when she touched the flame she at once withdrew her hand. At 164 days the little girl would again reach continually for the flame 'regardless of the fact that her fingers were often scorched'. By 178 days 'definite progress in avoidance was noted.' She reached out much more intermittently and tended to check her hand just before she would burn herself in the flame. On the final trial that day this now educated little child 'would not reach for it but looked at it and sucked her fingers'. Fear of fire had finally been forged. At 220 days L still reached for the candle but withdrew before her fingers met the flame. Only once in fifteen occasions did she actually put her hand near the flame.

The importance of the detailed analysis of this reaction, Watson claimed, was that it showed how slowly the child built up an 'avoidance reaction'. It was a gradual process. Watson argued that if the child had actually been allowed to burn itself severely once, the whole process might have been more rapid. But apart from the cruelty of it, the baby would then have probably become terrified of Watson and the whole experimental situation. It might have been elegant and effective but it would have meant losing a subject. Again, fifteen other children appeared to develop fear of the candle in a similar kind of way.

Impressive as Watson's detailed observations on the candle might be, they actually contradicted his view that fear was due either to the loss of support or to loud sounds. The children always sat on their mother's laps while the candle was placed in front of them. There was a proper scientific quiet in the laboratory. Watson had shown effectively enough that there was no instinctive fear of fire but the meticulousness of his observations also showed that his account of the origins of fear was rather inadequate. But neither Watson, nor, it must be said, his critics ever at that time appeared to notice this inconsistency.

Early in 1919 Watson did carry out a number of further tests on fear in very young children. Popular belief claimed that children were frightened of many animals. Three babies who were 165, 126 and 124 days of age were exposed to a number of animals including a black cat, a pigeon and a rabbit. In almost every case the baby 'reacted', Watson's word, positively. The baby would try and touch the animal. There was no sign of fear. At 172 days of age one baby was held by a stranger and in a darkish room in which she could not see her mother. Even under such circumstances there was no terror of cat, rabbit or dog. The baby did not try to touch the animals but watched them intently. Eventually a rabbit was brought in and the child did stretch its hands out to hold that. True to his faith in observation in real life, Watson then took the baby to the zoo. The baby's mother came too, as did Watson's secretary. The two women took turns at holding the baby. Monkeys, camels, brown bears and peacocks and ponies all made the child look intently. She was obviously curious. But none of these animals made the child the slightest bit afraid. Even when the monkeys made violent-sounding noises, even when an ostrich hit the wire of its cage, the baby was attentive rather than afraid.

These tests were repeated with two other small children and the results were identical. Tales of the fears of animals that children were born with appeared to Watson to be pure myths. He determined to make use of the fact that he had shown children were more curious than frightened of these creatures.

Watson spent a good deal of time talking to the mothers of the babies that he was testing. As he got to know something of their daily lives, he began to see how particular events might condition the behaviour of a child. For example, while he was showing that the babies were not scared of animals, one child that he knew had a small dog thrown into its pram. The baby became completely terrified. After this trauma, she showed marked fear not only of dogs but also of other animals and, even, of mechanically moving toys. Watson eventually tested this girl a year and three months later and, even with her parents present, she cowered in terror from a tame white mouse. 'She watched it for a moment, her lips puckered, she shook slowly from side to side, squirmed, retracted hands and feet, broke into a cry, scrambled to her feet and fell headlong into her father's arms,' noted the behaviourist. It made him all the more interested to observe how children's fears of one object seemed to develop into a fear of something else. Watson argued that fears transferred easily from one stimulus to another.

One child, for example, would cry at 67 days of age when the experimenter put a rod in her hands to test the grasping reflex. Her mother would take her up in her arms and crying would cease. By 115 days of age – the child was tested every day – the baby also cried when the experimenter put a stick of candy in her hands. Watson believed that this was a carrying over of the conditioned reflex. At first she had cried because the mother put her down on a couch before so that the experimenter could test the grasping reflex. This loss of support became associated first just with having the grasping stick placed in her hands, then with the stick of candy being placed in her hands and then, possibly, with just seeing the experimenter. Watson would make further, and much more convincing, observations of how fears were instilled in us later in 1919.

When he had completed his work on the candy and the candle, Watson decided to see what other kinds of objects the child might reach out for. He remembered that he had, as a child, loved to play with and manipulate things. Now babies were placed in front of a whole variety of objects, stop watches, toys, erasers, round metal balls, balls of paste, soap, the strings of a violin. All these objects made the child reach. After two or three attempts, the child usually began to play with the object in its fingers. Watson said that 'once the reaching co-ordination has been formed, infants respond positively to nearly all small objects which are given a high stimulating value by moving them.' There were far more positive reactions than negative reactions. The behaviourist believed that children were taught to be frightened of a whole host of objects and situations. The natural tendency of the child was to touch, to explore, to manipulate. Watson stressed the

121

importance of this for the development of the child time after time. Yet psychology became so arid after 1930 that it was hailed as a major discovery in 1959 when White claimed to show that animals and children were as motivated by curiosity and wanting to explore their environment as they were by hunger and thirst.

Crawling was also studied. Here Watson had to note a much more varied pattern than with reaching. Some of the children he studied did not crawl at all before they walked. Others crawled anywhere between the 180th and 280th days. Many children learned to pull themselves up to stand without showing the slightest inclination to crawl. Watson concluded that crawling was far from being the universal instinct that it had been made out to be. The issue did not interest him much more though he hoped, he said, to study the development of walking in much more detail.

Between November 1918 and July 1919, Watson was writing his old and new observations on children as well as pressing ahead with more research on them. These observations form the basis of three chapters of *Psychology from the Standpoint of a Behaviourist* which Watson was hurriedly finishing off in the summer. He read many of the chapters to seminars at the Phipps Clinic in which Adolf Meyer, Leslie Hohlman, a psychiatrist, and Curt Richter, a young graduate student, played a leading part. During the spring the energetic behaviourist had a new chapter for them to consider almost every two weeks. As usual, he reacted well to being criticised, as he acknowledged in the preface to the book. The chapters improved. Debate did not worry him.

But another project also interested Watson. While he had been in the Aviation Corps, he had seen the anti-VD film *Fit to Fight*. The American authorities were very worried that their soldiers, especially those innocents shipped to sinful Europe, might frequent brothels and catch the clap. To save them from this fate and make them able to face a decent fighting death instead, the Pentagon first produced *Fit to Fight* and then the even more rousing *Fit to Win*. In both these epics, young American soldiers are 'approached by bootleggers and prostitutes'. Watson was very curious to know just what effect this propaganda had. The films traced five young men. One hero, when he meets the prostitute, remembers his pure sweetheart back home and resists both her and the demon drink. The other four, more typical of what the Pentagon believed soldiers to be like, succumb at once and are pictured wallowing in wine, women and song. After this orgy, only one had the intelligence to go to a doctor to get 'medical prophylaxis'; the other three dumb debauchers catch VD and are discharged. They are no longer fit to fight. *Fit to Win* continued the tale. The uninfected hero returns to his pure sweetheart after a poignant scene in which he lectures the other four on how foolish they were. The boy who had the wit to be treated is cured and can now fight. One of those who caught VD is seen at home with his father 'heartbroken over his infection', trying to hide its true nature from his mother who would die of shock if she knew her son had VD.

There was science as well as sensation in these films – whose complexity is remarkable when one recalls that they were silent. Before going into the sad tale of those who were tempted and the hero who stayed pure, *Fit to Fight* and *Fit to Win* both devoted a thousand feet of film to showing the lesions caused by veneral disease, with full frontal graphic pictures of diseased genital organs.

The government wanted to know how effective these films were. Before he left the military Watson had proposed that he and Lashley be allowed to investigate their usefulness. After protracted negotiations (for it was, after all, a subject of great sensitivity), the US Inter-departmental Social Hygiene Board granted Watson $6,600 to examine the educational effects of the motion picture campaign against VD. The impact of the films had to be assessed in three ways. First, how much of the information that people were given did they retain? Second, what emotions did the films arouse and were those emotions the right ones for the message the films were trying to put across? Finally, did the films succeed on the practical level? Did men who saw them rush less often to prostitutes, bootleggers and sundry other temptations? Did the motion pictures make them more moral?

Watson and Lashley visited three towns in which the films were played. They estimated that between 4,800 and 5,000 people saw the films. The two psychologists distributed questionnaires to every member of each audience and they received questionnaires back from 1,230 persons. They analysed the questionnaires, interviewed many people and followed up a selected smaller sample of those who had seen the films.

The enterprise required also a detailed analysis of just what it was the films were trying to say. As Watson wrote, 453 seconds of film time were devoted to the 'lesson that continence is in no way injurious to health but that the continent man is physically superior to the incontinent'. Three scenes made that point. Another 75 seconds stressed that 'seminal emissions are not harmful unless occurring more frequently than twice a week'. In moderation, masturbation did not lead to madness, a message put over 'in fairly dramatic scenes'. A further 608 seconds of screen time were devoted to the main point that veneral diseases were serious and could lead to blindness, brain damage and other appalling disabilities. The photographs that outlined the physiological scars and lesions were none too clear.

The film could not just be factual, it had to horrify. And once the audience had been frightened, it had to tell them what to do. A passage of 131 seconds showed how easily one might catch VD. An innocent country boy was seen kissing a scarred prostitute. One touch of her sickening lips and he was a goner. You could not even trust your friends. One scene showed a soldier using a razor belonging to a friend who fornicated. From the infected razor, the friend caught VD. Watson and Lashley described these scenes as 'dramatic throughout'; they sound rather melodramatic throughout, and, in places, as if they exaggerated situations so much that no one could believe them. A further 150 seconds of the film made the point that if you thought you were infected you should seek immediate treatment, then 100 seconds then explained that both gonorrhoea and syphilis could be treated but the treatment was long, costly and painful. In one pitiless episode, a Federal medical officer told an infected soldier that the government did not have the time to bother with curing the kind of hopeless and immoral cretin he was. Washington was not after all bound by the Hippocratic oath. But in its wisdom, the Federal government did provide soldiers with an alternative to brothels. 'Wholesome recreation rooms' were available. In these clean places one could play darts and chess and get a mug of watered beer. With feeble optimism, the film concluded that these rooms 'may serve as a substitute for the bawdy house'.

It was a great deal of information to put across. But there were also many emotional points to take note of. The sweethearts of the infected idiots moped with their dreadful shame; the continent men appeared paragons of physical fitness; in a number of scenes, fathers warned their sons against the evils of prostitutes; very often blind children, the innocent victims of their fathers' uncontainable and indiscriminating lust, appeared on screen.

Watson and Lashley divided their questionnaire into two parts. In the first, they asked people what they remembered of the film. Of those who saw the films, 70 per cent had a fairly detailed and accurate knowledge of the points that were made; 48 per cent of the audience said they had learned something new from the films; 89 per cent of the audience knew that veneral diseases were communicable and that they should, therefore, not touch anything that had ever been touched by a prostitute.

The films did arouse emotions, especially a fear of infection, but not of 'pathological intensity'. Those who saw the films did not want to marry less. They had not been sexually excited by the films and they had not been put off sex by it. Mixed audiences in those fairly prime days found them disturbing. Men did not think that women should see films like that with men around. Among the younger members of the audience there was a certain flippancy. It relaxed their inhibitions in talking about sex with each other (which certainly was not the intention of the government). Also, a few of the young poked fun at some of the luridly melodramatic scenes in the films. All in all, it seemed to Watson and Lashley that the films did not really arouse emotions that were as strong and as anti-sexual as the film-makers intended.

Finally the psychologists turned to the proof of the pudding. Had the films affected the behaviour of those who saw them? Watson and Lashley had followed up those who answered their questionnaires for about six months. There was nothing to show the films made their audiences more continent. It was hard to know, of course, if subjects gave honest answers to questions that inquired whether they now visited brothels less often. But, given the prevailing primness, if subjects were going to lie, it would be plausible to suppose that their lies would make them out to be more moral. After all, the messages of these films were clear. But the evidence that Watson and Lashley obtained suggested that it took more than melodrama to make the American male a pillar of virtue. It seemed 'that there is no effect whatever upon continence or upon the use of prophylaxis.' Like anon, sex *floreat semper* even despite Pentagon propaganda. These moral melodramas did little to influence the behaviour of the audience.

In many ways this was an interesting piece of research. Historically, it seems to have been the first serious survey of sexual attitudes. The methods that Watson and Lashley used were a very sensible combination of observing audiences, using questionnaires and following up the questionnaires with detailed field work. The behaviourist knew quite well that subjects could give a great deal of evidence about their own thoughts, impressions and feelings. That kind of self-report, which was nothing like introspection, was perfectly acceptable to Watson. He would have preferred also to monitor the behaviour of some of these men but that was impossible. Their own verbal accounts of their ideas and behaviour would have to do and, for the moment, they satisfied Watson. The experience of doing this study also convinced Watson of the importance of researching sexual behaviour in more detail. He began to argue to a number of his colleagues that psychology needed to take a frank look at how people behaved sexually. Lashley was, of course, convinced; but many others thought that Watson was going too far. In this respect the differences between Watson and the psychoanalysts are really interesting. Since Freud posited our libido in the unconscious, in the fiery swamps of the Id, psychoanalysts did not really have to study sexual behaviour directly.

In fact it is telling the extent to which psychoanalysts did not make any empirical observations of how people behaved sexually. Watson agreed that sex was a, if not *the*, fundamental human drive and since he also agreed that society did much to repress sexuality, his own psychological position obliged him to try and study actual behaviour and attitudes. Dreams and symbols were interesting, he conceded, and he went so far as to argue that all politicians ought to be psychoanalysed before they were allowed to stand for office so that they could come to terms with the deformities in their personality. But, for the behaviourist, the proper study of sexual behaviour had to be much more direct. He was enough the son of Greenville to know that such ideas would outrage American opinion, both popular and academic. But the successful completion of the work on the VD films determined Watson to continue research in this area. He decided to tackle it obliquely though, for he knew that he could not yet get any financial backing for more direct research. Again with Lashley, Watson proposed to study the attitudes of doctors to sex and, especially, to sex education. The young, Watson believed, were not going to stand the moral conventions of the time much longer and he felt that they were quite right.

Hand in hand with all this work, Watson was completing his book. It was in September 1919 that he finished *Psychology from the Standpoint of a Behaviourist*. The book is really Watson's most complete statement of his psychological position. It was an attempt to see the whole of psychology from his own point of view. He offered, in the book, an approach to the whole field of human behaviour. Many of the themes and experiments that Watson discussed have already been examined but it is obviously important to look at it in some detail.

The interesting thing about Watson's first chapter was not that he repeated his now familiar claim that psychology ought to be an objective and a natural science; much more interesting were the methods to be used to achieve these ends. A correct psychology would need both observation and experiment. Experiments were not more important even though they could obviously be controlled far better than observations. Many ordinary people had long used psychology without knowing it, Watson said, and their psychology was based largely on observation. The behaviourist even touted the outrageous idea that businessmen, artists, artisans and other unqualified folk might have valid psychological understanding. 'It is possibly even a debateable question whether common sense has not kept closer to the fundamental truth underlying the psychology of reactions than the too detached psychology of the laboratory.' Watson had a healthy scepticism about the laboratory. He never meant to sacrifice observation to the laboratory gods. Accurate description of the most complex behaviours was vital to psychology; and the best descriptions came from observations of real life on the street, in the factory, in the classroom, in the office, in the lounge and even, in the bedroom. Field work should suggest what needed to be examined in the laboratory. The refined results of laboratory work ought to be taken back into the field and tested again there. Such a *va et vient*, shuttling between the field and the laboratory, has not even yet become fashionable though a number of influential psychologists now plead for it. For a long time, the laboratory was the supreme temple of psychology.

Watson not only wanted this kind of traffic, he warned against making too large inference from results of experiments on animals in the laboratory. Recently psychologists and ethologists have had a field day showing our every action to be either that of a super-rat or of a very intelligent baboon. We thirst for, and thrust for, simple theories that will explain all at the drop of an analogy. In his first chapter, Watson warned explicitly against such simplifications.

But for all this stress on observation, Watson was already convinced of the basic fact that he knew the nuggets out of which human behaviour, human reactions, were built up. 'Every one agreed that men's acts are determined by something and that, whether he acts orderly or not, there are sufficient grounds for his acting as he does, if only those grounds had been discovered.' Watson believed that he had discovered the basic grounds in the links between the stimulus and the response. For the behaviourist, life was a question of responding to stimuli. A psychology of *re-action*, as Watson termed his own, is a very apt phrase, for according to him we do not act. We react, we respond; confronted with stimuli, we flash various responses as a result either of our genetic make-up or the habits that we have formed. A detailed reading of Watson's books shows that he had a rather more sophisticated concept of the stimulus than we have been led to believe for he defined the stimulus as 'stimulus or situation'. This was provided either by the external environment, such as when one sees a pretty girl, or by 'movements of men's own muscles of the secretion of glands'. Watson was never clear. The examples Watson gave of *stimuli*, however, were broader than this definition suggests, for they often involved a person identifying a situation as being of a particular kind and acting, or reacting, according to the way that he perceived the situation. That kind of complex stimulus is really rather different from saying that a pellet of food is a stimulus. Equally, Watson's concept of a response was looser than modern behaviourists' for it could follow either immediately or after a while. Again, the examples Watson used were much broader than his theory ought to have allowed. Curiously, in the book, Watson actually spoke of the 'response or act'. Much of what Watson had to say about stimuli and responses was fairly loose. But that very looseness meant that his psychology was richer and more in touch with life than the logically tight systems of the 1930s and 1940s in which minute physiological stimuli led to minute physiological responses.

In the book Watson argued forcefully that James's idea that the task of psychology was to provide an account of the stream of consciousness was mistaken. The task of psychology was to provide an account of the 'stream of activity', of how and why people behaved. He hoped to extend his work on children because it would then be possible to trace the development of every kind of behaviour.

Watson often returned in the book to the notion that psychology ought to be of use to individuals. I suspect that Watson's ambiguities about the nature of the stimulus were due to this emphasis in his thinking. If our actions were completely determined, then it would follow that it was logically impossible for a person to choose to use psychology, or behaviourism, in order to improve or develop himself. In a time when there was great faith in the ability of science to improve the human condition, there had to be loopholes. Watson allowed such loopholes to creep into his psychology which stated, with mechanistic propriety, that it was a psychology of reaction, but he managed to leave some scope for human action. Later, behaviourists closed these loopholes. Possibly the best illustration of these aspects of the book is the section on the Determiners of Acts (p. 298).

The behaviourist began by making a what seems a damaging admission. Human behaviour is varied that it 'makes man's reactions hard to predict in a particular instance' and 'so varied is the shading of response' to any stimulus 'that habit seems at first to be a poorly chosen term to apply to it'. Nevertheless, Watson believed that we relied very heavily on habits in our behaviour. He then gave an example of observed behaviour. A man comes home and finds a revolver lying on the dresser.

> The usual reactions to a revolver lying on the dresser are possibly to polish and clean it periodically but if someone has been rifling your cash drawer or safe from day to day you may, on reaching home, pick up the weapon, load it, return to your office and lie in wait for the intruder.

If a person is sufficiently depressed, the stimulus, the revolver, might lead him then to contemplate suicide. An object can call out 'multiple responses' because 'man is prepared to meet any slight change in the situation or object with an appropriate change in the response. 'It is this complexity of possible responses that makes human behaviour so hard to predict.

Despite this, Watson tried to set out a number of rules which did determine actions. First, the response most likely to appear in a situation was that most recently called out by the same situation. When recency is neither a pertinent or a possible factor, 'the act which has been most frequently connected with the object is the one most likely to be called out'. A human being was a mesh of reflex pathways established by instinct, and habit. It was easier for an old response to an old stimulus to appear than for anything else to occur. But Watson was too much aware of the variety of reactions to similar stimuli to limit himself to these two laws. He added that 'the act called out is likely to be one which is most closely connected with the general setting of the situation as a whole.' This was more than mere habit for a person had actually to identify the sort of situation he was in in order to know what behaviour to put on. Watson wrote: 'We are expected to display church behaviour, funereal behaviour and wedding behaviour upon certain occasions. The situation as a whole envelops us.'

The traditional view has been that Watson put up a narrow stimulus response psychology in which human beings were meant to react like Pavlovian dogs, automata full of reflexes. But the last three determinants of acts show clearly that Watson did not believe there was an 'empty organism' between the stimulus and the response. Much of the psychology of the 1930s and 1940s was taken up with specifying the precise nature of the stimuli that would inevitably evoke the same precise response. The equation $S-R$ in psychology referred to such a psychology and Watson was said to be one of its founders. But his fourth determiner of an act was the state of the organism, both emotionally and physiologically. In different moods, after different experiences, the same situation would provoke quite varied reactions. Watson wrote that 'the situations which the individual has had to come against during the hours preceding the incidence of the stimulus to which he must now react and the amount of emotional tension those previous activities have aroused' do much to determine behaviour. Physiological factors also influenced behaviour. A philosopher with a toothache reacted quite differently to a volume of Plato than that same philosopher in no pain. Normal reactions might not be obtained from a seasick individual or one who had indigestion, Watson wrote. Later, he would go so far as to argue that the times of the day affected the way people responded to situations.

The last factor Watson emphasised was the previous history of the individual. A person's background, education, experience, illnesses, triumphs and disappointments were always there to limit potential responses. Watson argued that these six factors combined to limit the 'possibility of varied response' and also to 'rationalise behaviour and give it a causal basis'. The fact that human behaviour could not be predicted did not mean that it was uncaused. Watson did not develop this crucial point as clearly as he might have done, which was a pity, for many psychologists still believe that psychology can only be scientific in so far as it can predict human behaviour. The unpredictable is not the uncaused, however. Watson wanted to predict this but granted to human beings a range of complexity of action and reaction that made prediction, in practice, a naive pipedream for those who needed to predict in order to feel that what they were doing was duly scientific. Watson wavered in his views. He believed there were specifiable causes for human actions and reactions. Underlying all was the reflex; life was a pattern of responding to stimuli. But, as I have tried to argue, Watson's concept of the stimulus was so broad that his views are much less narrow, in fact, than they appear to be. Part of a person's response to a stimulus or situation depended on their reading of that situation and, also, of the state of the individual at the moment when he or she was required to respond. A boy who had had a series of unhappy sexual experiences might react differently if a girl would not neck with him at the end of a bad week at work than he would at the end of a good week. If he was in a labile state, he might start to cry or even to become violent; if he had had a reasonable week, he might control his disappointment and make sure that his next date was more willing. Watson smuggled into his account of reactions a great deal of potential subtlety including the way that a person saw a situation and the state of their body at the time.

Such an interpretation implies strongly that the behaviourist did not apply Pavlov's ideas about the reflex indiscriminately to all behaviour. The reflex was a basic unit out of which behaviour was put together. But Watson left plenty of room for all kinds of variations in the ways that different reflexes, different acts, might be the response to the same situations. Crude Pavlovian ideas could never properly account for the flexibility of human behaviour. Watson never offered a totally satisfactory account of what did determine human action, but it seems to me that it is incorrect to believe he was putting forward a psychology in which stimulus simply triggered response and in which psychology was concerned with specifying what stimuli evoked what response. Unfortunately, after Watson, behaviourists tended to forget all this messy complexity. It was more elegant to home in on the relationships that existed or could be made to obtain between one stimulus and one response. The discovery that objects looked different depending on people's expectations and experiences was in 1948 hailed as a discovery. Yet it follows easily from Watson's analysis of behaviour. Much of this thinking remains strikingly modern. But, by and large, it is the modern subtleties, the recognition of how flexible our responses to stimuli are, which Watson's immediate successors chose to ignore. (Skinner, for example, does not really dispute that he is a psychologist of the empty organism, concerned to crystallise the relationships that exist between stimuli and responses. Nothing else for him is really the province of the psychologist. Skinner's attitude typifies psychology in the USA from 1930 to the late 1950s.)

In *Psychology from the Standpoint of a Behaviourist*, Watson set out all his observations on children. He conceded that these were nothing but a tentative start to a vast subject. He used the research across three chapters in which he tried to tease out the relationship between instincts and habits. Watson put forward a list of 'asserted instincts' which included acquisition and possessiveness, hunting, collecting and hoarding, the search for a place to live, migration, fighting, maternal instincts, gregariousness, imitation, manipulation and play. This list was essentially Thorndike's. Thorndike also suggested as instincts greed, kindliness, teasing, tormenting, bullying, adornment and cleanliness. On the last, Watson was vicious. 'Psychologists persistently maintain that cleanliness is instinctive in spite of the filth of the negro, of the savage and of the child.' Emma K. Roe would have been proud of her son; he still had some slight relic of a scrubbed southern soul. Watson did not dismiss all of these as absurd instincts and it must be realised that Thorndike was quite modest in his list. William James had offered a yet longer catalogue of instincts and William MacDougall was to write a grand list in which just about every human action was due to some instinct, some flowering of Bergson's *élan vital*.

Watson did not put forward his own definitive list of instincts. He claimed that fear, love and rage were innate reactions to certain specific situations like being dropped, being stroked and being hampered. Fighting was, he granted, largely an instinct; the animal, including the human animal, is born with some tendency to defend itself even though all the baby can do is lash out with its arms and legs in an unco-ordinated frenzy. It is surprising to read that Watson accepted gregariousness as a well analysed instinct. 'Our cafés, boulevards, churches and county fairs are dependent upon it to a certain extent,' he pointed out. Manipulation and play seemed to Watson to be largely instinctive. Of manipulation, he wrote:

This instinctive tendency is sometimes exalted by calling it constructiveness. That there is an original tendency to reach out for

131

objects, to scrape them along the floor, to pick them up, put them back into the mouth, to throw them back upon the floor, to move back and forth any parts which can be moved is one of the best grounded and best observed of the instincts.

Play was an elaboration from that in which the child acquired certain habits.

In his view of instinct in 1919, Watson had much that was sensible to say. Most actions are 'really consolidations of instinct and habit'. It was hard to find where the instinct in adornment or cleanliness lay but manipulation, play, gregariousness and fighting, fear, love and anger seemed to Watson to have been largely innate. Not that it really mattered for scientists would see the role divide between the innate and the learned according to their prejudices. 'The geneticist is likely to over-estimate, to emphasise the number of original tendencies: the psychoanalyst to underestimate them.' Later, of course, behaviourists would also be accused of underestimating instincts. In daily life instincts often 'initiated the process of learning'. If a baby did not reach out for objects, he could not begin to handle toys. A child who did not handle all kinds of objects as a baby would find it hard to develop the co-ordinations that we take for granted. The plasticity of the human infant could be used 'in early youth to properly shape any child's future'. If you want your child to become a carpenter, give him or her plenty of manual experience: if, like James Mill, you want to turn your son into a great mind and advertisement for your own theories, stuff him full of Latin and Greek. In Watson's case, the toilet rather than logic was the great obsession. He was certain that children could be trained to be clean from very early on. And children could learn not to perform a plethora of nasty actions. They could be trained not to suck their fingers, not to touch their genitals too much, not to be too noisy, and to be either right- or left-handed. To break an instinct, the stimulus had to be changed. What the child usually sucks is his thumb. Change the thumb (the stimulus) by putting pepper on it or adhesive and the habit would soon alter. The child would no longer produce the sucking response because the stimulus was no longer bland-tasting thumb but glue-sodden thumb. (Naive Watson never had to cope with glue-sniffing.) The ways in which it is possible to build on and shape instincts would continue to fascinate Watson for a long time.

After he had dealt with instincts, Watson moved to habits. His arguments were simpler. Anything that is not instinctive 'must be looked upon as a habit. It is an individually acquired or learned act.' Even the embryo can form habits in the womb, for snug in the womb the embryo can rotate its head, flex and contract its fingers, kick and bend. Watson concluded that the baby at birth was capable of enough random movements so 'that in habit no new elementary movements are needed'. We are born with all that we need to carve out the most subtle habits like playing a Beethoven concerto. 'There are enough [movements] present at birth and more than will ever be combined into complex unitary acts.' From the physiological point of view, too, the baby was born complete with all the wherewithal to be conditioned. There was no need for the formation of 'new pathways'. Watson had observed far more than over a hundred separate, distinct movements in one-day-old babies. The mathematical permutations of a hundred different movements were staggering.

> One needs only to examine the five or six day old infant to be reasonably certain that there is no need for the formation of additional reflex arcs to account for all later organisation. The new or learned element in habit is the tying together or integration of separate movements in such a way as to produce new activity.

The details of how L came to reach for the candy seemed excellent evidence of how a child pieces together movements to produce an action.

A child can learn to respond to certain stimuli with the appropriate habit. For example, the mother cries, 'It's time to wake up' and the child gets out of bed, goes to the toilet, washes its hands and face and gets ready to dress. Watson argued that one difference between instincts and habits was that an instinct usually called forth only one behaviour. A hawk sees a small bird; it swoops to kill. But habits are much more flexible. I may usually respond to a train drawing in to the station at 8.50 a.m. by stepping on to it; but I can break such a habit. For Watson wrote: 'the same object can call forth from an educated man literally hundreds of different actions depending upon slight differences in its setting or upon his needs at the moment.' By contrast, instincts were more tyrannical. But habits were, for Watson, one of the main pillars of life. Among habits he included playing games, walking, working and 'in fact doing the thousands of things that we see individuals and groups doing from the moment of waking to the moment of sleeping'. Life was a matter of habits.

As a habit developed, a person had to shed many useless movements and to home in on the few actions that actually serve to, say, put on a gramophone record. At first the actions are clumsy and highly redundant; the process is slow. But as you get better at the habit, you lose most of these random movements. Watson tried to explain the formation of habits fairly fully and it is necessary to quote him at length to dispel the idea put about by many, including Herrnstein (1967), that for the behaviourist it was recency and frequency that caused an animal to learn. Watson, in attempting to explain how habits came to be fixed, offered the following causes:

(1)In most cases where random activity finally leads to success the successful group of acts is always the last one to appear; hence when the next trial is given the last group active in the preceding test (the successful one) is the one most recently exercised and therefore, other things being equal, it will be the one most likely to occur first or at least early in the second trial. [That is *recency*.] (2) In view of the fact that the random movements are infinitely varied the successful act is the only one performed each time the stimulus is presented. It therefore, becomes the most frequently performed movement.

As a result, it is more likely to occur again. But Watson was now willing to extend the boundaries of cause further than he had been in *Behaviour* in 1914. For he allowed a third and fourth potential cause. He wrote: '(3) By reason of the fact that the final group of acts always brings food, water, removes an irritating object, lessens emotional tension etc., the new state . . . brings heightened metabolism.' This Watson saw might be a form of reward. And, finally, as result of the final act bringing food or something else, 'it is possible . . . that the situation as a whole becomes an emotion producing one; internal secretions are set free which serve as reinforcers'. He did not expand on this idea but it seems clear that he realised that recency and frequency were not enough to explain learning (the limits of which were outlined in Chapter 4).

Once he had dealt with habits, Watson turned his attention to the emotions and outlined the three basic 'emotional reactions' of fear, rage and love. All other emotions stem from these, Watson argued, by means of the *conditioned emotional reflex*. At first, only a very specific stimulus, its movements being hampered, will make the baby rage. When that happens, certain reflex arcs are triggered. But, gradually, other stimuli come to set off the same reflexes. Just as Pavlov's dogs were trained to salivate to the sound of a bell, so children are trained, not necessarily consciously, to respond emotionally to very many situations. The innate fear of loud noises was the stimulus on which the behaviourist often harped. This generalised to a fear of being shouted at by parents. In turn, that made thechild afraid of various situations in which the parent shouted at them. For example, when the little boy knocks over his mother's fruit bowl, she yells at him. This loud yell evokes the same reflexes that were evoked in the neonate by any loud noises, reflexes that either mediate or 'are' fear. So the child comes to be afraid of any situation in which, generally, his mother yells and, second, any situation which seems likely to make his mother yell. When, therefore, someone hands the child another delicate bowl, he takes extreme care not to knock it over again. If the child is badly trained by a parent this emotional reaction may become pathological. Such a child, Watson suggested, might become so distorted by its conditioning that it would never touch a fruit bowl. His own fear of the dark seemed to him just such an excessive, absurd fear. But the basic model the behaviourist offered was one in which all our subsequent emotions stem from the three basic specific situations that evoke fear, rage and love. We learn everything else that we feel.

It is interesting here to compare Watson's doctrine with that of later behaviourists who often appear to deny that feelings cause anything. Skinner condescends to agree that he does have feelings only they do not matter. Watson was aware of his own emotions and the influence of Hume left him convinced that reason was, indeed, 'the slave of the passions'. Without conceding that feelings were anything to do with consciousness, Watson would have claimed that *rage* did, indeed, cause one man to lash out at another. The determiners of acts included how that fellow perceived the situations he was in, and how he perceived the events of the day had been and the mood he was in. It was necessary for people to understand their own emotional make-up, Watson argued.

The study of emotions in *Psychology from the Standpoint of a Behaviourist* was not meant to be only academic. Watson had had to analyse his own emotions when he had had a breakdown; he had often had to cope with periods of depression. Every student of psychology ought to be aware of his own emotional tendencies. To this end, Watson prepared a kind of quiz in the book so that each student could test 'the Efficiency of the Individual Emotional System'. (The word *efficiency* is, of course, telling; like a car, the emotions had to be in good gear.) The tests included asking yourself whether you showed anger too easily; whether you became frightened too readily; whether you became too attached to people too quickly; did it require 'adequate stimulation' for you to become 'hooked' either on people, places or things. Watson laid some stress on this, which suggests he knew how easy it was for him to become too attached to certain kinds of figures like Angell or Titchener. There were many other questions of the same ilk. How free were you from suspicion, embarrassment and a sense of inferiority? If you passed psychic muster on these, did you tend to be too garrulous, too exhibitionistic and arrogant? Physical control also came in. In a section entitled 'Freedom from Unusual Outlets', Watson set out questions on whether you had tics, twitchings or any other unusual physical problem. Among the unusual outlets that the perfectly adjusted person should be free of was that of talking too much about sex.

Two uses for these questions were suggested. Each student could test himself in private, of course, Second, every person in a psychology class could compare the way he rated himself with the way that others rated him. You would thus have some check on your delusions. Watson said that it was likely that the use of the test would show there was no one who was perfectly well adjusted. The majority of people have weaknesses but these are compensated for by other elements in their make-up that make it unlikely they will break down. Only a very severe crisis will destroy many of their defences and balances. Other individuals will turn out to be emotionally unstable. But to recognise that fact was the first vital step in coping with it. The unstable could either retrain themselves or be retrained. Armed with what Watson termed 'the balance sheet of the self', you can set about developing that strength, combating that foible, getting rid of that irrational fear, working on yourself as if you were a piece of clay to mould. The interesting thing about this idea is that, for Watson, it was the individual who could usually choose how and where to improve himself. His ideal society was one of self-shapers. People could use psychology to make themselves better, more 'efficient' than they were. Many of the questions that he asked individuals to confront themselves with are precisely the kinds of questions that occur in encounter groups or other forms of therapy. Each individual should exploit psychology. The science of psychology, like the other sciences, was there to enhance the perfectibility of man. That was Watson's fond hope. And, in that, is the paradox that he left it up to the individual to choose to use psychology. Despite all the attacks on consciousness, Watson wrote as if he completely accepted that individuals could decide that they needed to alter their personality and could choose to act in a certain way that would change themselves. How does a creature whose every action is a reaction determined by external forces decide to embark on a programme of changing itself? Watson never gave any attention to that point. Again, his ambiguity seems instructive. On the one hand, psychology had to be mechanistic and human beings had to be subject to laws not too different from other physical and biological laws; on the other hand, the whole ethos of Watson's time had faith in reform, in the power of the individual to make himself what he wanted to be. Many writers on behaviourism have claimed that behaviourism is a psychology which reflects American fear of the contemplative. To be is to do. Yet, few of these commentators seem to have realised that their explanation merely creates another paradox. For behaviourism has become not a psychology of action but of reaction. External reinforcements largely dictate what we will do. The rugged American individualists, the man who carved his farm out of the frontier, the great barons of business, all these legendary figures Watson admired were men who *acted*. The environment reacted to them. They knew themselves and had power. It is this tension between a psychology that is scientific and a psychology which allows people to master themselves and their situations according to the best traditions of the American dream which is at the root of the ambiguities in Watson's system. He felt as if people had the right to choose what to make of their lives. As a scientist, he ought not allow them that right. He never really resolved that ambiguity for himself and his psychology is, essentially, more closely in touch with life because he was not able to turn himself into a desiccated determinist.

But Watson did not believe it was only the individual who could use psychology. Society could also employ it to retrain those of its members who did not conform to civilised standards. The criminal, the lazy, the drifters and, even, the mentally ill could be turned into useful members of society. It would not be left up to them to choose that. More brutal than Skinner, Watson argued that those few criminals whose nervous systems were so askew that they could not be conditioned into decent members of American society ought to be 'etherised'. It was no good shilly-shallying sentimentally about a few misfits. Those sections of the book on the use of psychology for social control are extremely unattractive. Watson does not even consider the ethical and political issue of who is to judge what the right standards of behaviour are and whether a person so contravenes these that they should be sentenced either to retraining or, eventually, to the ether. Here again Watson was paradoxical. He often criticised the hypocrisy of society. Yet many of its standards seemed so obvious to him that he saw no need to discuss the political issues that such drastic social control might raise. The notion that behaviourism would allow the authorities to control the minds and behaviour of mankind frightened many intellectuals. Watson thought punishments were bad and unnecessary – a point Skinner makes much of in his Utopia *Walden Two* – but, otherwise, he firmly believed that society had the right to use knowledge in order to mould or control undesirables. This was a very rigid view and Watson did not in 1919 begin to handle its implications properly. In the 1920s, 1930s and 1940s a number of books, of course, exposed what such a behaviourally controlled world might be like. *Brave New World* and, later, *1984* depict mankind in the grips of a psychological terror that owes much to behaviouristic ideas. It is a horrendous vision.

The rest of the book was less interesting. Watson repeated his theory of thinking as silent speech. He had little new evidence though. He reported some new research in language and sketched out some areas for future research including how blind deaf mutes acquired language; stuttering, stammering and other defects; the consequence of lesions upon language; slang and profane words and the speech of psychopathic individuals. He also wanted to see work on the ways that manics and paranoid patients spoke. More unexpected, he urged study of 'the symbolic and folk lore side òf language' and 'the language system in day and night dreaming'. But he stressed that language should not be studied in isolation. Our speech is tied in with all our other 'adjustments'. To concentrate just on our utterances is to distort the role that speech plays in our lives.

Psychology from the Standpoint of a Behaviourist was an attempt at a grand psychological picture. It was meant to be not a total theory but a fairly full account of psychology. Everything was in it. Instincts and habits, thoughts and emotions, sensations and memory, sex and reflexes, children and fatigue all jostled in the book, in chapter after chapter. Watson felt that he had dissected the organism into its 'part reactions'. In his last two chapters, he aimed at synthesis 'to put the organism back together again and view him as an integrated biological concern'.

Laudable as such an aim might be, Watson did not really fulfil it. His last two chapters concern 'the organism at work' and 'personality'. They are both somewhat disappointing. The chapter on work is a summary of much contemporary research into human behaviour. Fatigue is examined in detail. Watson reported much research on 'the curve of work' and some of the military experiments on oxygen deprivation. He looked at how drugs and climate affected the performance of tasks and he even tackled the question of how diurnal rhythms of individuals altered the way they exercised skills. The variety of variables afflicted the supposedly pure relationship between stimulus and response. Watson wanted industry to make greater use of psychology but he warned against industries 'abusing the situation'. Abuse meant employing psychological knowledge 'to grind as much out of the organism as possible in the shortest space of time'. A person's work was a major part of his life. Psychology ought not to be employed to make him into a machine to the detriment of his happiness and comfort. The chapter was, in truth, a rather patched-up account of a variety of research. As a synthesis it was distinctly scrappy.

In his final chapter Watson turned to personality and its 'disturbance'. He did not offer any theory of personality and, in fact, he said very little that was new. Again, he urged that individuals should make use of psychology to understand themselves and their reactions. Vitriolic attacks were made on phrenologists and handwriting experts, though Watson had the honesty to admit that a certain M. Crépieux-Jamin seemed able to deduce sex and occupation astonishingly well from samples of writing. Otherwise Watson offered an expanded version of the questions he had suggested for students so that not only the would-be psychologist but also the ordinary person might get into self-scrutiny. Watson gave an account of Stratton's experiment on wearing lenses that made him see the world upside down. It was a rather odd chapter in which to insert this. Watson then repeated his interpretation of Freud which argued that we are left with all kinds of instincts and habits from youth and that we fail to outgrow them properly. They pop up and interfere with the mature flow of adult life. Society, Watson reiterated, had the right to take steps to improve the personalities of those of its members who were either criminal or beyond the social pale. Again, the chapter has a certain impression of having been thrown together in something of a hurry. It is neither systematic nor really synthesis.

Despite the disappointment of these two chapters, Watson's book was a very major work. It offered the outline of a complete behaviouristic programme. It had in it an attempt to provide a psychological account of the most diverse and complex human actions. The style of the book, the examples Watson drew on, were often from real life and they illustrated his commitment to making psychology not just objective but a reflection of the texture of everyday life. The 'too detached laboratories' were not his favourite haunts. Both here and in earlier chapters I have tried to indicate some of the problems of the ideas that Watson put forward. Almost no position that he espoused was totally right. But it was an impressive achievement and it is a pity psychologists attended mainly to small selected bits of it.

Reviews of the book were slow in coming. But the idea of applying behaviourism to various fields began to interest the public. With a number of colleagues, Watson published a small book on education. The idea, like James's *Talks to Teachers*, was to let teachers know how they could use psychology to good effect in the classroom. Watson recommended that information should be presented in such a way as to tug at the heart-strings. Facts that aroused emotions were more likely to be remembered. And the teacher ought to remember the basic reactions of fear, rage and love and use these insights to condition the children to their best advantage. Watson also used his work on the gradual formation of habits to show the basic pattern of learning. No punishments should be used in classrooms and, so that teachers should know the latest animal research that bore on learning, he summarised in his contribution much of his own and Ulrich's work on how rats learned mazes and problems. The interest of the chapter Watson contributed to this short book is mainly that it shows how he was beginning to be in demand as an expert on human behaviour.

Business also sought Watson out. He began to advise a life insurance company on various of its personnel problems. Life insurance salesmen suffered a very high turnover and Watson was asked to help. He was happy with the extra money it brought in. He wished to lead the life of a gentleman of easy means and that was proving impossible. Mary wanted to have a brighter, more social life. That, too, cost money.

There was every reason, therefore, for Johns Hopkins to be happy with its professor of psychology. With the war over, more students were enrolling. A lot of young people were attracted by Watson's vision of a scientific psychology. Moreover, Watson was sensing a certain mood of change. The moral climate of America seemed to Watson to be changing. His sense turned out to be an accurate one for the Twenties, that decade which is now seen as an early version of the Swinging Sixties, were about to begin. The young would rebel against the conventions, especially the sexual constraints, which society imposed upon them. It was in 1919 that Watson first began to speak of the value of 'wholesale necking' among students so that, before they married, they were competent smoochers at the very least. None of this endeared Watson to rigid men like Goodnow. But Johns Hopkins could not really complain too much since Watson had such an enormous national reputation and the wit to get very official backing for the research into sex that he did.

With the study of the VD films complete, Watson obtained a further grant from the Board of Social Hygiene to study the opinions of doctors regarding sex education and venereal disease. Cunningly, Watson made it seem that the only reason for studying sex education was to see if it could be used to prevent venereal disease among a population that was even more ignorant than it was depraved. But, in fact, the study that Watson and Lashley did was much wider in its scope than that. They prepared a lengthy questionnaire for doctors. The answers revealed clearly that doctors thought sex was a secret with which the masses should on no account be entrusted. A majority of doctors believed that young people should not be taught about the sexual anatomy of the opposite sex, and many thought that such knowledge among the unmarried would lead to an increase in sexual offences 'without a shadow of doubt'. Most of these medical men and women were afraid that sex education would lead to uncontrollable passions.

And who was fit to teach sex? Forty-six of them 'unhestitatingly affirmed that the average medical practitioner is completely incompetent to give such instruction.' It took skills such as those which they had as psychiatrists and gynaecologists to tell lay people the facts of life. One gynaecologist said of the average doctor: 'he has a narrow orthodoxy which is mostly false.' Yet many of these expert doctors thought that masturbation was evil or, as one man put it, 'not nice or decent'. One psychiatrist believed that it was the cause of sexual offences in men. Fifty-two of the sample felt that one great danger of sexual education was that it would arouse the young too much. Silence made for restraint. Many of the doctors worried that too much talk of sex, however well informed, would only lead the young into vice. 'Alcohol and bad companions' were often emphasised as stimuli that led to sex. In a section on VD, Watson and Lashley asked the doctors what their attitudes to the disease were. Most took a harsh line. One should exaggerate the dangers because that was the only way to force chastity from an immoral populace. One should be careful not to make it sound as if the disease could be cured too easily because that 'might lead to overconfidence'. 'Overconfidence' presumably meant outbursts of lust. Most doctors believed that any person who had VD should have to go through a special procedure before getting married; they had to be licensed to breed.

The study also shed light on medical attitudes to extra-marital sex and marriage. Half the doctors thought it was impossible for sexual problems to be so important as to cause marriage breakdowns. No one placed so much importance on sex. One gynaecologist answered that sex led to breakdowns 'rarely and only in psychopaths'. (If he could see the bookstands now.) The doctors had little good to say about extra-marital sex. Its causes were 'self indulgence' or a 'belief that intercourse is the thing everybody is doing' or 'inability to properly sublimate the sexual craving'. One gynaecologist expertly offered the following additional causes of extra-marital intercourse: feeblemindedness, evil associations, alcoholism, and a psychopathic personality.

Watson and Lashley reproduced verbatim many of the replies they got. What is apparent is the pious morality of most of the doctors who clearly appeared almost to view sex itself as a kind of disease. It was dirty; it was degenerate. Too much sex condemned you to the ranks of drunks and idiots. The replies convinced Watson that sex was too important to be left to the medical profession. The study took a long time to publish. He began to argue forcefully that psychologists study sexual behaviour. He wanted to find out what people's sexual relationships were like and what part these played in their lives. Such a project was not impossible. Watson hoped gradually to extend the studies

141

that he and Lashley had done so that, finally, psychology would study sex directly. He had definite plans.

But Watson returned, in the autumn of 1919, to the study of children. He embarked on one or two projects. First, after much difficulty, he persuaded Johns Hopkins to advance him $450 to buy film in order to make a motion picture of various aspects of the child's development. Watson was no great still photographer so it is unlikely that he took any of the film himself. No copy of the film appears to be in existence. Using slow motion it showed the basic reactions of rage, fear and love which Watson had made the basis of his theory of the emotions. Watson hoped to use the slowed film images to be able to describe in better detail the instinctive physical responses of rage, love and fear. It might offer a way of distinguishing rage and fear. The film was very successful, for Watson could write to Goodnow early in 1920 that it was being used in courses for nursery teachers and nurses by the philanthropist Mrs Dummer and others. It was probably the first psychological film to be made. Watson, as ever, loved using appropriate new techniques.

If the film that is now lost is an interesting curiosity, the experiment that Watson then embarked on was to become one of the enduring classics. In autumn 1919 one of the children of a wet nurse at the Phipps was brought to Watson's laboratory. His name was Albert and he is now enshrined in the history of psychology and psychiatry as Little Albert. Albert was eleven months old when Watson first began to work with him. On a number of occasions Watson showed the little boy a small white rat. As was expected, Little Albert reacted positively to seeing the animal. He stretched out his hands to touch it and, eventually, he came to actually try and hold the animal. Watson thus established that the normal response of the child was one of curiosity, of approach to the animal. Watson then waited a few days and brought Little Albert back into the same room. His friend the rat was again brought out. The little boy began to play with the animal. Watson then introduced a new stimulus. Just as the child put his hand out to touch the rat, he banged a long steel bar very loudly with a carpenter's hammer. 'The infant jumped violently and fell forward burying his face in the mattress. He did not cry, however.' The brave small boy reached out with his right hand for the rat again. Again, the hammer struck the bar just behind the boy's head. 'Again the infant jumped violently, fell forward and began to whimper.' Albert was so disturbed no further tests took place for a week.

A week later the boy was shown the rat again. He watched the rat but did not reach out for it. The rat was placed nearer; Albert, very gingerly, began to reach out for it. But when the rat nosed his hand, the hand was withdrawn. He tentatively put out a finger towards the animal but then took it away. Then, the child began to play with blocks quite normally. Both these presentations of the white rat had occurred in silence. Watson now showed Albert the rat three times at the same time as the loud sound was made. Each time, Albert fell over and turned away from the rat, though he did not cry. Then he was shown the rat in silence. The child 'puckered face, whimpered and withdrew body sharply to the left.' On the next three occasions the rat and noise were combined. The first time Albert whimpered; the second time he 'started violently and cried'. When the rat was shown to the child just by itself, 'the instant the rat was shown the baby began to cry. Almost instantly he turned sharply to the left, fell over, raised himself on all fours and began to crawl away so rapidly that he was caught with difficulty before he reached the edge of the mattress.' Watson's graphic description could come out of Brave New World. Little Albert had duly been conditioned to fear a thing he had started out by being curious about.

Watson claimed that this demonstration yielded 'an explanatory principle' of how our emotions originated. He went on, five days later, to see how effective the conditioning was. The child was placed in the room with blocks and played quite normally. This was an important methodological point for it showed that his fear of the rat was not a general fear of the experimental situation. Then the white rat was brought out. Little Albert 'whimpered immediately, withdrew his right hand and turned head and trunk away.' The blocks were offered to the child and he played quite happily with them. After a few minutes, the rat was brought into the room again. Albert leaned 'as far away from the rat as possible, then fell over, getting upon all fours and scurrying away as rapidly as possible.' The conditioned response had survived a five-day break.

The behaviourist then tested the child's reactions to a rabbit, a dog, a fur coat and cotton wool. The rabbit, not that unlike a giant rat after all, made Albert whimper, cry and crawl away. It was convincing evidence that fear of the rat had become also fear of the rabbit. The dog also made Albert cry as he did with the fur coat when it was placed close to him. After a while, the little boy did not seem to be afraid of the cotton wool though it is clear that he was in something of a volatile state for he cried when Watson gave him a Santa Claus mask. Before, Albert had always enjoyed handling the mask.

This study demonstrated, Watson argued, that our feelings are the product of conditioning. 'Our emotional life grows and develops like other sets of habits,' he would write later. Little Albert had been trained to fear a perfectly innocuous white rat and, as a result, was also

143

terrified of a rabbit and nervous of a dog and a fur coat. Now, one only had to play on these fears to make the child afraid of any other stimuli.

Watson had hoped to be able to retrain Little Albert into not being afraid of the white rat. He intended to do this by showing the child the rat far away in the distance while the child felt very secure and slowly building up his tolerance for seeing the rat. But Albert was adopted by a family that lived outside Baltimore and no further tests could be made. Somewhere, perhaps, there is a man of 59 whose name is Albert who maybe has a terror of white rats. Watson would pursue the question of eliminating children's fears later. The study seemed to him to prove the validity of his ideas on the origins of fear and to suggest very strongly that the kind of model of mental illness which he had put forward in his paper in 1916 was correct. Behaviour therapy, of course, proceeds just on those kinds of principles. Anxieties, irrational fears, phobias, even personality disturbances, are nothing but conditioned responses that are inappropriate. And it follows that what can be conditioned can be unconditioned, which is the task of the behaviourist therapist. Watson's contribution to this school of thinking is massive.

By the end of 1919, then, Watson was back in full action as an academic psychologist. There were few reviews of his book out yet but many young psychologists wrote to him to say they found it a major step forward. The research with children was going well. Watson had gone some way to persuading the National Research Council to add some rooms to a hospital in Washington so that children could be observed on a fairly constant basis from birth on. Only then would the descriptions of behaviour really be as accurate as Watson would like. Many of Watson's ideas and hypotheses had problems and flaws but he was revelling in his work. Since 1913 he had gone a long way not just towards establishing behaviourism as a method of psychology but towards investigating key areas of human development. He had not become entombed in the laboratory and he still argued fiercely that psychology should be practical and in touch with daily life, a point of view that later psychologists would ignore. He was feeling good.

But in the autumn of 1919 something else happened to Watson. He met a young graduate student, Rosalie Rayner, who had come from Vassar to do her master's degree in Baltimore. And, as we shall see in the next chapter, Watson's life suddenly became as much a matter of passion as of psychology.

6

1920: Divorce

Watson intended 1920 to be a busy year. *Psychology from the Standpoint of a Behaviourist* was well received. Bertrand Russell went so far as to say that Watson had made the greatest contribution to scientific psychology since Aristotle. High praise indeed. The success of the work with Little Albert meant that Watson now had to see whether children could also be cured of fears by un-conditioning them, a process which Watson had outlined already in 1916. Astute in academic politics, Watson was in the throes of pursuading the National Research Council to finance the special facilities he wanted to observe children from birth onwards. He wrote: 'I will never be satisfied until I have a laboratory in which I can bring up children from birth to three or four years of age under constant observations. By propaganda and writings I am bringing this about as rapidly as I can.' By April 1920 the National Research Council had gone some way to fulfilling the behaviourist's dream. It voted money to build some observation rooms on to the maternity ward of a Washington hospital. From here, Watson could monitor babies. There was also alcohol. Watson was curious about the effects of alcohol and other drugs on human performance. With drink now prohibited, this was a sensitive area. But Watson campaigned for the right to study the subject and in April he ran a complex and funny experiment on the effects of drinking rye whisky on dart throwing. This noble subject is a frequent study in British pubs but Watson had never had enough money to cross the Atlantic.

In 1920 the relationship between Johns Hopkins and Watson became remarkably cordial. On 12 January Watson outlined his plans for the next year in a letter to President Goodnow. The psychology department would give some new courses in practical psychology in the autumn, including one on the psychology of business efficiency. Watson believed the science should earn its keep by helping the world outside the university walls. Goodnow approved.

Through much of 1919 Watson had pleaded for a higher salary.

Academic salaries had not improved that much since 1905 and the inflation that came with the end of the war meant that they now bought much less. Watson was in debt. He was obliged to take on yet more outside work as a consultant for a life insurance company in order to make ends meet. In February Watson wrote to Goodnow to say that Angell and Harvard had both offered him very lucrative posts. Harvard had a chair for him with a salary of $9,000. He did not want to leave Johns Hopkins, for he said, almost meekly, that he was a Hopkins man, but he had to consider financial realities.

Goodnow replied that 'it would be extremely unfortunate for the University if you were to leave us to accept a call anywhere else.' After a few weeks, Goodnow wrote to Watson to say he would get a salary of $6,000. The behaviourist was delighted. He said it would concentrate his mind wonderfully. It helped make the relationship between Watson and Goodnow very cordial.

It was a sign of Watson's international reputation that he was invited to participate in a major international conference that would take place at Oxford in September of the year. Bertrand Russell would be there, as would Henri Bergson, Gilbert Murray and C. E. M. Joad. They would discuss problems of philosophy and psychology. Watson was asked to give a paper on the behaviouristic theory of thinking. It was a signal honour. But the problem was the fare. Watson wrote to Goodnow: 'Since I believe I am guilty of perpetrating behaviourism and since the British are really waking up to it, I think it would be very advisable for me to undertake the trip. Unfortunately they say nothing about paying my fare over and back and I doubt very seriously that the university would care to help me out in this matter.'

Goodnow replied that he would love to help but it was a question of the money. There was none. Watson then resorted to threatening the university with a peculiar disgrace. If Johns Hopkins was too mean, 'I am going to try and work my passage over on one of the boats either as an engineer's assistant or a carpenter's assistant or a husky freight mover!' He might turn up late for the October session if it was hard to get a passage back from England. But he did not mind working with his hands. If there was no other way to go, he would go that way. It was not only that going to Oxford would be good for him but 'it will be good for the university'. Goodnow replied that he was sorry he could not help. The two men seem to have treated the matter with fairly good humour. Watson was conscious of the hefty raise he had just received and did not press too much. He still meant to travel to Oxford though.

Goodnow was more helpful over alcohol. Watson needed Goodnow's help to get hold of rye whisky after the passing of the prohibition laws. Watson had told Goodnow that he had always believed that a moderate amount of drink was relaxing and did nothing to harm people. He meant to have subjects perform a number of tasks 'under the influence'. Watson did not add that one of the subjects would be his own thirsty self. Goodnow agreed and went through the bureaucratic manoeuvres needed to get hold of ten gallons of whisky. In April Watson had subjects drink 50 cc of rye whisky every two hours. In between gulping the precious prohibited booze they had to throw darts every three minutes. Watson wrote to Thorndike at Columbia that the alcohol did not impair their skill. Of his own ability, Watson said that 'I was shooting at an average from the bulls eye of 5 inches at 9 o'clock Sunday morning and around 4.8 fourteen hours later. One or two of the individuals became practically *drunk* but apparently the drunker they got the better they shot.' Watson wanted to have Thorndike's help in extending the work on the effects of alcohol. His letter to him is the only record that remains of the study.

But something quite drastic was to turn Watson's attention away from alcohol, child development and the trip to Oxford. In the autumn of 1919 a new graduate student came to study under Watson at the Phipps Clinic of the medical school. She was Rosalie Rayner who had just graduated from Vassar, that most élitist of American women's colleges. Rosalie came from a rich and distinguished family. Her uncle had been Senator Rayner who conducted the hearings on the sinking of the *Titanic*. He handled these tragic and epic matters so impressively that he seemed destined for ever higher office but he died before he could get himself elected to anything else. Rosalie's father, Albert, was an important Baltimore businessman. The family owned an imposing house on Eutaw Place. The house would loom large in the drama to come.

Rosalie was beautiful and lively. When she met Watson, she was just nineteen years old. She had a long oval face, blue eyes and brown hair. She was clever. She collaborated in the work on children and alcohol. She was funny, too. She fell in love with her handsome and impressive professor. It was to be a not unrequited passion.

In 1919 the tensions in the marriage between John and Mary Watson were not particularly evident to outsiders, even to their children. Polly recalls that her parents hardly ever quarrelled or, at least, that they took care to quarrel only when they were alone. Since Mary was rather nervous and frightened that Watson might leave her, it is not surprising that she suppressed many of her criticisms. Watson, for his part, had suffered enough quarrels between Pickens and Emma to know how bad they were for children. Curt Richter, a graduate student from Harvard who came to study under Watson, dined on a number of occasions in late 1919 and 1920 at the Watsons'. Both of them struck

147

him as people who would keep their rows very much to themselves and maintain the proper appearances.

But Mary Watson was becoming more and more upset by Watson's 'affairs of the heart', as Polly describes them, adding, 'which is a nice way of putting what Dad did'. Despite the fact that the couple kept their disagreements, Polly had got to hear from her mother of Watson's affair with Mrs Esselin, the glamorous redhead of Washington. So far Mary had always managed to get her husband back. And when she first suspected that Watson was being unfaithful again, she expected that this passion would pass, as previous passions had passed.

The romance between the forty-two-year old behaviourist and his young student blossomed, however. They spent most of the day together studying the children. Later, Mary Watson would say that the two of them spent all day 'together in her machine' but, alas, it has proved impossible to specify the precise mechanical contrivance that harboured the two lovers. However, the two of them left Rosalie's mysterious machine every lunchtime to eat together. They were seen in intimate *tête-à-tête* in a number of restaurants. Prim and conservative Baltimore began to talk.

Watson knew what risks he ran in having an indiscreet affair. He had seen what had happened to Baldwin. Yet Rosalie stirred something very deep in him. Partly it was her youth. He gave himself to her in a way that he had never given himself to anyone else. Within a few months he was signing himself 'your real husband' in his torrid, but amusing, love letters. Watson had always been more susceptible than one might expect. At Furman he had fallen passionately in love and been jilted; in Chicago there had been the mysterious woman of 1902 who jilted him. When he did fall in love, Watson had been impulsive and vulnerable. He had chosen to marry Mary at least partly because he wanted to be loved more than to love. Now he felt more secure in himself, more able to give of himself. And Mary had long ceased to call out anything in him. Rosalie could give him much and, not least, she could make Watson feel young.

His father, the rumbustious Pickens, had walked out on the marriage with Emma when he was in his early forties. It would be too glib to suggest that Watson was unconsciously imitating his father, but still the coincidence remains. Watson was very impulsive with Rosalie. By the start of 1920 they were often slipping away for deliciously illicit weekends in New York. A college friend of Rosalie's was kind and unconventional enough to put her apartment at the disposal of the lovers. Watson was so intoxicated with Rosalie that he actually told her when he saw her he did not even want to have a drink. She was exciting enough. In those dark days of prohibition, such a confession meant a lot!

Mary Watson probably suspected round the end of 1919 that her husband was having an affair. There were all the rumours of the couple lunching together. And Watson was away a great deal. Mary's reaction was a subtle one. She befriended Rosalie. Since Watson was one of the most distinguished professors at Johns Hopkins and since the Rayners were an important Baltimore family, the two families were on visiting terms before love flared up between Watson and Rosalie. Mary seems to have been cunning rather than outraged. She invited Rosalie, and also Rosalie's parents, to dinner on a number of occasions and these invitations were reciprocated. In late 1919 and early 1920 the Watsons dined a number of times at the imposing house on Eutaw Place.

Mary Watson did more than suspect and befriend. She started to search Watson's clothes for tell-tale clues. One day, probably in February 1920, Mary was rewarded. She found a love letter from Rosalie in Watson's pockets. It was passionate stuff and it was negligent of Watson to leave it in his clothes unless, of course, it had happened before and his wife had always loved him too much to end the marriage because of it.

Mary did not speak of the letter to Watson but she needed someone to talk to. She took her son and daughter to New York one week-end to see her brother, John Ickes. Mary was probably too proud to go and see her other brother, Harold, who had always warned her that Watson was an adventurer. John Ickes appears to have been a rather seedy unsuccessful man. He took Mary to see an attorney in Brooklyn. The attorney said that what she needed to do was to get hold of some letters which Watson had written to Rosalie.

I doubt that Mary wanted a divorce at this point. She hoped that if she got hold of the letters she would be able to persuade Watson to come back. When he had strayed before, they had remained somehow in touch. It was always clear that Watson's affairs did not really threaten the marriage. But Rosalie had a much more powerful grip on him. With letters in her hand, Mary thought she could cling on to Watson. John Ickes had more disreputable motives. If Watson had written love letters, such love letters would be worth mighty amounts of cash – either to Watson himself or to the rich Rayners who, being respectable folk, would pay a great deal not to have such letters made public.

It was after this meeting in New York that Mary Watson embarked on a new enterprise. She decided to get into Rosalie's room at the Rayner's house and search for those letters. Mary must have been very careful not to mention her suspicions about Rosalie to Watson because, if she had, he would hardly have accepted an invitation for the two of them to dine yet again at the Rayners'. After dinner Mary suggested that perhaps Watson and Rosalie might like to talk about their work at the Phipps Clinic. She had a raging headache. Could she lie down somewhere? For a few minutes. Skilfully, Mary managed to take her rest in Rosalie's room. She just needed a few minutes' quiet, she said. The moment she got in the room, she locked the door and began to search. Rosalie had not especially hidden the letters. She had no reason to suppose Mary suspected and even less reason to think that Mary would trick her way into her room. Rosalie was not thinking what would make good evidence in the divorce courts. A cool detective, Mary soon found fourteen letters. It is intriguing to imagine her reading them in Rosalie's room and coming across some of Watson's ardent phrases like the one where he said he was Rosalie's 'real husband'. But she concealed her anger and her bitterness superbly. She pocketed the letters and went back to the drawing-room. The dinner party was still in progress. Mary made no scene. She joined in the conversation with the other guests until it was time to go home with a man whom, she knew, no longer thought of himself as her real husband.

Soon after she had the letters, Mary left for New York with them. Her brother, John Ickes, made photocopies. Mary felt sure she could persuade her errant husband to come back. He would have to. There was in Mary Watson a dour and very determined streak. She had had enough of the other women. She loved John Watson and she could well understand why other women fell for him but she was confident she could win him back.

It must have depressed Mary to read the letters. The only one that was made public was declared to be tame, and that was tempestuous enough. It read:

Rosalie Mine,

I got another nice letter in the noon mail. It did my aching heart a lot of good. Tell me what happened at Ruth's party. I am so jealous. I know it isn't nice to have doubts and fears but they will grow up. That would be our hardest battle if we are married, wouldn't it? I have been an awful sinner, I know, and, in a way, so have you. We both have the power of getting what we go for and neither would take an inferior position to the other. I think this fear and the knowledge that the other one could do the same thing will be our salvation.

Watson was, obviously, head over heels in love. He was jealous; he was talking of marriage; he was acknowledging that Rosalie was his equal. Mary must have been galled by how graphically the 'awful sinner' went on to describe his jealousy. Watson continued to his Rosalie:

I just think I'll die if I don't hear from you. If I thought you were in, I'd call you dangerous as it is. Every time the phone rings I know I'll jump from my chair. My heart will be in my throat but I can listen anyway . . . do write to me that, no matter how long you stay, your heart and body will still be mine. They can't break it now can they? Only a change in one of us can do that. I know every cell I have is yours individually and collectively.

Even in his passion, Watson remained scientific. He added: 'My total reactions are positive and towards you. So, likewise, each and every heart reaction.' It is almost endearing that even when he was madly in love Watson.had to speak of 'reactions', as his theory demanded.

Watson's reactions were not just confined to his heart. He then said he had 'made enough love for one day to so young a girl' but proceeded to make yet more love! 'It makes me just mad when I come to the end of your letters. Does it to you that way? Could you kiss me tonight for a few hours without growing weary? I could kiss you for 24 hours and then find fault with the universe because the days are not longer. Let us go to the north Pole where the days and nights are six months long' and, he implied, could thus accommodate record-breaking kissing.

Watson ended the letter with a reference to one Hilda who had made the necessary arrangements for the two lovers to have an apartment to themselves. 'Everything will be lovely,' said Watson, 'and we ought to play safe. Still, play we will.'

The letter shows how lyrical and charming the behaviourist in love could be. Watson admitted all his passion, all his jealousy, all his fears. He was playful, but Rosalie had the power to hurt him in the way that no other woman had had for a long time. Watson never tolerated insecurity too well. Rejections echoed that first rejection by Pickens. In love, Watson fretted and brooded over whether Rosalie loved him.

The letter shows, too, that Watson realised how dangerous his position was. He knew they should play safe: he knew how damning it would be if someone listened to him and Rosalie on the phone. Everything in the letter suggests that, at this point, no one knew their secret. The only exception is the phrase 'They can't break it now can they?' But it seems that this was just an awareness of the pressure there would be to break their affair if anyone found out. Would the Rayners have received Watson and wife in their home if they knew what was going on? Almost certainly not. Yet John and Mary Watson dined there as a proper respectable couple at the end of March.

Reading the letters ought to have made Mary Watson despair. Her husband looked forward to being married to Rosalie. But Mary did not give up. She seems in her dour way to have tried to keep the marriage together. Back in Baltimore from the rushed trip to New York and John Ickes, Mary confronted Watson. She told him she knew everything about the affair. She told him he was running a terrible risk. He must know that Johns Hopkins would sack him. Was his 'crush' on the girl worth ruining his career for? According to Mary, Watson promised that he would have nothing more to do with Rosalie. He would not work with her, he would not see her.

If Mary Watson was telling the truth when she made this claim – and she may well not have been – Watson was really in no position to make the promise. His letters suggested that he knew quite well the hold Rosalie had over him and over every cell in his behaviouristic body. It would have been quite unrealistic of him to say he could drop her. It was not a flirtation or a fling; in Rosalie, Watson had found the love of his life. He may have dithered a little because he was not quite ready to face the consequences of that but every word of his letter to Rosalie suggests that he could not leave her.

But Mary did not just confront Watson. She did what must have been remarkably difficult for a proud woman like her to do; she went to see the Rayners. This time there was not a pleasant social dinner at Eutaw Place. Mary met with Mr and Mrs Rayner and, also, with Rosalie who was quite determined not to be left out of the proceedings. She told the Rayners of the romance. The Rayners should send their daughter away to Europe for a year, a modern version of the Grand Tour, so that the young hussy would have a chance to seduce and be seduced by plenty of other men. In her heart, Mary told them more gently, she did not blame Rosalie. Watson was very attractive. He had flattered Rosalie. Her 'crush' – this seems to have been Mary's favourite word for describing and, of course, minimising their relationship – would soon melt away. With cynical experience, Mary believed that with Watson it was out of sight, out of mind. Once Rosalie was gone, he would forget her. Whether she actually said this to the Rayners, and Rosalie, seems doubtful. It would only have egged Rosalie on to stay. Mary Watson must also have played on the respectability of the Rayners. Did they want their family to be mixed up in such a scandal? It was quite an impressive, impassioned plea she made.

Albert Rayner, Rosalie's father, agreed with Mary. A separation would be for the best. If Rosalie went to Europe for a year and, after that, she and Watson still loved each other then, perhaps, there would be no way of avoiding it. But it had all been too sudden to be all that serious.

But Albert Rayner was not the crucial character. And Rosalie simply refused to go. She had, as Watson noted, a way of getting the things she wanted and she wanted Watson as much as he wanted her. Even though Mary had not said that she had little belief in Watson's loyalty, Rosalie may have been worried that once she was in Europe her beloved would settle back with his wife who was fighting like a tigress for him. No one could force Rosalie to go. Her father went so far as to threaten to cut her off without a penny. It had no effect. Rosalie was firm. She loved Watson. She would stay in Baltimore. Mary Watson could make as many scenes as she wanted.

After this rebuff, Mary Watson tried again a number of times to get Watson to promise to drop Rosalie. She went so far as to give him back the love letters, though her brother prudently kept the photocopies in New York. Mary tried threats and she tried promises. She must have reminded Watson of how good their marriage had often been. But all this was to no avail. On 14 April John and Mary Watson separated.

It is very clear that in April Johns Hopkins were delighted with their professor of psychology. They had just voted him a large raise in salary to $6,000. If there was any public knowledge about the affair it did not reach the university. All through April, May, June, July and August, Watson was in polite correspondence with Goodnow. He kept on trying to persuade the university to give him the funds to go to Europe. He kept on planning his experiments on alcohol. As late as 20 September 1920 the university announced that Watson would teach three new courses in the session 1920–1. One of these was to be on the psychology of business efficiency. Mary Watson had not yet filed for divorce. It must have looked to Watson in the summer of 1920 as if he might manage to have his Rosalie without any gigantic fuss.

But this apparent lull between April and September 1920 is, I think, deceptive. The tale that follows relies heavily on Polly Hartley's account of what she remembers taking place.

For all the dramatic antics of Mary Watson, the children of the marriage did not know that anything critical was going on. Polly recalls that it was a tremendous shock to discover that her parents might be getting a divorce. She knew there had been trouble over other women but it had never been made to seem serious.

Throughout the summer Mary Watson kept on trying to persuade Watson to come back to her. She promised she would burn the letters and forget about the divorce if only he would come back to her. Watson was aware of the risk he was running. He asked Mary if she would go to Switzerland for two years. They would be separated and then they could get a divorce on the grounds of separation. There would be no great scandal. His position at Hopkins would remain safe. The settlement would be generous. Polly remembers that her mother, understandably, did not fancy the idea of two years in Switzerland in order to protect her husband who had betrayed her. Mary refused to go.

Moreover, Mary began to tell Watson that everyone was advising her to be really ruthless. It was a sign of how devoted she was to him that she did not apply for an 'alienation order'. Her lawyer was recommending that. Any psychologist who wrote about 24 hours of kissing and lust at the North Pole must be mad. (It is intriguing to wonder what psychiatrists would have been chosen to ascertain whether or not the great psychologist was crazy.) Mary always suggested that her fiendish advisers were urging her really to damage Watson's career.

So while Mary tried to persuade Watson to return, Watson was trying to persuade his wife to disappear discreetly in the direction of the Alps.

But there was also another reason for the lull till September. Mary's disreputable brother, John Ickes, was trying to blackmail the Rayners. He was, it seems, poor, dishonest and greedy. He saw in these fourteen letters his private pot of gold. Albert Rayner would eventually pay out vast sums of money to keep his daughter's name clean, Ickes believed. He spent much of the summer trying to persuade the rich Rayners actually to buy the letters. Then, if there were a divorce, it would be a quiet and civilised affair. There would be no scandal. Rosalie's name would be safe and, incidentally, so would Watson's career. Neither the Rayners nor Ickes cared a fig for Watson's career.

Through the summer, Watson became more and more worried. The situation with Mary made him drop his plans for going to Oxford. He could have raised the money on his new salary. Polly remembers a conversation her father had with Leslie Hohlman, a psychiatrist at the Phipps. Hohlman was a homosexual and, therefore, an odd friend for Watson who had a tremendous fear of homosexuality. Remarkably, Watson confided in Hohlman. Hohlman warned him that if the university found out it would be the end of Watson's career. Watson said, according to his daughter, that 'he was too big a cog for Hopkins to sack'. He was too important. Such arrogance was not unlike him. It was part of his defiance. Watson felt he had done nothing wrong. But he was nervous and rattled and he took refuge in bombast. Mary would not go to Switzerland. His beloved Rosalie wanted to marry and he could not do without her. Torn between love and reason as in a corny romance, Watson plumped for love. He scorned Hohlman's advice and pretended – it was a pretence he used to bolster himself – that Hopkins would not sack him.

It did not mean the end of work though. In May, June and July,

Watson was planning to extend his work on alcohol. We have seen how in April there had been the dart-throwing epic on which Rosalie had worked. Now Watson wrote to Thorndike to say that he wanted to look at the effects of alcohol on performance in mental tests. How did intelligence stand up under the influence? He asked Thorndike to supply some of the standard mental tests that he was then developing so that they could be tried out on subjects who had imbibed large quantities either of rye whisky or of absolute alcohol. On 1 June Watson was in New York – with Rosalie probably – and tried to see Thorndike so that they could discuss their plans further. Thorndike was out of town but he had by then agreed to collaborate on this extension of the work with alcohol. Thorndike wrote to Watson: 'I think your experiment is a very beautiful one indeed.' And, for Watson, its beauties were not just conceptual. It would allow him to get his hands on ten gallons of rye whisky from the 'prohibition guardians'. And that was precious stuff. It would be a complex experiment but it was worth pursuing.

In July Goodnow wrote to Watson that he wondered if this experiment was really safe. Watson pointed out what Thorndike said of it. He added that the design of this experiment would allow them also to investigate fatigue, which he intended to do. 'It is rather strange that this type of experiment has not been done before,' added Watson. If the eminent Thorndike was willing to put his name to it jointly with Watson, Goodnow need have no fear. All this would 'absolve the University from any criticism on our use of alcohol.'

But the weak Goodnow was not sure. He wrote to Watson on 16 July to warn it was 'rather a dangerous field'. He would much prefer it if no further research were done until the Academic Council of the university conferred and could apply to the dilemma 'the combined wisdom of the faculty'. Such wisdom would have to wait until September when the Council met again. The truth was that Goodnow was worried that such alcoholic experiments would tarnish the image of Johns Hopkins. But it was a friendly letter in all. It would be Goodnow's last friendly letter to the behaviourist. (Incidentally, Watson took no notice of it. Meyer approved of the project and Watson continued with it despite Goodnow's anxieties.)

Psychologists have assumed that Johns Hopkins sacked Watson because his divorce had hit the national headlines. His passion was front-page scandal all over the USA. But, in fact, by the time any news of the divorce became public, Watson had long since been dismissed by the university.

Sometime between 20 September and 28 September President Goodnow either heard of or saw some of Watson's love letters. To act as ruthlessly as he did, he must have had more evidence than mere rumour and since the letters were the only evidence, it seems reasonable to suppose that someone sent one or more of the photocopies to Goodnow. There might have been lots of gossip in Baltimore but gossip was not sufficient to sack professors of Watson's standing. Moreover, some phrases in a letter of Watson's to Goodnow seem to make it clear Goodnow had seen photocopies of the letters.

It will never be possible to be sure who, in effect, did the ultimate dirty on Watson by showing the letters to the University. Mary Watson might have been bitter enough to do it but she always said that she had done her utmost to protect her husband's career. The more likely culprits are either John Ickes or Albert Rayner who would have acted out of very different motives. Ickes was, by September, a frustrated blackmailer. His pot of gold had not materialised. He might have been frustrated and angry enough to inform Hopkins of Watson's affair. Rayner would have acted out of grander motives. He was a rich and influential man in Baltimore. He may have believed that if Watson was sacked from Hopkins and had no prospects, Rosalie (who was used to being a rich girl) would just have to give up her affair with him. Rayner had no interest in Watson's career but he did seem to feel he should save his daughter from him. Dismissed, Watson might be less attractive. If Rayner believed that, however, he did not understand his daughter well. Once she had given herself to Watson, she stuck to him.

Whoever did it, by 29 September the senior men at Johns Hopkins were in fevered discussion about what to do. If Watson expected his friends to rise to the occasion and to defend him, he would be disappointed. They all failed him, each and every one of them.

Goodnow did not feel able to act on his own. He circulated to a number of his colleagues a document that set out the sordid facts, as Goodnow saw them. I have not been able to locate this document. It is not at Johns Hopkins now and it seems likely that it was destroyed. But on 29 September Adolf Meyer, the head of the Phipps Psychiatric Clinic, wrote to Goodnow. He said the document should only be seen by the two of them, Lovejoy, the professor of education, and Willoughby, the Dean of the Medical School. It was too scandalous to travel further. Meyer was definite. Watson had disgraced himself, disgraced the university and disgraced science. Rather smugly, Meyer proclaimed: 'Without clean cut and outspoken principles in these matters we could not run a co-educational institution nor could we deserve a position of honour and responsibility before any kind of public nor even before ourselves.' This was probably just what Goodnow wanted to hear. He had been nervous of offending the public when Watson planned the alcohol experiments. Adultery was even worse than alcohol.

Probably the day after Goodnow had read Meyer's letter, he called Watson into his office. No one has left any full record of that meeting. But, I suspect, it was tempestuous. Watson felt that he had done nothing wrong. He had started an affair with a student who was well above the age of consent. He meant to divorce his wife. It was sheer hypocrisy to behave as if he were some irresponsible seducer. By the time he saw Goodnow, Watson must also have felt very angry at the way all his colleagues proposed to ditch him. Watson had never had much good to say of Goodnow but he had done a great deal for the reputation of Johns Hopkins. And there was a whole host of other men who had been Watson's colleagues for years; Meyer, Lovejoy, Willoughby, Jennings, Dunlap. When it came to this crisis they all behaved in a ruthless and conventional way. No one, certainly no one with power, spoke up for Watson. So he met with Goodnow knowing full well that he had no backing amongst all his friends.

Goodnow rehearsed all the familiar arguments. To sleep with a student was dishonourable; there would be scandal; the university had standards. We simply do not know what Watson said. He was bitterly disappointed that his friends had failed to rally round him. He did not think that what he had done was wrong. He was enough of Pickens' son to see how hypocritical Goodnow was being. The real offence was to be found out. Later Watson would ask Goodnow to tell him 'what the basis for the University's action was'. But he was too angry, too overwrought after a summer in which he failed to persuade Mary to go off to Switzerland tactfully to be calm about it. And he was also proud. If all his fine academic friends did not want to soil Johns Hopkins with his immoral presence, let it be. Goodnow was eager to settle everything at once. He demanded Watson's formal resignation. Watson had no option but to comply. The whole university backed the President. Goodnow insisted that Watson write a note there and then. So, in uncharacteristically shaky handwriting, Watson wrote out his resignation on the notepaper of the Office of the President. It was a brief note and said: 'I hereby tender my resignation as Professor of Psychology to take immediate effect.' Watson offered no explanation. As he saw it, the University owed him an explanation.

The strain of the summer had brought Watson close to breaking point. He was worried about money. He knew his career was at risk. He now was being abandoned by friends of long standing. The ruthless behaviour of Goodnow was a shock. Watson knew, in his heart, perfectly well why Johns Hopkins had sacked him but he pretended he could see no cause for the action. The whole saga left him, he wrote, 'stranded economically and to some extent emotionally'.

As soon as the interview with Goodnow was over, Watson packed his things and left Baltimore. He headed for New York. He felt he needed a change of scene.

It would be wrong to suggest that Watson left behind in Baltimore any kind of seething controversy. According to Curt Richter, people did talk about the scandal after Watson had gone but no one questioned what Goodnow had done. The rights and wrongs of it appeared clear. Dunlap succeeded Watson as head of the department of psychology. Adolf Meyer put the running of the laboratory Watson had built at the Phipps in the hands of Curt Richter. After Watson gathered up all his papers from Hopkins and the Phipps, he does not seem ever to have set foot in either place again, though he was often in Baltimore in the 1920s. I believe that Watson knew very well that Meyer had been one of the key figures who supported Goodnow. Yet Watson had read much of his 1919 book in seminars which Meyer had chaired. He dedicated the book to him. He looked upon him as a close colleague, a friend who should have been loyal to him. It hurt deeply that Meyer should have been so ruthless in calling for Watson's resignation. Watson met Richter again a number of times but he would never come to see him at the Phipps or talk about that institution.

Watson should not have been surprised by the official reaction. Academics in America in 1920 were far more restricted than they are now. Watson was always clearing his more contentious research projects with the President of Johns Hopkins. J. McKeen Cattell, the distinguished psychologist, had been dismissed from Columbia for his pacifist views and had written to Goodnow twice in one week to suggest they make him professor of psychology at Johns Hopkins. Cattell's plea came four years too soon. On 1 October 1920 Goodnow would have loved to get Cattell's letter: in 1916 it was embarrassing coming from a man as eminent as Cattell. And sex had destroyed even more academic careers than politics. Watson had seen two acquaintances, Baldwin and William Thomas, get dismissed for being caught, in effect, with their pants down. The amusing economist Thorsten Veblen had the same treatment from Stanford. (It is a good thing that after he was forty Freud gave up sex in the bed for sex in the head for if he had ever had an affair, it would have proved the critics' point that psychoanalysis was merely an excuse for pornographic behaviour.)

There was no press comment on what Johns Hopkins had done. Even when the divorce became public, no one asked whether universities had the right to control their professors' lives in so total a way. Neither the *New York Times* nor *New Republic* nor any more radical paper seems to have whipped up an editorial on the subject. It was just not an issue.

The simple fact was that adultery was not for academics. It might have been 'perversely unfortunate', as Titchener said, that the Baldwin affair should have happened at Johns Hopkins not so long ago (back in 1908). Otherwise Watson might have been dealt with more gently, he suggested. But this again seems to me to be Titchener's optimism. Everyone assumed that Watson had made himself too immoral to teach.

The most charitable interpretation that can be put on the actions of Watson's colleagues is that they felt there were more important freedoms to defend. Some American academics wanted more political and critical freedom. But none of the Johns Hopkins faculty were fighting for those freedoms in the way that Cattell had. They were creatures of their particular little patch of time. They were shocked. They knew Baltimore would be shocked. Watson had to go. There was no question about it.

When Watson got off the train in New York he had no money, no job and no prospects. His only friend was the sociologist William Thomas who had good cause to be sympathetic. Chicago had dismissed Thomas for transporting a woman across state lines for immoral purposes. Watson had done nothing so illegal or so geographic. Watson lived in Thomas's flat and borrowed Thomas's money. He poured all his woes out to Thomas. He paced up and down the apartment, unable to stop thinking about the whole affair. He was bitter and he was frightened. 'I was a product of schools and colleges,' Watson wrote, 'I knew nothing of life outside the walls of a university.' Confused, angry and depressed, Watson paced, brooded and wondered what to do.

It would have been a good moment for some of his eminent friends to offer help. It was his crisis. He had friends in most of the important positions in American psychology. He was waiting for them to come to his rescue. After all, Angell, who had been trying so assiduously to lure him away from Johns Hopkins with offers of $9,000, might now come up with something. There was Yerkes who now not only was professor at Yale but who also had much influence on the National Research Council – which, interestingly, did not ask for Watson's resignation. Surely, someone must come up with something. There is no evidence that Watson wanted to leave psychology. As he wrote: 'At this time, my infant work was in full swing as well as extensive work on learning – learning and performance under hypnosis, alcohol and drugs. All this work came abruptly to a close with my divorce in 1920.' If Watson could have found a way of carrying on he would have done so. But no university offered him a post. Yerkes does not seem to have written to his old friend though he knew quite well what was going on. Titchener had written to Yerkes. And though Titchener said he felt sorry for Watson, he accepted that 'he will have to disappear for 5 to 10 years, I am afraid, if he ever wants to return to psychology indeed'. Titchener blamed Meyer for much of what had happened: 'What makes me indignant is that Meyer and the Clinic in general couldn't have used their arts to keep W [Watson] straight.' Titchener was a sexual innocent if he believed any psychiatric arts would have kept Watson and Rosalie from seducing each other. Titchener added that as Watson was intrinsically 'a very decent and eminently likeable person', a little 'decent advice' would 'have prevented the family tragedy'. But, for all his sympathy, Titchener saw no way that Watson could continue in psychology.

As Watson paced up and down in Thomas's apartment, he began to realise quite bitterly that he would have to find a different way of earning a living. He once said that this came to him after three or four of the worst days he had ever lived through. He now faced the embarrassing problem of explaining why he, who had been the youngest person ever to make *Who's Who in America*, was now on his uppers looking for work. Watson wrote to Goodnow that he had been asked 'what I was forced to resign for' as he tried to make 'business connexions'. Watson added: 'When I have attempted to give the University's basis for actions, I find myself at a loss and it is not due to any inability on my part to face my own actions.' In fact, Watson wanted Goodnow to justify his injustice, as Watson saw it. 'I don't want it softened in any way.' If old friends like Lovejoy and Willoughby felt he should be sacked, then, 'I could have no wish to go on if my friends feel that way.' He was a Southern gentleman, sensitive to such issues of honour. He assured Goodnow that he did not want to re-open the question but he just wanted to know the formal reasons for the university's action. Of course, Watson was again pretending.

Goodnow replied stiffly to Watson. It must have been quite obvious to him that the university could not have a professor who had done what Watson had done. Goodnow was quite willing to write to anyone Watson wished explaining both Watson's intellectual reputation and, also, the nature of the scandal which had forced the university to ask him to resign. Watson had written his letter to Goodnow while he was still pacing up and down Thomas's apartment. The curt reply he got stiffened his resolve. He must have come slowly to see in those first days in New York that none of his powerful friends were going to have the courage to offer him a position in psychology. He now knew finally that he must resign himself to a different kind of life.

Thomas could see that Watson desperately needed something to do. He had to earn his living but, also, he had to be active. To brood over what had happened at Johns Hopkins would only depress Watson more. Watson knew that himself. He threw himself into the business of getting a new job. Thomas, who knew New York quite well, introduced Watson to a number of contacts. Two of Thomas's friends were Miss Alice Boughton and Miss Mildred Bennett. They were the personnel department of J. Walter Thompson which was then a growing advertising agency that employed just under 300 people. Miss Bennett liked Watson. She introduced him to Stanley Resor who was President of the company.

If Watson had been able to laugh at that point, he must have done so. Resor was a man who had graduated from Yale with no great distinction in 1901. He had sold stoves for his father and had gone on to run a twelve-man office in Cincinnati. In 1916 he had clubbed together with some friends from Yale to buy out the original J. Walter Thompson who had made the agency a small success. Now John B. Watson, who was recognised as being one of the greatest psychologists in the world, who was in the same intellectual league as Freud and Russell and Bergson, was asking Resor for a job. And Resor gave Watson only a temporary job. And what a job!

Resor had to address the annual convention of the Boot Sellers League of America. In order to have the most impressive paper at the convention, he wanted some quick research to be done on the boot market. John B. Watson was given the job of 'studying the rubber boot market on each side of the Mississippi River from Cairo to New Orleans'.

It is a measure of Watson that he took to this job without feeling humiliated. He set out to learn it. He did not feel bitter that he had come to this. He always believed in being adaptable, in coping with what he called 'life's little difficulties'. Most psychologists would have felt this little difficulty as a crushing blow. And, in many ways, it was crushing. Watson wanted to pursue his work on children; he enjoyed his status as a leading professor. But one had to deal with life and, for him, the best way of doing so was to plunge whole-heartedly into it adversity and all. He threw himself into the study of the rubber boot market on the Mississippi. To be immersed even in that was some relief.

It was hard for Watson to adjust. He had long been cocooned in universities. It was a long time since he had had to fend for himself in the way that he now had to. For a 'university man' it was, after all, a little humiliating to stop people to ask them about their boots. Watson wrote: 'I was green and shy but soon learned to pull doorbells and stop wagons in order to ask what brand of rubber boot was worn by the family.' Try to imagine Freud doing that. Or Jung. The mind boggles at such intellectual *lèse majesté*. But Watson coped. There was something irrepressible in him at his best. And this crisis called out much of the best in him.

It was while Watson was quizzing southerners about their boots that the divorce finally made the headlines. The *Baltimore Sun* reported the hearing on 25 November. The 'other' woman was referred to just as R. One of Watson's letters was read to the court and it was said that others were even 'more loving'. Mary agreed to spare Watson the embarrass-ment of having these yet more loving letters read and extracted punitive terms in return. Watson would pay her $4,500 in alimony. She would get their holiday house in Canada whose value was reckoned to be $10,000. Watson would also have to pay $1,200 per year for Polly until she was either eighteen or married. John, the other child, would also get $1,200 per year, in his case until he was twenty-six so that he could finish his studies. Mary also got the $10,000 insurance policy and all their furniture. It left Watson with nothing but debts. All these financial worries weighed on him too.

Though he was short of money, Watson agreed to such a punitive settlement because he believed it would buy silence. Mary Watson always said piously that she had not wanted to harm her husband's career with all that publicity. The sharp fact is that he bought that silence. He wanted to avoid publicity because he hoped to get back into psychology and every sensational headline made that more unlikely. And Watson did not want Rosalie's name dragged into it. So he agreed to the stiff terms set by Mary and her lawyer. When the papers started to carry the news on 25 November Watson was in the South investigat-ing boots.

The divorce hearing took place on 24 November in Baltimore. It was a formality. Mary produced the damning, though delightful, letters. An insurance broker called Arthur Magruder, who described himself as 'a good sport', gave evidence which suggested John and Rosalie had slept together though 'he hated like thunder having to tell'. The *Baltimore Sun* reported the case prominently on the front page. The other woman was not named. The press did not find out who Rosalie was till the night of the 27th.

Polly Hartley, Watson's daughter, is sure that the man who divulged Rosalie's identity was John Ickes. Ickes had failed to make any money out of the whole affair. With the case being heard, it was his last chance. He could not sell any paper the right to reproduce the letters since the letters did not belong to him. But he did the next best thing. He alerted the press and he offered to tell them the identity of Watson's mistress. On the evening of 27 November the *Baltimore Sun* sent a reporter round to the Rayner residence. He requested an interview with Rosalie. He was, the *Sun* said, 'emphatically denied'. Albert

Rayner had told the maid to keep all the press away and he said he was 'indignant' that the reporter tried to see his daughter. But the reporter returned the next day and tried, again, to talk to Rosalie. This time, the eager newshound was admitted into Mr Rayner's study. Rayner had finished his dinner and went to telephone. He held an extended conversation which the reporter did not eavesdrop on adequately and returned to say that he still had nothing to say.

But if the Rayners had any inhibitions, Mary Watson did not. As soon as the Rayners had been mentioned in public print, she granted an interview to a reporter from the *New York Herald*. He found her in quite good spirits, smiling bravely and sad. She was sad there had been all the publicity. She, still a good wife, wanted to protect her husband's name, to 'shield him'. As for Rosalie, she did have 'Jewish features' but in her magnanimity, Mary had also wanted to shield Rosalie because 'my resentment is tempered with pity. She is young and I was certain did not begin to realise the position she had placed herself in.' But now that the truth was out, Mary Watson was quite willing to spell out how foolishly infatuated John had been and how despite that, she had tried to keep the marriage together. Of course, the children had suffered. But men were so selfish. In their obsessive lust, did they care if their children suffered? Mary Watson recounted how she had offered Watson a number of times the chance to make it all up and how she had suggested Rosalie should go away, for with Watson it was 'out of sight, out of mind'. But all that was over. In her hard way, Mary added there was no chance of a reconciliation. But she did not hate Watson. She was too fine a person for that. Incidentally, the divorce did not distress Mary too long. Within eighteen months she remarried and lived to the ripe old age of eighty-eight. Her second husband was an insurance man.

Watson returned to New York round 15 December. He discovered he was notorious. His picture was in all the papers. He was making headlines all over America. He wrote to Goodnow and apologised for all the publicity. It was to be his last deferential letter. Watson expressed both bitterness and regret. He still felt he had been unjustly treated but he was willing to let bygones be bygones. If he could ever be of service to Johns Hopkins, Goodnow only had to write. After all the haggles over salary, Watson could not refrain from saying that Resor had offered him $10,000 'for life'. But Watson was trying to be gracious, to be the Southern gentleman who had it in him not to bear the grudge. His friends had let him down. But he would not let down his friends. He did not phrase it in that kind of condescending way but that was the feeling he expressed. I believe he hoped that Goodnow would rise to the graciousness in the letter and offer some hope of an arrangement whereby Watson could still do some research at Hopkins.

With brutal brevity Goodnow replied that he was glad Watson was now settled and that he had such an impressive salary. He wished him well. And he wished, though he did not quite say that, never to hear of Watson again.

In that letter to Goodnow, Watson had said that he was grateful to Resor because, though Resor hardly knew him, he had told him that he would stick by him through all the publicity. It did not bother Resor that his 'new man' should be making so much news. Watson could not but think how very differently he had been treated by his old friends and colleagues and by the total strangers of Madison Avenue. The letters which Watson and Goodnow exchanged on 15 December and 18 December were the last to pass between them. There was no further correspondence between Watson and Johns Hopkins. His name only crops up twice more in the university files. In the late 1920s, when Watson was writing on children and their education, the London *Sunday Express* carried a typically vitriolic attack on Watson. He besmirched Motherhood. He criticised the Holy Family. His outrages were as bad as those of R. D. Laing in later days. But the *Express* was none too accurate for the story still placed the infamous Watson at Johns Hopkins. Shocked *Express* readers wrote to Hopkins to say the man was a vile sadist, a monster who tortured children. Goodnow by then had retired and the new President of the university hastened to assure the outraged readers of London that Watson had no connection with the university. That was the last Johns Hopkins heard, officially or unofficially, of the great behaviourist.

During the whole critical autumn Watson had seen not all that much of Rosalie. But they spent Christmas together. The final decree for divorce had come through on 24 December. On 3 January Watson married, as the *New York Times* put it, 'his Rosalie'. It was a small and private ceremony. It had to be. The Rayners were furious. Watson never forgot how vicious Albert Rayner had been in threatening to cut Rosalie off. All the psychologists Watson knew wanted to forget him. Only in 1922 did he start to get into contact with any of them again. No doubt William Thomas who had helped Watson, was among the guests but that was all.

In many ways the wedding was a happy ending. In Rosalie Watson had met, loved and married the only person to whom he gave all of himself. As Polly said, she was the love of his life. While she was alive Watson never seems to have had the slightest affair. Polly adds, knowingly, that she would never have described the woman as the love of her father's life in 1920 for she had found the whole business of the divorce had been quite shattering for both her and her brother

John. But Polly's estimate seems right. Rosalie was the woman in Watson's life.

When Watson left Johns Hopkins and the academic life, he lost a great deal. I have claimed that Watson did his best work when he was tugged between his urge to defer and his urge to defy. I have charted the emotional sagas he went through from 1903 to 1913 before he could finally quash the hold that men like Angell and Titchener had on him. But once he stopped deferring to these patriarchs of psychology, Watson did not run riot. Most of his work from 1913 on was careful and considered. He was often revolutionary but he could not be totally self-indulgent. He talked and talked about his ideas with Lashley and Meyer and others. He felt he benefited by such debate. He mulled over his ideas and had to take academic constraints into account. He had to make a very powerful case, for example, to get the money for the sex research or the observation rooms in the hospital or, even, the finance for the film. If Watson had made it over to Oxford in 1920, he would have debated with what one may, with pardonable élitism, call some of the best minds in the world. He would have met Bergson, Bertrand Russell, Gilbert Murray, and Joad, a man with a far more florid reputation than Watson as a sexual desperado but who managed to stay an academic. And if the rest of the academic world as a whole provided criticism and competition, Johns Hopkins offered Watson a certain structure. There, he could not abandon all restraint. The position of being a 'university man' did something to curb the defiant streak in Watson and to make his work meticulous. But once he left Hopkins there was little to stop Watson being as defiant as he liked. Madison Avenue just could not provide the calibre of brains that Watson was used to. And, as we shall see, the majority of psychologists became so hostile to Watson that he had much reason for abandoning the caution and delicacies of 'university men'. They were so strident in denouncing Watson after 1920 that Watson, in turn, would become too strident.

But all this took time. After 1921, Watson still did much valuable psychological work. He continued to look at child development and he wrote provocatively on child care. Sexual behaviour and mental health still interested him. He wrote on them and he was to produce two more books *Behaviourism* and *The Psychological Care of the Infant and Child*. But much of the psychology he did outside advertising did not satisfy him. He felt that it was often skimpy and superficial. There was some truth in this though many of his ideas were worthwhile and became, as we shall see, remarkably influential.

In his autobiographical note, Watson said that he learned to get as excited by the upward curve of a sales graph as by the learning curve of the rat. But he was honest enough to admit that he missed the academic life. He continued until 1930 to do academic work in his spare time. It is sad that no university managed to take the greatly daring step of offering him any kind of position throughout the 1920s and 1930s. Paradoxically, because he was deprived of an academic post, Watson became very adept at popularising psychology. He wrote many articles for the better magazines like *Harpers* and he helped develop the huge market for popular psychology writings which exists in America. None of that endeared him to psychologists, of course.

Watson was a victim. But he was not blameless himself either. Advertising made him rich. He liked money and he got used to it. Even in 1925 he would have had to take a massive cut in salary to return to academic work if anyone had asked. Watson wrote to Yerkes once that he would give up all the money for the chance to complete his work on children. He wanted to be remembered and he knew that no one becomes immortal by having created a campaign for Ponds Cold Cream. Since no one made Watson an academic offer till the 1940s, it is hard to know whether he really would have given up so much money. I think he would have had that offer come in the 1920s or very early 1930s. But after 1920, Watson was never again a full-time psychologist.

If Watson suffered because he was excluded from psychology – and we shall see he spoke both of his bitterness and of his regrets – American psychology suffered too. As I have argued, Watson wanted to make psychology scientific and objective without divorcing it from real life. He seems to have been able to face complex messy data such as that which he and Lashley got in the sex research. Behaviour was all around him and it did not put him off. The psychologists who developed behaviourism after him were much more experimenters than observers. They seem to have been so eager to make psychology a science – and by that they understood an experimental science – that they were quite prepared to give up much of the data life had to offer. They made behaviourism not so much a method of doing psychology as a means of limiting what psychology was about. They almost ran amok in laboratories where behaviour could be confined in cages and mazes ironically generally far less complex than those Watson used in 1906. In this way the dreadfully complicated topic of how people live could be kept firmly under control. Watson's research often aimed at control. But he also had a great zest for life and for studying life. And he believed that people ought to be able to use psychology. He had, as we have seen, ambitious plans to study many aspects of real life. No psychologist really picked up Watson's vision.

In 1921, as Watson married his Rosalie, he was a happy man. He had had to choose between his love and his work. He had made an unexpected choice for so devoted a scientist. He had chosen love. Since Watson had started grappling with the problem of free choice back in 1897, he may have wondered if he really chose Rosalie or if, as behaviourism seemed to suggest, he had really had no choice but to choose her. Certainly very soon after they met they seemed fated for each other. And now Watson was happy. But he knew he had paid a very high price indeed for that happiness.

7

The Advertising Man

In November 1920 Watson felt completely depressed. Without money, without work and apparently without prospects, he had no idea where to turn. When William Thomas, who was putting him up, arranged for him to meet Stanley Resor of J. Walter Thompson, Watson was very grateful. The work that Resor was willing to offer, finding out who bought what brand of rubber boot down South, did not perhaps quite fit the dignity of a famous ex-professor. Academics later condemned Watson for stooping so low but, as he replied, he had no choice. He was glad to find any work.

Advertising was beginning to change in 1920 and Watson would make a very fundamental contribution to that change. While the academic establishment preened itself in its contempt for Watson and business, Resor was happy to try out the professor who was now beyond the academic pale. Watson brought a great deal to Madision Avenue. Apart from his ability and his intellectual prestige, he soon developed a real flair for advertising. He was determined not to feel ashamed and he refused to apologise for his new career. He had always respected industry as a source of American wealth. If one of 'life's little difficulties', as Watson put it, turned him into a eulogist for the products of industry, so be it. He would make the best of it. When Angell made a vitriolic attack on him, Watson replied: 'I just wonder whether any of my colleagues confronted with my situation would not have sold himself to the public.'

The next eight years would show just how great a success Watson was in advertising. The *New Yorker* in 1928 described the behaviourist as 'the chief show piece' of J. Walter Thompson and the advertising business as a whole. Watson did much to change the nature of American advertising and to make it the powerful force it is today.

The essence of Watson's contribution to advertising is that he made it much more psychological. Vance Packard in *The Hidden Persuaders* (1959) argued that advertising in the 1950s was beginning to make sinister use of psychology. Greedy Freudians were abandoning individual clients on their couches and turning to the more profitable trade of advising large advertising agencies. The 'deep motivations', as Packard put it, of the consumer were being manipulated. Psychological knowledge was being used to package products so that they would strike the consumer at some particularly vulnerable spot in the latter's Id, Ego or Super-Ego. Thus struck, the consumer would have at once to rush out and buy. Gleeful psychologists would crow over their triumph in persuading men and women that when they were buying a detergent they were really buying virginity, than which even Daz cannot wash whiter, or that when they were buying baby powder they were really buying motherhood, or that when they were buying a fast car they were really making themselves a motorised Casanova. In 1959, Packard was analysing contemporary advertising. He was not writing history. He briefly mentioned that Watson worked in advertising but this did not seem very important to his thesis. I shall argue, however, that many of the trends which Packard described in the advertising of the 1950s – and which have continued to develop – derive from Watson.

In Watson's *Psychology from the Standpoint of a Behaviourist*, one of the least attractive arguments is that society and business could make use of psychology in order to become more efficient and to control people more effectively. Watson had always believed in psychology being practical: he now had the chance to make very practical use of his psychology. And he was to make use of the chance, with some regrets, but none the less as effectively as one might expect of a man who had had from his youth the knack of 'getting things done'.

It was good luck that William Thomas was able to introduce Watson to Stanley Resor. Resor had bought a large interest in J. Walter Thompson in 1916 and had started to modernise the agency as soon as the famous J. Walter retired. J. Walter Thompson had joined the agency which was then known as Carlton & Smith in 1868. He was twenty years old and he was taken on as a book-keeper. The main business of the agency in 1868 consisted of selling space in religious publications owned by the Methodist Book Concern. It may be reckoned one of God's more mysterious moves that he helped set up the advertising business. Thompson was an energetic and brilliant salesman. He could sell space superlatively. He soon persuaded the bookish Carlton that the Methodists did not have the monopoly on messages. There were other clients in creation. Carlton realised that this was true, and that he did not like it, and he sold the agency to Thompson in 1878 for $300. Thompson talked more and more manufacturers into taking large amounts of space in general magazines like

Harpers and the quaintly named *Godey's Lady's Book*. Editors were worried that this craze for advertising might swamp their magazines. The editor of *Harpers* threatened to resign when he heard that his company had signed a contract which allowed Thompson to place 100 pages of advertising a year. *Harpers* was not 'a cheap circus magazine'. And there was indeed, something of the flavour of P. T. Barnum about Thompson and the advertisements he sold.

Today, advertising agencies like to see themselves as 'creative businesses'. There is art in it. The exquisite blend of the right copy and the right picture to produce the right image for the product is what the moguls of Madison Avenue aim at. One American told me that she thought the real American genius was for marketing and packaging. (That seems a little hard on America but that is a different story.) In many publications now, the ads have a quality sadly lacking in the contributions. J. Walter Thompson did not see the advertising agency in this light. His job was to sell space. What was put in the space was not that important. In 1886, for example, Thompson began to advertise Ponds Extract Company – a company whose stock in the world John B. Watson would mightily increase. The ads that year were crude. They proclaimed that Ponds Extract could cure everything including sore feet, diarrhoea, sunburn, toothache, dysentery and neuralgia. Only brain diseases didn't respond. No wonder it was called 'the wonder of healing'. In 1905, the wonder brew was nicknamed the 'family doctor'. If, indeed, it had been able to cure the whole catalogue of ailments it claimed to, doctors would soon have been out of work. But the actual advertisements were not the crux of the advertising business.

In order to sell more space in more magazines in more areas, J. Walter Thompson kept on opening branch offices. There were some in Detroit, Cleveland, Boston, Chicago and even London. In 1908, he decided to set up shop in Cincinnati, and to run this small outfit, he hired Stanley Resor, the man who would, in turn, hire J. B. Watson.

Resor had graduated from Yale in 1901. He had worked a few years for his father who had a stove business that was doing none too well. He then took a job with Procter and Gamble. Resor believed in organisation and saw clearly that much advertising effort was chaotic. Companies did not know who was buying their products. There was no clear idea of how many copies the magazines in America sold, let alone who bought them. Resor understood that if advertising was to become a really big business, it had to progress beyond the stage of selling space in any old publication for any old product. Resor also grasped that the actual words and pictures which praised the virtues of a product had to be a bit more subtle than the eulogies for Ponds. (Ponds were, of course, no more naive than any other company at the time.)

With this emphasis on helping companies to find out who they were selling their products to and what magazines might reach those people, Resor prospered. In 1912 he became general manager of the whole agency. In 1916 J. Walter Thompson believed that advertising had reached its ultimate peak because he had written just under $3 million in billings that year. He sold out for $500,000 and a peaceful old age. By 1917 Resor and his wife, Helen Lansdowne, had, in effect, control of the agency.

Resor was receptive to new ideas and so he was attracted to Watson. He hired him, as the *New Yorker* put it, so that 'the doctor could apply his scientific knowledge to the sale of commercial products.' Resor also had more complex motives. He was an educational snob. He wanted to turn J. Walter Thompson into the 'university of advertising'. He hired men from the best colleges, Yale, Harvard, Princeton and the like. It was his ambition to make advertising a profession with the high standards that were believed to flourish among doctors and lawyers. Resor helped found the American Association of Advertising Agencies whose charter spoke much of the purposes and ethics of advertising. Ethics were something of an obsession for Resor. He even lost business because of them for he declared dogmatically that J. Walter Thompson would never do 'any speculative work'. It would never tell a would-be client the kind of campaign he could have if he had the decent wit to hire J. Walter Thompson. That would be touting or prostitution. Resor even lost a $12 million account for Camel cigarettes because he would not do any such speculative work. Keen on education, aware that advertising was changing, Resor welcomed Watson. To have the influential and brilliant ex-professor working for him was almost a marvel.

But Resor was shrewd. He was not too enthusiastic too soon. While Watson was researching the rubber boot, Resor asked for references. Resor asked particularly if Watson had 'intellectual honesty' and 'sound judgment'. The first reference Watson gave was Philip Burnet who was president of the Continental Life Insurance Company. Burnet said that Watson had helped Continental Life. 'I have been profoundly impressed', said the insurance man, 'by the common sensical manner in which he has brought his science to bear' on problems that Continental Life faced. 'I have felt that Dr. Watson would be a very valuable man in a business organisation where he could have the chance to apply his scientific knowledge to the major problems of personnel, sales and advertising.' Behaviourism had been used in a very practical way. 'It is the best key we ever had to a working understanding of ourselves, our associates and those with whom we deal.' Watson would need time to make the change from the academic

171

life. But Burnet thought that the behaviourist would not cling much to the ivory academic towers.

Only one doubt was expressed. Watson was unsound on prohibition. Though Watson had marshalled impressive statistics to show that a drink did no harm, Burnet thought the scientist a little too strident on the point. Booze made him less then objective. But this did not worry Resor too much. There were few teetotallers on Madison Avenue. Burnet's letter pleased Resor. It showed Watson had commercial promise.

The other two references were academic. Shepherd Franz, the editor of the *Psychological Bulletin*, said that no psychologist, not even his enemies, doubted Watson's scientific integrity, scandal or no scandal. The other reference came from Titchener. It is a mark of the friendship between them that Watson turned to him rather than to someone like Yerkes. Titchener rose graciously to the occasion. He called Watson 'my friend' and spoke of his total scientific and intellectual honesty. Titchener was more reserved when it came to the question of sound judgment which mattered so greatly to Resor. He said: 'I have sometimes thought that Dr. Watson moved impetuously and I have put this down to the fact that he was a youth of quite unusual abilities who rose in his profession at quite an unaccustomed speed.' Such quick progress might well 'at times have tempted him to act a little hastily and over confidently.' Titchener knew little of the doubts and insecurities which had made Watson move so slowly between 1902 and 1913. But now Watson was 'a mature man; he has sobered down.' The matured and sobered Watson would show, said Titchener, 'poise of judgment though his temperament is aggressive and he will never judge phlegmatically.'

Watson was always deeply grateful to Titchener for consenting to write a reference and he wrote to him in 1922 that 'I know, in my heart, that I owe you more than almost all my other colleagues put together.' Watson's instinct was just.

The three references were, indeed, sound enough to make Resor hire Watson at the princely salary of $10,000 a year. But Watson was not to be an armchair expert. Resor insisted he learn the business from the bottom up. After the rubber boots, Watson would learn all about selling coffee to grocers. He spent nearly three months trudging from store to store in Pittsburgh, Cleveland and Erie trying to persuade grocers to stock more Yuban coffee because J. Walter Thompson were just starting a campaign for the brand.

Watson approached this work in good spirit. He had not been defeated by all the traumas of 1920. He felt he had an important contribution to make in business. Where most academics might feel that it was beneath their dignity to be reduced to the level of travelling salesmen, Watson was cheerful, even humble, about it. A letter that he wrote to Mildred Bennett who was head of personnel at J. Walter Thompson illustrates this nicely. After moaning about how much it cost to hire a stenographer to type out his report, Watson described what he called 'Yubanning' after the coffee he was foisting on the grocers. 'Yubanning is a strenuous job. We are up at 6.30 a.m., have a meeting at 7.45 a.m. and by 8.15 a.m. we are on the trail of the grocer.' The grocers were not, of course, told just what an important person out of *Who's Who* was pressing Yuban on them. Watson could not drive and, anyhow, this was before the era of company car. He had to walk to all the stores he visited or, sometimes, he took buses. It was 'hard work getting round them all' before the evening. By six at night he was tired. He would have a quick meal and then get on with writing a report about the day's work. On 20 January when Watson wrote this letter he was staying in Pittsburgh with a colleague called Walker. They had also started to pay 'back calls' to grocers who had failed to be persuaded the first time around of the wonders of Yuban. 'This is a thankless job and we are shown the door quite frequently.' He took it with good humour.

Watson had found that he was very 'green and shy' when researching the rubber boots down South. It was an effort to stop people and ask them what boots they bought and why. He had to steel himself to do it, at first. Now he was getting used to the knocks of a salesman's life and, typically, he saw it as an experience he could learn from. Watson added to Miss Bennett: 'Please don't think the strenuous life worries us. We are learning at a very rapid rate even if in a difficult school. What I am getting is invaluable.' And Watson would make it influential.

From Pittsburgh, Watson went a-Yubanning up to Cleveland and Erie. As ever, he worked hard and he finished his daily reports late at night. He intended to go back to Pittsburgh to see what effect the campaign for Yuban was having there.

On 15 March 1921 Resor announced publicly that Watson had joined the company. The internal bulletin that he issued to the staff showed how much of a catch he thought that Watson was. Resor said simply that Dr J. B. Watson had started to work for J. Walter Thompson. All he proposed to do to introduce Dr Watson was reproduce his not inconsiderable entry from *Who's Who*. Resor did not think he need say any more. Only, he asked, 'will not everyone in the company feel free to consult Dr Watson on any problems where he thinks Dr Watson will be of value.'

'It took me a year to find myself in the agency', Watson wrote. He had found the experience with the boots and with Yuban very useful. It was 'just what I needed to rub off the academic.' But he still felt that he had a great deal to learn. He spent the next few months in every department of the agency learning the skills of the copywriter, the researcher, and the media buyer who was responsible for buying space. He enjoyed learning. But, 'I felt one distinct need. I knew little about the great advertising god, the consumer.' So Watson arranged with Resor to spend two months in the summer as a counter clerk at Macy's, the famous New York department store. Watson worked in the groceries department. Before Macy's accepted him, he had to take a psychological test in which, he noted wryly, he did none too well. Watson had never had much faith in tests. At the counter, he was a polite, effective salesman. And it did for him what he wanted; he learnt about the consumer, the divine end to which all advertising is a means. Watson returned to J. Walter Thompson in September 1921, just when a new academic year was starting. He must have thought bitterly about the events of a year before, from time to time. But he threw himself with energy into his new career. To be absorbed by it was his only hope of being happy.

Resor did not give Watson an official position at once. Watson took on a whole variety of roles. He was consulted about various campaigns. He did a great deal of research on particular products. By 1922 he took charge of a number of accounts and acted as 'contact man'. Watson wrote a small paper on the function of this creature. The contact man had to analyse what the client really needed. He had to research the market the client could, and ought to, aim at. Having 'diagnosed' (and the comparison with the medical profession was quite deliberate sniffing after status), the contact man had to ensure that copywriters, artists and space buyers could deliver the right prescription for the product. 'Doctor' Watson would set his stamp on a number of historic campaigns. He also extended the nature of research in advertising. In a flurry of energy, he turned to various topics from the potential of radio to brand loyalties for cigarettes and how to break them to how consumers used leaflets. His scientific expertise meant that Watson was in constant demand as a speaker at conferences. His fellow persuaders wanted to know just how science could help them shift goods.

Between 1910 and 1920 advertising did change. There was some attempt to give the consumer more information about the particular product. It seemed to pay to research who bought particular products. The Audit Bureau of Circulations began to track how many copies newspapers and magazines sold. Resor's work was mainly organisational. For example, he persuaded the Scott Paper Company that it was irrational to manufacture 2,000 different brands of toilet paper. He rationalised this feverish toilet-roll activity so that the company only produced a few brands. The price of a roll fell as a result from 35 cents to 7 cents. But in such operations the idea of using psychological knowledge and research to promote products did not exist.

There were a few scattered writings on psychology and advertising before 1920. Thorndike contributed a brief piece in which he noted that advertisers made little use of current psychological work. Two books were entitled *Psychology and Advertising* but it cannot be said that they were very illuminating. One by Hetherington reported a study of how students had judged a variety of ads from newspapers. The book was lambasted because it was not introspective enough. Walter Scott, director of the School of Salesmanship at Pittsburgh, was a respected psychologist and, in his book, tried to apply the ideas of William James to advertising. Scott's book was full of references to the will. The best parts of it (which were only incorporated in the 2nd edition published in 1928) were those that reported results of a survey that examined what newspapers people read. Neither author was active in business. So when Watson went to Madison Avenue there really was no serious psychology in advertising.

Very soon Watson made his influence felt. Comparing Resor's speechs before 1920 with those he made after is enlightening. Little that Resor said before 1920 touched on psychology or the laws of human behaviour. But after 1920 he was always spouting the words 'psychology' and 'behaviour'. In April 1921 Resor told a convention that it was the job of the advertiser to 'guide human decision'. J. Walter Thompson, as a matter of empirical fact, were busily 'analysing and applying in actual practice' what psychology knew about such human decisions as buying. Grandiosely, Resor added that 'the laws that underlie all human actions are being applied to influence millions of buyers.' By 1924 Resor could be even more eloquent. He was invited over to London to address a number of British politicians and businessmen on the nature of American advertising. By this time he was mouthing the truths of behaviourism perfectly. He told his English audience that the key to advertising 'is in the better understanding and more effective use of the laws which govern human behaviour. . . . The actions of the human being *en masse* are just as subject to laws as the physical materials used in manufacturing.' Watson had, indeed, shifted the focus of American advertising. The potential buyer was a kind of machine. Provide the right stimulus and he will oblige with the right reaction, digging deep into his pocket. Resor's continuous use of phrases like 'the laws of human behaviour' reveal the extent of Watson's influence. And Resor was an important man to influence. By 1924 he was considered one of the leading men in advertising. And Watson had made a behaviourist out of him.

Watson's two months as a counter clerk at Macy's soon began to bear fruit. He soon observed that the way in which the goods were arranged on and behind the counter affected the way they sold. If an item was placed so that it was easy for a customer to pick it up, it tended to sell much better. Things that were put just by the cash registers (where a customer had to come actually to pay for his goods) also sold well. This fact appears utterly obvious to us now. Supermarkets always place sweets and books by the cashiers. As you wait to pay, you are likely to pick up a bar of chocolate that you don't want or a copy of the latest faddish paperback that you probably would never buy in a bookstore. Then, J. Walter Thompson at once made a great effort to persuade grocers to place Yuban coffee either just by the entrance to their store – where people would pick it up as they walked in – or on the counter by the cash register. In a letter to a student in 1956 Arno Johnson, who had worked at J. Walter Thompson's since the late 1920s, said that Watson had seen that *activation* was as important as *motivation* in selling. All the motivation in the world was of no ultimate use if it did not lead to a sale. And just as rats would tend to go for the nearest piece of food that was available in the wild, customers would tend to buy the nearest goods. The ethology of the supermarket was born!

The agency did not just capitalise on Watson's observation. In 1922 and 1923 he embarked on a number of research projects connected with advertising. Life, he would say a bit grandiosely, was his laboratory now. The first project was not quite into life, but rather into life insurance. Life insurance sales were not doing too well in the early 1920s. Watson conducted his own survey into why this was so on the streets of New York. The intrepid behaviourist stopped people at Grand Central Station and a few other locations. He went up to Columbia University and talked to twenty-three young businessmen who were making between $2,000 and $3,000 a year, which was then a very good salary straight out of college. He collared another eighty subjects in offices, stations and streets. He asked this motley crew whether they would ever consider becoming life insurance salesmen. Of his sample of 103, 86 said that they would never stoop so low. They felt people had a very negative attitude to life insurance salesmen largely because life insurance salesmen 'talk too long, stay too long and seek interviews too frequently'. Moreover, Watson noted, many of his interviewees said that life insurance salesmen had a whiff of death about them. They were always trying to persuade you that you might well drop dead any minute; this was macabre and not conducive to friendly conversation. Undertakers were more tactful and did not usually tout for business in advance of death.

There was also a very high turnover among insurance salesmen. Few could stand the social strains for long. As a result, 12 per cent of the agents wrote 60 per cent of the business, which indicated, Watson argued, that there was an enormous amount of waste. It was a cogent piece of research. Watson argued that there was room for a massive national campaign which would do something to combat this appalling idea people had of life insurance and its salesmen. The campaign would give the salesmen a little more status and something to talk about. You could introduce the risk of death a little more tactfully by tacking it on to the chat about the campaign. In fact what Watson was talking about was altering the image of life insurance. But he never used the word 'image', of course, because of its associations with introspection.

Watson was also intrigued to see what happened if you distributed a leaflet whose aim was to promote a product. In 1921 the Odorono Corporation had produced two cosmetic booklets. For women, they had 'The Appealing Charm of Daintiness' and for men, 'The Assurance of Perfect Grooming'. In 1922 Watson offered 25 cents to anyone who returned one of these booklets to him and answered a few simple questions. Forty per cent of the men and women to whom the booklet was sent remembered having read it and had found it of some value. About half of that number still had the book by their bedside. Three owners of the booklet went so far as to reply to Watson that it would take more than 25 cents to get them to part with it. It was a minor piece of research, of course; but it was an early attempt to check what use was made of such free booklets or coupons.

Resor, aspiring to a university of advertising, had always approved of research and Watson produced much innovative research. After life insurance and the fate of old leaflets, he turned to a problem which still concerns cigarette companies – brand loyalties. In 1922 no one had yet coined the term 'brand loyalty' though.

Watson set about the problem with much of his old ingenuity. He first tested whether smokers could identify particular brands of cigarettes which they had smoked. Twenty blindfolded subjects were made to smoke seven different brands including Camels, Tareyton and two exotically named brands, Egyptian Deities and Fatima. Before being blindfolded the subjects were all quite sure they could recognise different brands by taste alone: they turned out to be very bad at doing so. The men identified the brand they were smoking an average of 2.4 times: the women were even worse and only got the brand right 1.5 times. The only cigarette that was at all distinctive was Egyptian Deity which had a very strong flavour. Watson then made his subjects train.

For two weeks they smoked a variety of these seven brands and were told to concentrate on learning the different tastes. They were to become more sensitive to the individual flavour of each brand. Training had little effect. The subjects hardly improved and some brands, like Camels, became even less easy to recognise.

Watson then made subjects smoke through a cigarette holder. That did not help. He also – and his concern for detail recalls that of his work on the rats in 1906 – devised a screen so that subjects did not have to be blindfolded or smoke with their eyes closed. Placed between eye and mouth, the screen concealed the cigarette which the methodical Dr Watson placed on the subject's lips. Closing the eyes might somehow affect the judgment of taste. But puffing with their eyes open did not improve the extent to which subjects could tell the brand. Even when Watson just asked people to identify their favourite cigarette they did badly. Out of 36 choices of favourite brands, only 13 were correct. (Some subjects had two favourite brands.) Watson then asked people to roll their own cigarettes. Again, there was no improvement.

All this surprised Watson. He had expected smokers to be able to spot their own brand at least, because they would be conditioned to that. He said that he thought their intraorganic sensations – which, he had argued, guided rats round a maze – would equally guide a smoker to the brand which he was used to. All kinds of muscular responses ought to have been associated with the smoker's favourite brand.

As it seemed that this was not so, Watson extended the research. He persuaded seven of his subjects to smoke a different brand for a month. It caused more confusion than anything else. One person made a definite change to the strong and recognisable Egyptian Deity. The other six were undecided as to what brand was finally going to get their loyalty. Many, Watson confessed, complained bitterly 'of the experimenter's baseness in undermining their confidence in all cigarettes'. One subject said that his whole philosophy of smoking was 'completely up in the air'; even sadder was the man who said that his taste for cigarettes was 'completely ruined'.

Watson was, again, surprised. It should have been more difficult for people to give up brands that they were used to. Even if they could not recognise them, you would expect that they would miss them: at least, their intraorganic sensations deep in their muscles would miss the stimuli to which they had long become used. This experiment, of which Watson was always quite proud, pushed him to see that when people bought a product they were buying far more than the actual thing. A product was more than itself. It aroused feelings and emotions; it had an atmosphere around it. They were buying something like an idea. Watson was beginning to see that for many products, the emotions and associations that went with it were really crucial. Advertising was much less about information – which was what Resor liked to believe before 1920 – and much more a question of what we would now call images. Watson would not use the word *image* since that term for him, was linked with the old introspectionist belief in Images. It is ironic that Watson, the scourge of the image as a concept in psychology, was beginning to see that for advertising to succeed it had to create an image of a product.

Watson did not believe that you could manipulate images quite as cynically as Vance Packard argues modern advertisers do. The sensible manufacturer was sensitive to what his customers really wanted. And to this end, Watson argued, he should do decent research. Watson had a chance to make these points to the United Dressmakers of America in 1924. The American fashion houses paid proper obeisance to Paris then and when French couturiers brought out long skirts, American firms rushed to buy them. American people, however, were much more sensible in Watson's eyes. They refused to buy these clothes. Stores were piled full of unsold long, flowing Parisian clothes.

If only, bemoaned Watson, they had consulted a psychologist. A psychologist would have told them how futile it was to 'force long skirts on the American public'. But the fashion houses had bought 'apparently without a thought to the psychology of the people.' The fashion houses thought that with enough advertising they could shift these long dresses. Their mistake! 'You are beginning to find the resistance is too great,' said Watson, 'and that you had made a mistake in not consulting the desires of your public.' Watson then waxed lyrical over the beauty of the American woman and her leg. He did make it sound as if she had only one. Magnificently modern, the American woman was not 'shackled by the customs of the convent'. She saw no reason not to give men a decent sight of her good-looking legs: the virile American male enjoyed what the short skirt allowed him to see. As a virile American male, Watson added: 'We men like short skirts and wonder why we should not be allowed to gaze in admiration at something we want to see.' Long skirts were unconstitutional, for they hindered the pursuit of happiness – Watson would have loved the mini-skirt. But he had a more serious point to make. 'Sheer force of publicity' could have a great deal of impact but it would have been much better to consult the public, find out what they wanted and give that to them. It was vital to research the kind of product people wanted.

In 1924 Watson addressed a group of new men at J. Walter Thompson and gave them, as part of a course, an introduction to how the agency worked. Watson chose to illustrate many of the principles of advertising by referring to a campaign that he was planning for Johnson & Johnson's Baby Powder. It is a very modern document, well worthy of the strictures of Vance Packard.

Watson first outlined the main questions which had to be asked at the outset of any campaign. What are we selling? To whom are we selling? Where are we selling? How are we selling it? And, most crucial of all, how can we sell more of it?

The answers to the first question – what are we selling? – turn out to be largely psychological. They are selling much more than a talcum powder for infants and young children. Watson stated the main 'selling ideas' for the powder. First, it had to have *purity* – and the italics were his. The name of Johnson & Johnson helped for they manufactured many medical products which were used in the best hospitals. The copy had to build on this reputation for safety and hygiene. Second, the campaign should suggest that only a foolish and uncaring mother risked any old powder on her child. Watson might not be a Freudian but he knew how to tug at the maternal guilt strings. Next, the copy would claim that it was not only safe but advisable to apply powder before the child was twelve months old. In 1924 parents only used powder when their children were over a year old. To tell mothers that they ought to start using powder sooner would open a whole new potential market, Watson said. The behaviourist was not content to let the matter rest there. Mothers should use powder more often; children should be powdered not just once a day after they had a bath. Every time a baby was changed, he would be cleaner and more comfortable if he had some Johnson & Johnson's applied to his or her delicate bottom. To powder your child must make you feel like a loving, responsible mother. Sweet pictures of wonderfully clean, bright and happy-looking children would back up all these suggestions.

Watson would come back to psychological points later in his lecture. He now turned his attention to the potential market for the powder. A survey had been commissioned of 1,000 mothers: 83 per cent of them used some kind of powder. It was largely a middle-class and upper-class market at present. For the moment, they would concentrate on that existing market but Watson saw no reason why after 1925 they should not start to aim at the more working-class mother and, even, the coloured mother. His old fear of the dark and his black nurse and that old southern prejudice made him sound rather snide on the point of coloured mothers. Watson reckoned that there was a potential market of 40 million cans of baby powder a year.

To reach the most likely buyers, Watson planned largely to use women's magazines in 1925. There would be no newspaper advertising. Most of the advertisements would be placed in papers like

McCalls, *Cosmopolitan*, *Ladies Home Journal* and *Good Housekeeping*. Each of these retained a paediatrician who wrote a column and offered readers advice on their baby problems. Readers were obviously concerned about children.

After dealing with these points of marketing technique, Watson came back to the psychological 'selling ideas'. The copy would stress that the purpose of the powder was to better the child's health and to lessen the risk of disease. Watson told his audience that mothers wanted authoritative and practical advice – it was already the age of the expert. The copy had to be serious and informative. To add the final voice of authority, the baby powder would be endorsed by Dr Holt, who was in 1925 'a household word to every young mother'. His endorsement would help, therefore, to make every mother who did not employ it feel guilty.

Though Watson talked in terms of a 'selling idea', what he was really doing was developing an *image* for the product. It was clean, pure and hygienic. It fought disease. The mother who used it would feel that she was loving and responsible; the mother who did not use it would feel bad, that she was less of a mother, not really a good mother. All this is a far cry from the kind of thinking that dominated advertising before 1920 and it is, of course, in a completely different category from telling the public that Ponds Extract cured everything from sore feet to dysentery. Much of the image that Watson forged for Johnson & Johnson's baby powder is still there – even now.

But Watson went even further in his lecture to the young men at J. Walter Thompson. It was not enough for advertising to sell the products that were around. Advertising had to identify the need for new products, research those needs and then help companies to create the right products to fill that need. The manufacturer will then say, Watson assured his audience, 'Well, let's bring it out; what characteristics should it have?' For Watson, it is the advertising agency that has the ability to answer the question. 'In order to be able to answer fully, we have to make an investigation into various competitive products and actually try them out in use to show up their weaknesses. Then we are able to write him [the manufacturer] a general specification as to what the wished-for product should be like. He agrees to this and then engages his chemist. We go to the chemist together and talk to the chemist about the product.' The first chemist may say the task is beyond chemistry but one then tries a second chemist. 'He experiments and may actually make a discovery which makes the product we desire possible.' Once the product fits the conception that the advertising agency thinks will sell, it is time to start a campaign to launch it.

181

This lecture suggests that advertising should have a very central role in industry. Its job is not just to tell the public what is available – which was the essence of the view Resor and other advertisers held in 1916 or so – but rather to conjur up *images* to go with products and to work out what new products are needed. Watson often complained about how stale certain products became over time and of the 'morgue' of out-dated products.

Advertising is a business which does not go in much for history. The campaigns of 1920 may interest art historians but they are of little use to the moguls of Madison Avenue now. It has proved difficult to check whether anyone else was thinking along these lines before Watson came into advertising. Walter Scott was certainly not. In a *History of Advertising* published in 1928, Calkins does not point to anybody at all thinking in those terms. Calkins was curious about advertising through the centuries and his 400-page book has very little in it about the advertising of his own time. In a letter in 1959, however, a young man called Hanson who had just joined J. Walter Thompson wrote to Arno Johnson, who had worked with Watson, and thanked him for the opportunity to read Watson's files and speeches. Hanson said; 'It is amazing how much of what Watson said was necessary and ulti-mately came true.' Hanson's judgment seems to me sound: only Watson made much of it come true in the 1920s.

A year before his lecture that was such a manifesto of modern advertising practice, Watson had the chance to help create a new product. He was working on the account of Lehn & Fink who, amongst other things, made Pebeco toothpaste. Pebeco tasted revolting, apparently. People bought it because they thought it was good for their teeth. Watson made a number of colleagues at J. Walter Thompson brush their teeth with it and few of them found it a pleasant experience. Watson persuaded Lehn & Fink to hire a physiologist who would have the job of working out what was wrong with the taste of Pebeco and how it could be altered. The physiologist, with a little scientific help from Watson, solved the problem. A new Pebeco was launched.

To launch it Watson chose the then new medium of radio. He cashed in on his reputation as a scientist and made one of the first advertising broadcasts. He was introduced as a man who had been professor of psychology at Johns Hopkins, an eminent scientist who would now give a talk on the care of the teeth. The talk, it was said, was sponsored by Pebeco. The announcer then faded out and Watson himself never uttered the word Pebeco. The behaviourist gave a ten-minute lecture on teeth. To keep the glands of the mouth active and healthy and the mouth moist, said Watson, it was good to brush the teeth after every meal. (Like baby powder, toothpaste should be used more.) A toothpaste worthy of the name should polish and clean the teeth without scratching the delicate enamel. Use a paste, he recommended, that will mildly stimulate the glands because their secretions will help keep the teeth wonderfully clean.

Cunning magazine ads appeared the next day which pointed out that only Pebeco, new improved Pebeco, stimulated the glands mildly and thus helped keep the teeth clean.

Watson liked the radio; 133 listeners wrote in to ask about Pebeco. J. Walter Thompson published the talk in their bulletin as an example of how advertising could use radio. Throughout the 1920s J. Walter Thompson helped develop radio as an advertising medium. Watson became a competent broadcaster and, as we shall see, often gave radio talks on behaviourism and the care of children.

All the energy, intelligence and flair which Watson poured into advertising was soon recognised. In 1924 Resor made him a vice-president of the company. There were only three other vice-presidents. Titchener, generous as ever, wrote to congratulate Watson. No doubt the new job meant 'a fabulous salary'. But it grieved Titchener, for Watson's elevation 'will give you even less time than before to devote to what you are pleased to think is psychology.' No other psychologist seems to have congratulated Watson, not even Yerkes.

Watson told Titchener that he was happy enough in his work now. He had become used to it. He had learned 'that it can be just as thrilling to watch the growth of a sales curve of a new product as to watch the learning curve of animals or men.' But advertising did not totally satisfy him because he still continued to do some psychological work. However, Watson was determined not to feel ashamed. In 1924 he took a number of professors from Columbia round J. Walter Thompson to show them what an advertising agency did. What they saw, he wrote, was a man rushing madly from the copy department to the art department to the client in order to weld a finished product that persuaded. Again, Watson invited Titchener to come up and see the agency. When he had been an academic Watson had always believed that it was important to have links between business and universities. He was now in a position to help develop those contacts.

There is no doubt that Watson had a great flair for advertising. He said that while he hoped that advertising would one day become 'an exact science', that day was really a long way off. Often what he did was just a question of intuition, he admitted. He liked to use large spaces in newspapers and magazines, for instance, but he did not have experimental evidence to justify that. He believed that copy in newspapers had to read as if it was part of the paper. Again, there was no evidence for that. A number of campaigns that Watson ran show how acute his nose was for what would interest people.

Take testimonial advertising. The patent medicine salesmen had got a bad name for testimonial advertising. Watson, however, believed in the value of using testimonials. He said that people were interested in what other people did or used. He really had no evidence to justify this but he pulled off a spectacular coup.

One of his accounts was Ponds. So far in this chapter I have had some fun at the expense of their Extract. By 1925 they had a new product from the Extract: Ponds Cold and Vanishing Cream. Watson decided that the right way to advertise this was by getting attractive and admired women to praise it. The message would be clear. If you, drab ordinary housewife, used Ponds your complexion would glitter just as if you were in Hollywood or High Society. But Watson went better than mere film stars, for the behaviourist persuaded the Queen of Romania and the Queen of Spain to appear in advertisements. Each of these royal ladies told the public that she used Ponds because it was so wonderful. What better image could a cosmetic have than to adorn regal skin?

After the advertisements appeared – and, apparently, each Queen got $5,000 for her work – Watson faced the problems of success. Who could follow such models, he told the *American Press*. After the Queens, the only way was down. Watson found a number of other highly respected society leaders to endorse Ponds but he told the *American Press*, 'we have used so many of these prominent names that it is difficult to continue to find names of equal value.' Did Watson then approach Buckingham Palace to see if the Queen of England would follow suit? Certainly, Queen Victoria would not have been amused to find her fellow royals (even if they were foreign) demeaning themselves so.

Despite all these problems, Watson told the *American Press* that he believed testimonial advertising had another fifteen years in it, at least. In 1948, in fact, Ponds ran an identical campaign. Glamorous society women endorsed their cold cream. By then Watson had long left J. Walter Thompson. But while he was still publicising Ponds he helped them to develop two new products – a skin freshener and tissues to cleanse the skin. He was practising what he had preached – the creation of new products.

Two other campaigns that Watson master-minded are of some interest. He worked for the Pennsylvania Railroad and he used in this campaign an idea derived directly from his psychological research. He had written in 1919 that one of the few instincts babies are born with is rage if their movements are hampered. Crowds and traffic jams hamper movement. But the image that J. Walter Thompson offered of the Penn was of a comfortable railway where there was plenty of space for the traveller so that there were no crowds, no hampering of movements.

From a visual point of view, one of the most beautiful campaigns Watson devised was for Maxwell House Coffee. He decided to appeal to the snob in the consumer. The advertisements all pictured splendid historical scenes. At high society balls in the nineteenth century what was it that the butler brought round on a silver tray? Why, Maxwell House. In the best southern mansions, the belle of the ball always asked for Maxwell House. The elegant advertisements may have in them something of Watson's fantasies of what it would have been like to grow up rich in the South in the 1880s. Even O. Henry was dragged in. He was quoted as having said that the original Maxwell House inn served food that was 'worth travelling a 1000 miles for'. Even the Michelin Guide doesn't recommend such extensive detours but O. Henry was clearly what P. G. Wodehouse called a discriminating trencherman. Another advertisement showed coffee being served to courageous cavalrymen.

As the *New Yorker* wryly observed in 1928, 'he has conditioned housewives and commuters into all sorts of prejudices about coffee.' It was not a drink that the advertisements were selling, it was a dream. The Maxwell House campaign suggested that if you only tasted that miraculous brew your living-room would be transformed into a palace where the rich, famous and beautiful dallied. The men were all dashing officers, the women all stunning. Drink Maxwell House and project yourself into a world of superb elegance and gorgeous glamour. Sip Maxwell House, slip into the dream.

Watson directed advertising more and more towards what we now call *the image* of products. He became enormously successful and wealthy. The *New Yorker* described him as the 'chief show piece of J. Walter Thompson'. In 1928 Watson was being paid over $50,000 a year by the agency, and by 1930 his salary was close to $70,000 a year. In the late 1920s such sums were quite fabulous. And the agency housed Watson in style. The *New Yorker* man who wrote the profile on Watson found him thus: 'after a journey past a row of Spanish grill cages inhabited by high-placed executives and high-priced copywriters finds the Doctor sitting – in quite a private room – at a desk which cost the agency more than half what Johns Hopkins paid him as a professor's salary.' Also lavish was the ornate door of Watson's room.

With money came social success. Rosalie liked entertaining and parties. Now that they had money, they did a lot of that. But very few of the people who were invited or who came were intellectuals. Watson tried very hard really to befriend some of his advertising colleagues. But he made only one lasting friendship, with James Young, another vice-president at J.W.T. Watson worked perfectly well with Resor but the two men were never close. Watson had found many of the great psychologists of his era a little dull. Madison Avenue was not the place for him to find like, or equal, minds. He knew it too. And he was not such a saint that he did not at times resent his intellectual exile. In 1928 Watson joined the Mid York Club which was a very snobbish club for the rich in Manhattan. It was no place for a 'university man'. But that had become his scene.

When Watson had been sacked from Johns Hopkins he soon behaved in a way that, I must confess, I find very appealing. He did not stand on his dignity. He did what he had to do in order to survive. He did it as cheerfully as he could and he did it well. There was no pretentiousness about it. The American dream depended on people being able to adapt to and make the best of circumstances. Watson had done just that. Now he was in the best of financial circumstances. He was getting a lot of attention in the press. But neither money nor adulation spurred him as much as crisis had done. He missed the company of really good minds. It was too easy. And after 1928 Watson very gradually became too confident, too cocksure and too conservative. He would, as we shall see, eventually realise that.

It must also be said that Watson came to advertising at the right time. Between 1925 and 1928 advertising was the fastest growing business in the whole of the USA. Advertising billings rose by 498 per cent in that period. There were enormous amounts of money available. There was an enormous need for new skills to promote an endless stream of new products and Watson capitalised on this expertly. His daily concern with what the public would and could be made to buy turned Watson's attention to the psychology of the consumer.

Watson developed what one might call a rudimentary psychology of the consumer and of the salesman. He never published much material on either topic but after 1925 he delivered a number of speeches on both subjects. His analysis of what the consumer wanted and how to influence him or her was powerful both in theory and in practice. And Watson practised it aplenty. For he directed the advertising of Odorono, one of the first deodorants, Ed Pinaud's Eau de Quinine, Baker's Coconut, Lux and Unquentine as well as Maxwell House, Ponds, and the Penn Railroad. He had enough to experiment on. As well as 'dissecting the consumer', Watson also had much to say on the psychology of selling. It could be argued that Watson created the ethos of what selling was about which destroyed Willie Lomax in *Death of a*

Salesman, Arthur Miller's play.

Let us, first, dissect the consumer according to the behaviourist. To dissect him, argues Watson, you must first get to know his habits and customs. Life is your laboratory here. Watson added:

> By laboratory, I do not mean the lab of the colleges. Your lab may be in crowded city quarters, pulling doorbells, wandering over the country talking to consumers, finding out what they do, what papers and magazines they read. It may be standing in the street corners watching what people wear and how they wear it or in the great stores, markets or restaurants. No matter what it is, like the good naturalist you are, you must never lose sight of your experimental animal – the consumer.

As ever, Watson was preaching the value of observation in real life.

But now, of course, observation was not enough: Watson was out to modify the habits and customs of the consumer. To do so, the advertiser had to keep abreast of any changes in the habits of the consumer. 'The morgue of outlived products is huge,' said Watson, because no one understood how, and how quickly, the tastes and needs of the consumer change. Obsolescence was only just round the corner of his mind.

All this knowledge had, of course, only one purpose. The advertiser wants to get sales. 'We want the man to reach in his pocket and go down and purchase. This is the *reaction*' (my italics). Watson was still not prepared to see that what the advertiser wanted to do was to get the consumer to act and to act by buying. It remained a reaction for Watson. He added: 'What we are struggling with is the finding of the stimulus which will produce that reaction.'

Science was in a position to help with this but only, Watson said, to some extent. For example, Watson drew on some early research on language use to show that almost everyone had the same basic vocabulary of about 500 words. Those who had finished high school tended to have a vocabulary of about 2,000 words. 'The most cultivated', added Watson, 'know something between 10,000 and 15,000 words', while he added there was always the person like 'George Bernard Shaw who claims to use and understand 400,000 words'. To reach the consumer, messages had to be put in such a way as to make him understand precisely. He should not be stretched or confused by words whose meaning he did not know exactly. (Products whose only market was Shaw could be handled differently.)

To be comprehensible was basic. The far from elementary Dr Watson perceived that the way to make the consumer act, or react, was to appeal to his emotions. People did not buy things because they were the best buy. It was not a question of reason and advertisers, he warned, should not let the 'thinking processes' of the consumers 'buffalo you'. The rules of how to manipulate the emotions of the consumer stemmed from Watson's own psychological thinking which, as we shall see, had become more crude than it was in 1919. There were only three human instincts – rage, which was caused by having one's movements hampered; fear, which was caused by loss of support; love, which was caused by stroking of the skin, and, especially, of the sex organs. Every other emotional reaction had been conditioned from these. It was the aim of advertising to get consumers to buy by playing on their fear, rage and love.

'Take rage,' Watson said. 'Hampering of movement is the fundamental stimulus. Show individuals herded or being crowded into cars as in our own subways in New York, show people confined in close position or tied to the stake or tied down with water dripping on them and you are touching fundamental situations which call out rage.' If an advertisement for railways or cars or holidays advertises that product as a way of avoiding being hemmed in it will do well.

Another way to get at the consumer was to make him afraid. Fear loss of support was the original fear, Watson argued. But from that people were taught to be afraid of many other things. Well before Watson arrived, J. Walter Thompson had had the business of the Scott Paper Company which made toilet paper. In 1931 Watson was involved with a campaign whose final copy is a masterpiece of arousing fear. We are in an operating theatre. Surgeons peer at the patient. The headline reads: 'And the trouble began with harsh toilet tissue.' The ad goes on to say that 'surgical treatment for rectal trouble is an everyday occurrence in hundreds of hospitals.' If only the poor patient had had the sense to use Scots instead of some pebble-dashed toilet paper, he would never have been in this mess. In a hypochondriac culture, it appealed.

The other basic emotion was love. Watson argued that this was due, initially, to stroking of the skin and sex organs. It generalised to mothers and sweethearts. The convincing advertisement had to conjure up these powerful females, 'arouse the love' which was associated with them, and suggest that by buying that product you would be loved or get loved more.

If these three instincts of fear, love and rage were basic, so were three human needs. Human beings needed food, shelter and sex. It is a mark of Watson that while most psychologists put sex a little below food and shelter in the hierarchy of needs, Watson saw it as being a priority of existence. Good copy had to harp on fear, love and rage and be linked with food, shelter and sex. 'Can't the position be taken that every piece of good copy must be some kind of combination of these factors.' It was because he saw advertising in such terms that Watson liked to make copy feel like news. Any news tended to provoke fear and anxiety. In the days of the radio and telephone, he felt that this was still true of some people. 'We now react to all news, good or bad, in an emotional way.' Many newspapers thrive on arousing our fear, lust or disgust.

Watson did not make a fetish out of his formulae. But he did repeat that to get the consumer to react, and buy, it was only necessary to arouse his emotions. To do that, there were those six elements you could combine in, he smiled, a total of 720 ways. 'Don't let us push mathematics too far,' he added. But the position he took was clear. Advertising worked not so much by giving information as by arousing emotions.

When it came to selling, Watson also developed ideas that influenced America very deeply. He often started by telling salesmen that they tried too hard to sell. They did not know themselves well enough. A typical analysis was one Watson gave a conference in April 1934:

> You should watch yourself like a Cadillac or a Ford. . . . It has always been a curious thing to me that people don't know more about themselves. If I started asking you searching questions about yourself now you would find yourself pretty dumb. You have never looked at yourself in this critical performance way. Then, too, there are many painful things about yourself that you do not want to face and that you never have put into words. We know less about ourselves than we know about almost any other thing in the world.

This is stirring stuff and, pushed in one direction, it might have led Watson to start a kind of encounter movement in which the accent would have been entirely on externals and performance. (In place of *insight*, that current cliché, maybe Watson would have given us *ex-sight*, the skill to see yourself from the perspective of the other.) But that was not what Watson was selling to the salesmen. His point was that a salesman should first of all get to know his own strengths and weaknesses well. 'When you are able to understand, predict and control your own behaviour, you will be in a good position to start understanding and controlling the fellow you do business with.'

One of the main problems that salesmen faced was that they were actually more afraid than they dared to admit. They lugged around all kinds of inhibitions from their past. Watson had seen some salesmen who were terrorised by customers with loud voices; the loud voices reminded the salesmen of their severe fathers and, then, all they could do was quail, which sold few items. Watson urged salesmen to observe their 'difficult dealers'. By making a study of the difficult dealer, 'an inventory of his emotional liabilities and assets, you get to the point where the man is not a monster to you. You understand him. You can flash out some phrase of your own organisation which will bring out some kind of flash in his,' said Watson. Flash out and overcome your fears! Watson had learned from being green and shy at the end of 1920. Once the difficult dealers were overcome the rest would be much easier. Salesmen would understand that 'the man you have to sell to is cut out of the same piece of cheese you are with the same kinds of holes in him as you.'

So eager and anxious were they that many salesmen tried to sell in far too brash a way. They bored their would-be customers by going on and on about the qualities of their product. It was much better to be subtle, to get yourself in conversation, to become, in that phrase out of *Death of a Salesman*, 'well-liked'. Watson spread the idea that you sold by being well-liked. He said, 'this ability to get along with people, to sell yourself, is probably the most important single asset that any salesman or business executive can have'. If a salesman can establish a relationship with a client, if he can make himself liked, then a sale will follow. You have to be well-liked; your goods don't matter nearly as much. 'You are primarily selling yourself to these fellows and anything else you may be selling, any product you may be selling is simply secondary and if you can sell yourself, you will have no trouble in selling them 12 dozen.'

The hearty American salesman who sees to it that he is 'well-liked', who takes all those courses that are supposed to help him strike up instant relationships seems to me to have imbibed much of Watson's teaching. It was a philosophy of selling which *Death of a Salesman* showed to be a cruel myth in 1960. However 'well-liked' Willie Lomax was, nobody cared once he was out of a job. No one bought his goods. He was sacked. His world in which he was well-liked crumbled about him. He could have had a few harsh words to say to John B. Watson who, as he spoke to many salesmen's meetings from 1924 on, continued to argue that you had to sell yourself to sell your product. Watson's influence probably produced more salesmen who were superficially cheery than who were really self-aware.

His business career was not confined just to advertising and its problems. As a psychologist, Watson felt it was his duty to cast a critical eye on certain industrial problems. Before he was sacked by Johns Hopkins Watson already had that in mind. With a number of psychologists including Thorndike and Titchener, he had founded the Psychological Corporation. The aim of the Corporation was to make psychological skills available to industry. The Corporation planned to develop tests for various jobs. Watson never became that involved with the affairs of the Corporation, largely because the psychologists who ran it distrusted him. It did not matter much. Watson could now use other platforms to propose his ideas. In 1927, he delivered three lectures on personnel to the convention of the National Advertisers of America. He was a big draw. And he was concerned to debunk a few myths.

The myths Watson was after were those to do with how to choose staff – one of the perennial problems of industry. New York in the 1920s was a city which worshipped experts. Since 1880 science had produced so many marvels, from electric lights to telephones to cars to airplanes, that it seemed able to solve any problems. People had extraordinary faith in the promised potential of science to solve any problems. When Edison announced in 1920 that he was working on a new telephone that would enable him to dial the dead and make trunk calls to ghosts, few scoffed. Such faith generated a boom in experts. Agencies grew up that offered industry scientific accuracy in choosing staff. Watson was particularly acid in 1927 at the expense of these 'head hunters, skin and hair searchers and bump measurers and handwriting students'. 'There is not one grain of truth in their claims,' he said. These 'fakers' wasted time and money. They made business feel that selection and promotion 'ought to be done by some kind of prestidigitation or even by the use of miraculous methods.' The worst effect was often on individuals. 'I cannot tell you how many times I have had individuals come to me,' Watson said, 'who were seriously disturbed about their vocations. They were doing well in their work but some characterologist had informed them that their future lay in grand opera, in diplomatic work', in anything but what they were doing. He often had a hard time trying to talk them out of dropping their careers for a 'roseate future' in some new field. It caused much suffering. Watson added that he had issued a challenge to one company in this selection game. They would take twelve photographs. (Many of the companies claimed to be able to select good executives by the shape of their faces alone thanks to new scientific principles!) Six photographs would be of successful men in the prime of their professions: six would be of 'jailbirds', washed, shaved and beautified and dressed in clothes as good as those of the other six. All characterologists would have to do was to pick out which were convicts and which were sound men. Watson grinned as he said that his challenge had been ducked.

Watson argued against too much faith in any kind of tests. Intelligence tests only tested 'verbal organisation', a familiar critique now. Few skills were so specific that you could construct tests which would predict how well individuals would do. Many people failed in business because of their emotional make-up. Past educational and work records offered clues but there was no 'well developed study of the personality which enabled one to make scientific predictions about particular individuals. Industry has no ready made tool the exclusive use of which will enable it to select and promote its personnel with any degree of surety.' The best way of seeing how a person coped with a job was to observe him on the spot, under pressure, having to make decisions. Then, one could judge if his emotional make-up would withstand the pressures or if it would crack. Instead of relying on utter quacks and inadequate tests, Watson wanted to see particular industries develop special training schools. These could be run jointly by experienced industrial men and psychologists who did not disdain business.

Watson's sharp criticism of much personnel selection was well received. By 1927 he had already great public status as an expert on all things psychological. 'The world has gone psychology mad,' he said. His list of speaking engagements was always very full. He could be witty, provocative and practical. What more could one ask of a psychologist speaking about business?

Watson's success in advertising affected his life in many ways. He became rich enough to fulfil his childhood dream of living on a farm. But instead of being down South, it was a farm in Westport, Connecticut. Watson and Rosalie bought a magnificent 40-acre house and farm there in 1930 so that Watson commuted every day by train to New York. Money came to matter more to Watson and he started to invest on the Stock Exchange. He was clever and cautious; he was not too much affected by the great Wall Street crash of 1929. He invested mainly in blue chip stocks. But if the money was nice, the company was less stimulating. Most of the advertising men did not have his kind of mind. They drank a lot, too. Watson had always liked a drink and had argued fiercely against prohibition, but in New York he started to drink heavily. After what had happened at Johns Hopkins, he had plenty to drink about. One of the first memories that Watson's youngest child, Jimmy, has is of the bootlegger coming with booze to the door of their apartment on Fifth Avenue. The great god, the consumer, had made Watson so rich that he lived at one of the best addresses in Manhattan and employed a butler. So much money brought out his vanity. He began to dress in a very dandified fashion. He had his shirts hand-made and his trousers and suits cut by L. Bean, a fashionable New York tailor. He had his shoes made by hand in London and shipped across the Atlantic. It all made him look all the more attractive, but it gives him a slightly ridiculous air in retrospect.

His success in advertising also made Watson feel oddly inferior as far as academic psychology was concerned. We shall see, in the next chapter, how he tried to continue doing some psychological research and how dissatisfied he was with it. It did not feel to him to be really good enough. Because he published some of it and met with a hostile reception – much of which had nothing to do with the quality of the work – Watson did not want to risk publishing his views on advertising and psychology. This seems to me a pity for he had made a major contribution to shaping American advertising in to the industry it is now. He had booted it out of the patent medicine era.

In one of his last articles, 'Influencing the Mind of Another' (1935), Watson said; 'As a psychologist, I decry the fact that we are all trained so much alike – that there is so little individuality in the world. But, as an advertising man, I rejoice; my bread and butter depend on it.' At $70,000 a year, it was some bread and butter! But the more important point was that in this article Watson summed up many of the ideas that I have discussed in this chapter. Watson's whole approach rested on the idea that people were very much alike. There were the same human emotions waiting to be aroused in New York, Rome and Addis Ababa. Good advertising had to create and push 'selling ideas' which made products far more than what they really were. The art and the science lay in finding ways of generating 'selling ideas' that touched people and Watson made advertising into much more of a psychological activity. You first had to understand that what you were selling was more than a mere thing. 'Selling ideas' gave a product, a personality, an *image* like that of purity which Watson gave Johnson & Johnson. Once advertisers knew that this was what they were doing, it became much more a creative business than before. The 'selling ideas', or image, had to arouse the emotions of the consumer. If you did not use Johnson & Johnson's, you were a bad mother; if you did not use Scott's toilet tissue, you might become diseased; if you drank Maxwell House, you would circulate among the glamorous; if you used Ponds, young men would desire you. Watson played on fear, love and rage.

J. Walter Thompson formally recognised Watson's importance by the money they paid him. By 1930 the agency employed 440 people; the salary of John B. Watson amounted to nearly 4.5 per cent of the wage bill for the whole company.

Watson believed that he had in no way been able to turn advertising into an exact science. It would need a great deal of sophisticated methodology to achieve that. Even today, despite a plethora of Institutes of Marketing, sales and business schools, only an optimist employed by the advertising industry would claim – and then to a client – that it was a science. Watson brought to Madison Avenue as much sheer flair as psychology. He played his hunches as to what would persuade people. He certainly did much to make advertising desperately concerned with the psychology of the consumer, the image of a product and how the right image might trigger the 'buying reaction'. But any campaign remained a matter of intuition and luck as well as of exact science. Watson was too good a psychologist to think you could always predict how well a campaign would work. His contribution to changing the nature of American advertising remains a very considerable one. And yet the work never satisfied him as his rats or terns or babies had done. With the arrival of the Gallup polls, of course, marketing would become far more sophisticated in its initial research into who wanted and who bought what.

In the next chapter, we shall see how Watson tried quite hard not to make the advertising world his only world. In 1920, when he had been sacked, he had buckled down to surviving. He had not stood on his dignity. He had coped. He had made his way in the world again. In the best tradition of the American dream, his brains, his hard work and his refusal to lie down and be licked had been rewarded. He was rich; he was famous; he said he was happy. Psychologists liked to believe that he had found his true vocation. It was just his style to sell Maxwell House or some other glossy product and that was much more lucrative than behaviourism. Certainly Madison Avenue was a good place for him to use his energy and his flair and his intelligence. But for all the success that he had, Watson was dissatisfied and he knew it. He often tried to avoid thinking about the fact, for he did not want to admit that he missed the psychology which attacked him so. But he was an honest and a critical man and he knew quite well that an important part of his personality was not being fulfilled.

8

Children 1920–30

Despite all the aggravations of 1920, Watson had carried on his observations on young infants. It was while he and Rosalie had collaborated on these that their passion had flared up. In spite of everything, the couple still managed to do a good deal of actual research. They made the film on infant development for which Watson had prised $450 out of Johns Hopkins. But with all the strains of 1920 Watson had found no time to actually write up the work.

When Watson left Baltimore in 1920, the one psychological project he was determined to complete was the one on children. The hostility of psychologists was such that it would have given Watson a perfect excuse to stop doing any psychological work. Advertising was new, interesting and tiring. If his true vocation in life had really been devising dreams about Maxwell House, which was what many psychologists claimed, Watson need never have made another observation or toyed with another experiment. But the behaviourist did not suddenly give up doing psychology. He devoted a good deal of energy between 1920 and 1930 to the question of the development of children. He often referred to this as his pet project. He wrote to Yerkes in 1923: 'I have lost interest in university work. If I could get the baby work going, I would starve to death.' But the baby work was, of course, university work. Though no university would invite Watson back, he still did his best to get the baby work going.

The work Watson did on children between 1920 and 1930 is a curious mixture. He spent a good deal of time arguing the very simple case that psychology needed to study the growth and development of children. He said, acidly, that more was known about the development of monkeys than of children and he usually failed to add that he had been responsible for much of the initial work on monkeys. The facilities now existed for studying the behaviour of monkeys in something like their natural habitat. But, Watson complained, there did not seem to be much sign of anyone financing similar facilities for studying children.

After Watson's dismissal from Johns Hopkins there was much less enthusiasm on the National Research Council for the project on observing children in the Washington Hospital.

But not all the work that Watson did was polemical. He tried in a number of ways to keep on observing and experimenting. Both he and Rosalie made a number of notes on the development of their own children. Watson drew on some of these notes both in *Behaviourism* (1930) and in *The Psychological Care of the Infant and Child* (1928). Otherwise the notes were never published. And, apart from studying his own children, Watson managed in 1923 to raise some money from the Laura Spellman Rockefeller Foundation to finance the study of the development of children. Watson did not have the time actually to run many of the experiments himself. They were done by a friend of Rosalie's, Mary Cover Jones, who was working for her PhD at Columbia. Watson acted as a kind of mentor and unofficial supervisor. He insisted, according to Mary Cover Jones, that she get the credit because she had her name to make. Much of this work was a direct continuation of the observations carried out at Johns Hopkins both on the ordinary development of children and on their fears. A little boy called 'Peter' succeeded Little Albert though Peter has never become one of the classics of psychiatric literature.

Practical as ever, Watson was not willing to let his research be just of purely academic interest. His results suggested ways in which children might be raised more effectively. From 1924 on Watson began to talk about the implications of his research, and from 1926 he began to publish articles which offered, in effect, advice to parents. He found an appreciative audience. The man who had given Johnson & Johnson's an image of purity and had had the product endorsed by a leading paediatrician found himself, by 1928, acclaimed as an authority on how to bring up the young. His fame became international. Queen Marie of Romania, who had starred in the ads for Ponds, sent her grandson to see Watson so that the behaviourist would condition the boy with all the qualities that would make a great king. The Communists, however, took over Romania before Watson's client had the chance to show off his mettle on a throne. To some extent Watson became the Dr Spock of his generation.

But all this lay in the future. Soon after Watson and Rosalie were married at the start of 1921, they prepared an article for the *Scientific Monthly* in which they assessed current knowledge about children. The paper stressed that 'on the psychological side our present knowledge of infant life is *nil*' (their italics). Because of that, 'if an anxious mother wishes to determine whether her infant is developing normally along psychological lines, there are no data to guide her.' No doctor, no psychologist could honestly pretend to know what it was normal for a baby to do at three, six or twelve months. Despite the lack of data, Rosalie and Watson claimed their work at Johns Hopkins suggested very strongly that a child's personality was determined by its experiences in its first five years, if not earlier. 'We believe that by the end of the second year the pattern of the future individual is already laid down,' they wrote. They said that their research showed that babies were born with far fewer instincts than William James would have saddled them with, but that it was not possible to be definitive. They stressed how tentative their work was. Watson was far from being dogmatic at this stage. The paper added: 'Verified conclusions are not possible; hence this summary, like so many other bits of psychological work, should be looked on merely as a preliminary exposition of possibilities rather than a catalogue of concrete usable results.' Watson still hoped to do the research that would yield concrete results. He knew precisely the work he had in mind, detailed observations of children over a long period of time. That should make it possible to establish what a normal child at each stage of development should do and 'what additional complexities of behaviour should appear as the months go by'. Once norms were found it would be possible to test very young children who did not seem well 'to detect feeble-mindedness, deficiences in habit and deviations in emotional life'. Observation would have its practical uses.

In 1921 Rosalie had her first child. Billy was born on 21 November 1921. As was usual then for the rich, Rosalie had him in hospital. After about two weeks she returned to the cottage, as Watson called it, on Long Island where the couple had made their home. Watson liked having a baby around again. He told Titchener that it renewed his youth. He was only sorry that he had to go to work every day rather than being able to stay at home and watch him grow day by day.

Later, by 1923, Watson would be quite wealthy and from then on there were always nurses to look after the children. But though the Watsons had a maid out on Long Island in 1921 it was Rosalie herself who did most of the baby-minding. Rosalie was Watson's psychological assistant as well as his wife, so it meant that they could observe Billy's behaviour from the moment that he was born. The plan Watson had in mind, it seems, was to do a systematic study of how their child developed, precisely the kind of study which Piaget was to publish. But only part of the notes that were made survived. It seems probable that Watson destroyed many of the notes when he had his papers burned. He did use some, however, as a basis for comments he made both in *Behaviourism* and *The Psychological Care of the Infant and Child*.

In November, when Billy was only a few weeks old, Rosalie

observed that singing could be used to quiet him. She then tried to see what would happen if he were made to listen to music – a stimulus that seemed to be soothing – while his movements were hampered, a stimulus that had provoked rage in the babies at Johns Hopkins. So Rosalie restrained Billy's head, hands and feet while someone played the Victrola. Despite the soothing music, Billy raged.

By February 1922, Billy weighed 11 lbs 1 oz. Now that he was three months old, the Watsons tried to condition their son's bowel movements. Watson's mother, the fastidious Emma, would have approved of that. But for all the scientific expertise that was lavished on trying to train his bowel, baby Billy would not co-operate at all. Despondently Rosalie noted in February: 'I thought I had succeeded in conditioning bowels to move but it was a false observation.' Billy was constipated and had to have laxatives which made the whole under-taking more chancy but 'he is still made to "try" every morning at the same time'.

Later that month, the notes refer to the baby movements other than those of the bowels. Billy was using his hands. He was not quite reach-ing for objects which Piaget noted that his children started to do at four months but the hands no longer 'waved at random on each side of the body. They seem more stable to work towards each other.' By 11 March at 110 days, reaching was almost established. Billy had his thumbs out and could manipulate. When he was unsuccessful in reaching he began to whimper. By May the infant had developed considerable manipulative skills. Billy no longer just 'fingered' objects when reaching out. He now grasped them and swung them about. He took things like a doll or toy rabbit and swung it. The notes also show that by then Billy was using his hands more and more in order to explore objects. The baby's curiosity was growing like that of the young rats back in 1902.

In March at four months, Billy was 'beginning to show sensitivity of erogenous zones'. He cooed or cried in the bath when the foreskin was pushed back and he smiled when he was stroked. Watson was to experiment on himself, his wife and his children in ways which neither Freud nor Piaget dared or, at least, ever admitted that they had. Later Watson would tell both that if society were properly organised and not so infested with inhibitions, he would like to provide both his sons with mistresses once they reached the age of puberty.

The notes on Billy show that as well being constipated, he was beginning to make sounds. In April, he was cooing, laughing out loud and making 'Ah' sounds. Rosalie picked up her son once saying 'Da' and repeated it back at him time and again. She tried to condition him to say 'Dada' and Watson also tried. But, at first, they had little success.

The attempt to condition Billy to produce 'Dada' continued throughout May and June.

In April also, Billy tried to raise himself from his pillow a number of times; by May he was crawling. In May, Rosalie left him for a few days, which seems to have been her first absence. When she got back a few days later, Billy seemed 'very cute' to her but he did not seem to recognise her. She had to recondition him, she said, though she failed in her notes to specify to what. There is no doubt, however, that she was close to her son. When Billy was eight months old Rosalie and Watson had to go to a party. When Watson put on his coat, there was no reaction from the baby. Watson left the room. Rosalie tip-toed away out through the back door hoping that Billy would not realise that she had left. Billy started to howl and the Watsons had to tell the nurse to let him 'cry it out'. Watson disapproved and was amused. He did not want his child to be so emotionally dependent on his parents.

Language progressed. Billy often said 'Boo-boo' or 'Goo-goo' though he rarely produced the 'Dada' phrase his parents tried so hard to condition him to. But on 24 June they succeeded. On that day, baby Billy said 'Dada' and also finally managed to 'have a natural stool' at the right and proper time in the morning. In the next weeks, 'Dada' soon became the sound Billy used to refer to a bottle.

But after this linguistic and rectal triumph, the notes on Billy seem to come to an end for about 18 months. Then notes begin again. Some of the material in *Behaviourism* and in articles produced by Watson or by Rosalie drew on observations made when Billy was two or three years old.

The unpublished notes make little mention, however, of the emotional climate in which Billy was brought up. As a couple, Watson and Rosalie were happy and affectionate. He shed some of his shyness for her sake and went out a good deal to the theatre and parties though he really had very little feeling for drama. They hardly ever quarrelled. They would seem to have had a good love life since Watson was completely faithful to her, a fidelity he had never achieved before.

But their baby was not supposed to get much affection. We have seen how Watson did not go in for kissing or hugging the children in his first marriage. Mary Ickes was also not a very demonstrative person and Polly recalls how rare it was to be hugged as a child. By the time Billy was born, Watson was beginning to believe that the scientific evidence showed that children should get very little kissing and hugging. His research had shown that children loved the person who stroked them first. The way to make a child really yours was through its body. Touch it, treat it sensually and you would make sure that it loved you. But Freud had shown that many children were hopelessly fixated on either their mother or their father. In their most secret unconscious dreams they longed to be seduced by them. That Watson seems to have believed, was the consequence of so much infant hugging, kissing and coddling. There were commercial effects, too. Many adults never seemed really able to grow up. They remained stuck with their infantile emotional problems, forever dependent and unable to handle a job maturely. That, too, came from being loved too much, protected too much. Watson was determined that his own children would be brought up in what he considered to be a healthy way. If their parents did not drool emotionally over them, they would grow up independent, competent and without complexes or fixations. He put his theory to work on his own children.

Theoretically, too, child development continued to fascinate the behaviourist. It was, he knew, one of the central questions in psychology. It offered him the chance to show the validity of his ideas. For example, if it were possible to condition and 'un-condition' children into a variety of habits, fears and skills, it would powerfully suggest that we were, indeed, born a *tabula rasa*. Throughout 1921 and 1922, as he settled into his advertising career, Watson looked for money to enable him to investigate child development. He was spurred on by meeting a young psychologist called Mary Cover Jones who was a friend of Rosalie's from Vassar. Mary Cover Jones had been deeply impressed by Watson's writings. Behaviourism seemed to pave the way for a scientific psychology. Mary Cover Jones wanted to work with Watson, whom she regarded as a kind of mentor. In 1922 Watson wrote to Titchener about getting money to carry on studying children. Titchener had no practical help to offer though he wished Watson would do it. Watson also wrote to Yerkes. Yerkes could not help either, though Yerkes did happen to be on the staff of the National Research Council at the time and its director of information! But Watson did not give up.

Watson eventually persuaded the Laura Spellman Rockefeller Foundation to finance the work. He found a nursery, the Manhattan Day Nursery, where he could arrange for children to be observed. Most of the work would have to be done by Mary Cover Jones but Watson went as often as he could during the week. Every Saturday he went faithfully to the nursery and he spent many evenings with Mary Cover Jones looking over and analysing the results of the work. It shows how much he wanted to do the work. He was very busy at J. Walter Thompson. Rosalie liked to lead a busy social life. They were always going to parties, especially as many of her friends worked in the theatre, a business that thrives on parties. In the midst of all this, Watson made the time to pursue the research on children.

Conditions at the Manhattan Day Nursery, however, were not the ideal ones Watson had managed to organise at the Phipps Clinic in Baltimore. He did not have the academic weight he carried then. Neither he nor Mary Cover Jones could have total control of the children. They had to fit their studies into the way that the nursery ran. Often, they did not know too much about the background of the children. It was impossible to assess, for example, why a girl who was frightened of rabbits was frightened of rabbits. Epidemics spread through the nursery from time to time and removed all the subjects they were studying. Watson told Yerkes what the problems were but, he added, 'at any rate it is a start'. And, despite the handicaps, Watson and Mary Cover Jones managed to complete quite an impressive programme of research in the next two to three years.

They looked in particular at two topics. How could children be cured of particular fears? Was the case of Little Albert a good model for how children acquired and could be made to lose all manner of anxieties? Second, Watson encouraged Mary Cover Jones to carry out naturalistic observations of how children behaved in a normal day.

The first set of trials they carried out at the Manhattan Day Nursery tried to test other ways than 'un-conditioning' of curing children. Watson was too acute methodologically to expose himself to the accusation that he only worked with his own pet technique. Simply removing children from the feared object had little effect. A little girl called Rose burst into tears when she saw a rabbit. She was 21 months old. Watson and Mary Cover Jones talked to her parents and ensured she did not see a rabbit again for two weeks. But then again, the sight of a rabbit made her cry and tremble. A further thirty children on whom this method was tried did not respond any better. Watson pointed out that these thirty cases 'incline us to believe that the method of disuse in the case of emotional disturbance is not as effective as is commonly supposed.' It was not enough simply to do nothing. Fears did not disappear just by themselves. There had to be active intervention as there had been in the case of Little Albert.

Watson and Mary Cover Jones then tried a number of possible methods other than conditioning. They tried talking a child out of its fears. There was a bright five-year-old girl who was also scared of rabbits. They read her Beatrix Potter stories; they explained to her that rabbits were nice creatures; they got her to make Plasticine rabbits; they managed to get her to say that she liked rabbits and was not frightened of them. But next time she saw the rabbit, all this travail was to no avail. She jumped up, screamed and stopped playing. So much for words and positive thinking!

Social pressures did not seem to succeed either. A boy called Arthur was called 'a fraidy cat' every time he showed himself to be afraid of frogs. Arthur on seeing a frog would always yell 'They bite' even when they were in an aquarium. Making fun of Arthur had no good effects. Other cases were not much more promising.

The trend of all these results was clear. The only way to get rid of fears was to use the kinds of conditioning which Watson had used on Little Albert and which, incidentally, he would use on Billy when Billy developed an extraordinary aversion to goldfish. But before looking at how Watson used therapy on his own children, let us consider the case of Peter.

Mary Cover Jones recently explained that, as she did most of the work, Watson accepted her wish not to 'create' any fear in a child. They only worked on children who were already exhibiting fears. Whilst admiring the ethics, it deprives one of the elegance of Little Albert. Peter was three years old when he came to the day nursery. He was a bright child who seemed to cope quite well with life except for the fact that he was afraid of white rats, rabbits, fur coats, feathers, cotton wool, frogs, fish and mechanical toys! To go through life in fear of feathers, fish and fur coats may not be too arduous but to fear toys and cotton wool seems, frankly, to bode ill.

When Peter first saw a rat under observation he was with a two-year-old girl called Barbara. Barbara picked the rat up in her hands and played with it: Peter screamed and fell flat on his back in a paroxysm of fear. The rat was taken away. Peter would not move and it took twenty-five minutes before he was calm enough to start playing normally again. The next day it was seen that he was nearly as frightened of all the other items listed above.

Watson and Mary Cover Jones first started by trying to show Peter that other children could play with animals and mechanical toys. There was some improvement. But then Peter had to go into hospital for scarlet fever. On his way home from hospital he and his nurse were attacked by a large dog who barked viciously at them. The nurse and child just got into a taxi in time. Peter was, very understandably, terrified. There was no previous evidence that he had been frightened of dogs but when he next came to the nursery, all his fears of animals returned, magnified. All the improvement that had been made was lost. He was even more frightened of the animals than he had been before. It was decided to try 'direct un-conditioning'.

Watson wrote:

We did not have control over his meals but we secured permission to give him his mid-afternoon lunch consisting of crackers and a glass of milk. We seated him at a small table in a high chair. The lunch was served in a room 40 feet long. Just as he began to eat his lunch, the rabbit was displayed in a wire cage of wide mesh. We displayed it on the first day just far enough away not to disturb his eating.

They marked the spot on the floor where that was. Every day after that, the rabbit was brought closer and closer. At last the rabbit could be placed on the table close to Peter and, finally, Peter would eat with one hand and play with the rabbit with the other. Evidence, surely, Watson wrote in triumph, 'that his viscera were retained with his hands'.

Once they had cured the boy of his fear of rabbits, they wanted to see how that had affected his other fears. Peter was no longer afraid of cotton wool, fur coats or feathers. Some progress towards normality. Peter went so far as to pick up a fur rag and bring it to the experimenter. In the past this limp rag had made the little boy whimper with terror. Peter was also no longer afraid of the white rat though he was not very interested in playing with it. He also enjoyed playing with earthworms and could watch a mouse without any signs of distress.

Watson noted that they did not know the circumstances in which Peter's fears had first come about. If they had, they might then have been able to spot which was the primary fear and how this had been 'transferred' to other objects. He thought it vital to do more work in this line. He wrote: 'Not until we have had more experience with building up a primary fear, noting the transfers and then uncondition-ing the primary, will be be working upon sure ground in this interesting field.' He believed that it might be possible that there was a difference of intensity in the fear (as exhibited in behaviour, of course) that the primary stimulus and other stimuli aroused. By seeing what scared a child most, one might be able to learn what his basic fear was and cure him of that. Then, other fears would wither away. In *1984* George Orwell used this idea in a grotesque way for the State through its tentacular mind probes could tell what was for each of its citizens 'the worst thing in the world', your own tailored terror that lurked in Room 101, and use it to destroy dissidents.

Watson and Rosalie hoped to bring up their children free of all such fears. As Rosalie noted in an amusing article, 'I am the Mother of the Behaviourists' Sons', she was a little too affectionate always to stick to the conditioning rules. Billy was so fond of her that he would cry when they went out. Later on Billy became terrified of goldfish. Watson exposed his son to goldfish just as Peter had been exposed to the rabbit. The phobia disappeared. Watson was less successful with his son's nail-biting. Rosalie wrote 'our older son bites his nails which is a very bad symptom in a behaviourist's family'. They tried punishment and reward, pasting adhesive over his fingers, sending him to bed with gloves on, and trying to make him what they called 'socially conscious' about his hands. But all these stratagems failed: Billy bit on.

But Watson did not just try out his therapeutic ideas on his children. They were his experimental subjects, too. When Billy was eleven months old, Watson and Rosalie decided to see whether any show of love between the parents would, as Freud suggested, make the baby angry and jealous. This was, in 1922, one of the first experimental attempts to verify Freudian ideas. 'When father and mother embraced violently,' Watson wrote, 'the youngster could not be made to keep his eyes on his parents. Love making between them was nothing in his young life.' But if the father, the great behaviourist, and mother attacked one another, Billy looked fixedly at his mother, whimpered and cried out aloud several times, but Watson observed that it seemed that the noise and the sight of his parents' angry faces were in themselves stimuli enough to make him whimper and cry. 'His behaviour was of the fear type. . . . There was apparently no jealousy behaviour in this infant.' Watson, who had been so jealous as a young man, was understandably interested in the genesis of this emotion but he never really did more than account for its early appearances.

At the age of two years Billy first exhibited signs of jealousy. Then, whenever Rosalie embraced Watson, the child began to attack the father. Billy pulled at his father's coat, cried out 'my Mama' and pushed Watson away and crowded in between them. If Rosalie and Watson continued embracing or kissing the reaction would become quite intense. On Sunday mornings Billy would always come into his parents' bedroom before they were up and be fussed over (which sounds a most unbehaviouristic way of proceeding, Dr Watson). And yet, at 2 years 9 months, Billy would say to his father 'You going to the office, Dada' or instruct his poor father actually to get going to J. Walter Thompson.

Freud suggested that one of the first experiences to make a child jealous was the birth of a brother or sister. Watson noted that no Freudian had ever put this idea to experimental test. When Billy was two years old, Watson and Rosalie had their second child, Jimmy. Rosalie went away to hospital for two weeks. 'The day the mother returned, his own [Billy's] nurse kept B busy in his room playing until the conditions for the test were all set.' Even in his own home, with his own children, Watson remained conscious of methodology. Rosalie nursed the new baby with her breast exposed. When Billy walked into the room, he went up to his mother, leaned against her knee and said 'How do Mama'. Billy did not try to kiss her and, for 30 seconds, he seems not to have noticed the baby. Then he saw it, said 'Little baby', took the baby's hands, patted them and said 'that baby, that baby'.

Billy was very gentle and tender. The new baby nurse then took the baby, which distressed Billy who called to his mother 'Mama, take baby!' Watson noted that his son's behaviour quite contradicted the Freudian hypothesis. Billy showed no signs of jealousy. In fact, he tried to get his mother to 'take' the baby. When he had to give up his room for a while to the new nurse, Billy helped pull all the furniture out of his room. He did not pay excessive attention to the new baby but soon turned back to his toys. Watson noticed only one occasion when jealousy flared. When Billy was three and Jimmy was one, a nurse said, 'You are a naughty boy. Jimmie is a nice boy – I love him'. 'For a few days jealousy threatened,' Watson wrote. But then he and Rosalie sacked the nurse who had tried to control Billy in such a crude way.

Watson believed that his work on jealousy was just preliminary but thought jealousy was a 'bit of behaviour whose stimulus is a [conditioned] love stimulus the response to which is rage'. Because Billy first reacted only when there was fighting between mother and father, Watson suggested that it was the sight or sound of the loved object being tampered or interfered with that led to jealousy. It was not because of being deprived of the loved one that you became jealous but because you seemed to see them being threatened. It remains a curious idea.

When Billy was 37 months old, his mother had to go away for a month. On her return the child was not very jealous if she and Watson embraced. Watson then tried to see what would happen if he attacked Rosalie. The child stood this for a few minutes but then began to attack his father 'tooth and nail'. Next, Watson remained passive while Rosalie assaulted him. 'She inadvertently punched below the belt, causing the father to double up in no simulated way,' Watson said. But his father's pain did not make Billy sympathetic. While the behaviourist was trying to soothe the injured parts, his son started to attack him. The experiment had to be discontinued for Billy was quite disturbed – and so, it seems, was Watson. Next day, the child showed no jealousy when Watson and Rosalie kissed.

Family life with the Watsons cannot be said to have been boring. Both Watson and Rosalie were willing to take considerable risks in the way they treated their children.

The notes on Billy suddenly resume again when he is about four. They are rather less technical. Rosalie made some interesting notes on his use of language. Billy was at the stage when, if he read a book, he had to describe every picture he saw. Rosalie showed him some pictures of himself and Jimmy. Billy pored over the photograph album. Half an hour after she had left him in the room, he was still sitting there enthralled saying, 'This is Jimmy – this Billy.' Nothing could dissuade him that the pictures of Jimmy as a baby were not him as a baby. But he recognised himself between one year and two years old, which seemed to be connected with beginning to speak.

The notes also reveal a good deal about routines the behaviourist imposed on his children. After breakfast, Billy used to sit on the toilet. He did not produce but he did protest. As soon as the children could toddle, Watson insisted that they go to the bathroom each morning at 8 o'clock prompt and 'take care of the matter themselves'. (There were a number of bathrooms, of course, in their flat on Fifth Avenue to which they moved after Watson became a vice-president of J. Walter Thompson.) The boys then had to go back to their parents and make a verbal report. The Watsons had no way of being sure if the children told the truth; they did not go to inspect the toilet before it was flushed. Their policy was to trust their child. An admirable idea but, according to Jimmy, both children often lied. When Jimmy was three, Rosalie had to take him to the doctor because the child had a pain in his stomach. The doctor asked about Jimmy's bowel movements and Rosalie had to admit she could not be sure about them. The doctor laughed and said, 'I suppose that it is more important to go through life independent and well adjusted if a bit constipated.' When the children were older Watson could apparently laugh at his bathroom obsession.

Sex was also very much a matter of concern. Watson and Rosalie never felt that their children should not see them embracing or 'love making'. It is not clear from the context whether, by this, Watson meant hugging or kissing or actual intercourse. Billy certainly saw his mother naked and was taught the right words for his genitals quite openly. One evening when Rosalie asked him if he wanted to 'tee-tee' (the euphemism the Watsons seem to have used despite all their progressive thinking), the three-year-old said, 'My penis don't feel liken to.' Later when Billy saw his mother naked he told her that she had big black breasts and that he had little white ones.

The notes also show that while Billy and Jimmy continued to like each other, Watson was determined not to allow them to become too dependent on each other either. They were not allowed to kiss each other or to fight. Billy had to ask quite forcefully to be allowed to 'shake hands with Jimmy when he was about to be put to bed.' The spectacle of the three-year-old Billy shaking hands with the one-year-old Jimmy is a ludicrous one to conjure up. But it was all part of the behaviourist's plan to make his children well adjusted and independent, to which he devoted an enormous amount of thought. We shall see later on what the effects of all this were.

If his home was his own private laboratory, Watson also continued to work with Mary Cover Jones. He told both Yerkes and Titchener that the work was progressing somewhat though research ideas were slow to form as so much of his brain was taken up with business. Unable to do much observation, Watson encouraged Mary Cover Jones to carry out observations of children in their homes. It proved impossible to get parents to agree to such intrusion in those days. So, instead, Mary Cover Jones followed a group of nine children who were living temporarily in the Hecksher Foundation. The children were between sixteen months and three years of age. Every cry, every laugh, was timed and noted. Most important, the general situations that evoked these reactions were carefully monitored.

These observations allowed them to arrive at a list of behaviours which seemed to evoke crying. These were having to sit on the toilet chair, having property taken away, being left alone in a room, having the adult leave the room, working at something which did not work out properly, failure to get other children to play with them, being dressed, failure to get an adult to pick them up, being undressed, being bathed, having the nose wiped. In all, there were some hundred situations which called out crying. Watson believed that many of these situations were actually basically rage responses which had been conditioned. Being dressed, undressed, washed, having one's nose wiped, were all instances of being hampered in one's movements which was, Watson claimed, the origin of rage. Equally losing property or being unable to work something out properly were also a kind of hampering. Some of the other cases of crying were due to love or grief such as when the child failed to get an adult to pick him up or a child to play with him. The observations also revealed that most tears occurred between 9 o'clock and 11 o'clock in the morning. These results made Watson suggest to the nursery that the rest period for the children should be moved to before lunch because when children were less tired and less active, they were less likely to respond to particular situations by crying. Under different conditions, responses to stimuli varied. There was not a fixed and immutable connexion so that stimulus, S, invariably produced response, R.

The laughter of the children was also observed. Again, Watson and Mary Cover Jones established a list of situations in which the children laughed. Being tickled, running and romping with other children, tossing and trying to catch a ball, teasing other children all made the children laugh. So did success. When a child was trying to make a toy or a piece of equipment work and finally managed to do so, the child often laughed. It is a pity Watson never pursued this observation, for the stimulus here was an action on the child's part rather than anything external. Other situations that provoked laughter were banging to make sounds, crashing on the piano and blowing through a mouth organ. Watson noted how laughter could be used 'to change the whole tenor of the room, changing distress into laughter'. In all, there seemed to be eighty-five situations that led to laughter.

Watson made use of some of this material in a series of lectures that he gave in 1924 at the New School of Social Research. He looked upon it as work in progress. In 1926, the collaboration between Watson and Mary Cover Jones came to an end because she and her husband moved to California. Watson was never to find another collaborator like her. Once she left New York, his psychological work became almost entirely theoretical. He could only offer explanation, not experiments.

In a recent article Mary Cover Jones has discussed her debt to Watson. Watson influenced her whole approach profoundly and contributed a very great deal to her research, she emphasised. She suggested, too, that if he had had the time to immerse himself in the work on a full-time basis, he would soon have started to modify his ideas somewhat. For example, Watson was with Mary Cover Jones in a child's home when there was a very loud noise much worse than those Little Albert was exposed to. The child was startled but he did not become frightened. They discussed the possibility that children might react very differently in their own home and in a strange environment like a laboratory. The idea tallies well with Watson's strictures about how artificial laboratory situations were. But the observation was never pursued.

Nevertheless, the work on children that he did after 1923 is still of considerable interest. He and Mary Cover Jones had shown clearly that a number of children could be conditioned out of their fears, the very premise of behaviour therapy today. The results with that seemed to be much better than other methods of cure. The work at the Manhattan Day Nursery was also one of the very first attempts to observe children's behaviour in natural environments. None of this work was really completed. There needed to be far more observations of children in all kinds of settings. A purist would say the work on using 'unconditioning' to cure children of phobias needed controlled trials to prove its worth. But, for all that, Watson was pointing the way forward. But with the departure of Mary Cover Jones the emphasis of Watson's work on children changed.

From 1926 on, Watson began to tackle the subject of how children ought to be brought up. He had always had strong feelings about how to raise his own children. They were to be trained to be independent and unfixated. John and Polly, his children by Mary Ickes, had been brought up in this kind of regime. They received little physical affection. Polly remembers that her father only kissed her once, the day that he left to fight in the First World War. Since there were no wars to fight in the 1920s, he never kissed Billy or Jimmy during the whole decade. Jimmy recalls that his mother sometimes 'bootlegged some affection' but such outbursts were rare. Hugging your children conditioned them to love you more than was good for them. It bound them too much to the nest. Watson's own childhood told him how difficult life was for children who loved their parents too much. He had had terrible problems in coping when his father left home.

But by 1926 Watson had two strands of research which suggested that too much love harmed children. Freud had shown that many neurotics had failed to resolve their early Oedipal or Electra complexes. Their adult problems were rooted in being too close to parents to be able to grow up and grow away from them. Watson's own work at Johns Hopkins offered reasons as to why this happened. Anyone who stroked a baby gently and softly conditioned that baby to love him or her. Smothering your child with kisses was an excellent means of making him or her totally dependent on you. Watson read, or misread, Freud in accord with his own gut feelings about keeping a 'healthy' distance from his children. His research showed babies loved to be stroked but he took that to mean that any physical affection was an overdose. It would prevent normal development. But his advice on how to achieve perfect parenthood reflected more than either research or his own personal fears.

Watson's advice reflected his concept of the ideal person. He had always admired a kind of naive and rugged individualism; now he thought he had a blueprint that would enable parents to produce children who were independent, individual and who could stand on their own two feet from an early age. But in order to be able to rear such children parents would have to cut loose from many traditional attitudes.

Throughout 1926 and 1927 Watson addressed teachers' groups and medical groups on his theories. From time to time the press got wind of them and there were outraged editorials. One paper in Florida referred to the psychologist as subnormal; another paper called him sub-human. What particularly irked many parents was that Watson suggested the love they lavished on their children was not good for the children but gave the parents intense pleasure. In 1928 Watson began to organise his ideas more formally for a set of six articles which first appeared in *McCalls* and then came out as a book under the title, *The Psychological Care of the Infant and Child*. Rosalie co-authored the book. It is worth looking in some detail at the book, for it was the last long piece of really original psychological work that Watson did.

Parenthood was a science, Watson declared. He personally would prefer to live in a society where no mother kept a baby for more than three or four weeks because after that all kinds of attachments were almost bound to develop. But the behaviourist realised that, for the time being, children would be brought up by their mothers and fathers in their own homes. 'Mothers should see it as an experiment,' he said, and the most important experiment of their lives. There was no responsibility greater than that of bringing up a child.

Watson then argued that still far too little was known about the normal course of growth of the child. Psychology needed to study that, and to do so intensively. For all that lack of finalised research, Watson was confident that he had shown that babies are born with precious few instincts. Their behaviour is built by their parents. Gravely, he told parents: 'You daily slant your children. . . . Truly do we inevitably create our young in our image.'

It was precisely because parents so influence their children's behaviour that they had to guard against showing them too much love. Watson said that most mothers should be indicted for 'psychological murder. . .I know hundreds of mothers who have slain their young. They want to possess their children's souls.' Fathers were little better in Watson's view. 'Most fathers should be punished for the idiotic parental duty dogma they try to instil in their young.' Parents loved their children so much, Watson suggested, because there was something missing in their own lives and because they hoped to make the children feel indebted to them. Parents, he added, 'build for their own future happiness by making their children believe something is due parents for having brought children into the world. This is bunk. Children don't owe their parents anything.'

This was strong and unpopular stuff. The Housewives' League reacted with outrage to the first *McCalls* article. At a lecture Watson gave about that time, a woman said she was glad she had had her children before she had ever heard of John B. Watson and his blasted behaviourism because, that way, she had been able to enjoy them. Precisely my point, riposted Watson. And he often used that story in subsequent lectures to show how parents used their children selfishly as a means of enjoying themselves.

The third chapter had the ominous title, 'The Dangers of Too Much Mother Love'. Watson warmed to his theme. Editorials provoked by the articles in *McCalls* showed that 'kissing the baby to death is just about as popular a sport as it has ever been'. He had gone for a three-hour drive with some friends and during that period the mother had kissed her boys thirty-two times! It was not odd that America was losing all its rugged virtues. Watson went further. He claimed that the reason why mothers indulged in so much baby-loving was sexual. 'It is at bottom a sex seeking response.' With rather endearing naiveté, he said if it was not sex-seeking why did mothers kiss their offspring on the lips? Sexual responses were so precisely located. Watson suggested that children should never be kissed, never be hugged and 'never let them sit in your lap'. If there has to be any kissing, let it be on the forehead. It was far better just to shake hands. That was not as difficult as it seemed. 'Try it out . . . in a week, you will see you can be perfectly objective and yet kindly.' The baby who was coddled too much would become an adult who always needed to be pampered and coddled. But, as adults, 'there is no one to baby us', mourned the behaviourist.

Watson also warned against 'unscrupulous nurses' who knew the facts of sex perfectly well. In order to get babies down to sleep quickly, they often stroked their sex organs.

And parents, Watson said, were also incapable of leaving their young alone. They were always keeping an eye on them, never giving him or her any freedom. Parents should learn not to always watch their children. Constantly watched the child would never learn to cope with problems by himself for he would always run to Mummy or Daddy who would do it for him.

If parents could not stop themselves watching their young, said Watson, 'use a periscope'. At least the child would not know you were watching and might develop a few independent habits.

In March 1928, in *McCalls*, Watson came to the logical conclusion of his thinking. If mothers were incorrigible, always kissing, hugging and babying their babies, then their babies would have to be taken away from them. In an ideal world, Watson argued, no child would stay with its natural mother too long. Plato made the same suggestion, of course. Watson recommended that a child would stay with its natural mother for three or four weeks. After that a baby would go either from one home to another or be brought up in communal homes which would be run on psychological lines. He believed that such a system would not make the child insecure but rather independent. A very modified version of these ideas was, of course, pioneered by the *kibbutzim* in Israel.

The ideas Watson put forward again owe a surprising debt to Freud. The seven-year-old boy who loved his mother too much and could not free himself, the seven-year-old girl who loved her father too much, these were the neurotics of the future. All their complexes unresolved, they would become frigid or homosexual or compulsive hand-washers. That was the drift of psychoanalysis. Moreover, in their dreams, Freud's patients had reported fantasies of being seduced by their parents. Watson took this idea and, characteristically, placed the unconscious out on the surface of the skin. The reason children had

211

these dreams and fantasies, the reason that they could not detach themselves enough from their parents to get over their first, infantile loves, was because they had been so strongly conditioned to love their parents who stroked them incessantly. Given Watson's own rigorous scientific standards, he cannot really have been just convinced by the rational evidence. The theory appealed to him. His own experiences as a child left him with the fear that he had been too close to his mother for a well adjusted psychologist. Then his father, Pickens, whom he loved, left him. This was enough to make him fret about making children dependent on parents. Curiously, at the time when Watson was expounding these views, Pickens did get into contact with him. Watson sent money but he would not see the old man. What better way was there of proving he was no longer dependent on Daddy!

There is no doubt that Watson's views shocked the American public. Much of what he said would not be out of place in David Cooper's *Death of the Family*. Watson accused the American mothers of 'loving their children to death', he meant they could never become adequate adults. And, of course, Watson enjoyed shocking the conventions. It gave him an excellent chance to be defiant.

Mothers hit back. Mrs Julian Heath, president of the Housewives' League, affected pity. On 8 March 1928 she said that Watson must be a very unhappy man to offer such ideas. An editorial in the *Florida Times* said that the 'theorist' should be 'backed against the wall and let him have it full force from the shoulder in plain speech that he is plainly wrong.' Watson's ideas provoked a considerable storm which, of course helped to sell the book. There were some women who thought it an interesting idea though, as a Mrs Jean Bull said, 'our civilisation has not yet reached a point where it will admit such a revolutionary proposal.' Watson was also mocked by some women for concerning himself so much with children. A Mrs Laidlaw referred to him as the man 'who wants to be mother to the whole world'.

Watson knew, of course, what the reaction would be. He understood the temper of the times perfectly well. But it was both fun and a duty to shock. The duty to shock came from the fact that Watson believed his research, taken together with the insights of Freud, revealed most parents to be a menace. They spent their time making sure their children loved them too much or inculcating them with absurd fears such as those of the dark, spiders, Satan, sin, God, rabbits, feathers or whatever else. The great American family was a myth that needed debunking. And Watson was only too happy to do the debunking.

Marriages were harmed by so much love between parents and children. Watson believed that too close a bond with the mother especially made it hard for sons to form proper relationships with women. Again, there seems here to be the edge of personal experience.

Watson ended the chapter with an almost Ciceronian plea. He said, and the rhetoric is not without cadences: 'Mother love is a dangerous instrument.' It may 'inflict a never healing wound, a wound which may make infancy unhappy, adolescence a nightmare, an instrument which may wreck your adult son's or daughter's vocational future and their chance of future happiness.'

These ideas, of course, shocked Americans who believed that family life was at its best when it was warm, cosy and loving. But, as we shall see, Watson also had a number of allies.

Having warned against excessive love, Watson turned to the topic of how to control children's fears and rages. One chapter in *Psychological Care* was devoted to fears and one to temper tantrums. Watson's views on these subjects were much more popular.

Fears, Watson explained, were largely the result of conditioning. The case of Little Albert showed that. He warned against loud noises. Slamming doors and yelling at babies and young children was a wonderful way of instilling all kinds of terrors into them. Parents tended to be far too authoritarian, Watson implied. They said 'Don't' to children too often and too loudly. 'Satan' and 'sin', he added, recalling his own youth, were words that were often barked in just the same kind of tone 'Don't' was and with the same effect in mind. Don't say don't, said Watson. Parents should only prevent children doing something if it was really dangerous or harmful. With his own children Watson felt able to be even more revolutionary. His own children were never told that anything was good or bad in itself. There were no sins for them or, at least, there were not meant to be any sins. But parents tended to be far too emotional in the way that they punished their children. They hugged them or hit them. This was very repugnant from a scientific point of view. Less emotion and more objectivity, Watson recommended. A parent should never punish a child.

Watson was not suggesting that parents should tolerate any kind of behaviour. But he felt that the process of teaching a child what he could and could not do should be regarded as an experiment. He wrote:

> The behaviourist advocates the early building in of appropriate
> common sense negative reactions by the method of gently rapping
> the fingers or hand or other bodily part when the undesirable act
> is taking place – but as an objective experimental procedure, never
> as a punishment.

The perfect parents can, of course, always tell one situation from the other. Watson argued that such a cool attitude was much healthier. He also stressed that it was not effective conditioning to slap, rap or tap the child hours after the wicked deed – if I may slip into Satanic language – had been done. It was no good waiting till father, the dispenser of discipline, got home. To make its point on the organism the child had to be disciplined then and there, as soon after the act as possible.

And if a child developed unreasonable anxieties or fears because his conditioning had been awry, Watson offered a number of case histories of how children had been un-conditioned. There was no need to go to the doctor for advice. Sensible parents could un-condition their child themselves if he was frightened of the dark or of dogs or of whatever. Psychological knowledge was now available for people to use. Let them use it to raise and to help their children.

Watson added that children often put on tantrums because they know that it is a way of getting adults to coddle them. In one case, he told readers, a mother had been sent away for a few weeks because her child was always making scenes to which she responded. After a few weeks away the child was cured. Watson seemed to suggest that such an absence had no adverse effects at all.

There were also a number of very practical suggestions on how to run a child's daily life. Watson stressed, as ever, the importance of toilet training. 'The problem of cleanliness should intrude from birth,' he wrote. From three to five weeks the child should start to be trained. Children should be woken up at 6.30 in the morning. At 6.30 they should have orange juice and a pee. After that, they should play till 7.30. Breakfast was at 7.30 sharp and Watson said very sensible things about making it a nourishing meal. Eating was followed by excreting. At 8 o'clock, the child should be placed on the toilet 'for 20 minutes or less till bowel movement is complete'. The child should be left on his own, without any toys, to concentrate on this important ritual. Then until 10 o'clock the child should play indoors. At 10 o'clock, he should be taken outside to get some exercise. A healthy child got fresh air even in New York. The Watson children always went to play in Central Park, which was conveniently close to their apartment on Fifth Avenue. In the afternoon there should be a short nap after lunch and then 'social play' with other children.

Bedtime also had its schedule. After its bath the child should not be allowed to romp around or to get too excited for then it would find it hard to sleep. At 8 o'clock the child should be put to bed, without a kiss or a hug, of course, but with a handshake or, at most, a pat on the head. In the book, Watson made no great play on the use of powder before bedtime. He was not selling Johnson & Johnson now. The psychologist even touched on the controversial question of whether children should be allowed to take toys with them to bed. In itself, this was not harmful but, he warned, 'often such habits are carried over into adult life. Then, they may become troublesome.' If you insist on taking a teddy bear to bed with you, it's not surprising you might have difficulty with your 'marital adjustment'.

But the public seems to have wanted expertise desperately. In a world where science seemed to make everything possible, there was very little of the scepticism with which we tend to treat experts today, seeing them as all-too-human beings who market their particular brand of wisdom. Watson was listened to as a man who knew.

Watson used his position to promote his own vision of what the American child should be like, an independent and self-reliant creature with no emotional problems. It was not enough not to mollycoddle. Parents had to strive to make them do things for themselves from the earliest possible age. As soon as physiology permitted let the child try to feed itself, clothe itself, bathe itself. By 12 to 18 months any self-respecting parent would have toilet trained a child; at 18 months the child should start to feed itself with a spoon; at 22 months parents should start letting the child use a blunt fork; at 30 months the child should start to dress itself and to butter its own bread. By 3 years of age 'children should begin to dress and act like youthful young men and women and should be scrupulously treated as such.' Dressing would be made much easier, Watson claimed, if only fashion houses would design clothes 'which toddlers themselves can operate'. Watson toyed with the idea of starting to design such clothes himself but he never seems to have carried out this plan.

Sport was also recommended. 'There is no reason why children as young as three or four shouldn't have instructions in boxing, baseball, football, tennis, dancing and nature study,' said Watson, 'though, of course all this can be carried to extremes.' His own children were taught to play many of these games when they were very young. Playing such games was a way of using up the children's aggressive energies, Watson felt. Billy and Jimmy were never allowed to fight.

Parents were also chided for buying too many toys. Christmas was especially appalling, Watson felt. 'It is not a foolish guess to say that many millions of dollars' worth of property are destroyed each Xmas Day, destroyed as utterly as were by high explosives during the World War. And with just as poor results socially.' Watson believed that toys should have a function beyond that of mere play. Children should be encouraged to use their toys in such a way as to develop their skills. Parents should give the child materials with which to make toys. It would make children handy and creative.

Sex, of course, also came into the book. As we shall see, Watson wrote a great deal on the subject of sexual freedom. If a child was to be treated as scrupulously as a young adult, he or she had to learn the facts of life early on. Billy and Jimmy were often sat down by their father to discuss sex. The average American family should do the same. Watson said that the child has a right to expect proper and interesting information about sex from his parents if they wanted his respect. It sounded daunting. But it was less daunting 'if you start, early, to form a club to talk it out with your children. When the club is going well, it is a safeguard to health and sanity.' Part of the talk-it-out club would tell the children about sex.

It was only intelligent to talk to children about sex. Otherwise, children would talk to each other. Relying on doctors was, said Watson, worse than useless. The doctor usually 'has a narrow orthodoxy which is mostly false.' Parents should get their facts right and pass them on to their children.

Despite stressing this, Watson was far from recommending that children should be allowed to indulge in sexual activities. He suggested that parents do their best to discourage thumb-sucking because 'parents whose children suck thumbs are condemned in progressive communities'. That was enough. Thumb-sucking was liable to lead to 'misshapen mouths' and worse complications. If a child sucked his thumb 'the outside world doesn't get a good chance at him. He doesn't conquer his world. He becomes "exclusive", an auto-erotic.' Again Watson spoke with the voice of Freud. On masturbation Watson was also conservative. He denounced those doctors who claimed that masturbation led to madness. But if a child masturbated, it tended to make them withdraw, and massive masturbation 'may make heterosexual adjustment difficult or impossible'. Too much auto-eroticism was bad for the routines of everyday life.

Watson was also very worried about homosexuality. He drew on some recent experiments in which rats had been conditioned to be homosexual to argue that institutions like the Boy Scouts and the YMCA led to dangers of homosexuality. Girls were in even more danger. 'Our whole social fabric is woven so as to make all women slightly homosexual,' Watson said. Girls held hands, kissed and even slept in the same bed together. Mothers believed that this was a natural form of relationship but it was, in reality, an excellent way of making all women more than slightly lesbian. Watson did not approve.

The whole emphasis of Watson's advice was that parents should be honest about sex with their children. And the older they grew the more should be permitted. When young people went to college, Watson believed, that ought to be a period for them to play around with sex.

He wanted each university to set up a Department of Sex Instruction so that ignorance would be banished. The moral atmosphere on campuses should also be different so that students could take part in 'wholesale necking'. And, certainly, Watson wanted them to go further than mere necking. No one could make a good sexual partner in marriage without previous experience. But young children should be prepared for all this by getting the facts of life honestly and accurately. Watson told Jimmy that he would have liked to have been able to arrange for him and his brother to have mistresses when they were about fourteen but that would have no doubt led to a scandal even worse than the divorce. And Watson desisted, for once.

The message of *Psychological Care of the Infant and Child* is clear enough. To bring children up is a responsibility. Science now showed that many traditional notions were wrong-headed. In order to raise independent children who could cope with life's problems, parents had to be much tougher with themselves. They should not regard their children as toys from whom they got pleasure. They should look on the parental task as a long and very worthwhile experiment. Children had the right to expect that their parents would prepare them for the modern world, rather than molly-coddling them into neurotics. The book sold well. It became a best seller and within a few months had sold over 100,000 copies. It was extremely influential.

Reaction from the academic world was very mixed. Many psychologists felt that Watson was using his talents as a persuasive salesman. They decried him for writing anything so popular. It was yet another sign of how timely his exit from psychology had been. But Watson found a number of champions. George A. Dorsey called his study a great contribution to knowledge. Dorsey compared the importance of Watson's observation on children with Darwin's on flowers and birds. The ideas on sex were 'astonishingly frank', added Dorsey.

The most prestigious supporter of Watson was Bertrand Russell who wrote a long review of the book. Russell took issue on a number of points. He believed that there were children who were born with exceptional abilities, like Mozart. Watson did not distinguish enough between the natural unfolding of growth, the genes flowering, and the effects of education. The behaviourist seemed to assume that all changes after birth were to be regarded as effects of the environment. Russell disagreed. On the dangers of too much mother love, however, Russell was in whole-hearted agreement. Russell believed that Watson was a little too extreme in his ban on kissing and hugging. A little tenderness was needed for the person to mature into a healthy sexual being but Watson was still 'wholesome' for most parents. But Russell also praised highly the scientific approach of the book. He warmed to

217

Watson because the man was not afraid to suggest that he wanted to spend so much time in a children's nursery. Most scientists would fear ridicule if they suggested that. No well trained man has watched a child develop from 0 to 36 months which, Russell agreed, was a key project that needed to be carried out.

The honesty in sex education which Watson demanded seemed wholly admirable to Russell. Watson had also revived Plato's argument that perhaps it would be best for parents and children not to know each other. While this was bound to shock the American public, Russell believed this was an issue that was worth discussing. He ended by saying that no one since Aristotle had actually made as substantial a contribution to our knowledge of ourselves as Watson had – high praise indeed, from a man who was then regarded as one of the greatest minds in the world! None of this impressed most psychologists who complained that Watson had demeaned himself, which was only to be expected, and demeaned their science, which was only to be deplored.

Popular reaction was also very controversial. *McCalls* said that Watson's articles had set off a nationwide debate. *Parents Magazine* called *Psychological Care* a necessity. It ought to stand 'on every intelligent's mother's shelf'. The hardly unintellectual *Atlantic Monthly* said it was 'a godsend to parents'. But for all this praise, Watson could not shake out of his mind the harsh criticisms of psychologists like Angell who felt that to write such a book was to renounce your status as a serious scientist.

In 1929, when the book was published, Billy was seven and Jimmy was five. They continued to be educated on behaviouristic lines. Watson was living out his own ideas. Their life was far from being the cheerless routine that one might imagine. Though neither of their parents were very affectionate, the boys were encouraged to live a very full life. They learned how to swim, to skate, to box, to hang from trapezes and to stand on their hands. Every weekend they went off to camps which were rough, cold and fun. They had been trained to be adaptable children. They could sleep on the floor, in an Army cot or in a cosy bed. They could wash themselves in a fancy bathroom on Fifth Avenue or in a cold lake. Hardy souls they were. To be happy, Watson felt, was to be able to adapt. You had to be able to make do in a whole variety of environments.

Rosalie was, Jimmy recalls, 'very much a fun person'. Though she was not as strict as her husband, she was not often affectionate. But she loved talking with, not *down to*, she emphasised, her children. And being merry she loved playing with them. She sometimes helped Billy and Jimmy tie the behaviourist's pyjamas in knots. She had been known to put hair brushes in people's beds and, with her children, to hide behind doors and jump out at people. 'I really control this one,' she wrote. Watson, too, believed in talking a great deal with his children. They had their own talk-it-out club on Fifth Avenue, though, Jimmy recalls, his father very rarely talked about his own feelings. Billy and Jimmy were also encouraged to make friends with other adults. To ward off the dreaded dependency they had to know that their parents were not the only adults one could talk to. There were no rights and wrongs in the life of the Watson children. They were never told they were *bad*. Many nurses were dismissed because they could not cope with bringing up children without using that handy word. Rosalie wrote in 1930 that 'their moral prejudices were still in a fluid state.' She compared this happy state of affairs with the daughter of a friend of hers who when she saw Rosalie wearing red nail polish, exclaimed, 'Mummy, do nice women do that?' The Watson boys were allowed to smear themselves with blue nail varnish, which they thought great fun, while that girl could only view nail varnish as a mark of incipient evil because her 'behaviour is fast being poured into lead molds'. The Watsons made a definite attempt not to give their children contemporary moral prejudices.

But the Watson children also suffered from the fact that their parents believed they had the right to go on living their own lives. Children should not swallow their parents' lives whole. The Watsons went out a great deal. The children were expected to be very polite to their parents. They ate together rarely as a family. Rosalie felt there was some danger that their sons were not enough part of their lives. She wrote: 'I would like to feel our sons are a little more part and parcel of our home . . . I think lots of people are forgetting in this epoch of scientific rationalisation what fun a home can be.' In their home, some of the formalities strike one as absurd. Rosalie and Watson knocked before entering their children's rooms and expected, of course, their children to knock before entering their quarters. They treated their children as young adults and they expected their children to return the courtesy. But to expect children to behave like this was to place enormous demands on them, demands of which both Watson and Rosalie seem to have been blithely unaware. He was so sure that he had the way to raise independent children who could make do in whatever life threw up at them and she was always a little guilty because she was, as she said, 'not the perfect behaviouristic wife'. She liked to giggle, a bad sign, and she was 'still too much on the side of the children', a telling phrase. She could not resist kissing and hugging 'her two little pieces of protoplasm' sometimes. Watson had no difficulty, however, in remaining aloof.

The two little pieces of protoplasm became infant celebrities in New York. The newspapers photographed Billy and Jimmy as the models of modern children. They were behaviourism on trial, 'the unwitting subjects of experiments'. Reading the stories I get the feeling that the press was just waiting for one of these unconventionally educated children to show some sign of going to the bad. But Billy and Jimmy did not oblige. When Billy was five and Jimmy was three, the *World* carried a photograph of them on a bicycle. 'They are free from fear and temper tantrums. They are happy children.' Not coddling his own children seemed to work. When the boys went to the exclusive Bovee School at 836 Fifth Avenue the press duly noted the fact. The *World* added that most of the children at Bovee were 'the offspring of solid millionaires', and the Bovee never advertised. Billy and Jimmy were 'well built, bright, healthy and apparently good advertisements for behaviourism'.

By the end of the 1920s, then, Watson had concluded his research on children. The work that he did with Mary Cover Jones was very novel and important but he never really carried it on. The plan of observing children in their natural environment from birth on was one psychologists should have carried out. Some of Watson's actual observations remain useful: for example, no one else has till now looked at the situations that make children laugh. If Watson had systematically carried out observations on his own children as he planned, we would be able to compare Piaget's account of the development of his own children with those of other children. This would tell us much about children and about psychologists. Watson had more observations but they were destroyed. After the frosty reception *Psychological Care* received among psychologists, some of Watson's feelings of inferiority returned. For all his success, he felt out of psychology. He knew better than anyone else the imperfections of his research. After the departure of Mary Cover Jones, he could no longer do experiments that satisfied his high standards. Still, many of his ideas on observation seem to me to be of great value and his work on using conditioning techniques to cure children of their fears and anxieties was successful and years ahead of the rest of psychology.

The impact of Watson on the American baby was also not negligible. He was constantly asked for interviews and articles on how to bring up children. The 1920s were hungry for new knowledge. Science seemed to have limitless potential. It was plausible to assume that a scientific psychology would soon offer a way of rearing perfect children. The US Department of Health adopted some of Watson's ideas in their pamphlets for parents. Huxley's *Brave New World*, which was published in 1934, shows how great the impact of Watson was. Huxley foresaw a world in which children were conditioned to hate beauty and to fear themselves. Behaviourism would be a wonderful tool for dictators. Society was also changing. Families moved into cities and had money to spend on more than mere necessities. Women were becoming restless and wanted to do more than just bring up children. Watson spoke with authority and had a message which was not without advantage for all that it shocked. You could bring up your children to be healthy and independent by using the insights of science. Furthermore, the way you instilled independence also gave you time to lead more of your own life. It was the best of both worlds. The responsible parent took plenty of time away from its offspring. In a world where there was money enough to buy servants – and Watson said that no one should have a child unless that child could have a room of its own – all that meant that parenthood could be caring, intelligent and somehow less all-consuming. The reason that Watson made many Americans angry, of course, was that he suggested many mothers and fathers were so insecure that they clung to their children, loved them to if not literal death at least to utter dependency. It sounded true and it was a little too uncomfortable. But, wrote the behaviourist, no man had ever forced people to confront themselves in the way that Freud had. And that idea was a peculiarly Freudian one.

Watson ended the 1920s, then, not just as the man who had done much to shape American advertising but also as one of the nation's most influential and controversial experts on child care. He also, as we shall see, was not quite finished as an academic psychologist.

9

The Last of the Psychologist 1920–30

As well as pursuing some research on children and using psychology in advertising, Watson tried quite hard to remain something of a psychologist after 1920. It was not easy. The reaction of most psychologists to the divorce scandal was so pious as to be hard to credit now. Yerkes, his friend since 1904, does not seem to have written Watson any note; Dunlap, his old pupil, was only too glad to inherit his chair, Angell, his old professor, did not lift a finger to help him. The loyal Titchener did write Watson a brief note after he had furnished Resor with the reference Watson had asked for, but Titchener was convinced that it would take five or ten years for Watson to resume respectability. That was the vital qualification an academic student of human behaviour needed.

It was not only Watson's old friends who denied him. He aroused a great deal of general hostility among psychologists as a whole, as Titchener observed sadly in a letter to Herbert Warren, the owner of the *Psychological Review*. There were, it seems, a variety of reasons for the attitudes of psychologists. First, many were genuinely worried that the divorce scandal would give psychology a bad moral name. The psychoanalysts were always being accused of turning psychology into pornography. Here was the founder of behaviourism revealed as an adulterous sex maniac. The psychologists of the time were too deeply conventional actually to raise the question of whether what Watson had done was really so wrong. Second, many psychologists who were opposed to behaviourism could not resist the temptation to pillory Watson. If one could smear the reputation of the behaviourist, then one could sneer at the value of his ideas. Some of the attacks on the man were such as to give vitriol a bad name. When Watson became financially successful, and found he could command a wide audience through books like *The Psychological Care of the Infant and Child*, many psychologists also became jealous. Their only tactic was to outlaw Watson as being beyond the psychological pale. It must also be said, finally, that Watson was not a total victim. As the decade wore on, he became more flamboyant and less scholarly in the exposition of his own ideas. Slowly his isolation was taking its toll.

After twenty years in psychology it took some time for Watson to cut all the bonds with the discipline. At the time of the divorce he had two learned papers in press. One, written with Rosalie, resumed the work on children and added details of the experiments with Little Albert. The second paper appeared in the *British Journal of Psychology*. It should have been Watson's contribution to the seminar at Oxford which he never reached. The paper offered the behaviourist's latest ideas on thinking. It began with an outline of the theory of thinking that Watson had been putting forward since 1913. But the prospect of a meeting with the sharpest minds in the world had clearly made Watson take a long and critical look at the theory so that his arguments are somewhat more convincing and a trifle less dogmatic than they were before. After he had outlined the basic behaviourist line of thinking, Watson went on to say: 'In advance of any argument I think we can say that he [the behaviourist] has never really held the view that thinking is merely the action of the language mechanisms.' Watson admitted that his 'own loose way of writing' might have encouraged such a view. But the behaviourist was not about to allow back into the limelight any of the nefarious central processes that he had started to dislike so. Thinking, argued Watson, involved the whole body. He added:

> The behaviourist believes that thinking in the narrow sense where new adjustments are made corresponds to the trial and error process in manual learning. The process as a whole consists in the organised interplay of laryngeal and related muscular activity used in word responses and substitutive word responses; that is, the motor stage is not always situated in or even near the larynx.

Again, Watson pointed to the fact that children first had to think aloud in words before they could think silently. One of the reasons why his emphasis on muscles raised hackles was that many psychologists made a very fine distinction between a thought and the expression of a thought. They granted that the expression of the thought might involve some action, explicit or implicit, but which was in principle observable; but the sacrosanct thought itself was more remote than its expression and in all its cerebral purity it could only be observed by introspection. Watson argued that there was no real distinction between a thought and its expression.

Watson offered the symposium some recent results of Lashley's. Lashley had recorded tongue movements and shown that 'overt but whispered repetition of a sentence produced a tracing on the smoked drum which was wholly similar except for amplitude to that obtained when he told the subject to think the same thing without making overt movements.' For Watson, this was obviously crucial. The silent thought produced a physical and muscular response very like the pure spoken, but whispered thought. Watson's theory did not strictly demand that the unspoken thought 'bananas' should be accompanied by the same physiological responses of the tongue and larynx as when the spoken thought 'bananas' was uttered, but, obviously, any evidence to that effect would boost his theory. Watson and Lashley did, in fact, try to show that. If when I say 'bananas' and when I am asked to think 'bananas' my tongue and larynx do the same things, then it would really suggest that thought lay in the muscles.

Watson's paper was well received in Oxford. It led to much comment especially by Frederic Bartlett. For many years, the motor theory of thinking, the thesis that we think with and in our bodies rather than in our brains, remained influential. Subsequent research showed that there was a relationship between thinking and the state of tension in the muscles. Completely relaxed, people did not appear to have any thoughts. To show that is quite different from showing that we think with our viscera. George Humphrey, who was no behaviourist, devoted a long chapter in his important book on thinking to the motor theory of thinking which stemmed from Watson's ideas. He even found parts of it proven.

Watson's paper in 1920 was scrupulous, scholarly and reasonable. For Oxford, he pulled out all the academic virtues. It was not to be his final contribution to the study of thinking but he was already close to what became his final position later in the 1920s. Watson was certainly not right in his ideas and the current situation is paradoxical. Today, academic psychology tends to celebrate the cerebral with our new-found faith in cognitive psychology, though, of course, there is a whole range of encounter and growth groups that hold that really we think too much with our brains and that we should express ourselves more with our bodies. Not quite Watson's idea but an interesting evolution of the motor theory of thinking.

Despite the divorce, there were two official positions that Watson retained in psychology. Well before the divorce scandal, a number of major psychologists including Thorndike, McKeen Cattell, Dunlap, Angell and Watson had banded together to form the Psychological Corporation. The aim of this Corporation – which still exists today – was to make available to industry all manner of psychological knowledge and insight. Personnel selection, tests of particular skills, help with various problems would all be provided, for a fee, of course. Watson himself had long advocated that psychologists develop closer contacts with industry and the setting up of the Corporation owed much to him. The main work of launching it was done in 1920 while the behaviourist was still respectable but only in 1921 did the Corporation actually go into business. By then, it seems, the Psychological Corporation felt that it was vital to exclude the disreputable Dr Watson from the Corporation. He did little work for it though he was much concerned with the whole field of industrial psychology.

The psychologists could also not quite immediately divest Watson of the editorship of the *Journal of Experimental Psychology*. There had been a plan as far back as 1913 to divide the *Psychological Review* into two so that one of its journals would deal with theoretical contributions and the other with experimental ones. The war made this plan impossible. But in 1918, after much deliberation, the *Journal of Experimental Psychology* began to publish with Watson as its editor and a board of assistant editors which included Jastrow, Tolman and Dunlap. Energetic and by now expert in the arts of publishing learned journals, Watson made the new publication thrive. In its first years it attracted a number of major contributions including papers by Dunlap, Lashley, Weiss and Hunter.

Since the attitude of psychologists to Watson after he was dismissed was so negative, it is rather surprising to find that he was not asked to resign as editor of the *Journal of Experimental Psychology*. Shepherd Franz, one of the references for Resor, appears to have been instrumental in persuading the board of the journal to stay with Watson. It may well be that this show of loyalty was due to the fact that by now Watson was so expert at editing. And also, as Titchener shrewdly remarked, Watson had so great a reputation that his name on the masthead of the journal probably sold some 1,000 copies just by itself. It might be the wish of psychologists to remove him but common and commercial sense suggested that was a bad idea. For the time being, Watson remained editor of the journal.

The only psychologist with whom Watson stayed in close touch was Titchener. On 15 December 1921 he wished Titchener 'general good wishes' of the season and added enthusiastically: 'Incidentally I am to renew my youth in watching the antics of my infant son.' Watson told Titchener too that he had just received $55 for a review of a book by Bertrand Russell, a sum 'which seems to me almost unbelievable'. The divorce left Watson in need of money. On 14 March 1922 the behaviourist explained that he could not spend more than $20 to commission a young man to compile a bibliography of behaviourism because the alimony payments were so heavy. Titchener was a little offended by this since he had encouraged the young man to work up the bibliography and the two men did not write to each other for five months.

By the end of 1922 Watson was beginning to find his feet in the advertising business. But he knew quite well that there was not enough on Madison Avenue really to satisfy his intellect. In the autumn of 1922, after much soul searching, three teachers at the New School asked Watson if he would like to give a series of evening lectures. The three intrepid men were Horace Kallen, Leo Wallman and Alvin Johnson. The behaviourist was deeply grateful to them. He wrote to Titchener in October:

> My work started off at the New School quite auspiciously. About two hundred people in the audience, largely Columbia trained students, some Freudians, a few just interested and interesting people and the like. I lecture every Monday evening. I know I shall enjoy it but I am pretty tired when five o'clock comes and I lay down the business yoke for a while.

At the New School Watson performed two roles. He gave his own lectures which were largely based on the material in his book of 1919. And, sometimes also he acted as a kind of psychological impresario. He invited a few other psychologists up to the New School to give evening lectures which would often end with lively discussions. Watson took the opportunity of these lectures to write again to Yerkes. His fifteen lectures on behaviourism, he said, 'looks like a gradual return to respectability'. He told Yerkes a little defensively that he had 'lost interest in university work'. But then universities had lost interest in Watson, of course. But 'the baby work', the bulk of his university work since 1916, was different. 'If I could get the baby work started again I would starve to death,' he said. As we saw in the last chapter, Watson did not fail entirely with that though he did not, alas, give up money on Madison for romantic dedication to the study of child development.

As Yerkes was chairman of the Research Information Service of the National Research Council, one might have thought he could help his old friend. It was not to be. In fact, the reverse happened. Yerkes told Watson of his own problems at the National Research Council. His salary was too low – again. Were there any business contacts that Watson had who might be interested in Yerkes's services? By January 1923 Watson was in an excellent position to assist. He arranged for Yerkes to come and talk to the board of Macy's. After his spell at the counter, Watson had become very friendly with a number of directors of Macy's and had given them excellent advice on how to 'activate' the consumer. The activated consumer bought, bought and bought. Yerkes was delighted. He came up to New York. He talked at great length to the men at Macy's. They made him an offer. Yerkes threatened the National Research Council with his resignation. Terrified by the idea that another scientist would turn super-salesman, the National Research Council caved in to many of Yerkes's demands (imagine for a moment what might have happened to psychology if Yerkes had gone to work for Macy's and had triggered an exodus of exasperated scientists from universities to business. Where would psychology be now?)

But Yerkes had no real wish to go into industry. He had just wanted to find a way of improving his bargaining position. That done, he was very glad to get back to the academic way of life. Despite all this assistance from Watson, Yerkes remained fairly aloof in their relations and did nothing to aid the behaviourist. They stayed now in inter-mittent contact.

Early in 1923, as part of his programme at the New School, Watson invited MacDougall to come and address his class. If the behaviourist was the fiery evangelist who could not stand any criticism, it is really odd that he should have invited MacDougall. What MacDougall had to say could not have surprised Watson for in October, in a letter to Titchener, Watson said he had appreciated 'a nice little dig' that MacDougall took at both of them. 'One I thought rather clever, to the effect that in this country the student apparently was expected either to become a Titchenerian or a Behaviourist. He suggested that there was another possibility, namely, to become a Psychologist.' Though that seemed a sharp dig, Watson thought that the rest of the article was 'cry baby' and he particularly thought little of 'the idea of bragging on the second page that his book had gone through many editions and distinguished gentlemen support him.' Most of those distinguished gentlemen were not even psychologists, Watson pointed out. Despite all these reservations about MacDougall, Watson felt he should expose his class to his ideas. On 5 February 1923 MacDougall addressed the Monday night students at the New School.

MacDougall was not a total failure at the New School. 'The class liked his talk very much but they were not convinced,' Watson reported to Titchener. MacDougall lumped these two very different men together as prime perpetrators of mechanistic psychology even though a few months back he had jibed that students had to be either with Watson or with Titchener. MacDougall saw human purposes and human motives as the unfolding either of the divine will or of the *élan vital*. To understand human action in any other way was wrong. Mechanistic psychology could never unravel human motives or purposes. 'And he begged the class to accept that dictum while they were young.' This would spare them a lot of unnecessary effort. 'In other words, after you spend a busy and active life on psychology, you

227

have to lie down, admit that everything is futile and rest on the bosom of the Lord.' That was no resting place for Watson. He wanted Titchener to come to the New School to rebut MacDougall and hoped also to show him round J. Walter Thompson.

The relationship between Watson and MacDougall developed into further acrimony. MacDougall made a few more jibes in print at the expense of behaviourism. Then later in 1923 Watson was asked by *New Republic* to review MacDougall's new book, *Outline of Psychology*.

Watson first accused MacDougall of trying to put the scientific clock back thirty years. He claimed that any work in the laboratory that smacked of 'mechanical psychology' was useless. Watson went on to object to MacDougall investing organisms with purpose. To allege that the Divine Will injected purpose into biological creatures was 'an insult to the corporate body of facts and deductions we call science'. Stronger stuff was yet to come. Watson asked the reader to imagine he was watching an earthworm. As proof of omnipresent purpose, MacDougall had stated that an earthworm will explore a piece of paper before drawing it into its burrow. Witnessing this creative scene must be very touching, according to Watson for, if we follow the purposive MacDougall; 'all we can do when we see the earthworm tugging a triangular piece of paper into his burrow is to take off our hats, glance humbly downwards, point the facts out to the youths who look to us for guidance and say, "What an example of foresight – what beautiful proof of the wisdom of our Creator in endowing so lowly a creature with purpose" and then pass on to our Sunday dinner of fowl and mutton.' Such an attitude would soon starve the scientific journals of any new papers, especially as, Watson accused, 'Nor shall we let the youngster stop to try out a few things on the earthworm.' Experimenting on the earthworm was out of the question. It should not be painted with cocaine, soaked in whisky, given drugs or even cut in half to see how such manipulations affected its behaviour. The reason why MacDougall was hostile to experiments, Watson argued, was that he was a religious maniac. 'From his earliest writing he, like many Englishmen, has been a telepathist at heart.' MacDougall believed both in consciousness, the mind, spirit and the soul. His psychology was full 'of the mystical connotations that Hume so valiantly combated,' said Watson.

Watson's verdict was the sort that is usually reserved for pornography. He said 'the book is unsafe.' It should not be given to elementary students or to the general public. 'It breeds a lazy, genial, speculative arm-chair attitude.' It is not surprising that MacDougall was so bitter towards Watson.

It is interesting that before he published this review Watson sent it off to Titchener. 'If you think I am too rough on him I could modify it somewhat, but before you make me soften it, please look up the rotten things he has been saying.' Titchener replied quickly to say that he thought the gist of the review was fair but that, at four points, Watson had really gone too far. Watson answered to say that the review was now, alas, in proof because *New Republic* had rushed it into print quickly and that there was no real chance to alter it. Watson was apologetic, he said; 'I see now, in the light of the few days that have elapsed since I wrote the review, that I was hasty and that when I take the review up a year from now I shall be ashamed of the spots you mention.' In a corner of the page, Watson scribbled that he had not meant 'to rub it in' on the English by calling them telepathists. 'God knows I like them better than they like themselves,' quipped Watson and he excluded the British Titchener from the criticism.

The hostility between Watson and MacDougall was far from being at an end. After this review, it was suggested that they debate in public. This gladiatorial contest would take place in February 1924.

But other psychologists than MacDougall were at odds with Watson. He had made many academics angry with his review. Titchener had to write to Professor Raymond Dodge of the National Research Council explaining that Watson 'had had extreme provocation; but no amount of provocation excuses bad taste.' Titchener pointed out that Watson had wanted to make alterations but the review was already set in proof. Titchener told Dodge all this in confidence 'since as you say, you have been predisposed towards MacDougall by Watson's invective. For my own part I had a good deal rather be Watson than MacDougall.'

In 1923, a few months after this skirmish with MacDougall, there was a concerted move on the part of the board of the *Journal of Experimental Psychology* to have Watson removed from the editorship. Professor H. C. Warren, who had personally bought the *Psychological Review* in 1908, now still controlled most of the shares in the new experimental journal. Warren was worried by the condition of the journal. Since he had gone to work for J. Walter Thompson, Watson had antagonised many psychologists. Though the papers published between 1920 and 1923 include some interesting contributions on a whole variety of topics including Lashley's paper on a behaviouristic interpretation of consciousness, Tolman on emotions and a good deal of work on social psychology, there was a feeling that the journal was a disappointment. Warren wrote to Titchener who was one of the editors of the *American Journal of Psychology*, one of its main rivals. Titchener said he had to admit that the journal 'is generally looked upon as not having fulfilled its original promise.' Titchener felt Watson 'is under a double disadvantage as editor: first, he has no interest in experimental psychology and therefore in all probability does not command the confidence of experimentalists; and, secondly, there is still in certain quarters, a very strong and bitter feeling on personal grounds.' Some experimental psychologists were clearly offering their papers to other journals because they did not care for Watson. Titchener's curious point that Watson was not interested in experiments can be explained by recalling that, for Titchener, proper experiments were introspective. He saw Watson as a man carving out a 'technology' of behaviour.

Titchener was careful, however, to point out the merits of Watson. As 'his name is very much to the forefront in newspapers and magazines', it was likely that he attracted readers. Might it not be possible to get Watson to 'spruce up' the scientific character of the journal rather than ask him to resign? Warren was not content, however, to do just that. He asked Watson to give up the editorship on the understanding that the behaviourist would become one of four co-editors of the journal. Though Watson was not very happy with that proposal he had no option but to accept. In practice Bentley became editor and Watson played less and less of a role in the journal he had done so much to create.

In 1923 Watson also began to find himself under fierce personal attack. He was quite used to attacks on behaviourism. But now that he was no longer an academic psychologist some of the attacks were extraordinarily personal and hostile. In 1923 A. A. Roback, a disciple of Titchener, accused Watson of all the scientific sins possible. Roback was doing work which might be described as the fag-end of introspection. He read to his subjects bits of Aquinas, Anselm, Nietzsche and other great thinkers. Subjects were to introspect with particular attention to their sensations when they agreed or disagreed with a particular philosophical gem. When subjects agreed, Roback found, that was 'characterised by a tingling in the chest' so that we may take intellectual agreement really *to be* a feeling round the solar plexus. (Is not this view even more bizarre than Watson's that we think with our larynx?) Thus, according to Roback, to tingle is to agree but to disagree *is* to feel all stuffed up in the chest as if I have a bad cold. If only Nietzsche had been alive to see to what pettifogging use Roback was putting his bitter maxims whose butts were often psychologists. Enough, though, of Roback and his intellectual tinglings. The point is that Watson aroused all the ire Roback could muster. Roback argued, first, that behaviourism was wrong; second, that it was not Watson's idea anyway; and, third, how dare the commercial creature! Watson was running an advertising agency and so he could hardly be considered a qualified psychologist or a man fit to have views on human nature. He was no psychologist but a puffed-up salesman with delusions of intellect. Roback could hardly contain his fury. Why did anyone bother to discuss Watson's views?. They were not psychology. Madison Avenue had metamorphosed Watson into a psychological non-person.

Roback's attack was particularly vitriolic. But many other psychologists were, as Titchener had noted, surprisingly hostile to Watson. Watson wrote to Titchener about Roback and said the attack was so intemperate, it really did not bother him too much. But others like his one-time colleague Arthur Lovejoy also attacked Watson in a 'vicious' way, as the behaviourist put it. To some extent Watson could shrug off these attacks as being just too personal and hysterical. But he did feel wounded and he missed the cut and thrust of intellectual debate. By the end of 1923, Watson was heartily disliked by most other psychologists in America. Titchener was really his only loyal friend.

While all this was going on, Watson continued to teach one evening a week at the New School. He was still feeling the urge to make useful contributions in the field and, in 1924, he published a revised edition of *Psychology from the Standpoint of a Behaviourist*. He altered much of the opening chapter, brought the chapters on the sense organs up to date with the help of H. M. Johnson and added a preface. Watson wrote that since the first edition

> behaviourism has been passing through an emotional and logical evaluation. Whether it is to become a dominant *system* of psychology or to remain merely a *methodological* approach is still not decided. The strong reaction for and against behaviourism points to the fact that psychological students are restless. . . . Most of the younger psychologists realise that some such formulation as behaviourism is the only road leading to science.

Functional psychology could not help for 'it died of its own half-heartedness before behaviourism was born'. Freudian ideas, though useful, could 'never serve as a support for a scientific formulation'. The structuralists, like Titchener, who were interested in the anatomy of consciousness were impaled 'upon a crude mystical dualism, the roots of which extend far back into theological mysticism'. Behaviourism has to make 'a clean break with the whole concept of consciousness. Such a clean break is possible because the metaphysical premises of behaviourism are different from those of structural psychology.' Watson was worried by psychologists who were 'half-way behaviourists' and believed both in some objective study and some introspection. They would dilute behaviourism and it ran the risk that it would lose its very identifiable ruthlessness.

231

In this preface, Watson also made some valuable historical notes. He said he had first raised behaviouristic ideas in conversation back in 1903. 'This formulation was not encouraged,' he commented tersely. 'He was told that it would work for animals, but not for human beings,' he noted tersely. Later in a seminar at Yale in 1908, when he tried out these ideas again, he was informed that such a psychology would be only 'at a descriptive level'. Psychology had to offer explanations though, 'How a parallelistic psychology could be explanatory was not brought out.' The preface also made a realistic acknowledgment to Knight Dunlap. Dunlap's treatment of the image was an important factor in helping Watson frame his own ideas on the image as expressed in *Image and Affection in Behaviour* but Dunlap contributed nothing more.

The alterations in the text are largely predictable. New material from the work on Little Albert was included. The extended theory of thinking which had been evolved for the 1920 Congress replaced the earlier and rather tedious section on thinking. As well as these additions Watson totally rewrote the first nine pages of the book, but he really did not revise his main arguments much. He renewed the plea that psychology should be a natural science. As usual, he put forward a good critique of introspection, and added one new barbed assessment. 'All that introspective psychology has been able to contribute is the assertion that the mental states are made up of several rather than irreducible units.' The atoms of the mind were elusive yet. Psychology should 'study man in action' rather than in the laboratory and such inquiry ought to be of use. Every person 'needs the data and laws of behaviourism for organising his own life.'

Changes in the book reflect two factors. Watson was very much concerned to keep the book up to date. He did not want to be accused of having lost touch with recent developments in psychology. Also, very many students were buying the book and the ex-professor felt he had a responsibility to them. They had to have the best possible text going.

Late in 1923 the Psychological Club in Washington decided to make the most of the skirmishing between Watson and MacDougall. The club invited the two men to debate with each other. At the end of the debate the club would vote. The winner of that vote would presumably be consecrated as the man with the true theory. Watson, who never shied away from debate, looked forward to this encounter. Though he attacked MacDougall he took care not to be too vicious or too personal in his attacks on MacDougall's ideas.

On 5 February 1924 the two psychologists confronted each other before a full house of the Psychological Club. Over 300 people were

232

there. It was an impressive occasion. Watson was the first to speak – and one wonders if they tossed for who was to go first. Watson did not want to be as vitriolic as he had been in *New Republic*. He outlined his own ideas stylishly and had some fun at the expense of MacDougall. If everything was the unfolding of the Divine Will, were we to imagine the Lord tugging at each arm to make it reach out for a plate? Watson was really rather restrained.

On the other hand MacDougall was neither accurate nor restrained. He accused Watson of being 'unfeeling' because he denied the existence of emotions; he accused Watson of denying that people dreamed which was rather absurd since Watson had called for a study of how language was used in dreams. Behaviourism, said MacDougall, 'knows nothing of pleasure and pain, of admiration and gratitude. He has relegated all such "metaphysical entities" to the dust heap.' Watson did not dump them on the dust heap, of course. To offer a radical new interpretation of what love is, and what causes love, is not to deny the fact that the emotion exists. MacDougall seemed not to be able to catch the distinction. He suggested that behaviourism would have bad social consequences. 'If all men believed the teachings of the mechanical psychology, no man would raise a finger in the effort to prevent war, to achieve peace or to realise any other ideas. . . . So I say the mechanical psychology is useless and far worse than useless. It is paralysing to human action.'

That last phrase highlights again the peculiar paradox of behaviourism. It has always been argued that behaviourism appealed to America because Americans distrusted contemplation. The USA was the land of action. Yet any close reading of behaviourism would suggest that the theory promotes a model of mankind which does not act but react. Watson, as I have argued, was eager to have individuals use psychology to better themselves and to know themselves better. His mechanical psychology and its in- or ex-sights would free human beings for greater action. MacDougall did not really properly exploit this inconsistency in Watson's thinking; he fell back on inaccurate railing.

Towards the end of the debate MacDougall tried hard to be adroit. The idea that psychology should not use introspection led MacDougall to say: 'I am moved almost to break into song, to exclaim: "Oh, Mr Watson, what a funny man you are." ' A few moments later the generous MacDougall, who believed in human and divine purpose, was asking the audience to yield 'these natural human of impulses of pity' to the unnatural Dr Watson. Out of such pity for man who clearly had no idea of what it was to be a man, MacDougall pretended to urge the audience to vote for Dr Watson. The irony was rather infantile.

And MacDougall brought the last few sneering minutes of his talk to an end with the following invitation: 'Vote for Dr. Watson, for Behaviourism and for men as a penny-in-the-slot machine. In a few years, if my reading of the signs of the times is not wholly at fault, the peculiar dogmas for which he stands will have passed to the limbo of the "old forgotten far off things and battles long ago".'

The vote went against MacDougall by a short head. But he was not too dismayed. He noted scornfully that all the ladies, of whom there were a fair number, had voted for Watson and implied that this was because the behaviourist had the better looks. Both authors had prepared written contributions for the great debate; eventually the text of the whole encounter was published under the stirring title of *The Battle of Behaviourism*. (It must now rank as the longest battle ever for Chomsky and Skinner are still fighting much of it.) In 1929 MacDougall added a postscript in which he bemoaned the fact that behaviourism was still thriving and he regretted that it had not done the decent thing he predicted in 1924 – withered away. MacDougall added that when he had said it would soon wither away that opinion 'was founded upon a too generous estimate of the intelligence of the American public'. MacDougall did not feel that it was under the aegis of the divine will or purpose that the Americans listened to Watson. It was still five years to that postscript, though, and throughout 1924 Watson continued to attract large audiences to his once-weekly lectures at the New School.

In 1924 Watson published what would be his last research papers. 'The Unverbalised in Human Behaviour' and 'The Place of Kina-esthetic, Visceral and Laryngeal Organs in Thinking' appeared in the *Psychological Review*. In them he put forward an extended, challenging account of his ideas on language and thought. He argued from his and Mary Cover Jones's observations that an 'almost unbelievable amount of organisation goes on in infants too young to talk'. By organisation he meant development of physical co-ordinations and of 'conditioned fears, loves, rages'. Watson said that as he wrote he was observing a child – his son – who was 2 years 3 months old and who had an enor-mous range of physical skills. He could pedal a large toy car up a hill, guide it, drag it, steer it and coast down hill on it. But 'the only *verbal parallel* [Watson's italics] to these physical feats is the sentence "Billy ride kiddy car".' The words were very imperfect by comparison with the movements. Watson argued that this example showed that the manual habits that very young children learn are unverbalised. That meant, he claimed, that they had no memory of them in the sense that an adult has memory of how to play golf. For if you ask an adult to describe either what golf is or how he played that wonderful round last Sunday, the adult can paint a good picture in words. That picture *is* his memory, Watson asserted. But the three-year-old child has very little of such a memory.

For Watson, the importance of this was that it allowed him to claim that Freud's 'unconscious' could be explained in less mysterious ways. It was not necessary to assume that society repressed the child's memory of his free, pleasure-strewn early years and it was not to assume 'that these childhood memories are lost until the analyst gives the mystical phrase which opens the cave where the memories are stored. The unsatisfactory ground for this assumption is now apparent. *The child had never verbalised these acts.'* Watson went on to give an example of an experiment he and Rosalie tried on Jimmy and Billy. Billy was 2 years and 3 months old. He had been weaned from a bottle at one year. He now had a baby brother, Jimmy. On 17 February 1924 Rosalie called 'Dinner, Billy', laid him flat in his crib as she had when she had given him a bottle and handed him the warmed milk. Billy began to cry. When told to 'take his milk', he put the nipple of the bottle to his mouth and began to chew it. 'Nursing could not be called out,' Watson claimed. Before this test, the Watsons had done their best to stir up their son's memory of bottle-fed days by talking about bottles. To no avail. Billy reacted to the whole situation just as if he had no memory of what to do when confronted by a bottle. It was not a question of repression. Rosalie even offered her son the breast but, again, the child would not suckle. He could not remember what to do.

The concept of repression is, Watson argued, misconstrued. The very young child never has the memories to repress. The behaviourist noted too that while children were not encouraged to organise their 'incestuous attachments' verbally, the whole notion of mother love meant that children were kissed, hugged and petted, if not to death, at least to perversity. Watson never pursued this interesting explanation of Freud's unconscious any further. In his summary, he repeated the claim that 'unverbalised organisation makes up the Freudian unconscious'. Watson's faith in the body and its muscles did not mean that he played down the importance of words. He recognised that as soon as a child did learn to speak quite well 'word organisation soon becomes dominant because man has to solve his problems verbally'. Watson presumed, rather than proved, that particular point. Later Watson was always urging parents to help their children by getting them to name the actions they performed so that the development of language skills would soon catch up with manual skills.

In these papers, too, Watson attempted – rather in passing – a definition of what it means to be conscious. Given that we learn to name the exterior actions we perform, psychologists would come to see 'that being "conscious" is merely a popular or literary phrase descriptive of the act of naming our universe of objects both inside and outside, and that "introspecting" is a much narrower popular phrase descriptive of the more awkward act of naming tissue changes that are taking places like movements of muscles, tendons etc.' By the age of ten, we are well practised at catching a flutter in the foreskin or tension in the toe. But, of course, the explanation is defective. For what causes the act to be carried out?

This final paper contains controversial ideas that are not followed through, powerful suggestions that could do with a more critical scrutiny and has a certain strident tone which now began to spoil Watson's work.

Throughout this period Watson continued to give lectures at the New School. He was also asked to lecture at the Cooper Institute in 1924. But though he enjoyed lecturing, he could not now give his ideas the concentrated attention they needed in order to develop. Titchener asked him for a paper for the *American Journal of Psychology* and referring to his brain as a vegetable, Watson replied wryly: 'Formulations grow very slowly in my bean these busy business days. It seems to be a long while between drinks. In the event, however, that my laryngeal and related apparatus do become active enough to start the writing habit, I shall certainly ask the Journal to read the result with a view to publication.' But the writing habit never re-asserted itself in this vein though Watson did promise Titchener to try and have something ready for the July 1925 issue of the *Journal*.

One of the reasons why Watson had nothing to offer Titchener was that he was already committed to writing up four lectures for publication. A young publisher, W. W. Norton, 'got hold of me and practically forced me to write up a course of lectures I was giving at the Cooper Institute.' And while Watson was disgorging these words he had also promised to contribute a chapter to a volume called *Psychologies of 1925* which was being edited by Carl Murchison of Clark University. The chapter would be based on a lecture Watson would give at Clark. Norton, an aggressive salesman, rushed Watson's lectures into print as pamphlets. Since the material of the lecture at Clark was identical to the material in one of the pamphlets, Watson felt very embarrassed. He confessed to Titchener, who was having his own problems with Murchison. 'Now the hell of it is the book will be out, in lecture form at least before I lecture at Clark. I guess the only thing I can do is to have a nervous breakdown and get out of it that way. I have been known to do that before,' commented the behaviourist who was far from unaware of his own foibles. Titchener counselled British moderation. It would be preferable to admit to influenza.

In the end Watson did not put on a nervous breakdown. He

managed to explain to Murchison that he had agreed to let Norton publish these lectures a long time previously. If that meant that Murchison preferred not to have him give that one lecture, that would be fine. Murchison, however, was very eager to have the behaviourist expound his views and so Watson went up to Clark in February 1925 to deliver yet another talk on behaviourism and its benefits. He eventually let Murchison have two more chapters, one on Little Albert, the other on the emotions. Later that year Norton's published in book form the lectures that Watson had given at the Cooper Institute. Watson was not pleased with the book because it was 'strictly a rush job' and showed only too clearly 'its hasty origin'. He rewrote it a great deal for the second edition which appeared in 1930. By then he had new material and some new ideas to incorporate.

It will be clear by now that Watson devoted much energy to keeping his ideas before academic psychologists even though many of them appeared to detest him heartily. He also, as we shall see in the next chapter, began to do a great deal of popular writing that expounded behaviourism and its uses. Watson might have lost the writing habit for academic papers but he trained himself to write well for the intelligent magazines of the 1920s. Rosalie helped him to some extent. As a result of that, a number of Watson's articles for *Harpers* were collected together into a book called *The Ways of Behaviourism* which was published in 1928 though all of the material and ideas in it stem from the previous years.

With Watson propagating his ideas so actively, he roused into critical fury a whole variety of writers. One colleague wrote that 'Dr. Watson was once a good scientist' but he was now preaching vulgarly as if behaviourism were 'an evangelical religion and he preaches it with all the dogmatic zest and vulgarity of a Billy Sunday.' And if psychologists objected to this religious fervour, many religious people complained, in the words of one article, 'behaviourism is a theory entirely contrary to the psychological theory teaching of the Lord.' (It seems to me, incidentally, quite wrong as a criticism. Jehovah in the Old Testament was frequently trying to condition the Jews into obedience by thrusting fire, brimstone and prophets at them when they disobeyed Him: in the New Testament, a form of delayed reward dear to Skinner's heart is given. Be good now and, ultimately, in Paradise, rewards will be eternal. Both techniques owe a lot to behaviourism or vice-versa. But, this is by the way.) The ministers of the period saw behaviourism as dreadfully wicked. In November 1926, in the *Christian Register*, a more subtle approach was taken by Richard Boynton, professor of philosophy at Buffalo. Boynton disliked behaviourism but argued that it would not do too much harm because 'man is incurably religious'. The modern Christian could view it as a new psychological technique rather than a moral or mortal threat. In March 1927 Bishop Henry Mikell, who was said to be 'the most intellectual bishop in the US', claimed that behaviourism was responsible for a wave of student suicides. The reason shows how very different Watson's behaviourism seemed. The mind-throbbing bishop claimed that behaviourism made students 'indulge in a great deal of self-introspection'. Examining their personalities as recommended in Watson's quizzes made these young men and women so depressed that, the bishop said, 'the student says "Oh what is the use! I'll end it all!" '

In 1927 a number of books were published that attacked behaviourism. Louis Berman's *A Religion Called Behaviourism* seemed to generate the most attention at the time and attracted a number of prestigious reviewers. Berman's book cannot be said to be critically sound. After objecting that behaviourism robbed man of all dignity because it reduced us to the level of rats, Berman went on to say that behaviourism was partly responsible for 'making pessimism fashionable and suicide contagious'. It is intriguing to think that a mere theory of human behaviour could be thought to lead to such drastic consequences. More interesting really than Berman's book were the reviews of it.

Jastrow, the sociologist, believed that Berman was largely correct. Behaviourism was a 'barren theory in which purpose is hokum; feeling is verbalised sentimentality and elaborated visceral reactions and imagination, inspiration, creation nothing but the swiftly evolved patterns of something like a rat running in an infinitely complex maze.' These points, judged Jastrow, 'strike the inner ring if not the bull's eye'. Henry Hazlitt was much less favourable to Berman. Hazlitt thought that Watson's work 'stands in need of a thorough drubbing' but Berman had signally failed to provide it. Hazlitt believed that behaviourism undervalued the role of heredity. The theory of thinking put forward by Watson was inadequate and the various attempts to test it were not serious. He made fun of Watson's last experiment (reported back in 1920) when he had asked subjects to think aloud and had been gratified to find they thought aloud 'in terms of words'. How else were they to think aloud? In grunts? In musical snatches? Hazlitt quipped: 'Was there anything ever more naive in all "scientific" literature?' Hazlitt also took the behaviourist to task for stating that because it was impossible to tackle consciousness in the laboratory, consciousness did not exist. Perhaps if Watson had been able to pursue his academic career, his observations out in the world might have softened his position. With all these reservations Hazlitt felt that

Watson still had much to offer, though the true psychologist 'must be more of a scientist and less of a showman'. Hazlitt ended his review by comparing behaviourism and psychoanalysis. Psychoanalysis, Hazlitt said, reads into the human mind many things that are not there: behaviourism reads out much that is there.

Behaviourism was attracting so much publicity that it made a cautious man like Yerkes nervous. Watson invited him up to the New School to take part in a seminar which would also include Walter Hunter, an arch-behaviourist and Edward Boring, a pupil of Titchener's. Watson told Yerkes that 'what you say to them will be a good corrective to the type of propaganda that I have been feeding them.' Yerkes agreed but made Watson promise that the seminar would not be reported. He did not want to find his views either on the New School or the battles within psychology publicised. Watson agreed. The two men enjoyed seeing each other and Watson seems to have taken no offence at what might seem to be Yerkes's failure to help his friend in times of need. They discussed Yerkes's work on the gorilla. The behaviourist said that to hear Yerkes talk of that work made him very envious. 'It would be a real treat to do such work', but though Watson was by now able to give the odd academic lecture, no university ever considered hiring him for a full-time job. Yerkes was surprised by how little Watson had been sucked into business life. 'It seemed very much like old times,' Yerkes wrote after the seminar, 'to be talking shop with you and to find your interests so little changed.'

But many psychologists preferred to suggest that Watson had found his true *métier* on Madison Avenue. MacDougall, in a review of the first edition of *Behaviourism*, gave vituperative vent to such thoughts. MacDougall wrote:

Dr. Watson knows if you wish to sell your wares you must assert very loudly, plainly and frequently that they are the best on the market, ignore all criticism and avoid all argument and all appeal to reason. The response of the American press to his new book shows how sound these methods are. The susceptibility of the public to attack by these methods in the purely commercial sphere is a matter of no serious concern. When the same methods make a victorious invasion of the intellectual realm, it is difficult to regard the phenomenon with the same complacency.

Watson's contribution to advertising was, of course, just that he did not merely brag repetitively that his product was the best. But in his *brio*, MacDougall was only concerned to vilify the behaviourist. No one seems to have felt that MacDougall was in poor taste for Watson had few friends among professional psychologists.

The lack of any facilities to do research, the hostility of most psychologists, the time he had to spend on Madison Avenue, all combined to make Watson gradually more rigid. He could see more and more that he had no real chance of ever making his way back into science. In 1922 he had seen the lectures at the New School as marking a gradual return to respectability. He had hoped that he might be able to set up something more permanent as a result of the work with Mary Cover Jones. But his friends singularly failed to oblige. Yerkes and Angell were both in positions to help him. Neither offered to do so. Watson was too proud to ask too much. And his own life had also changed so that he would have had to persuade both himself and Rosalie to cut their living standards mightily. Some time in 1928 Watson set about one final attempt to put his psychological ideas in order for he began to revise the first edition of *Behaviourism* into the final and definitive statement of his psychology.

In many ways *Behaviourism* followed the same plan as *Psychology from the Standpoint of a Behaviourist*. The first chapter deals with the general theory 'the old and new psychology contrasted'. Then there are three chapters on techniques of doing psychological research and two chapters on the human body and its physiology. There was very little that Watson said in these chapters that was at all novel. Much more interesting were his chapters on instincts which show change in emphasis in his views and on emotions which incorporated all the new research that he had done with Mary Cover Jones.

Not surprisingly, Watson began again by attacking introspective psychology. But Titchener's death in 1927 had 'left introspective psychology without emotional leadership'. Watson now pointed out the errors of introspective psychology in historical retrospect. After '30 odd barren years' of introspection, the behaviourists had decided in 1912 that it was no longer possible to do psychology in that kind of way. Watson did not specifically mention his own paper as the starting point of behaviourism. He went on to sketch a few specific problems which had been studied objectively. Then in three short sections he mentioned issues that I have picked out as important in his psychology. He said that 'to understand behaviourism begin to observe people.' But while he still stressed observation, he was much now less willing to allow people to begin by studying themselves. He said that this was very difficult, if not impossible. Equally, his concept of the stimulus became less liberal. He now defined a stimulus in the narrower, now orthodox way. A sound of a gun going off; the smell of hydrogen sulphide; small pellets of rat food, these are stimuli. The complexities of 'determiners of acts' in 1919 were by and large lost.

But while Watson was becoming more rigid in his specific ideas, he was clear now that behaviourism was an approach rather than a total system of psychology. The method did not entail one model of humanity once you accepted the basic proposition that we were soft biological machines. For all the useful results objective psychology was beginning to notch up, Watson wrote: 'It may never make a pretense of being a system. Indeed systems in every scientific field are out of date. We collect our facts from observation.' Experiments refine hypotheses. Conclusions have to be modified.

> Every scientific field, zoology, physiology, chemistry and physics is more or less in a state of flux. Experimental technique, the accumulation of facts by that technique, occasional tentative con-solidation of these facts into a theory or an hypothesis describe our procedure in science. Judged upon this basis, behaviourism is a true natural science.

It was a modern and realistic approach.

Most of the second chapter was devoted to an exposition of Pavlov conditioning including Pavlov's own techniques. But, again, Watson repeated his case for observation of real life. But, once more, by now, his impatience was showing through in places. He argued that large political experiments, like the overthrow of the Tsar in Russia, were too haphazard and he seemed to say that the behaviourist offered a more sensible method of social planning. For example, he pointed out that the Bolsheviks in their revolutionary fervour set about a whole series of experiments on a vast scale. They made divorce easy, argued against the family, liberalised all manner of Tsarist laws on sex, redistributed property, abolished inheritances. But they did all this without proper prior testing. If only Lenin had been familiar with behaviourism he would have acted more objectively, Watson seemed to suggest. Pro-hibition was another case in point. Religious fervour changed social conditions radically. 'In this type of social experimentation society often plunges – does not feel its way out by means of small scale experimentations. It works with no definite experimental programme in front of it.' As a result, complained Watson, 'its behaviour often becomes mob-like which is another way of saying that the individuals composing the groups fall back upon infantile behaviour.' If politicians would only take psychology seriously, change could be better managed. Most social experiments had been carried out in the 'interest of some nation, political group, sect or individual rather than under the guidance of social scientists, assuming their existence.' Watson promoted the behaviourist or social scientist as the person with the knowledge and, therefore, the right to create new social structures which would 'perfect' society. Only in his last paragraph did Watson concede a shred of modesty for he admitted there that 'we know far too little of the make up of the human body' in order to be able to declare 'what is "good" or "bad" for the human organism – to know how to guide man's conduct on experimentally sound lines is beyond us at present.' Skinner, of course, took up this challenge and in *Walden Two* offered a behaviourist Utopia. But the arguments that Watson outlined reflect his growing stridency. He made many digs against the ignorant and corrupt politicians of America and against 'labor propagandists' and 'religious persecutors' who prevented the kind of intelligent social experiments he was advocating. He was too forceful for the good of his own points.

In the next two chapters, Watson dealt with the physiology of the body, and he then came to the most interesting part of the book, that on instincts. From a historical point of view Watson's chapters were to influence how people perceived behaviourism. Since 1914 Watson's views on instincts had hardened considerably. He was now willing to be fairly dogmatic about the number of instincts human babies had and how they used them. It was Watson's final dogma which was remembered and then caricatured into the position that behaviourism believed babies were born with no instincts, conditioning fodder for the environment to mould entirely in its wisdom. But still in his two chapters 'against' instincts in the book, Watson listed a whole variety of 'unlearned behaviours' that the baby is born with. These included reflexes that enabled it to grasp objects, the first basic arm movements that would later allow the baby to reach and a whole catalogue of other embryonic skills. Knowledge of the abilities of the new-born infant was still very limited because society did not seem to want scientists to study the development of the baby in too much detail. But, Watson said, there had been enough observations – and Mary Cover Jones had added to the stock of data here – for it to be clear that among the 'relatively simple human responses there is none corresponding to what is called an "instinct" by present day psychologists and biologists.' Watson went on to attack the notion that 'mental traits' are inherited. He admitted flying in the face of such eugenicists as Galton but he believed that early training of the child is the crucial factor in determining both its intelligence and the talents of that it will come to have. But even here, Watson was not quite as much of an environmentalist as we have come to believe. He did introduce his discussion with a section on 'Differences in Structure'. Watson never defined what he meant by *structure* here but it appears to refer to the whole biological make-up of an organism. He wrote:

The fact that there are marked individual variations in structure

242

among men has been known since biology began. But we have never sufficiently utilised it in analysing man's behaviour. I want to utilise another fact only recently brought out by the behaviourists and other students of animal psychology. Namely that habit formation starts in all probability in embryonic life and that even in the human young environment shapes behaviour so quickly that all of the older ideas about what types of human behaviour are inherited and what are learned break down. Grant variations in structure at birth and rapid habit formation from birth and you have a basis for explaining many of the so-called facts of inheritance of 'mental' characteristics.

It seems to me that because Watson was read rightly as having debased the value of instincts, he was taken to have debased the importance of heredity. Instincts are inherited: Watson being hostile to instincts, he must be hostile to and dismiss all heredity as zero. There is no doubt that Watson believed that a normal child could be conditioned to become anything from a lawyer to a miner by his environment and that he felt that conditioning was more important than heredity. But he did not lapse into the absurd position of believing that conditioning is all.

In *Behaviourism*, however, it is clear that the position he had taken on instincts is much more ruthless than before. In 1914, he had adopted a long list of instincts, by 1919 there seemed to be a few instincts. By now he did not see the value of the concept at all. Watson accepted that the behaviour of the infant was a product of 'the way he is put together and of the material out of which he is made – he must act (until learning has reshaped him) as he does act.' But one may argue: 'That gives your whole argument away – you admit he does a lot of things he is forced to do by his structure – this is just what I mean by instinct.' But Watson said that the kinds of acts that James, for example, listed as instincts were distinctly different. They were complex whole acts – like instincts for hoarding and walking. Relying on the observations of children made at Johns Hopkins, his work with Mary Cover Jones and Mary Cover Jones's own separate work, Watson claimed that the baby's early actions are simple responses, nothing like these elaborate chains of responses that were the actions of James's instincts. 'All complex behaviour is a growth or a development of simple responses,' said Watson. And the particular complex responses a child develops will be due to conditioning. 'The infant is a graduate student in the subject of learned responses (he is multitudinously conditioned) by the time behaviour such as James describes – imitation, rivalry, cleanliness, and the other forms he lists – can be observed.' Instinct is a confusing concept, therefore. And just as Watson had swept consciousness out of the thoughts of psychology, he now hoped to do the same with instincts. But I have tried to show that even now, as his position had become more controversial and strident, he was not denying heredity a role. Only the role of heredity was not to deliver us in the maternity ward with well-meshed well-developed instincts.

In his account of the emotions Watson also put forward the new research he had done with Mary Cover Jones and concluded that our emotions were, again, largely the product of conditioning. You could train children to fear and to love rabbits. Because our emotions were so malleable, it must follow that our personality was also infinitely changeable. Watson never tackled the problem of how we hang together as individuals. He said that from birth on, we learn more and more responses and that these responses develop 'into an ever expanding system'. But what connects or interlocks different parts of the system to make an identity, he never stated. Instead, Watson showed how any deficiencies in a part of the system could be remedied. You could train yourself not to be so frightened of men with loud voices or when you go into a strange new house. Here Watson added nothing to the thinking he had formulated in 1919.

But there were two points Watson made which were novel. He claimed that certain situations switched us from one habit system in our personality to another, that personality was made up of various habit systems. There is the monk – an odd example to use – with a manual system which dominates when he is tilling the fields. But when the Angelus rings, the rival religious habit system which has been lurking dormant throughout takes over and the peasant drops his tools and troops obediently, out of habit, into church. Invoking such competing systems of habits, each one triggered by some set of stimuli or situations, allowed Watson to get rid of the concept of attention. But it left him with a problem he never faced up to. How does a person get a sense of himself, or herself, if all that he or she is is a bundle of competing bits of personality? And is it realistic to view all life as switching, at the drop of one stimulus, from religious behaviour to commercial behaviour to sexual behaviour? If Watson had still been functioning as a full-time psychologist it is hard not to believe he would have examined that idea rather more critically.

Before the end of the book, Watson also put forward his theory of thinking again. There was little novel added to the ideas of 1920 and 1924. The very last paragraph of *Behaviourism* has a definite messianic tinge. Watson claimed that behaviourism was 'a foundation for all future experimental ethics'. He repeated his belief that behaviourism 'ought to be a science that prepares men and women for understanding the principles of their own behaviour.' That way, they could use it to 'rearrange their own lives' and to teach them how to bring up their young in a healthy way. But Watson did not want psychology to affect only the individual. He wanted to reshape society as well. In the unlikely guise of a very premature flower child who would not have been too out of place in San Francisco in the heady 1960s, Watson wrote at the end of what was to be his last book that he wanted to see:

> a universe unshackled by legendary folk lore of happenings thousands of years ago; unhampered by disgraceful political history; free of foolish customs and conventions which have no significance in themselves, yet which hem the individual in like taut steel bands. I am not asking here for revolution; I am not asking people to go out to some God-forsaken place, form a colony, go naked and live a communal life, nor am I asking for a change to a diet of roots and herbs. I am not asking for 'free love'. I am trying to dangle a stimulus in front of you, a verbal stimulus which, if acted upon, will gradually change the universe. For the universe will change if you bring up your children, not in the freedom of the libertine, but in behaviouris-tic freedom – a freedom we cannot even picture in words, so little do we know of it. Will not these children in turn, with their better ways of living and thinking, replace us as society and in turn bring up their children in a still more scientific way, until the world finally becomes a place fit for human habitation?

Of course, Watson was here being grandiose. But he had faith that a psychological theory, if consistently applied, would provide us with a better world. Utopia was no longer political or economic but to be sought in psychology. The importance of this emphasis for behaviourism was very considerable. *Walden Two* owes enormously to Watson. And many who are not behaviourists have succumbed to the idea that it is in psychology, in the modification of behaviour, that political happiness lies. Freud, for example, tended to be much more restrained in his claims.

The reactions to *Behaviourism* were interesting. On the one hand, many American psychologists felt that Watson had now become really far too crude in his thinking. The book did not have the weighty academic feel of his 1919 book so that his controversial ideas were easier to attack. Even the highly respectable Pavlov was attacked, for on 24 May 1928, Cattell refused to introduce a film on Pavlov's work at the American Society for Cultural Relations with Russia and Watson had to fill in at very short notice. Introducing the film, he called for 'large reconditioning plants' to which people could choose to go to be improved. Watson said nothing about the political dangers involved but went on to praise Freud whose methods 'give some mental release' but fell short of the practical excellence of total reconditioning. The *New York Times* reported the speech but the learned journals continued to ignore Watson.

The journals that appear to have carried no review of *Behaviourism* were the *Psychological Bulletin*, the *American Journal of Psychology* and the *Journal of Abnormal and Social Psychology*, all of which published book reviews as a matter of course. William MacDougall did pillory the book and there were reviews in the popular press which were often favourable to the book. Bertrand Russell wrote a favourable review of it in the *World* in which he praised Watson's whole behaviouristic approach, his stress on observation and his feeling that parents should be more frank and less sentimental in dealing with children, Russell, of all people, was so dazzled by the prospect of a genuine and sensitive science of human behaviour that he said little of the danger inherent in 'reconditioning plants'.

But even though psychologists chose to ignore the book, it failed to disappear. It became a steady seller and is still in print now which is more than can be said of most of the volumes that the learned journals, in their wisdom, reviewed between 1930 and 1933. Whatever the faults and crudities of the book – and I have hinted at enough – it had much of interest in it. It had the best account of the work on children with Mary Cover Jones. Psychologists should have considered it. That they did not do so was a sign of the extent to which, after his divorce, Watson was divorced from psychology.

It is, of course, tempting to portray Watson as the total victim. However, that would not be true. Most psychologists behaved very badly towards him and he did make a number of valiant attempts to keep on doing psychology. But he never took the romantic, though reckless, step of resigning from J. Walter Thompson and just doing research on his own. He became less and less critical of his own ideas, an understandable reaction when he was being constantly attacked or ignored by his former colleagues. He became more and more strident in the way that he put forward his own views. Watson must bear some responsibility for his own decline as a creative, working psychologist. But, as we shall see, even by 1930 he was not completely and finally played out as a psychologist. He had made *Behaviourism* in its revised edition what he believed to be the final statement of his ideas as a psychologist. But he still had one small, but vital, spark left in him. Before he was finally silent he had one last study which, like so much of what he did, was surprisingly modern and very unlike what we imagine behaviourism to be about. But, as we shall see, hardly anyone knew a thing about this study.

By 1930, then, Watson was becoming less and less of a psychologist.

The conventional psychologists had triumphed – at the expense of psychology. In 1930 Watson was fifty-two years old, an age at which very many psychologists are just beginning to produce some of their best work. But Watson never had, and never managed to make, the chance to execute his rich psychological ideas. Soon they were to become neglected.

10

The Great Populariser 1920–30

Psychologists may have denied Watson a serious audience: the public, however, lapped up his every bit of prose. After 1920 Watson became a very successful popular writer. Long before he had been ejected from psychology he had written for magazines. He contributed an article to *Harpers* in 1910 on the 'New Science of Animal Behaviour' and was delighted to receive a cheque for $75. Watson always felt the public had a right to know what psychologists were doing and thinking. And, apart from his noble informing impulse, he needed the money. After 1920 he did not need the money so much, but he needed an audience very badly. Between 1920 and 1930 Watson wrote often for *Harpers* and, his work also appeared in *McCalls, Liberty, New Republic, Dial, Cosmopolitan*, and the *Saturday Evening Post*. Watson often wrote on child care. But he also applied his expertise to sex, marriage, the role of women, how to succeed in business and a pot-pourri of other topics. He also used these magazine pieces to communicate what behaviourism was really about as a theory and what its implications for the ordinary man or woman were. Watson had always enjoyed persuading people of the validity of his views. He became increasingly fervent through the 1920s in trying to make the public see the benefits of behaviourism. Partly, of course, he wanted to prove that he was right but, partly too, he believed that people should be able to make use of psychological knowledge to improve their lives.

In the articles he wrote for magazines like *Harpers* Watson said nothing that he had not said before for psychological audiences. His tone tended to be sharper, however. He was extremely definite about the rightness of his views and harsh about those of his opponents. For all the stridency of some of his writing, especially after 1926, Watson performed a useful service. His articles were widely read. They made his ideas easily accessible to a wide public. In most countries of the world today psychology is really not news; in America, the press reports psychological research with considerable eagerness. There is a massive market for magazines that bring psychology to the public – *Psychology Today* sells well over 1 million copies a month. In the rest of the world there is no such mass market. Of course, many factors have combined to create such an interest in psychology in the USA and Watson's popular writing was just one of those early factors. His articles read well. Editors paid him very large sums to write. By 1928 he was getting around $1,500 for a long article. He made behaviourism news.

Watson could make fun of this trend. He opened an article called 'Feed Me on Facts' in the following way:

> I am sick of 'psychology'. I can't move without somebody confronting me with the word. I go to my office, the phone rings – 'Dr. Watson, the Philadelphia *Blade* is on the wire and they want to know whether you ever saw a robin get drunk from eating decayed china berries.' It rings again – 'The New York *Ledger* wants to come in for an interview on "Whether women dress for men or for each other".' 'The St. Louis *Herald* wants to know if you agree with Count Keyserling when he says that American men are being made neuters by American women – the Boston *Times* wants to interview you on "Whether easy divorces will finally do away with marriage" – the Pittsburgh *News* wants to know whether children who grow up without being kissed by their parents will know how to neck when they grow older.'

And that last vital question led to the one which, it seemed, the press was always throwing at Watson. Was 'behaviourism ruining the moral fibre of the nation and if not why not'?

Certainly, Watson had put behaviourism on the map.

He was not content to campaign in his articles for a scientific approach to behaviour: he also attacked art. The trouble with art was that it was based on lazy armchair thinking. Many novels and plays announced themselves as being 'psychological' but, said Watson, 'I started to read and wonder when the psychology is about to begin.' It was always over the page. Watson wanted writers to devote part of their apprenticeship to just watching people. Then they might stop producing utterly implausible characters. One play Watson went to was about a young woman who pined and pined and pined away for the love of a young man. Psychologists and psychiatrists diagnosed that she was dying 'from lack of will to live'. Her inferiority complex robbed her of all incentives. 'I have searched into human nature quite a bit and never found a character like this,' Watson said. Moreover, the play was set in New York and most New York women 'would snatch the hair off the hero's head in her haste to get him'. The pining virgin, if she ever existed, went out with Queen Victoria. But artists had not noticed because they were too lofty actually to look at how people behaved. Watson thought that modern writers used words with great charm and skill but they could not create psychologically plausible character or situations. He met more interesting, more true-to-life situations a dozen times a month in his work. Most plays struck him as infantile and 'most of the actors producers and actors are children'.

Watson had no objection at all to novels and drama. He liked Sinclair Lewis because he could portray accurately the life of Elmer Gantry. He liked *Tom Sawyer* and *Peter Pan* and *Treasure Island*. Literature did not just have to be sombre realism. Watson was quite pleased by Jules Verne. But, wrote the behaviourist, 'when we write about life – about how people live together, let's weave accuracy of observation into our story or plot.' The failure of writers to do this seemed a pity to Watson for 'the human being is an interesting and fascinating animal when adequately portrayed'.

It was fun, of course, to take writers to task for not knowing what life was really about. Watson was impatient with much of it. He could hardly ever sit through a whole play. Rosalie often took him to see thrillers but he was apt to leave at the end of the first act saying that he had guessed the mystery. 'Drivel' was the right word, he felt, for most of the literature of the time.

All this made Watson, of course, even more of a celebrity. Rosalie was friends with Judith Anderson, the actress, and the Scott Fitzgeralds. Many of the parties that she dragged Watson to were full of theatrical folk. It must have made for some lively rows at parties.

But while it was fun to decry writers, it was not really shocking. And as if Watson had not shocked the American public enough by out-lawing the soul and claiming parents were a bad idea, he started to write about sex. During his time at Johns Hopkins Watson had felt there was a need for serious research on sex. In Watson's own life sex was clearly a major concern. He wrote often about the need for sexual freedom. He talked about it in his home a great deal. Jimmy recalls that when he was a teenager his father stressed the importance of perform-ing well sexually. As with many aspects of his life, this concern surfaced in his work too.

Soon after he had completed his pioneer work on the VD films and sex education Watson told a New York paper that he believed the young people of 1920 were 'too alert and too wise to follow the dictates of their parents'. Dictates meant morals. Watson said that young men 'now would release the forces of nature' without feeling guilty about it. In 1920 Watson had not yet suggested that each university should set up its own Department of Sex Instruction – President Goodnow would have riposted that maybe Watson would like to run it considering his interests. But it seems clear that Watson was beginning to think along those lines. Shame about sex was as antiquated a notion as the soul.

In a number of Watson's articles before 1926 there were asides that hinted that science should look at sex and that the old morality about sex was foolish and not fit for the modern world. In 1926, two New York journalists, G. V. Hamilton and Kenneth MacGowan, who wrote a profile of Watson for the *New Yorker*, asked the behaviourist to write an introduction to a book they had written. It was called bleakly *What is Wrong With Modern Marriage?* Watson jumped at the opportunity.

The Introduction started with the statement that 'sex is admitted to be the most important subject in life'. Yet sexual behaviour had been ignored almost entirely by science. Watson told how he had been recently invited to work on a committee on sexual research. He was delighted but then it turned out to be 'rats, rabbits and guinea pigs again'. He refused to join in. Ironically, he noted 'the study of sex is still fraught with danger. It can only be openly studied by individuals who are not connected with universities.' It pleased him to introduce the work of Hamilton and MacGowan because they added considerably to the stock of meagre information on the subject.

Briefly, Watson outlined the conclusions of the book. They interviewed 200 people. Only 29 per cent of women felt they were successfully married; only 21 per cent of men felt that too; 49 per cent of men felt there were temperamental problems in their marriage and so did 37 per cent of women; 30 per cent of women and 39 per cent of men felt there were sexual problems in their marriage. Jealousy was also a problem and many married people felt trapped. The authors had gone so far as to ask women if they had climaxes. Watson approved. Fifty-four per cent of women said they often did not have a climax and most of them claimed they could be happy without it. 'I believe that this is far too high,' wrote Watson. He doubted a woman without climaxes could really be that content in her marriage. And there was evidence to support his contention. More women than men were 'experimental', which seems to have meant unfaithful. The psychologist felt it was good that 'extramarital experience is becoming quite general (I am sorry the authors have to use the word adultery)', for adultery had moral connotations, being one of the Ten Devine Don'ts brought down in the desert.

There were problems about how the authors had selected their sample. Their questioning was, perhaps, not designed to make people completely frank. But, Watson argued, there was no reason to delay publishing the work until enough cases had been amassed to churn out statistically reliable results. One white rat, 'observed carefully from the moment of birth to death', he said, was as likely to offer data as rich as two thousand rats opening a puzzle box. It was a 'scientific crime' that the authors could not continue with their work. Universities and foundations were too frightened to allow research into this most basic of human behaviours because they were obsessed with the need to keep up moral appearances. 'We as human beings should be allowed to catch up on the science of living,' fulminated Watson.

One lesson of this research was that divorces should be made much easier. Watson argued that most divorces and marital problems stemmed more from 'what I call infantile carryovers than from any other reasons'. Couples wanted to be coddled; they refused to give each other any independence; often, there were sexual problems. The arguments for easier divorce seemed to him quite obvious.

Watson took these admirably progressive views even further. Marriage would wither away.

In 1928, in *Cosmopolitan*, Watson predicted that by 1978 men would no longer marry. Unless women took to marrying each other, this male boycott would spell the end of matrimony. In the place of marriage, which made so many people miserable, there would be real, sexual freedom. Watson told the *Independent Woman* in 1928 that because of the 'unintelligent sex life of the average person', many suffered. Ignorant, frightened of sex, people missed out on the best things in life. In order to remedy this sad state of affairs (or non-affairs) a new breed of experts had to inform the public about sex. In the nineteenth century frustration had made many women neurotic invalids because of their 'gross ignorance of the facts of life'. These poor women had been made to feel so guilty about sex that they could not face it and, without sex, they became ill. Watson pitied them. He acknowledged, too, the great debt owed to Freud who had 'broken down the secrecy surrounding sex'. It was, at least, a subject that could now be discussed even in the *Independent Woman*. Watson looked forward to a time when people would rationally enjoy their sexuality. He dreamed even: 'Perhaps it will not be long before colleges will even take steps to teach a course on the art of living together. That will be the dawn of experimental ethics. Then we shall have men and women leading richer and more satisfying sex lives.' Watson's higher men and women would not require the ritual of marriage. The world, he knew well enough, was not going to change that fast and it would be a long time before society allowed 'such almost perfect human beings' to come into existence. But it would happen, eventually, when people were not conditioned into the most bizarre puritan customs. Watson remembered enough of *Folkways* to know that in some parts of the world people were much freer sexually.

Before we worship Watson as an early exponent of radical chic, it should be pointed out that, as well as being so sexually progressive, Watson was very ambivalent about the role of women. On the one hand, they were free and sexually equal beings in his passionate paradise; on the other hand, women existed to serve men. With fairly strident male aggression, he added that women were so strident and aggressive because they had failed to make 'a proper sexual adjustment'. His motto might have been 'sex gives you serenity'. Watson doubted that the modern woman for all the triumphs of her emancipation was any happier than the cave woman or the frontier woman who accepted, of course, that submission was her duty. In the early 1920s Watson himself had not been so aggressive. He had argued that women could compete with men for jobs. He had, after all, encouraged a number of able young women like Mary Cover Jones. But by 1928 Watson's views had hardened.

When he wrote his article forecasting the end of marriage, Watson believed that women who immersed themselves in work and a career could not give their husbands the love and comfort they deserved especially when they got back from commuting. Home from the train, the male of the species expected a drink, some charm and some solicitude about the hard day he had had in the office. A working woman might not be able to give all these out; she might be too concerned with her own work to ask him about his. It points to an increasing rigidity in Watson. The 'macho' side of his personality was making itself felt more and more.

The ultimate masculine insult, perhaps, was when Watson claimed that women reached their prime between sixteen and thirty while men reached theirs at forty-odd and stayed at their peak for a good twenty years. Watson, who had always favoured contraception, suggested that no woman should have a child before she reached the age of thirty. Her first wrinkle was the sign she ought to get pregnant. And men in their prime should, naturally, marry women in their prime. So men of forty-odd should, as Watson had done, marry women who were eighteen or so. What happened to men under forty and women over thirty Watson did not care to elaborate. Watson was recommending that the world should take his life as a model. He had divorced his first wife when he was forty-two and in his prime while she was thirty-seven and out of her prime. The young Rosalie had made him happy. He felt very vital and alive. In his own life, this sort of marriage seemed to have worked well. It followed, therefore, that this was a universal principle. (When Rosalie would be forty, he would be close to sixty: past their primes, they could moulder together.)

Jimmy Watson believes that his father's private conviction was even more radical. There should be no marriage at all. People should be free to change partners as and when they wished. Watson may have pushed his ideas so far when talking but he never actually published anything quite so extreme. What he published was controversial enough. And in 1928 a New York paper had the bright idea of pitting the brainy behaviourist against a distinguished society lady, Mrs James Laidlaw. Mrs. Laidlaw was outraged by almost everything Watson had to say. He wanted 'a world without ecstasy and a world without despair.' In her rich mansion where the meeting took place, despair must have given such a delightful *frisson* to life. Moreover, the behaviourist was sex-crazed. Everything he said 'emphasises sex and minimises humanity'. So crazed, added Mrs Laidlaw, were the psychoanalysts. She was offended by the idea that couples needed to learn to make a 'sexual adjustment'. She was appalled by the idea that mothers might love their children too much. Watson contented himself by pointing out where his research showed how ignorant Mrs Laidlaw was and pointed out what the results of his research suggested. But Mrs. Laidlaw brought out the snob in Watson. He did concede that his views were for the privileged. 'People who live in slums will go on repopulating the world.' he snorted, and without having made an efficient sex adjustment at that.

The emergence of Watson as a kind of instant commentator on many aspects of life delighted Rosalie. It made their social life brighter and more exciting. They continued to go out a good deal. Watson continued to drink more. The constant pressure of the advertising business and of producing instant expert opinion on a whole range of subjects meant that he had less and less time for serious psychological thinking.

There is one other strain of thinking in Watson's popular articles which is worth looking at. Watson tried to make psychology useful to the lay public. The main points that Watson always stressed were that we were all conditioned by our past and that we needed to know ourselves more. He told the *Erie Despatch Herald* in 1927 that no one could be really objective in studying themselves because it was impossible to make 'accurate allowance . . . for the effects of his own past habit system.' At other times Watson was more hopeful. He often told salesmen that if they studied themselves, they would soon be able to come to identify their own fears. Once these were identified, they could be cured. Having hacked off one's 'infantile carry overs', one would be able to be a freer person. In a radio talk he gave on station WEVD New York, Watson made a plea for 'psychology as a background for life'. Lest anyone think that Watson was advocating some kind of charm school for salesmen, it is important to realise how fundamental this idea was for him. The point of studying psychology was that it would enable one to come more to grips with one's life. By observation rather than by introspection, you could know yourself.

In his talk on WEVD Watson praised Freud highly precisely because he forced people to analyse themselves. Watson said of Freud: 'He is a great teacher and deserves to go down in history with Mahomet and Confucius. . . . He has taught us as no one had before him to face ourselves, to strip ourselves of our compensations and rationalisation.'

'Psychologist, know thyself' is not usually a motto we associate with behaviourists. When Skinner speaks well of Freud, for instance, it is on the totally different grounds that Freud was a thoroughgoing determinist. Watson's idea are still quite original now when most psychologists urge students that the discipline they are about to study is, at best, only remotely connected with life. In 1930 it was a very radical idea, for the scientist was still hallowed as an expert. The psychologist like Watson was an expert on human beings. To then suggest that human beings, without degrees, might employ psychological knowledge on themselves by themselves was dauntingly modern. But Watson never really followed through this idea, except in one too glib interview in 1928 for the popular *NEA* magazine.

In this article, Watson advocated the setting up of Personality Clinics where people could go to get advice on how to improve their personalities. He did not really elaborate that idea, and it seems not to have been too serious. But he then went on to offer a number of psychological rules for business success. First, he enjoined the young man to watch all those around him. But from that point Watson's advice became mere common sense. You should be willing to work overtime, you should not expect to become president of your company overnight, you should dress well and talk neither too much nor too loud. You should learn about the whole area of business you were in, you should avoid slang, you should be 'thick skinned' and develop your ability to get on well with all kinds of people. Two last points. You should not marry too soon and you should not get the reputation while young of being a boozer, a gambler or a 'fast' man. Cynically, Watson said 'you will have plenty of time to do these things once you have established yourself.' None of this is very remarkable advice.

From 1919, then, Watson had always suggested that students should learn psychology in order to use it. In his books he suggested the same thing and in the magazine writings that he did through the 1920s. But he never really developed a structure to help people do that. To know about behaviourism was insight enough. Again, Watson seems here to have missed an opportunity that he saw and which psychology was not to begin to explore again for many years. Self-therapy has only recently become an acceptable idea.

255

But though he failed to develop his ideas at all fully, Watson continued to be in great demand both as a writer and as an interviewee. He became quite cocky about this third career of his. In the early 1920s he had been delighted to receive a cheque for $55 for a review of a book by Bertrand Russell; by 1928 he was commanding fees of between $750 and $1,500. He was said to be the highest paid writer for his kind of article in the whole of the USA. If the professional psychologists would not listen, then at least the public would. And they listened to Watson on the radio as well for he often appeared to give talks on particular aspects of behaviourism or of child care. It was success of a kind.

But it was not success of the kind Watson really wanted. One of the few bitter sections in his autobiographical note deals with his career as a popular writer. He said he wrote articles for magazines like *Harpers*:

> I received pay for them – generous pay. I had learned how to write what the public would read, and, since there was no longer opportunity for me to publish in technical journals, I saw no reason why I should not go public with my wares. Yet these articles have brought criticism greater than the offense, I believe, from no less a person than President Angell of Yale. His Commencement Address at Dartmouth some years ago left me with no bitterness but rather with poignant sadness. I just wonder whether he or other of my colleagues confronted with my situation would not have sold himself to the public.

The criticisms hurt Watson quite deeply. He not only had to live with the fact that he felt he had been unjustly dismissed from Johns Hopkins but his late colleagues now condemned him for writing untechnical articles. As we shall see, this affected the opinion he held of one of his own books.

Nowadays, of course, academics are expected to appear in any kind of print. Short of being published in the *Sun* or the *Philadelphia Inquirer*, any publicity is good publicity. In 1930 academics were much more aloof. Science was seen as much less of a public domain. It was in 1934 that J. G. Crowther, doyen of science correspondents, walked into the office of the editor of the *Manchester Guardian* and informed the august man that he wanted a job which did not exist – that of science correspondent of the paper. Watson was breaking new ground in making himself and his ideas so accessible to the press and the novel medium of radio. It did not improve his relationships with the men of science.

Much of Watson's popular writing was ephemeral, much clearly came from the top of his head. But, still, as I have tried to suggest, he did touch on a number of interesting and original ideas which psychology scorned to develop. And psychology was the poorer for that.

11

Suburban Silence 1930–50

In 1930 Watson was fifty-two years old. He had led a very frenetic and fragmented life through the 1920s. He was trying to do so much. An advertising man by day and a psychologist by night, a popular writer and an expert on child care, his life buzzed with activity. On top of his work, Rosalie expected her husband to go out and glitter in the society she loved and thought such fun. Because his career through the 1920s was so diverse it seemed better to look at it in its various separate bits. After 1930 the behaviourist's life became rather less broken up. This unity was not all to the good.

Many psychologists and psychiatrists do their best work in their forties and fifties. Unlike mathematicians and physicists, psychologists take time to mature. Life has to keep at them, it seems, for them to grow wise enough to produce their own particular truths about human nature. Watson had no reason to suppose he would do no more productive psychological work. I shall argue, in fact, that he tried very hard to give himself the circumstances in which he could again do some serious scientific work. He had a lot going for him. He was happy with Rosalie, he was famous, he was rich because he had invested conservatively so that the Wall Street crash did not wipe him out. He wanted very much to produce some psychology that would stun and silence his detractors. But to do this he had to make a firm, and difficult, choice. External circumstances, J. Walter Thompson, another speech, another article, another evening out on the town, all conspired to make that hard. New York took up a great deal of energy.

Watson was always critical of his own performance and he knew that he had to take some dramatic action in order to make serious work again a possibility. For some years after 1930, we shall see that he took a number of steps in this direction. He cut down on the numbers of speeches and articles that he wrote. He tried to arrange another programme of psychological lectures at the Rand School and invited Yerkes, Brill, the psychoanalyst, Koffka, the *gestaltist*, and a number of others to participate. He was making a particular effort to keep up with the latest psychology and to give himself some time in order to think.

It was not easy. The press still clamoured for Watson and it was not so simple to refuse them. Their attention was flattering. On 27 February 1930, for example, Watson went to Princeton to give a lecture and he told the university newspaper, the *Daily Princetonian*, that family life was on the wane in large cities and that the 'American home remains nothing but a place to change one's clothes in, to have cocktails in before going out to dinner, and a place to get a few hours' sleep'. Watson did not entirely disapprove. He returned to his theme of a new breed of person. He wanted to see a new individual who needed no country, no party, no God, no law, and could still be happy – a free individual. The American child was unlikely to be elevated into this emancipated creature for that infant was nothing but 'layers of obsolete religious and political bandages wrapped round the semblance of life'. In May 1930 Watson spoke in New York on 'After The Family – What?' He hoped that his kind of free human being could take over the world.

There were also trips abroad that had to be taken. In the autumn of 1930 Watson and Rosalie were in England, France and Spain. He was looking after the international General Motors account. In Paris Rosalie was especially happy. They met Ernest Hemingway who deeply impressed Watson. Hemingway was his kind of man, rough, rugged, boozing, cursing, a 'macho' man's 'macho' man. Early in December the Watsons sailed back to New York.

In New York, too, advertising took much time and energy. In the Depression agencies had to work especially hard in order to keep accounts. As one of the most experienced men at J. Walter Thompson, Watson had to work really very hard. He was in great demand as a speaker to professional groups. Salesmen and executives hungered after those magical pieces of psychological knowledge that would make business boom in difficult times. Advertising men were nervous, on edge because there was so much less money around, and the authoritative Watson was comforting as he often told salesmen that their worst fault was their fear and that, if they used psychology, they could conquer their own fears.

The environment on Madison and Lexington Avenue was not a pleasant one. There was a lot of bankruptcy. People drank a great deal. Watson had started to drink more and more throughout the 1920s. He had never minded drinking in his academic days but a professor needed a sharp, clear mind. Drunk to the gills, Watson was quite sharp enough to be successful in advertising. And he had his reasons for drinking. He suppressed most of the anger he felt about the way psychologists treated him. The odd vituperative article, like his review of MacDougall's book, was the only way in which he had countered what the psychologists now said of him. He defended his ideas stridently but, also, defensively. He was more worried than he ever admitted that he might be wrong. Hence his fervour and, hence, too, another reason for drinking a little bit more. In a typical day, Watson would have three or four drinks at lunchtime and at least as many in the evening

Money had also made Watson more vain. He preened himself rather, as befitted a man in his prime. He had plenty of spare cash to indulge in hand-made shirts and suits. As for his shoes, there was no shoemaker in the whole of New York who could rise to the challenge of Watson's feet so he sent to London for his footwear. To St. James, of course. All these delicacies were effective. At fifty-two, Watson remained a handsome man. He danced well still and Rosalie made him dance often for she was always eager to be out and be bright about town.

Towards the end of 1930 Watson made a crucial decision. He decided to move out of New York. He would keep a small *pied-à-terre* in New York for when he had to work late at the office but that would only be for emergencies. Jimmy was doing none too well in the city. Doctors thought the country air might do him good. And Watson himself, I think, wanted to withdraw a little from the city. He persuaded his socialite wife that she would not miss New York too much. They found a small and pretty town, Westport, Connecticut, and they started to look for a property there. Soon they found one that suited them perfectly – a forty-acre farm with a modern farmhouse. An architect had just designed and built it for himself but, for some reason, he now had to sell. The Watsons snapped it up. The young man from Greenville who had been brought up on a farm had now made it rich enough and big enough to buy a large farm of his own as a hobby. It was something of an achievement.

In a number of his writings Watson stressed how important it was to change your environment when you were depressed. This move seems to have been an effort on his part to get through his own growing feelings of depression. He took care to buy a place where there was plenty of land and plenty of room to keep animals. Here he hoped, I think, to start doing some research on his own again. The country life would give him more time to think and, somehow, would make him creative again. And so he and his family moved with enthusiasm down to Westport. He kept a small apartment in New York.

In 1930 Westport, Connecticut, was not the dream commuterland it is today. It was a 90-minute ride from New York by train and it was pretty much open countryside. Watson's farm was a good way up a hill and the family lived, in effect, in the country. A few acquaintances lived nearby, notably James Young, a friend of his who was also a vice-president at J. Walter Thompson. But it was really a very distant spot for such a socialite couple as the Watsons to move to. The reason was deliberate. Watson, who had always had an instinct for knowing when to move, felt that unless he made a supreme effort now to change the way he lived his life as a psychologist would be finished for good. He also sensed it would not be so easy for him to change. William James always warned that after the age of thirty habits set like cement. At fifty-two, Watson would need utter dedication to do real research again. But the defiant side in him would really enjoy cocking a snook at people like Angell. Some new, incontestably important piece of research, the continuation of his work on children, would serve. But it required more discipline and concentration than teaching at the New School had done. That meant so much to Watson precisely because he had not given up on himself as a psychologist.

His ambivalence is perfectly caught in a letter to Yerkes who, after a six-year silence, suddenly wrote to Watson in 1932. Watson had asked him to take part in a series of psychological lectures with Brill and Koffka. Yerkes ended his letter in reply by asking why Watson did not think of doing some observational work again. Watson was, at first, harshly realistic: 'I am afraid there is too much water under the dam for me ever to be able to think of going back to university work.' His tastes were too lavish 'even if a university were so misguided as to offer me a job'. But resignation was not all. In the next sentence, Watson said he still really wanted to do the work on infants, to finish it, and added 'I think I still have the guts to do it'. It would need much money and staff and, as ever, Yerkes made no practical suggestions to his old friend.

As Watson struggled with the idea of doing some real academic work again, he became depressed. Even out in Westport he could not stitch the time together quite enough to concentrate. His failure to come to grips with the dilemma, to make any positive decision even if only the modest one of starting some small project out on his new farm to get him going again, depressed the behaviourist. We have seen that Watson had, in previous crises in his life, been acutely depressed. There is much evidence to suggest that in 1932 and early 1933 Watson was again extremely depressed and, possibly, even suicidal. He realised fully he was at another crisis. He knew that he could not really go on for much longer relying on research that he had done in 1920 and claiming to be a psychologist. He had actually to tackle some new research. The idea depressed him. He had so many things tugging against it. J. Walter Thompson needed much time. There were new accounts which required travelling to Chicago and California. Watson, who had tested aviators in 1917, discovered again that he hated flying. Westport proved to be quite a busy social place in itself. It would need enormous effort to get to grips with a project against all these odds. Watson responded to this dilemma in an intriguing way. In order to fight his own depression, he decided to study depression or, at least, suicide. In 1932, the Depression was not merely economic but psychological. The numbers of suicides were rising steadily. Young people seemed to have lost their sense of direction. Watson struggling with his own bitterness, suggested to the editor of *Cosmopolitan* that he wrote an article entitled 'Why I Don't Commit Suicide'. The premise embodied in that title is remarkably bleak. Most people leave suicide notes explaining why they took the awful final step. We tend to view life as the usual human condition. Not so Watson in this title. Suicide was the norm; living required the explanatory note.

The article (which is a long one running to over 25 typed pages) was a strange mixture of research, personal history and political critique. Watson began by pointing out that there had been a vast increase in suicides in 1926, 1927 and 1928. There had been another rise between 1930 and 1931. In 1932 suicides had been up a further 6 per cent. The ages at which people were most likely to do away with themselves were between 35 and 54. Watson had just passed the latter age by a year.

Statistics having been rendered, Watson began by taking a very general look at the state of American life. His opinion of it was pessimistic. The good old virtues had gone, Patriotism seemed to him defunct. He noted that 'Napoleon, if he came to life, couldn't muster a regiment if he marched from California to New York.' Historians had discovered that Washington had told lies. The country was no longer the sacred entity it had once been. If that sounded like the lament of a conservative, Watson admitted to being positively glad that the churches had also lost their influence. But the loss of faith seemed to have sapped people of the will to live. Other institutions that were once holy and reasons for struggling with and through life had also been called into question. The family was no longer worth fighting for. 'Mother love, father love, brotherly and sisterly love all have been deflated or are in the process of being deflated,' mourned Watson who had, of course, done much of the sharpest deflating himself. Marriage was no longer a mystery. There was little glamour left in it. Four out of five marriages went wrong and the best ones ended in divorce. 'I do not decry this. In the end, I think it will work for more independent and more happy lives,' he said, but it still was a factor. The world was becoming different and was changing

261

much more quickly than it had done before.

Science appeared to Watson to be one of the few things which still retained its undeflated value. 'There is real romance in Chemistry, Physics and Biology,' he noted and added that no one complained of medicine's 'too rapid control of disease. I notice that every time science creates a better car, a refrigerator, an air conditioning unit, a vacuum cleaner or cold cream, people rush out to buy and enjoy them.' Aided, Watson failed to point out, by advertising skills that made these products seem essential to modern life.

Modern life was particularly hard on the young, Watson felt. Colleges were not preparing young people for the realities of life, especially in business. 'There is something awry.' Rather romantically, Watson went on to compare the life of the college graduate with that of the American Indian. 'The Indian lad was all in a dither about becoming a recognised man of the tribe; he had to learn to shoot, ride, swim, hunt, track, look for signs, fight his enemies. Every day was fraught with new dangers.' On each new day, the lad 'could be a hero. . . . He lost himself completely in the vicissitudes of everyday life.' The college graduate had neither the training nor the exciting vicissitudes to be so absorbed. It was not surprising, felt Watson, that so many of them should be miserable and depressed.

It was against this background that Watson set out to do his research. He wrote to 100 people asking them to explain in a brief statement why they went on living, 'to dramatise for the discouraged adults of 25 to 35 years of age' the reasons and values 'that keep us carrying on when the road is rough'. Though Watson never said so, he was clearly at this point one of the discouraged for all his success.

Watson received replies for every person he wrote to – they were people he knew in all walks of life. He trumpeted the originality of the enterprise and said: 'Here for the first time, I believe, in history is set down the motives of why people go on living.' This is a subject with which psychology has not tangled much subsequently. Suicide is a respectable subject; life is much less so. Watson tabulated the answers as follows;

Enjoy life too much even fighting against odds	32
Love of family, of use to family	32
It is a cowardly thing to do, not good sportsmanship, not playing the game (!)	24
Religion	21
Health too good to contemplate suicide	14
So many things I still want to do	14
Afraid I won't succeed in act of suicide	12

Afraid there is no future life. This is only one we know	6
Don't like to make a mess	5
Wouldn't so gratify my enemies	4

Three people said they were 'just an optimist'; three others replied, with little respect for Watson's views, they had an 'instinct to live'. Two replied that they wouldn't profit by it; two others moaned that they had actually tried to kill themselves but had failed and they were now too frightened to have another go. Two said, histrionically, 'as soon as life gets tedious I shall leave before the final curtain.' One person replied that 'living is just a habit'; another one said that her life insurance was in her husband's name and she would stay alive just to make sure he never got his hands on the money; the final reason one of the correspondents gave was also hardly a message of hope. 'We are tricked into being born and tricked into staying alive.'

Watson was disappointed by how negative the responses were.

> I hoped to draw out of the material a wealth of positive material
> on why one should fight to live. The material was disappointing to
> an extent, I believe, because when the environment has been
> continuously depressing for a period of years everyone thinks of
> suicide at some point or another.

The psychologist did not exclude himself at all.

There were a few replies that were more encouraging. A psychiatrist replied that he had never killed himself when he was depressed because he recognised depressions for what they were, transient, and waited for them to pass. Watson endorsed this as sensible advice. Watson also approved of one person who wrote that

> life, if lived dramatically, is too exciting and interesting and
> stimulating a business to stop it until the game has been played
> out. I have a belief that around every corner may be interesting
> adventures and when suicide notions occur I recall the dramatic
> experiences that have made life glamorous to me.

The whole subject of suicide seems to have been very much on Watson's mind at this time. He certainly commented a great deal on it. One of his few statements to the press in 1932 was on five wealthy suicides. Watson attributed their deaths to the fact that they had all spent their whole lives amassing money. They had no contact with women; they were desperately lonely; in the end, death seemed better than life to them.

Watson even went on the radio to talk about suicide. He believed psychologists had a responsibility to help people who felt suicidal. He advised listeners who felt suicidal not to commit suicide while they felt suicidal. When the depressed suicidal mood had lifted, then was the right time to make the decision. He counselled that one should get into a new environment. 'Leave a letter for your loved ones saying you are going away to get sane again but go away and don't come back till the depressed state is over and courage again oozes from your elbows.' Watson went on to say that each conquest of such a depression makes you stronger and 'conquer a few such states and you are forever free of the germ of suicide'. The advice sounds very heartfelt. Watson had conquered such depressions himself. He had confronted himself in such moods. And in 1930 part of his reason for moving out of New York was to get out of such a depression. He wrote so much on the subject because it was so much with him.

At the end of 'Why I Don't Commit Suicide' Watson offered some ideas on how to improve the state of the union. He wanted colleges to be modernised to prepare young people better for life. He wanted business to become more glamorous. He yearned for 'the old buc-caneers and pirates who used to make industry as interesting as war'. But those glamorous nineteenth-century industrialists were an extinct species. Politics also needed purification. Watson argued that if the civil service had 'half the romance [that is] built around the Marines, thousands of people seeking modest careers would go into it', and be happy. It is a pity that Watson was never asked to mastermind a government campaign that turned being a clerk in some agency in Washington into a career charged with mystery and romance. The great sexual reformer also hoped to inject some new life into marriage. He hoped 'marriage could once more be made enduringly romantic. The task is herculean though,' he concluded. It would take at least two generations and well planned training to achieve that end.

The final fate of this article was bizarre. *Cosmopolitan*, who commissioned it, refused to publish it. They told Watson it was too depressing. A few months later, the editor of *Cosmopolitan* himself committed suicide.

Watson, however, was deeply hurt by the fact that it was not published. He offered it to other magazines: they all refused to touch it. He believed that it was because the pessimistic and critical tone of the paper would offend President Roosevelt. Watson never had a good word to say for Roosevelt. After it was not published, he just about stopped writing. Certainly, it was a gloomy piece, a just reflection of gloomy times and *Cosmopolitan* may well have felt that the depressing nature of the survey gave people only too many reasons for throwing themselves out of windows.

Whatever the reasons for its not being published, it is an interesting piece of work. Watson was certainly correct in his claim that no psychologist had previously enquired why people lived. It did not seem the right kind of question. Even psychologists who were wedded to the idea of purposive behaviour, like MacDougall, did not ask what human purpose was about. Purpose was a sign either of the *élan vital* or of the divine design. It is, of course, extremely paradoxical that Watson, the creator of behaviourism, should have himself asked people what gave them the will to live and accepted as valid the most subjective of replies. 'I live because I like the struggle' is really not at all a logical answer for a determinist to give because the determinist must know that all his responses are really conditioned, prompted by externals and beyond the control of anything as subjective as enjoying the dramas of life. 'He' cannot really struggle. But Watson always felt and wrote as if people could choose more than his theories allowed them.

But the paradoxes of the piece were more than merely philosophical. They show, in many places, that Watson was close to despair in his criticisms. He was not prepared to say that old-fashioned marriage or old-fashioned religion have anything to commend them but their decline has left a vacuum. Once they are not the holy and sacred things they once were, how do you replace them, how do you give people the framework within which to live, to organise their lives? Watson came close to understanding the problem that is central, namely, once you are free of everything that shackled you, how do you cope with that freedom? He had sensed in this, his last piece of research – this central problem of psychology and metaphysics. But, again, he lacked the stamina to pursue it. When the article was refused for publication, Watson felt very angry, and, in fact, he never again wrote an article for the rest of his life. He was moving into silence.

Oddly, too, this article was the occasion of Watson's last exchange of letters with Robert Yerkes. He asked Yerkes to give his reasons and Yerkes replied that 'despite psychological ills, difficulties and disappointments, I find life intensely interesting, a game in which by matching my wits against the universe I may oftener win than lose and enjoy the risk.' Watson thanked him for that reply and added that Yerkes seemed to have a more positive attitude than most. The two men who had first corresponded as bright young psychologists who planned to co-operate to revolutionise psychology never wrote to each other again. Another silence was developing in Watson's life.

Between 1933, when *Cosmopolitan* rejected his article, and 1936 Watson did still make some public statements. He was still a very polished speaker. He gave a number of radio talks including the one on suicide. He gave a talk in 1935 on a programme called *The Magic of*

Speech in which he argued that it was extremely important for parents to help their children to verbalise their experiences. Watson prefaced these remarks with his usual points about training children to be independent. He added 'from the first year he should be helped to name the things of his world, to build his Word World.' If parents wanted their children to be well-organised and 'integrated,' they would spend time with‌ them talking over work and play, plans and problems and so 'will help them get words for new things and new situations'. Such verbal training would teach children to think for themselves, Watson argued.

Watson also drew on the observations made in the Manhattan Day Nursery to trace how children first talk incessantly to themselves when playing and then this 'talking aloud' goes underground. They no longer talk out loud. They can think silently. Piaget, of course, and Vygotsky arrived at the same observation but came to quite different conclusions for it. Real thought began when thinking ceased to be tied to words and verbal structures. But here, as in most of his utterances in the 1930s, Watson was merely repeating himself. His one original piece of work, on suicide, could find no publisher. After December 1935 Watson does not even seem to have taken part in any further radio programmes though he was an experienced radio performer and, apparently, a good one.

The work at J. Walter Thompson became less exciting. There were no further innovations for which Watson was responsible. He was still good at his work but he no longer felt that involved in it. He could do it but it no longer challenged him as it had done in the early 1920s. Oddly, in the mid 1930s Watson's fate inspired a play called *The American Way of Scandal* in which hypocrisy about sex makes a university sack a professor. Sacked, the professor turned to what the author clearly considered an anti-social career – advertising. The author blamed the hypocritical conventions of American life for forcing his hero into this position. Watson never said anything about this play and it is not even certain that he saw it. But the excitement of advertising faded for Watson. And he drank more.

He still did make a few public speeches to advertising conventions in 1934 and 1935. He addressed the Direct Manufacturers Association at White Sulphur Springs on 18 April 1934 and urged their salesmen to become aware of their fears. 'There are many painful things about yourself that you do not want to face and that you have never put into words. We know less about ourselves than we know about any other thing in the world.' On 26 September 1935 he gave a lecture on influencing the mind of another. In October that year Watson was one of the main speakers in Toronto at the Advertising and Sales Club of that city. His presence was hailed as a coup. He also gave a talk on the psychology of the consumer. It was largely repetitive stuff. On 15 January 1936 Watson yet again urged salesmen to know themselves and rid themselves of their fears.

In one speech Watson also developed some of the ideas in his suicide article. He wrote that youth was suffering from doing nothing. Business should take young people if only to run errands. College students were too pampered. But it would be better for them to run errands than to be unemployed. In this speech, Watson returned to a favourite hobby horse of his. Education was hopelessly impractical. It was based much too much on English ideas. He wanted to reform high schools so that they were more like the real world, one of the increasing number of ideas that he failed to do anything with. Watson ended that speech by saying that he wanted to see youth blaze a new path in politics, putting through the reforms which were needed. This was all rather vague bombastic stuff. With the rejection of that article the heart had somehow gone out of Watson's thinking.

And here at this time of dilemma, Watson repeated a familiar pattern in his life. He took to his hands. When the family moved into the house in early 1931 it was a splendid property. Watson set about improving it, with his own hands. He first built the stucco garage. Then, with Jimmy and Billy, he set about building a barn with a gothic vaulted roof. I have been in this building and all I can say is that it is breathtakingly beautiful. It is large, 31 feet wide and 71 feet long. It is designed to exquisite perfection. Watson put on a copper roof and, for years, pilots at American Airlines used it as a landmark. Watson also built a number of outhouses for animals, the animals which he still vaguely toyed with using as experimental subjects. The carpenter psychologist built a number of other buildings and also constructed an ingenious motorised trolley which wheeled hamburgers into a gigantic outdoor barbecue. You put the hamburger on the metal tray, pressed a button and the trolley chugged on into the barbecue, tilted like a dump truck and deposited the hamburger in the flame. When it was done, it picked the meat up out of the barbecue. Remote control cooking was here.

As they became more at home at Whipporwhill Farm, the Watsons invited people up there more often. Harvey Carr, the psychologist with whom Watson had done the work on blinded rats, visited them. Leslie Hohlman, Watson's homosexual psychiatrist friend, visited the farm a number of times with his boyfriends. Hohlman often quarrelled with Jimmy who did not like him because the psychiatrist tried to force him to eat things he did not like. (Jimmy once vomited in Hohlman's face.) There was a good deal of drinking and eating and social jollying at all these parties. Polly, Watson's daughter by his first marriage,

267

came to work nearby and was often at the farm. Rosalie and Watson were anything but lonely.

For Billy and Jimmy it was in many ways a good life. They enjoyed the country. Watson, true to the traditions of his youth, believed that a father should teach his sons how to ride and shoot and hunt just like the hypothetical Indian lad he had conjured up in the article on suicide. Watson also taught his sons to build things with him. It was a much better way of being together, much more wholesome and practical. Billy went off to boarding school when he was eleven.

When the children became used to the country, their father encouraged them to explore, to feel at home in it. This led to a near disaster just after Christmas 1933. Billy had gone for a walk when a snowstorm blew up. Around two in the afternoon, Billy had left the farm and, very soon after that, the weather deteriorated. After he had been gone for two hours, a distraught Rosalie sent the hired man to look for him. Jimmy, who was only ten, was sent out with him. Jimmy and the man got into trouble in the bad weather themselves. Around four o'clock, Rosalie rang Watson in the office and he at once hurried to catch a train home. By 7.30, Watson was home and a frozen Jimmy had also returned but there was still no sign of Billy. Everyone was getting more frantic with worry. The snowstorm was still raging outside.

Billy had, in fact, gone into the woods close to Westport and come out five miles away from his house. He had turned the wrong way at a long stone wall because, under the snow, it looked like a different landmark. The neighbourhood grew less and less familiar. After two hours, Billy had found a farmhouse. The adults there rang the Watsons. His father came to fetch him.

The press, who were still very interested in Watson, made much of the story. The *Sun* ran the headline that Billy 'was recovering today from his attempt to master his environment in the form of a snowstorm'; the *Herald Tribune* claimed Watson had been worried his son would die. In fact Watson told the press that he had every faith that his son would pull through. He had been schooled to look after himself and could handle himself sensibly in any emergency.

The press gloated rather more in January 1934 when Watson's son by his first marriage, John, 'showing a burst of speed and self reliance', married Joan Wallance, a belle of the Westport art colony. Watson stayed away in 'high dudgeon', reported the papers, though Rosalie attended. The man who preached that children should be independent was said to be muttering and complaining that his own eldest son was 'an improvident young puppy who couldn't earn his own living'.

These were, of course, the dramas which the press used to try and mock Watson. Nothing is so funny as a discredited expert, the guru caught with his hands up his lady disciples' skirts. If Watson's children were unemployed or lost in a snowstorm, it humbled the behaviourist and showed him to be all too human after all. Just what readers wanted.

Jimmy Watson's recollection of the years between 1930 and 1935 is ambivalent. On the one hand, he enjoyed the countryside. He liked his father teaching him all those skills from riding to carpentry. That was good fun. But the behaviourist's emphasis at this time on punctuality, on going to the toilet, on eating this and not eating that, made him fret. He felt, also, the lack of affection in the home. 'I respected my father as a man but not as a father really,' Jimmy said. The psychologist, for all his talk of talk-it-out clubs, was hard to talk to. He talked wonderfully, amusing and frequently but he hardly ever talked about himself. He never let his feelings show, even when he drank a great deal. To his children, he never seemed to have drunk too much because he was never out of control.

As Billy and Jimmy grew older, the emphasis in their education shifted from toilet training to sex. Jimmy recalls that their father often sat the two of them down together to tell them of the importance of sex in human existence. A man had to be virile or he was not a man. Homosexuality was always referred to as something to be dreaded. A proper man was a good lover and devoted much time to learning how to be a lover. It was very much sex seen as a matter of mechanics, of superior performance. You had to perform well sexually in order to be a proper man. As Billy and Jimmy reached their teens, they were often treated to evening lectures in this vein as they sat round the fire in the elegant living room at the farm. Neither son felt that close to their father though both of them respected much in him. But he remained very aloof to them.

Late in 1935 Watson did two things which were of some importance. First, he decided to leave J. Walter Thompson. It was, I think, a sign of his boredom with the place. A fellow vice-president at J. Walter Thompson, William Esty, broke away from Resor's agency. Esty was able to do this because Resor refused to do any speculative work. The makers of Camel cigarettes, Philip Morris Ltd, were looking for a new agency and Resor went down to talk to them. He told them they knew J. Walter Thompson were good but he refused to budge from his principles. He would not give any idea of the campaign they might do in order to win the account. Philip Morris would not sign on those conditions. Esty either approached or was approached by Philip Morris. He did not have the ethical niceties Resor had and he gladly submitted a campaign speculatively. Esty won the account which was worth an enormous amount in billings. He started his own outfit and invited Watson to join. Watson had recently quarrelled with Resor a few times. He decided to go with Esty, even though he did not like him that much on a personal level. Watson told the *World Telegram* on 3 February that he was going to join Esty's, and that he was going to use psychological principles in his new job. Grandiosely, Watson added: 'The university psychologist deals with a few individuals, the *advertiser* with millions. The scientific approach is equally applicable in both fields.'

The other significant thing to happen to Watson was that he was asked to contribute an autobiographical note to a series called *A History of Psychology in Autobiography* which was edited by Carl Murchison of Clark University. Watson wrote this late in 1935 and it was published in 1936. Watson wrote much less about himself than all the other psychologists who were asked to contribute. Angell devoted some 38 pages to his career and Dunlap could not tell his own story in less than 25 pages. Yet Watson, who had really done so much, crammed his life into 10 pages. The first 8 pages dealt with his early life and his career as a psychologist and said nothing that has not, in some way, informed this biography. But in the last 2 pages Watson turned to his life since he had been sacked by Johns Hopkins. He told of his career at J. Walter Thompson. He added how glad he had been to be able to teach at the New School. He explained how W. W. Norton published *Behaviourism* very much from his lecture notes. So far, it was all fairly dispassionate stuff.

But then he became tetchy and defensive. He apologised for *Psychological Care*. It was a 'book I feel sorry about – not because of its sketchy form but because I did not know enough to write the book I wanted to write. I feel I had the right to publish this, sketchy as it is, since I planned never to go back into academic work.' It was a ridiculous justification and the book had been praised enough by men like Russell and Dorsey not to need such endorsement. But Watson felt very vulnerable, far more vulnerable than he admitted, to the attacks of his psychological colleagues. He devoted his next paragraph to defending his popular articles and to clearing himself of the infamous charge of having sold himself to the public. Few psychologists will not sell themselves to the public but there are many psychologists whom the public won't buy.

At the end of that, Watson said starkly: 'I have reached the end of my psychological career. . . . My life is taken up with business, my family, my farm.' He was retreating into suburban silence. He did not do so without regrets. He added that: 'I sometimes think I regret that I could not have a group of infant farms where I could have brought up thirty pure-blooded Negroes on one, thirty pure-blooded Anglo Saxons on another and thirty Chinese on a third – all under similar conditions. Some day it will be done, but by a younger man.' The notion of finishing the work on infants was still there but Watson, realistically, resignedly, relegated it to the status of a dream. He no longer had the will really to do it.

Watson concluded this piece with what was his last statement on psychology and it deserves to be quoted in full. He wrote:

I still believe as firmly as ever in the general behaviouristic position I took overtly in 1912. I think it has influenced psychology. Strangely enough, I think it has temporarily slowed down psychology because the older instructors would not present it whole-heartedly, and consequently they failed to present it convincingly to their classes. The youngsters did not get a fair presentation, hence they are not embarking whole-heartedly upon a behaviouristic career, and yet they will no longer accept the teachings of James, Titchener and Angell. I honestly think psychology has been sterile for many years. We need younger instructors who will teach objective psychology with no reference to the mythology most of us present-day psychologists have been brought up upon. When this day comes, psychology will have a renaissance greater than that which occurred in science in the Middle Ages. I believe as firmly as ever in the future of behaviourism – behaviourism as a companion of zoology, physiology, psychiatry and physical chemistry.

Watson was careful not to appear too bitter. He had not dwelt on the fact that Johns Hopkins sacked him. He said nothing about the abuse psychologists heaped on him apart from his one restrained reference to Angell. It was typical of Watson to make the best of things and, also, there was no reason why he should give psychologists the pleasure of seeing how much he had been hurt by having to leave his work unfinished. Apart from Harvey Carr and Hohlman, he hardly ever saw psychologists after 1932. Polly Hartley remembers one dinner party to which an old friend – possibly Karl Lashley – came and how the two men talked for hours in terms which none of the rest of the company could begin to understand. 'Dad loved that,' she said. But he had fewer and fewer opportunities to pit his mind in really sharp academic conversation. In Westport they preferred gossip and drink. And by 1936 he was too much a rich suburban commuter really to fight his way back into the academic world. It was, he said, a reason for becoming silent. There was nothing valuable that he now had the knowledge to say.

But it was not just a careful appreciation of his own growing distance from psychology that made Watson silent. He was, not for the first time, a victim of terrible ill luck.

In the summer of 1936 Rosalie caught dysentery. She had got it, it seems, from eating some bad fruit. For the first two weeks, she was ill in the house. She received all kinds of colonic irrigation in an effort to get the sickness out of her system. After two weeks of this treatment she was much weaker and she still had dysentery. The doctor recommended that she go to hospital.

Rosalie did not improve in the hospital. In 1936 there were no drugs that coped effectively with dysentery. Watson went every day to the hospital for many hours. But Rosalie was deteriorating. Her son, Jimmy, was taken to see her by his father some two or three days after she went to hospital. She seemed gravely ill. In the next two weeks she did not get any better. Jimmy went again a number of times. She could hardly talk after two weeks. She looked very grey. Rosalie held her sons' hands. The children felt frightened.

In a final attempt to help, Watson gave her a blood transfusion in the hope that that would make her stronger. But it did not. His beloved Rosalie was slipping away.

The farm was gloomy, fraught with the likelihood of Rosalie's death. Watson must have known there was little hope for in June, after Billy and Jimmy had seen their mother, they were sent away to camp. 'I can remember being afraid she was going to die,' Jimmy recalls. On 19 June Rosalie Rayner Watson did, indeed, die. Watson was with her.

The children were brought back from camp. Before they could see their father, the cook, Anna, told them that their mother had died. Five minutes later they stood outside the house with Watson and, for the only time ever, he put his arms around his children. He looked up at the gothic barn they had all built and he said: 'Somehow we'll get by this.' Watson was crying. He had lost the love of his life, the woman for whom he had risked and lost so much.

Rosalie had asked Watson not to allow her, if she died, to be buried under the earth. So Watson built a rather ornate mausoleum for his wife in a nearby cemetery. Rosalie was placed in that mausoleum on June 1936. Once she was in that vault Watson never discussed with his sons the blow that her death was. He did not cry ever again or, at least, he did not cry when there was anyone there to see.

But after Rosalie's death Watson was never the same again. He was lost without her. He had relied on her for love, fun, laughter, companionship. They had been very close and very happy. They had never been unfaithful for all their progressive ideas. Rosalie's death marked Watson terribly. He brooded a great deal after she died and he never talked much about her death. He took to drinking more and more so that it was not unusual for his sons to find him having a glass or two of bourbon before breakfast. Not that he ever lost control even now, however much he drank. But there was no real reason for him to try to restrain his drinking.

Throughout his life Watson had faced a number of acute crises. He had always managed to pull himself out of them. He had buried himself in work or he had gone away to a new place to put himself together again. But this time, after Rosalie's death, he seems to have lacked the will to do any of those sensible, psychologically healthy things which had been such a help to him before. He withdrew more and more into himself. He never seems to have written another article or made another speech. He continued to work as a vice-president of ˙ William Esty's but, it seems, he got little joy out of the work.

With the death of Rosalie, Watson's creative life was finished. Before she died, as I have tried to suggest, Watson's last effort to do some serious academic work – an effort that he never publicly admitted – had been flickering out. With her gone, any energy, any determination that he might have had left was snuffed out. The elaborate mausoleum that he built, an edifice that was somehow slightly grotesque for such a non-believer, was odd in itself, out of character with the man. He was, indeed, losing many of those rugged, tough, active traits that had so marked him out as a man. His habits were wearing out.

Watson had once said that if either he or Rosalie were to die while their children were still young, it would be better if it were Rosalie. He could cope with the tragedy without spoiling them for ever. And, in the aftermath of their mother's death, he did try very hard to be kind and exceptionally affectionate. Jimmy felt that his father found it awkward to be so affectionate but he did attempt to be close to his sons in this time of crisis. He was willing to give them his strength which was only what they had a right to expect of a father but there was no one that he felt able to open his own heart to very much.

Meanwhile, there were arrangements to be made about the children. Watson could not cope with an important business job at Esty's and two growing boys. He was now completely used to a lavish style of living. He brought his sons back to schools in the Westport area for a while and asked a secretary of his, Ruth Lieb, to come and live at the farm. Until 1950 Ruth Lieb saw him every single day. She had first met Watson in the late 1920s when she went to work for J. Walter Thompson. When Watson moved over to Esty's, he took her there with him for the brief period before Rosalie's death. She became very much a mother figure to both Billy and Jimmy.

Watson retreated into himself, his drink and his farm. He continued to make improvements to the property. He bought more and more animals, horses, cows, dogs, ducks and would tend them all himself. He had always felt at home with animals and now they pleased him much more than people did. He still took his sons riding and shooting sometimes but he was often depressed. He did not, as his sons got older, find it any easier to talk to them about his feelings. He was proud of them but silent. And they found him rather awesome. According to Jimmy, it was not that difficult to see when he was depressed because he behaved in such a depressed way. But if you had asked him if he was depressed, he would have denied it.

When Rosalie died Watson was fifty-eight years old. He did not see himself as an old man though he felt sad, sad about his work, sad about his wife, sad about himself. He clung to his interest in his appearance. The shoes and shirts and suits were still hand-made. Every morning a dapper Watson arrived at the offices of William Esty. He spent a good deal of time in the company of women who continued to find him very attractive. And he was tragic now as well. Many women apparently were eager to marry him but Watson remained true to his criticisms of marriage and refused to be a husband again. But he did not stop having affairs, even though Ruth Lieb lived in his house now. And his teenage sons continued to be treated to sermons on the importance of potency.

Life in Westport tended to be quiet and conservative. Watson did not give parties though people sometimes visited him at his farm. It was Rosalie who had pushed into society. Without her, he tended to withdraw. As Westport grew bigger, as more commuters bought property there, Watson became something of a local character. Gracious, interesting, he had once been a great man but now, by the end of the 1930s, he had dwindled into a man much like the other executives and businessmen who lived in the town. In Jimmy's apt words,'Dad became suburbanised.'

His politics, which had never been radical, became more and more conservative. He was an arch Republican. Roosevelt was the dreaded enemy. The New Deal would sap the rugged virtue of the nation. It was pampering adults. But though Watson was religious about voting, he never felt any urge to devote his skills to aid the cause of the Republicans. His politics reflected what he had become, a rich businessman who wanted to protect his property.

After 1936 Watson did not write again. It is impossible to know what he thought of psychology, if, indeed, he still thought of psychology at all. When the subject came up he defended his old ideas as fervently as ever; 'he was a holy terror in defending behaviourism,' according to Jimmy. But he was never the one to start talking psychology. And yet, as we shall see, he would not be able to forget it, to drive the subject out of his mind. His vision of a psychological renaissance spurred by behaviourism must have seemed unlikely in 1938 or 1939. If Watson had been keeping up with the literature – and by now he was not – he could have read an article entitled 'The Rise and Fall of Behaviourism' in which behaviourism was declared dead and buried. His moment had gone.

To his sons, Watson did not speak much of psychology. He did not go out very much with them now. He wanted to be close to them but it ran against his grain. And he thought they were closer to him than they really were. He and Billy often laughed together and the tight disciplines of the early behaviourist upbringing had slackened somewhat. But it was not a happy house.

Watson continued to be proud of his sons. According to his own lights, they were too old now to be conditioned and the tight disciplines of the home seem to have slackened somewhat. But the rigid upbringing they had had, the stream of governesses, and the death of their mother had all combined to make them rather fretful children. Jimmy felt he was a rather neurotic boy, aware of how distant he was from his father and not sure that his father understood that that distance existed. Jimmy looked up to Billy as his hero, too. There was tension on the farm, too. Ruth Lieb and Polly who lived close by did not get on at all well. It did not make for an easy adolescence for either Billy or Jimmy.

Oddly, too, for a man who had so raged at the academic way of life and so attacked the futility of colleges, Watson was very determined that his children should get an education. They had to have proper careers. He was always rather annoyed that his eldest son, John, did not have a proper profession and he kept on pressuring him to go back to college. He did finally persuade the boy to do so and prevailed on Cornell to accept him though he was over thirty. But within weeks John was back at his father's door saying he could not stand learning from books. With Billy, Watson was to have more luck. When Billy was eighteen or so, he decided to go to medical school. Watson was delighted. One regret about his period at Chicago was that he had not had the money to finish his medical education. To become a psychiatrist had always been an ambition. It was fitting that one of his sons, the product of the behaviourist system of child education, should become a psychiatrist himself. It was arranged that Billy should go to the Columbia Medical School.

When the war broke out, Watson was worried about all his three sons. Even Jimmy was, at eighteen, old enough to go into the service. Alarmingly, Jimmy chose to go into the Air Force. Watson did not like that. He had his own fears of flying and he did not like his son to go up in the air. Jimmy would ring his father at a set time every Sunday evening. It was a ritual, a ritual that Watson cared for and insisted upon. And Jimmy was too much in awe of his father to disobey. Like Billy,

Jimmy was consistently nagged to go to college. In his father's eyes, an uneducated man was not much a man at all. This was, again a contradiction in Watson's character for the typical 'macho' American male with his love of guns, alcohol, women and the rugged life is not usually devoted to education. 'Intellectual' is a term of abuse. But Watson, like any ambitious father, wanted his children to be educated and to make it. He hoped, of course, that Billy would make a contribution to psychiatry which would cap his own contribution to psychology.

Eager for his children to do well, Watson also continued to be competent at his own job. His drinking did not impair his performance at work. He had taken a number of accounts from J. Walter Thompson's including much business with Lehn & Fink, the makers of Pebeco, the toothpaste Watson had made taste better. He also worked on the Camels account on which the Esty agency greatly depended. The behaviourist was responsible, it seems, for another priceless consumer innovation. He helped develop underarm deodorants and made us all fear that we smelled just like people do. The underarm deodorant was one of his important new accounts. With touching brand loyalty, Watson started to shave under his own arms and to spray his armpits with the stuff. He also changed to smoking Camels.

Advertising often took him away from Westport. There were clients all over the USA to see. With Rosalie, Watson had quite enjoyed travelling. But now he grew to dislike it. He was petrified of planes. But he had no option but to fly.

And flying was not the only disadvantage to working with Esty. The two men needed rather than liked each other. Esty was a graduate of Amherst and Watson did not care for what he described 'as all those damn New England airs'. The two men did not work too happily together. But Watson was still competent and the war meant that the firm needed him. He stayed on past the normal retiring age. He was sixty-five in 1943, but he did not stop working for another four years.

The war made Watson's life less active. Even though Roosevelt was President, he was very patriotic. But his house in Westport was usually empty now. The children were grown up, gone. Ruth Lieb lived with Watson at Whipporwhill Farm but few people were around. From time to time, people did write to Watson but when people addressed him it was usually as a psychologist of the past. He was asked bizarre questions like What novels best exemplified the behaviourist approach to life, or Could a book be translated into Russian? Two books which considered Watson and his ideas – *The Mind Explorers* by Winkler and Bromberg (1939) and a French tome called *Le Behaviourisme* by Neville (1942) – already treated him as an historical figure, rather as if he ought to be decently dead already. He hardly ever met a psychologist now.

Even Curt Richter, his old student, who had seen him a few times in the 1930s, did not come to see him now. Watson could not have foreseen in 1930 how small, how parochial his life in Westport could become.

Paradoxically, it was now that a university finally made Watson an offer. According to Polly, he was asked again to teach at the end of the war. But Watson felt he was much too old, too much past it to be able to tackle academic work again. He must have paused for a wry smile before declining the invitation. In 1930 it might have made all the difference. It might have pushed him to choose to be a real psychologist again. It came far too late. The one consolation perhaps was that it began to seem likely that Billy would specialise in psychiatry when he finished medical school. The two of them started to talk, and to disagree, about psychiatry. But when the last chance came to be academic, Watson lacked the will and the confidence. He preferred the life he was now used to.

In 1947, Watson decided that the time to leave Esty's had come. Quarrels had increased there. The very proper Mr Esty objected, of all things, to Watson's dress. Watson was always impeccably dressed for he was now very rich indeed and continued to have all his apparel hand-made. There were serious questions raised in the agency about the fact that Watson refused to wear a hat. A hat, it seems, was the *sine qua non* for an advertising man. It seems that Esty, for some reason, started to make fun of Watson's way of dressing. Watson had no reason to put up with all these snide jibes and he quit the agency in 1947 after a few rather angry, bitter months. Ironically, it was in 1947 that *Fortune* had run a big article on J. Walter Thompson in which Resor prided himself on the fact that his firm was 'the university of advertising'. Resor had been very angry when Esty and Watson left with the Camels account which had been obtained by speculative work, that unethical form of labour, and he did his best to conceal how much Watson had done to make J. Walter Thompson 'the university' of Madison Avenue.

So, finally, in 1947 at the age of sixty-nine, the behaviourist who had done so much retired. More than ever, he spent time with his animals and tending his farm. He was still in quite good physical condition despite the drinking. He went out a little in Westport society. He saw his children and his grandchildren as often as possible. But, more and more, he withdrew. In 1950, he decided that it was time to sell the magnificent farm with its forty acres and all the lovely buildings he had added. He was winding down his life – and he knew it.

As the estate agents noted the wonderful particulars of the property – it fetched $90,000, a near fortune in those days – Watson must have

277

thought with much sadness of his life since 1930. He had come to Westport in the hope that, away from the distractions of New York, he could perhaps come to grips with some work again. He had not really managed to do that. His depressions had deepened. After Rosalie died he became more and more enclosed in himself, bitter and brooding.

In 1950 the Psychology Club of Furman University wrote to Watson to ask him to contribute a letter to a new magazine they were going to publish. Watson was glad to oblige. His letter ran to no more than a page and a half. He said, with some amusement, that he had always been a bitter critic of his time at college but now he looked back with some fondness on his college days. He still had a sense of humour about the accidents in his career. He noted that when Mark Baldwin told him he was the new editor of the *Psychological Review*, 'I was about as well prepared to undertake this work as to swim the English Channel.' But he had coped. He had always coped. He even felt he had coped with his inability to keep on doing psychology. Tersely, he said, that once he went into advertising, 'I had no lab and no ready reference library. Under such conditions, one dries up. I had nothing more to say.' It was only too true.

By then he had long been dried up though not dried out. But as Watson sold his house and prepared for a peaceful old age, he could not know that he would have to deal with a few more cruel ironies.

12

The End 1950–8

Watson had decided that it was time to sell his grand house with its large expanse of land. The estate agents issued a magnificent prospectus that praised the beauties of the property and the many cunning improvements that had been made. For one year, Watson let the house to a lady crime writer. During this time he went to stay in Woodberry, Connecticut, with a lady called Miss Ayman. With no particular work to do, he became very much an ageing gentleman. He was now completely out of touch with developments in psychology. And though he was growing very fat he still retained much of his manual skill. He did a good deal of handy work fixing up Miss Ayman's house. In 1951, finally, the house at Westport was sold and Watson found himself living, more or less permanently, in Miss Ayman's home. He did not seem to be bothered by this slightly odd arrangement.

The years after 1950 were, essentially, quiet ones. Watson pottered in the garden and round the house. Gradually he became a little more withdrawn than he had been. Ruth Lieb answered most of the letters that he still received. It was only with his son, Billy, that he still talked about psychology. Much to his father's chagrin, the child who had been brought up by behaviourism was now turning against behaviourism. Billy was a psychiatrist and, as such, he was getting more and more interested in Freudian ideas. Jimmy recalls that father and son had very heated arguments on the subject of the nature of the proper psychiatry. Watson kept on trying to talk his son out of these Freudian ideas: Billy resisted. It led to a serious rift between them which, for a few years, meant that they really did not get on too well and no doubt the two of them were very relieved when they came to an accommodation allowing each other their prejudices. But it caused Watson a good deal of pain to realise that his eldest son believed in a very different view of psychology. While Freud had had the initial merit, as Watson saw it, of letting sex into science, by the 1950s psychoanalysis must have seemed to Watson to be steeped in all kinds of mysticism.

Watson also saw something of his other two children, Polly and John, especially, was still a rather rootless person who often sponged on his father. Polly had married and gone to live in Hollywood.

Until 1955 Watson remained fairly healthy. He lived an active life between his garden and his do-it-yourself work. He saw a good deal of Ruth Lieb. Jimmy also came to see him quite often. But by 1955 when he was seventy-seven years old, Watson's health began to fail.

Paradoxically, it was in these last two years that Watson's name began to surface again in psychology, though commentators wrote of him as a dead master. In a way it was embarrassing that he was still alive. Watson was suddenly given two honours. In 1956 a paper appeared in the *Psychological Review* in which Gustav Bergmann argued that Watson's contribution to psychology had been second only to Freud's. Bergmann offered an interesting appreciation and critique of Watson. He wrote, rather hesitantly, that the subject of his paper was actually still alive. In 1957, prompted by the appearance of Bergmann's paper, the American Psychological Association (APA) finally decided to award Watson one of its gold medals, as the citation read:

> To John B. Watson whose work has been one of the vital deter-
> minants of the form and substance of modern psychology. He
> initiated a revolution in psychological thought and his writings have
> been the point of departure for continuing lines of fruitful research.

When Watson was approached by the APA about this he was very pleased. He decided to come down to New York from Woodberry in order to appear at the meeting of the APA and collect the medal in person. It would have been thirty-seven years since he last went to one of the meetings of that august association. Billy, Jimmy and Ruth Lieb came down to New York with him where Lashley joined them. They stayed in an hotel. But when the day of the presentation came, Watson could not bring himself to go. Ruth Lieb recalls that he said that it was because he no longer had hand-made shoes or hand-made shirts; Jimmy says that it was because his father felt so fat. These rather trivial reasons – Watson was a rich man and he could have easily had shirts, shoes, suits made for the occasion – surely mask the fact that so much hostility from psychologists had had its mark on Watson. After all that he had endured he just refused to go out and accept the medal from them now as he was doddering towards his grave. He sent Billy to the convention instead to accept the gold medal on his behalf. Given the general manner in which psychologists had behaved towards Watson, it was a bit much to expect him docilely to lap up the belated honour they bestowed on him. This action, this refusal to accept the medal in person, was Watson's last mark of defiance. It shows, to me, a certain decent contempt.

In the summer of 1958, Watson fell ill. He was suffering from a stomach infection and had to go to hospital. In early September he was allowed back home. He still received letters and among the letters that he received was one which asked him to state for publication which short stories he felt best reflected the ideas of behaviourism. But, by now, his health was failing. Watson was admitted back to hospital later in September. Just at this moment his old student, Curt Richter, wrote to him saying that he was sorry he had been out of touch for so long. Ruth Lieb replied to Richter that she had had time to show Watson the letter before he died. He had died on 25 September. He was eighty years old. His death affected his children, especially Billy and Jimmy, very deeply. It freed Jimmy to go into psychoanalysis. Billy, tragically, committed suicide a few years later.

The obituaries on Watson were either brief or bitchy. The *New York Times* carried a short piece about him which recounted his influence as a psychologist and as an advertising man. B. F. Skinner wrote an obituary for *Science* in which he stressed only one aspect of Watson's contribution – his methodological impatience with introspection – as a 'brilliant glimpse'. Skinner said almost nothing about the complexities of Watson's position or of the many areas into which he brought psychology. There was also an obituary in the *American Journal of Psychology* by Watson's contemporary, R. S. Woodsworth. Woodsworth meant to show that Watson had been influential but that behaviourism had not triumphed too much. He stressed that once Watson had gone into advertising, behaviourism seemed to fade somewhat. Woodsworth conceded that consciousness had departed from psychology but went on to mention as an instance of Watson's decline that verbal reports were not allowed. Watson had, of course, used such reports himself. Woodsworth then referred to Watson's 'extreme environmentalism' as also being at a low ebb. He then quoted from a number of sources to arrive at a consensus of Watson's importance. Clark Hull had been 'repelled by Watson's dogmatic claims' though the dogmatic criticisms of Koffka had made Hull a bit more sympathetic to Watson. Tolman granted that now all psychologists were behaviourists but he did not like Watson's 'muscle twitches' as the roots of all behaviour. As far as Woodsworth could see, European psychology had largely ignored Watson. Jersild regarded Watson's theory that emotions are located in the muscles – a theory that Watson never held or propounded – as being 'unfortunate'.

Woodsworth did quote Skinner who said that Watson was right in his general approach but wrong in detail. The grudging obituary ended with two quotations on Watson's ideas on thinking. One condemned Watson's ideas as a total menace; D. O. Hebb, on the other hand, just thought that while the theory was largely wrong, it had introduced some important concepts concerning sensory feedback. Woodsworth's final comment is hardly generous:

What shall we say then? Watson's mistakes have not been forgotten; every recent comment takes note of one or more of them. It would not be safe to overlook them unless we were prepared to overlook Watson, altogether; and that we are not prepared to do – not in America anyway.

Finally, Woodsworth said that psychologists were 'gravitating' together and that even non-behaviourists were employing 'functional concepts – which were after all the positive core of Watson's system'. Watson, who attacked functionalists like Woodsworth for being half-hearted, would have minded not being able to have the last word to tack on to this unglowing obituary.

A more generous estimate of Watson came in 1956 from Gustav Bergmann. In many ways Bergmann provides a better obituary though he was not specifically writing one. Bergmann saw clearly that there were many facets to Watson. He criticised his fear of the central nervous system and also what he considered to be Watson's meta-physical naïveté. But Bergmann praised many elements in Watson's work. He realised that Watson was a more complex psychologist than was usually allowed though he did not argue any one example in depth. 'Watson's psychology was not, at any stage of his thought, one of "muscle twitches".' But Bergmann never elaborated the point. He guessed, rightly, that if Watson had been practising psychology in 1956 he 'would not be today, a doctrinaire advocate of physiological reduction. He was, quite to the contrary, a vigorous and, if anything, overoptimistic advocate of behavioral research clinically as well as in the laboratory.' Bergmann stressed the importance of behaviourism as a method rather than as a system. He saw something of the flexibility of Watson's ideas and suggested that those who had followed him had not perhaps served his thinking best. In a short paper, of course, Bergmann's main purpose was to make people aware again of Watson's contribution. He had to ram the point home rather than refine it. And just as if it were an obituary, Bergmann concluded his article by saying

...he is a very major figure. Psychology owes him much. His place in history of our civilisation is not inconsiderable and it is secure. Such men are exceedingly rare. We ought to accept them and appreciate them for what they are.

Since his death, Watson's reputation has been stagnant. He is quoted, according to the computer, in 215 sources but none of these articles actually appear to evaluate his contribution. Cedric Larson has, in a number of papers, attended to details of Watson's life such as his relationship with Titchener, and his holiday home in Canada. An unpublished paper on the psychology department at Johns Hopkins includes a section on Watson's tenure of the chair. Mary Cover Jones has written briefly on their collaboration. But the only major consideration has been by Herrnstein in *American Psychologist* and in an introduction to *Behaviour*, a reissue of the text. Herrnstein criticises a great deal of Watson's work but points out that he did seek to achieve a 'botany of behaviour', by listing all the reflexes people had and all the acts they performed. This was grandiose, but we seem destined to undertake Watsonian botanising but with much better prospects for success than Watson would have had 50 years ago. These additional skills would give 'parameters that would make behaviourism truly practical'. Herrnstein called Watsonian behaviourism less 'modest' than its modern counterparts and argued that part of its merit, and present timeliness, lay in that.

Throughout this book I have argued that Watson should be viewed as more than just the man who founded behaviourism. His behaviourism was not the rather constricted thing the word is now taken to mean. At his most imaginative, Watson looked forward to a kind of botany of behaviour, a logging of all that men and women do. He stressed observation in real situations as well as experiment. He even practised what he stressed for he studied aspects of behaviour which psychology then proceeded to neglect for many years. He did work in industry, and work on sexual attitudes and behaviour. All this amounts to a much more expansive psychology than that common in the 1930s and 1940s. He saw clearly too how central developmental psychology was to psychology as a whole. He saw the need to study children from birth on. He did not achieve everything he set out to do but, incomplete as it is, his work on children was a very important new departure from the anecdotal tittle-tattle of most developmental research. Piaget might not have suffered from reading some of Watson's 'naive' and simple observations. I have also argued that Watson, in effect, created behaviour therapy – a fact that most behaviour therapists seem conveniently to bypass. The elegance of the work on Little Albert was acknowledged by Wolpe and Rachman who seem never to have read *Behaviourism* in which Watson outlined cases of positive cure from phobias – using the 'modern' techniques of behaviour therapy. Making Watson out to be a man with just one vital idea at the time when the paradigm of psychology was ripe to change is, really, to do him an injustice.

Watson was not perfect, of course. He had a crude belief that psychologists could tinker with the environment in order to produce the perfect environment to be inhabited by the now perfectly conditioned species. His views on language and thinking appear strange though the motor theory of thinking was an influential one. But even with all the criticisms that can be made, it must be said that Watson's ideas were very important in their time and remain so for the progress of psychology today. By and large, his views have been simplified or plainly misrepresented. A great deal of his work points to much less rigid and artificial psychology than that we have today. He founded behaviourism but he founded a behaviourism that was both more ambitious and more realistic than behaviourism is today. Watson deserves to be remembered for what he said and did rather than as being the originator of a caricature of what psychology should be like.

Sources

The material, other than books and articles, which bears on Watson's life is not all that extensive but it is quite scattered. I have relied for much basic information on Watson's own autobiographical note in *A History of Psychology in Autobiography*, ed. Carl Murchison, Clark University Press, Worcester, Mass., 1936. This is referred to as 'Watson's note' in the subsequent sources. Much valuable material is also to be found in the Library of Congress MS division, both in Watson's own papers and those of Jacques Loeb. The correspondence between Watson and Yerkes is at the Yale University Medical Library MS Division. The correspondence between Titchener and Watson, and Titchener and other psychologists, which bears on Watson is in Cornell University Library MS Division. There is much illuminating material on Watson's early life and circumstances in the MS division of Furman University Library in Greenville, South Carolina. Letters relating to Watson's career at Chicago are in the papers of Angell at the University of Chicago and in the files of the President's Office. The archives of Johns Hopkins have much useful material, including the papers of the Office of the President, the correspondence of the actual Department of Psychology, in which a number of Watson's papers still survive, and a few references to Adolf Meyer. There are also a few letters in the Mrs Dummer papers in the Radcliffe Library MS Division at Harvard, the Hunt and the American Philosophical Society. There are also some unpublished private papers and notes held by the Watson family.

On Watson's advertising career, there is some useful material in the archives of J. Walter Thompson.

As well as consulting these written sources, I have made use of material gathered in interviews with Watson's children Jim Watson and Polly Watson, his long-standing friend Ruth Lieb; Curt Richter, the psychologist who was his student, and Dean Schiffra who studied at Johns Hopkins in the 1920s.

1 The Making of a Behaviourist 1878–1900

On Watson's childhood: his note, recollections of Ruth Lieb and Jim Watson; material in the MS division of Furman University. On Greenville background: material at Furman University. On Watson's university career: papers in the MS Division of the Library at Furman including a tape by Dr Ben Field. On

285

death of Watson's mother: letter to Yerkes. On Batesburg Institute: Ben Field. On leaving for Chicago: letters in MS Division of the University of Chicago Library. Charles Brewer, unpublished paper read at History of Psychology in the South Conference, 1976, Atlanta, Georgia.

2 Chicago

On Watson's career at Chicago: letters in the MS Division of the University of Chicago and Watson's note. On Angell: Watson's note, and Angell in *History of Psychology in Autobiography*. On the origins of behaviourism: Watson's note; preface to the 2nd edition of *Psychology from the Standpoint of a Behaviourist* and *Harpers* 1924. On Watson's marriage: recollection of Jim Watson, Polly Watson and Ruth Lieb and letters to Robert Yerkes. On Watson's holiday home: Polly Watson and Cedric Larson. On Watson's slow disenchantment with contemporary psychology: especially letters to Titchener and Yerkes; Titchener in Cornell University Library. On the noddy and sooty terns and on leaving Chicago for Baltimore: Watson's note and letters by Angell, Donaldson and Baldwin are in the Archives of John Hopkins.

3 The Young Professor 1908–13

On Johns Hopkins at the time: Philip Pauly of the Psychology Department at Johns Hopkins (unpublished talk) and material in the archives of Johns Hopkins. On Baltimore: *Baltimore Sun*. On how Watson developed the department: Watson's note; material in the archives of Johns Hopkins; letters to Titchener and Yerkes. On the struggles towards articulating behaviourism: letters to Titchener, Yerkes and to other psychologists in the archives of Johns Hopkins. On Dunlap: Dunlap in *History of Psychology in Autobiography*. On Baldwin: his *Between Two Wars*, Stratford Co., Boston, 1926. On Sumner: *Folkways*, Yale University Press, New Haven, 1907. On home life: Polly Watson and letters to Yerkes. On the Congress of Psychology: letters in Johns Hopkins archives and at Cornell University and Yale University. On the work with the terns: Carnegie Institute publication No. 211, *An Historical and Experimental Study of Homing*, 1915. On pressures of editing learned journals: letters to Yerkes and at Johns Hopkins. On psychology for medical students: Watson in *Journal of the American Medical Association*, 1911, vol. 58, p. 916. On Meyer and the Phipps Institute, Johns Hopkins archives, recollections of Curt Richter and Watson's note. On the lectures at Columbia: Watson's note, notes in *Psychological Review* and letters to Yerkes.

4 Towards the Psychology of Real Life 1913–18

On success of the Columbia lectures: letters to Yerkes. On accolades: *Psychological Bulletin*, 1914 and 1915. On Mary's illness: letters to Yerkes. On Phipps Clinic: Watson's own note and material in the archives of Johns Hopkins. On Watson's war: correspondence between Watson and Thorndike; and Thorndike and Johns Hopkins and Watson's note.

5 The Complete Behaviourist Programme 1918–20

On the relationship between Watson and Goodnow: correspondence in Johns Hopkins archives. On the alcohol experiments; letters with Thorndike in Johns Hopkins archives and Curt Richter. On the experiments with children: *Psychology from the Standpoint of a Behaviourist* and notes by Rosalie Rayner in the possession of Jim Watson. On the projects about veneral disease and sex: *Social Hygiene* and correspondence at Johns Hopkins. On education: see Watson's contribution to *Thoughts on Education*, Macmillan, New York, 1918 – Watson's was one of five chapters. On his business relationships: correspondence with Philip Burnet of the Continental Life Insurance Co. On the film: correspondence with Goodnow in Johns Hopkins archive. On the plans for observing children 24 hours a day: letters to Goodnow and Thorndike in Johns Hopkins archive.

6 1920: Divorce

On the divorce: contemporary articles in *Baltimore Sun, New York Herald, New York Times*, the *World* as well as the recollections of Polly Watson, Jim Watson and of Curt Richter. On the relationship between the Rayners: the *Baltimore Sun*. On Mary: the *World*, 27 November. On the way the university behaved: corespondence in the archives of Johns Hopkins between Watson and Goodnow, and Goodnow and colleagues; also recollections of Curt Richter and Dean Schiffra of Johns Hopkins. *Baltimore Sun*, 23 and 28 September, 27, 28 and 29 November, 24 December. On the Oxford conference: letters at Johns Hopkins, *British Journal of Psychology*, 1920, vol. XI, pp. 87–104; *Mind*, 25–26 November 1919, vol, 29, pp. 383–84. Account of the divorce hearing from *Baltimore Sun*. Other papers on John Ickes: Polly Watson. McKeen Cattell's letter: Office of the President, Johns Hopkins. Watson's reactions: Watson's autobiographical note; Polly Watson. On Titchener's reactions: Titchener to Yerkes in Yale and Yerkes's response.

7 The Advertising Man

On the state of J. Walter Thompson: the archives of J. Walter Thompson and a centennial article in *Advertising Age*, 7 December 1964. On Resor: *Advertising Age*, 7 December 1964; *Fortune* 1947. On Watson's first dabblings in advertising: his note.

On advertising in general
On Watson's entry to advertising: letters to Mildred Bennett. On the background to contemporary advertising: *Advertising Age*, 7 December 1964. Calkins, *History of Advertising*, American Library Association; Walter Scott, *The Theory and Practice of Advertising*, Small, Maynard & Co., New York, 1919. On Watson's achievements: various bulletins of J. Walter Thompson as cited. For Resor's speeches: papers at J. Walter Thompson and reports in the *New York Times*. On Titchener: correspondence between Watson and Titchener, Cornell

University Library MS division. On Watson's fame: the *New Yorker*, 6 October 1928, and *Saturday Review of Literature*, June 1928. On the psychology of selling: papers to National Conventional of Advertisers in Library of Congress MS division and similar papers to the 1934 Canadian convention. On the Psychological Corporation: *New York Times* 1921. On his financial situation: Jim Watson; Ruth Lieb; *New Yorker*, 6 October 1928.

8 Children 1920–30

Mary Cover Jones in *American Psychologist*, 1974, vol. 29, p. 581. On attempts to do the baby work: letters to Yerkes and Titchener. On Billy and Jimmy: unpublished notes by Rosalie and John in Library of Congress and others in the possession of Jim Watson. On the Manhattan Day Nursery: Mary Cover Jones, op. cit., and letters to Yerkes and Mrs Dummer. Much of the material used in *Behaviourism*. On giving advice to parents: *McCalls* in 1926 and 1927–8, *Baltimore Sun*, 11 November 1928 and Rosalie Rayner in *McCalls* 1930. On reactions to this: the Housewives League in *New York Times*, 8 March 1928, editorials in *Jacksonville Times* and *Scranton Republican*, March 1928. On being brought up by a behaviourist: Jim Watson and radio talks whose transcripts are in the Library of Congress; *New York Times*, 3 February 1929. Bertrand Russell in the *World* and an introduction to *New Generation*, Allen & Unwin, London, 1929. On reactions to Watson's views see also *Parents Magazine*, 1930, *Atlantic Monthly*, June and July 1929.

9 The Last of the Psychologist 1920–30

On relations with psychologists: letters to Titchener and from Titchener as well as letters to Warren and Dodge by Titchener. George Humphrey, *Thinking*, Methuen, London, 1951. On the New School: Watson's own note and his letters to Yerkes, Titchener and reports in *New York Times*. On MacDougall: Watson in *New Republic*, April 1923, and letters between Watson and Titchener. Roback in *Behaviourism and Psychology*, Sci-Art, Cambridge, Mass., 1923. On Norton: Watson's note. On reactions to Watson: Richard Boynton in the *Christian Register*, November 1926; Berman's *A Religion Called Behaviourism*, Boni and Liveright, New York, 1927; Hazlitt in a review of Berman in the *World*, 1927; MacDougall in a review of *Behaviourism* tacked on to *The Battle of Behaviourism*, Kegan Paul, London, 1929. On the film: *New York Times*, 24 May 1927. Bertrand Russell in the *World*. Other material in the Library Congress from contemporary papers kept by Watson.

10 The Great Populariser 1920–30

There is no way of being sure that one has covered every single article Watson wrote. The bibliography has tried to include the most important. On top of this, Watson often gave interviews on various subjects like changing your personality given to the *Independent Woman*. On life in New York: Jim Watson. On radio talks: material in the Library of Congress.

11 Surburban Silence 1930–50

The *Daily Princetonian*, 27 February 1930. On Watson's home life: Jim Watson and Ruth Lieb. On remnants of psychology work: letters to Yerkes. 'Why I Don't Commit Suicide' in Library of Congress, and on that MS: Ruth Lieb. On radio talks: material in the Library of Congress. On continuing work in advertising: material in the Library of Congress, including a number of press reports of his speeches to advertising conventions. On building: Jim Watson and Polly Watson. On Watson's isolation and drinking: Jim Watson and Polly Watson. On Billy and the snowstorm: *New York Herald*, 27 December 1933 and other papers, *Herald Tribune*, the *Sun*; Jim Watson. On leaving J. Walter Thompson: *Advertising Age*, Watson's note and Jim Watson and *World Telegram*, 3 February 1936. On Rosalie's death: Jim Watson, Ruth Lieb and *New York Times*, 1936. On the relationship with the children: Jim Watson. On his continuing career in advertising: *Advertising Age*; *Fortune*, 1947. On his politics; Jim Watson. Letter from Watson to Furman University in Library of Congress.

J. B. Watson: A Bibliography

Books

Animal Education, University of Chicago Press, 1903.
Behaviour, Holts, New York, 1914.
Chapter in *Thoughts on Education*, Macmillan, 1918.
Psychology from the Standpoint of a Behaviourist, Lippincott, Philadelphia,
　1919: 2nd edn revised, 1924; 3rd edn, 1929.
Behaviourism, Harpers, New York, 1925; revised, 1930.
The Ways of Behaviourism, W. W. Norton, New York, 1928.
The Psychological Care of the Infant and Child, W. W. Norton, New York, 1928.
The Battle of Behaviourism (with contribution by W. MacDougall), Norton, New
　York, 1928.
Preface to *What's Wrong with Modern Marriage* by G. V. Hamilton
　and Kenneth MacGowan, Harpers, New York, 1929.

Periodicals and learned papers

Editor, Comparative Psychology numbers, *Psychological Bulletin*, III, 1906,
　and V, 1908.
'Some Unemphasized Aspects of Comparative Psychology', *Journal of
　Comparative Neurology and Psychology*, XIV, 1904, pp. 360–3.
'The Effect of the Bearing of Young upon the Body-Weight and the Weight
　of the Central Nervous System of the Female White Rat', *Journal of Compara-
　tive Neurology and Psychology*, XV, 1905, pp. 514–24.
'The Need of an Experimental Station for the Study of Certain Problems in
　Animal Behaviour', *Psychological Bulletin*, III, 1906, pp. 149–56.
'A Comparison of the White Rat with Man in Respect to the Growth of the
　Entire Body' (with H. H. Donaldson and E. H. Dunn), *Boas Anniversary
　Volume*, New York, 1906, pp. 5–26.
*Kinaesthetic and Organic Sensations: Their Role in the Reactions of the White Rat
　to the Maze*, Psychological Monographs, VIII, 2, whole no. 33, 8vo, vi+100,
　Psychological Review Co., 1907.
'Condition of Noddy and Sooty Tern Colony, Bird Key, Tortugas, Fla.',
　Bird Lore, IX, 1907, pp. 307–16.

'Imitation in Monkeys', *Psychological Bulletin*, V, 1908, pp. 169–79.

'Behaviour of Noddy and Sooty Terns', *Carnegie Publication 103*, Washington, 1908, pp. 187–255.

'Orientation of the White Rat' (with H. A. Carr), *Journal of Comparative Neurology and Psychology*, XVIII, 1908, pp. 27–44.

'Experiments Bearing on Color Vision in Monkeys', *Journal of Comparative Neurology and Psychology*, XIX, 1909, pp. 1–28.

'A Course in Psychology for Medical Students', *Journal of the American Medical Association*, vol. 58, 1911, p. 916.

'Psychology as the Behaviourist Views it', *Psychological Review*, vol. XX, 1913, pp. 158–78.

'Image and Affection in Behaviour', *Journal of Philosophy, Psychology and Scientific Method*, 1913, p. 421.

'Notes on the Development of a Young Monkey', *Journal of Animal Behaviour*, no. 3, 1913, pp. 114–39.

'Conditioned Reflex in Psychology', *Psychological Review*, XXIII, 1916, pp. 89–117.

'Behaviour and the Concept of Mental Disease', *Journal of Philosophy, Psychology and Scientific Method*, vol. 13, no. 22, 1916, pp. 587–96.

'The Psychology of Wish Fulfillment', *Journal of Philosophy, Psychology and Scientific Method*, 1916, p. 5.

'Does Holt Follow Freud?', *Journal of Philosophy*, vol. 14, 1917.

'The Effects of Delayed Feeding upon Learning', *Psychobiology*, vol. 1, 1917, pp. 51–60.

'Emotional Reactions and Psychological Experimentation', *American Journal of Psychology*, vol.11, 1917, pp. 163–77 (with J. J. B. Morgan).

An Historical and Empirical Study of Homing (with K. S. Lashley), Carnegie Publications, Washington, 1915, no. 211.

'The Opinion of Doctors regarding Veneral Disease' (with K. S. Lashley), *Social Hygiene*, 1919, vol. 4, pp. 769–847.

'A Schematic Outline of the Emotions', *Psychological Review*, vol. 26, 1919, pp. 165–77.

'Is Thinking Merely the Action of the Language Mechanism?', *British Journal of Psychology*, vol. XI, 1920, pp. 87–104.

The Effects of a Motion Picture Campaign on Sexual Hygiene (with K. S. Lashley), US Interdepartmental Social Hygiene Board, 1920, pp.1–88.

'Studies in Infant Psychology' (with Rosalie Rayner), *Scientific Monthly*, 1921, December.

'The Unverbalised in Human Behaviour', *Psychological Review*, vol. 31, 1924, pp. 273–81

'The Place of Kinaesthetic, Visceral and Laryngeal Organs in Thinking', *Psychological Review*, vol. 31, 1924, pp. 339–48.

'What the nursery has to say about instincts' and 'Experimental Studies on the Growth of the Emotions', in *The Psychologies of 1925*, ed. Carl Murchison, Clark University Press, Worcester, Mass., 1925.

'John B. Watson' in *A History of Psychology in Autobiography*, ed. Carl Murchison, Clark University Press, Worcester, Mass., 1936.

'The Origin and Growth of Behaviourism', *Archives of Gestalt Philosophy*, vol. 30, 1927, pp. 247–56.
'Behaviourism, a Psychology Based on Reflex Action', *Journal of Philosophical Studies*, 1926, pp. 454–66.

In J. Walter Thompson Bulletin

'Smoking', July 1921.
'On the Use of Booklets', September 1922.
'The Contact Man', July 1924.
'Use of Radio in Advertising', May 1923.
'Life Insurance', April 1923.
'Can Psychology help the Study of Personnel', April 1927.
'On Influencing the Mind of Another', September 1935.

Unpublished

'Why I Don't Commit Suicide', 1932, held in Library of Congress MS Division.

Popular articles

'The New Science of Animal Behaviour', *Harpers*, March 1910.
'Instinctive Ability in Animals', *Harpers*, September 1912.
'Review of Outline of Psychology', *New Republic*, April 1923.
'Behaviourism', *Harpers*, May 1924.
'What is Behaviourism?', *Harpers*, May 1926.
'How we think', *Harpers*, June 1926.
'The Myth of the Unconscious', *Harpers*, May 1927.
'On the Weakness of Women', *Nation*, 6 July 1927.
A series of six articles on children in *McCalls* from September 1927 to March 1928.
'On Reconditioning People', *New York Times*, 4 March 1928.
'Feed Me on Facts', *Saturday Review of Literature*, 16 June 1928.
Encyclopedia Britannica, 1929 edition, entry on 'Behaviourism'.
'Why 50 years from now Men won't Marry', *Cosmopolitan*, June 1929.
'After the Family – What?', in *New Generation*, ed. Bertrand Russell, Allen & Unwin, London, 1929.
'Women and Business', *New York Telegraph*, 16 September 1930.
'I am the Mother of the Behaviourist's Sons', by Rosalie Rayner Watson, *McCalls*, December 1930.

Radio talks

'How we think', December 1927,
Pebeco advertisement, 11 April 1923, WEAF New York.
'Psychology as a Background Life', 19 April 1933, WEVD New York.
'On Children', 6 December 1935, WEAF New York.

Contemporary books on Watson

A. A. Roback, *Behaviourism and Psychology*, Sci-Art, Cambridge, Mass., 1923.
Louis Berman, *The Religion of Behaviourism*, Boni and Liveright, New
    York, 1927.

Articles on Watson

E. Titchener, 'On Psychology as the Behaviourist Views It', *Proceedings of the
    American Philosophical Society*, vol. 53, 1914, pp. 1–17.
C. Diserens, 'Psychological Objectivism', *Psychological Review*, vol. 32,
    1925, pp. 121–53.
E. G. Boring, 'The Society of Experimental Psychology', *American Journal
    of Psychology*, vol. 41, 1938, p. 410.
W. Harrell and R. Harrison, 'The Rise and Fall of Behaviourism', *Journal of
    General Psychology*.
J. R. Winkler and W. Bromberg in *The Mind Explorers*, Reynald & Hitchcock,
    1939.
Gustav Bergmann, 'The Contribution of John B. Watson', *Psychological
    Review*, vol. 63, 1956, p. 264.
R. S. Woodsworth, obituary for John B. Watson in *American Journal of
    Psychology*, vol. LXXII, 1959, p. 301.
B. F. Skinner, obituary in *Science*, no. 3343, 23 January 1959, p. 197.
Cedric Larson and John O'Sullivan, 'Watson's Relationship to Titchener',
    Journal of History of the Behavioural Sciences, vol. 1, 1965, p. 338.
R. J. Herrnstein, preface to re-issue of *Behaviour*, Holt, Rinehart and Winston,
    New York, 1967.
John C. Burnham, 'The Origins of Behaviourism', *Journal of History of the
    Behavioural Sciences*, vol. 4, 1968, p. 143.
Mary Cover Jones, 'Albert, Peter and John B. Watson', *American Psychologist*,
    vol. 29, 1974, pp. 581–83.
R. J. Herrnstein, 'The Evolution of Behaviourism', *American Psychologist*, vol.
    32, 1967, pp. 543–603.

More recent works related to Watson

Pierre Neville, *Le Behaviourisme*, Gallimard, Paris, 1942.
Andre Tilquinu, *Le Behaviourisme*, Libraire Philosophique Uvin, Paris, 1950.
Lucille T. Birnhaum, 'John B. Watson and American Social Thought',
    Doctoral Thesis, University of California, 1963.

Index

Index